3

Swinging Pendulums of Destiny!!

ORIGINAL CONCEPT BY **Kazuki Takahashi**

PRODUCTION SUPPORT: **STUDIO DICE**

STORY BY **Shin Yoshida**

ART BY **Naohito Miyoshi**

DUEL COORDINATOR **Masahiro Hikokubo**

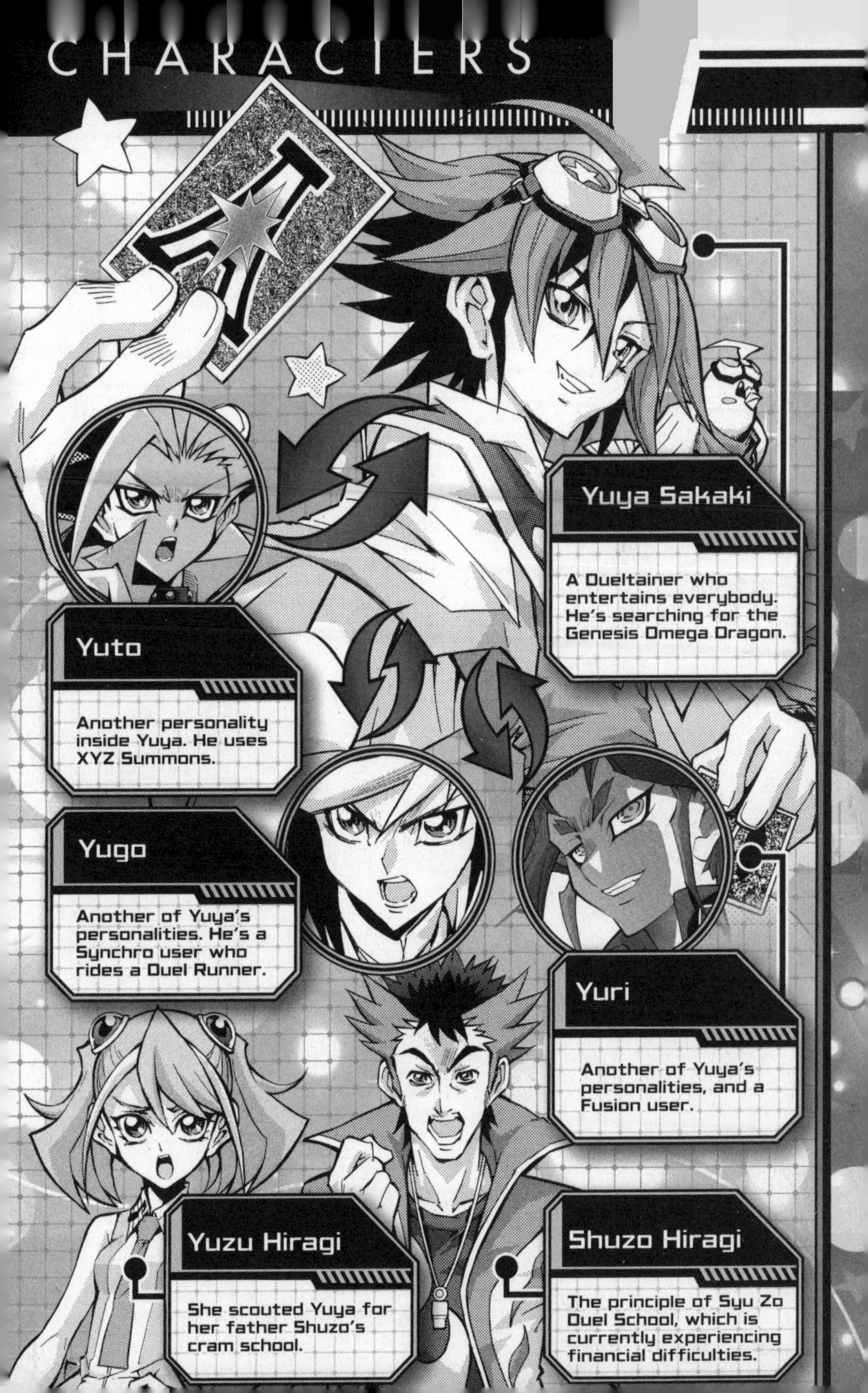
CHARACTERS
Yuya Sakaki
A Dueltainer who entertains everybody. He's searching for the Genesis Omega Dragon.
Yuto
Another personality inside Yuya. He uses XYZ Summons.
Yugo
Another of Yuya's personalities. He's a Synchro user who rides a Duel Runner.
Yuri
Another of Yuya's personalities, and a Fusion user.
Shuzo Hiragi
The principle of Syu Zo Duel School, which is currently experiencing financial difficulties.
Yuzu Hiragi
She scouted Yuya for her father Shuzo's cram school.

Reiji Akaba

President of the Leo Corporation. He's using his company to hunt Yuya.

Shun Kurosaki

The Leo Corporation's second assassin. He challenged Yuya to a no-holds-barred Duel!

Sora Shiunin

Although he wants to duel Yuya, he is concerned about Akaba's enigmatic behavior.

Ren

A suspicious character who infiltrated Yuya's memories.

Shingo Sawatari

The first Leo Corporation Duelist to face off against Yuya.

STORY

Solid Vision with mass has plunged the world into the era of Action Duels. The Duelists of the Leo Corporation are in hot pursuit of Yuya Sakaki, a Dueltainer who can hack that technology. The Leo Corporation's first assassin, Sawatari, squares off against him only to discover that the person he has been chasing is someone else—a guy who introduces himself as Yuto! However, during the Duel, Yuto transforms into Yuya, who wins and escapes. Yuzu Hiragi, who happens to be present at the Duel, becomes Yuya's manager and joins him in pursuit of the Genesis Omega Dragon [G.O.D.]. After his Duel with Sora, Yuya passes out, which allows Ren to infiltrate his memories. In a Duel in his mind, Yugo defeats Ren. Meanwhile, Akaba has also begun to act...

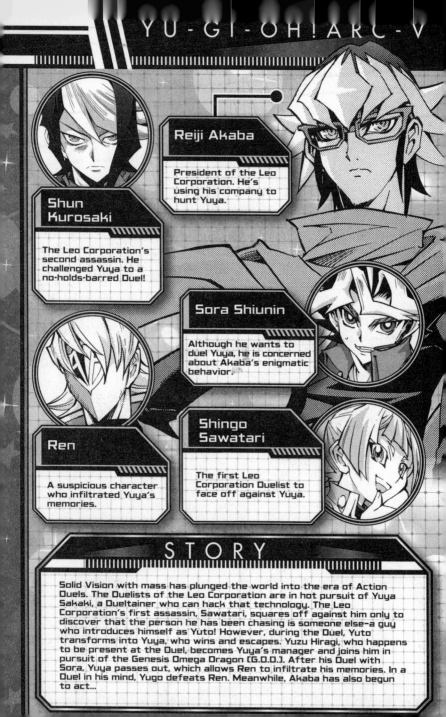

Yu-Gi-Oh! ARC-V

3 Swinging Pendulums of Destiny!!

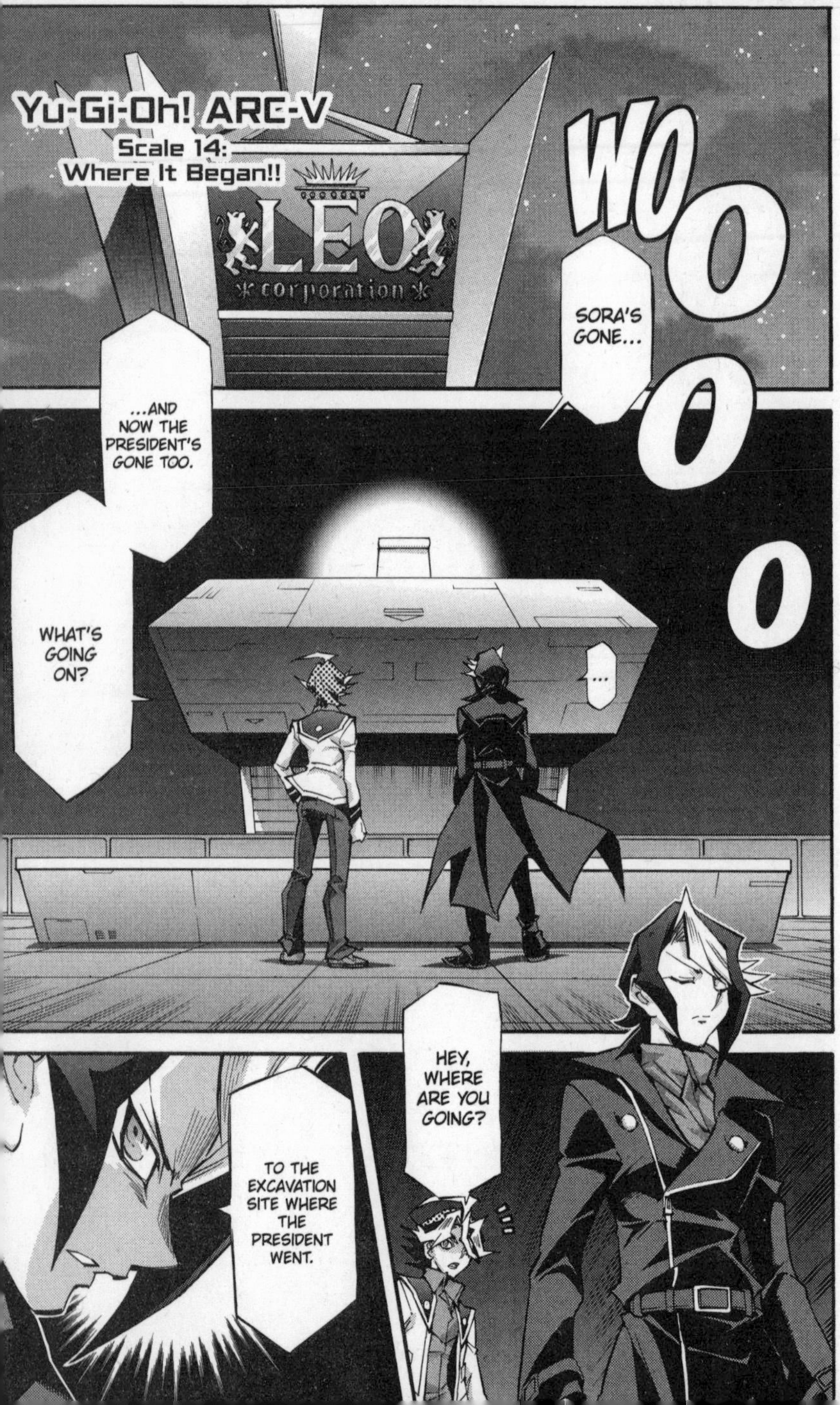
Yu-Gi-Oh! ARC-V
Scale 14: Where It Began!!
LEO corporation
WOOOOO
SORA'S GONE...
...AND NOW THE PRESIDENT'S GONE TOO.
WHAT'S GOING ON?
...
HEY, WHERE ARE YOU GOING?
TO THE EXCAVATION SITE WHERE THE PRESIDENT WENT.

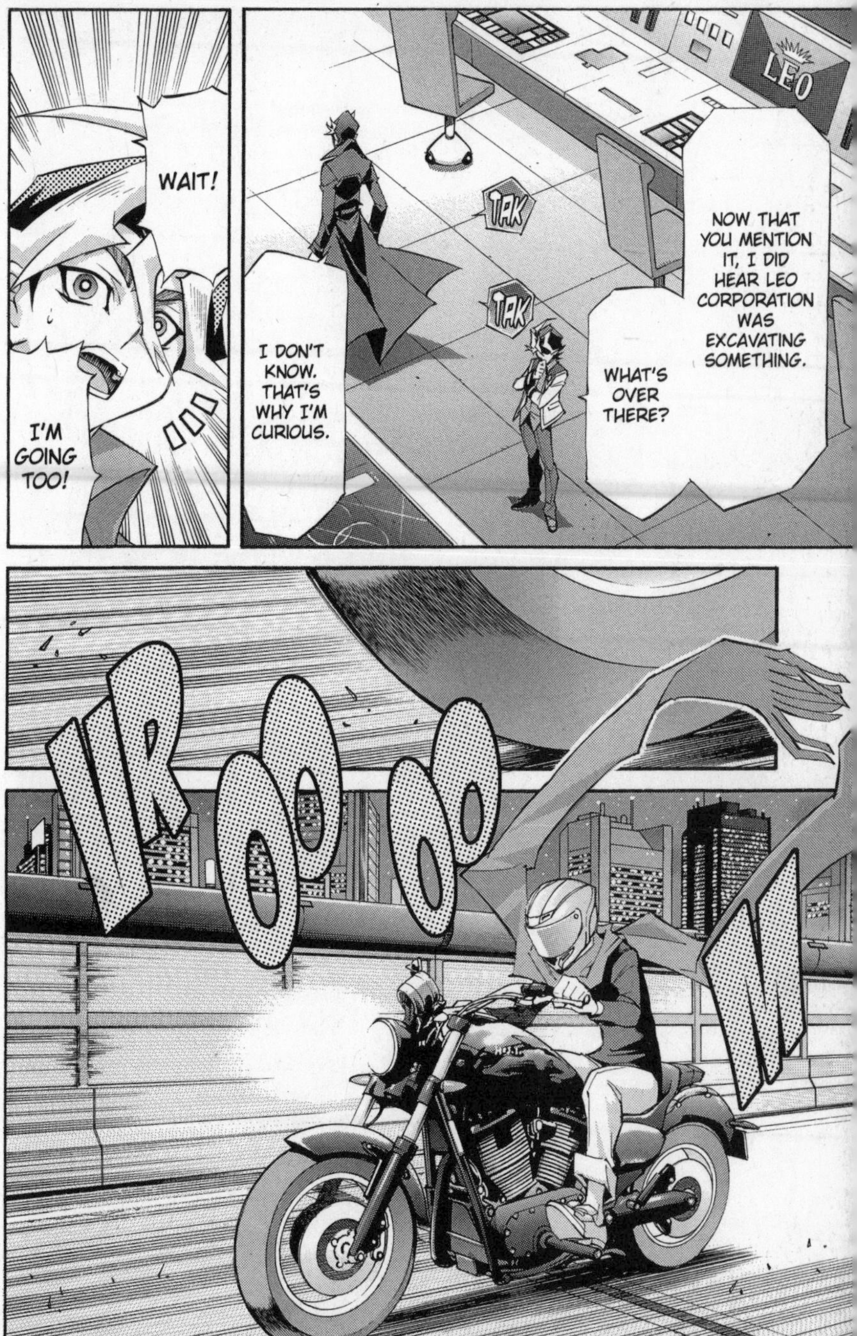
LEO
NOW THAT YOU MENTION IT, I DID HEAR LEO CORPORATION WAS EXCAVATING SOMETHING.
WHAT'S OVER THERE?
TAK
TAK
I DON'T KNOW. THAT'S WHY I'M CURIOUS.
WAIT!
I'M GOING TOO!
VROOOOM

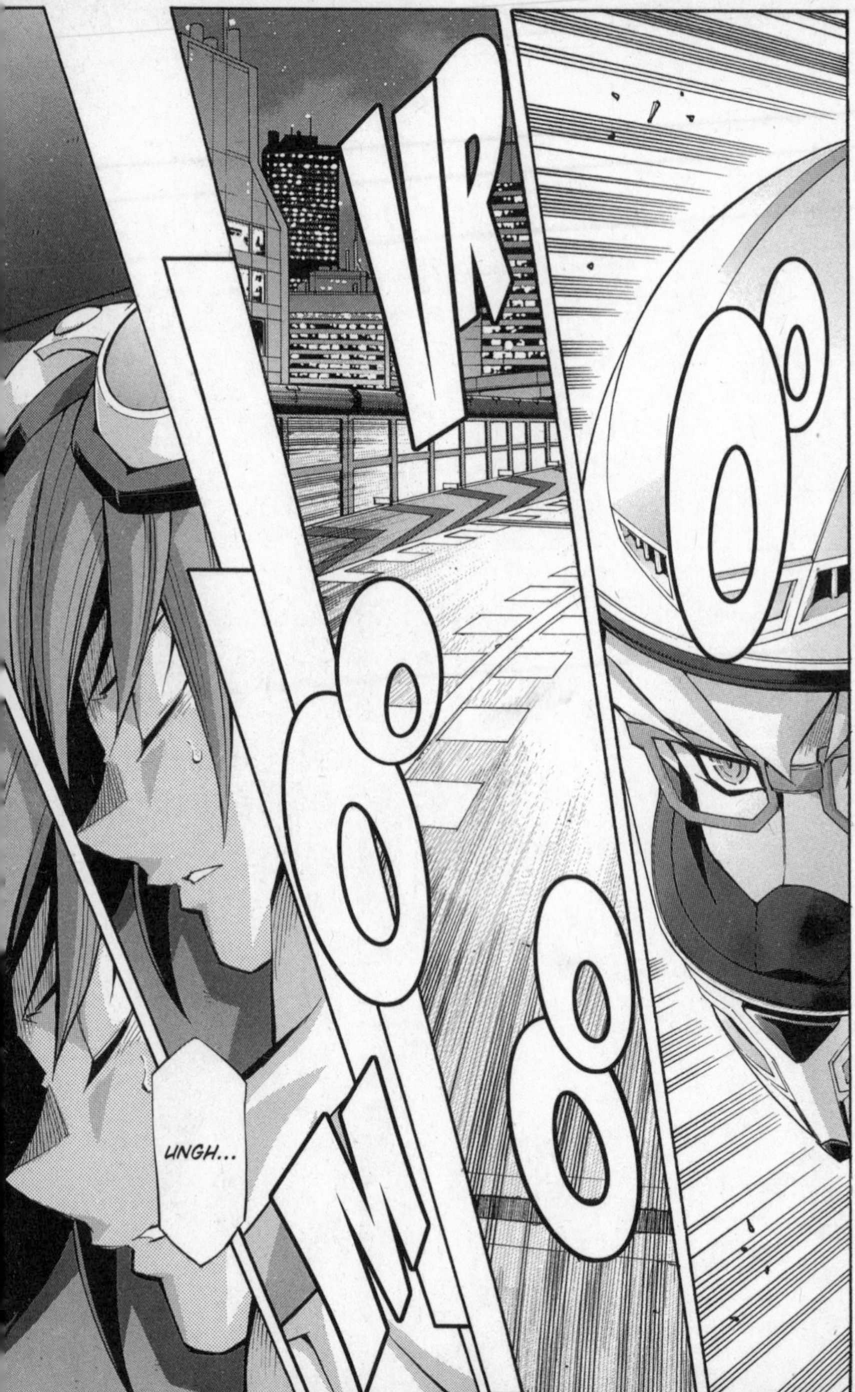
UNGH...

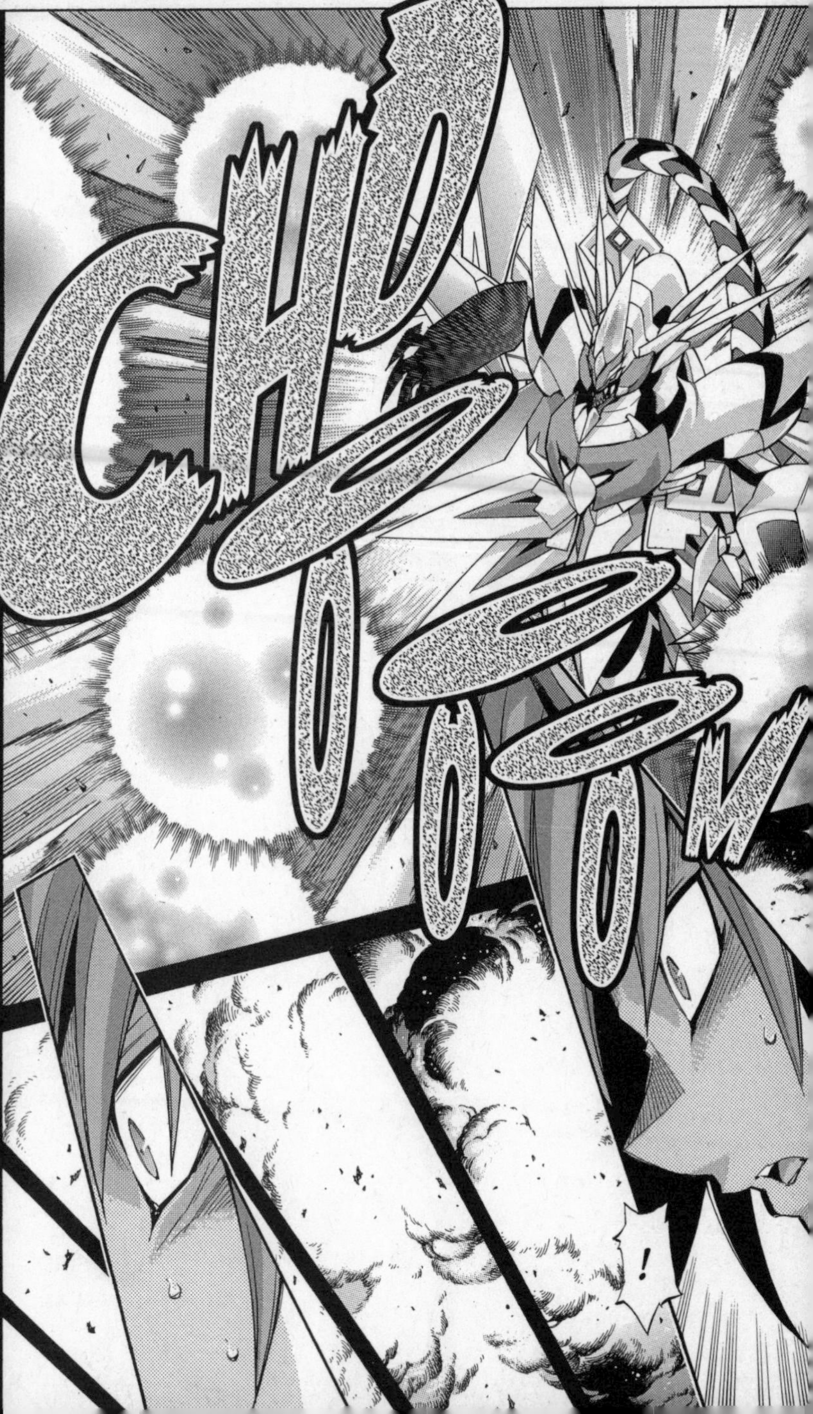
CHOOOOOM
!

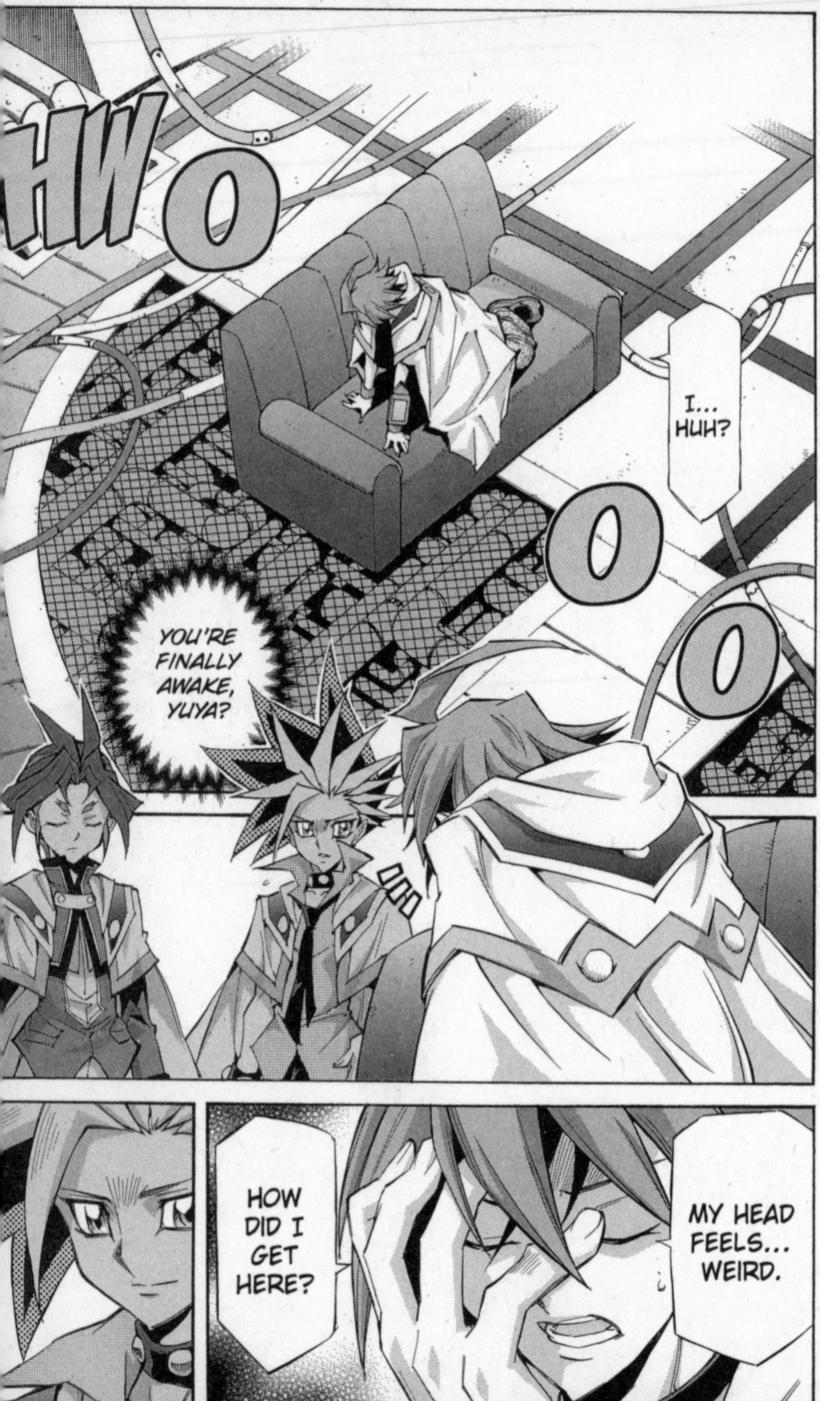
HWOOOO
I... HUH?
YOU'RE FINALLY AWAKE, YUYA?
MY HEAD FEELS... WEIRD.
HOW DID I GET HERE?

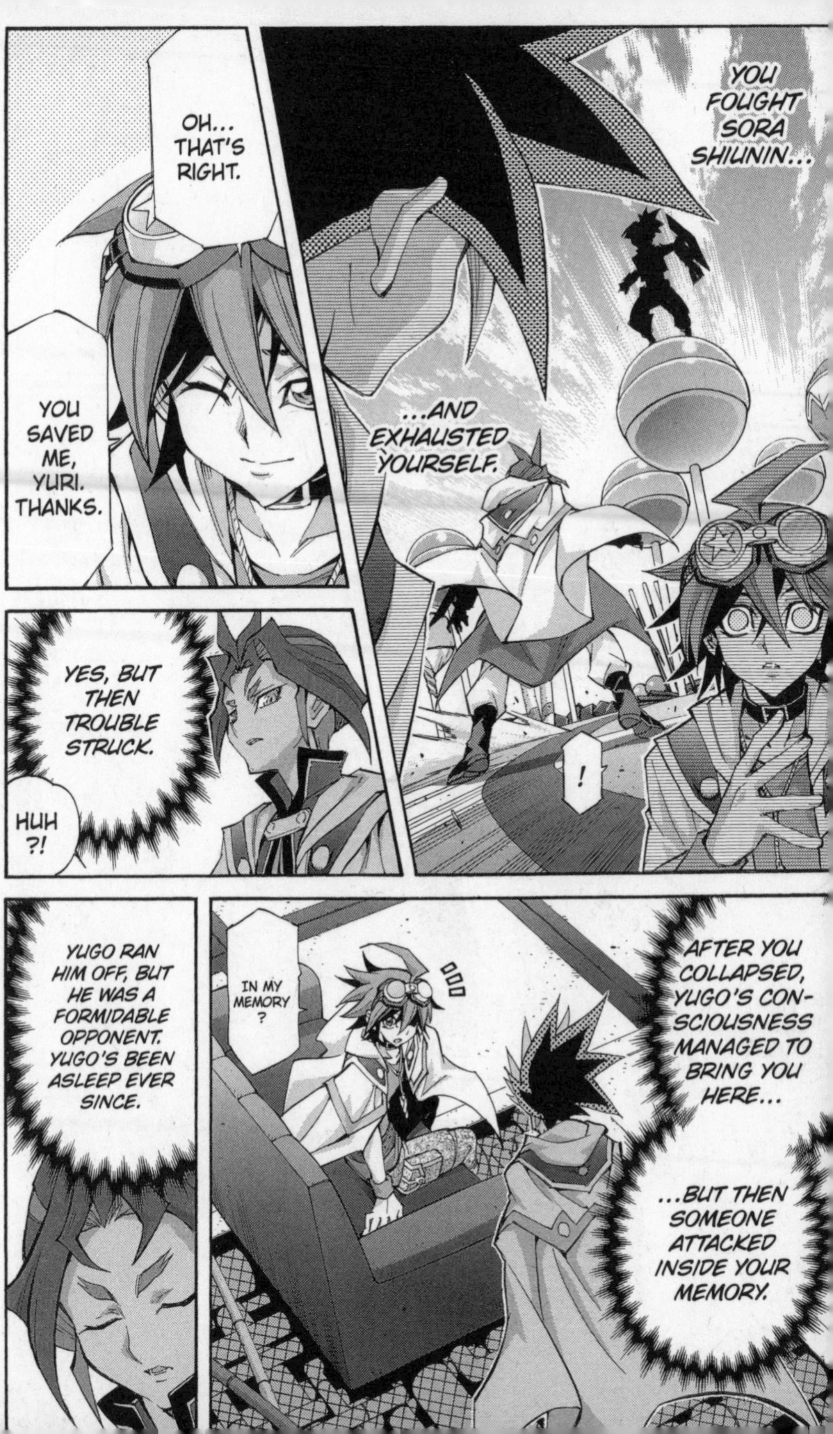
YOU FOUGHT SORA SHIUNIN...
...AND EXHAUSTED YOURSELF.
!
OH... THAT'S RIGHT.
YOU SAVED ME, YURI. THANKS.
YES, BUT THEN TROUBLE STRUCK.
HUH?!
AFTER YOU COLLAPSED, YUGO'S CON-SCIOUSNESS MANAGED TO BRING YOU HERE...
...BUT THEN SOMEONE ATTACKED INSIDE YOUR MEMORY.
IN MY MEMORY?
YUGO RAN HIM OFF, BUT HE WAS A FORMIDABLE OPPONENT. YUGO'S BEEN ASLEEP EVER SINCE.

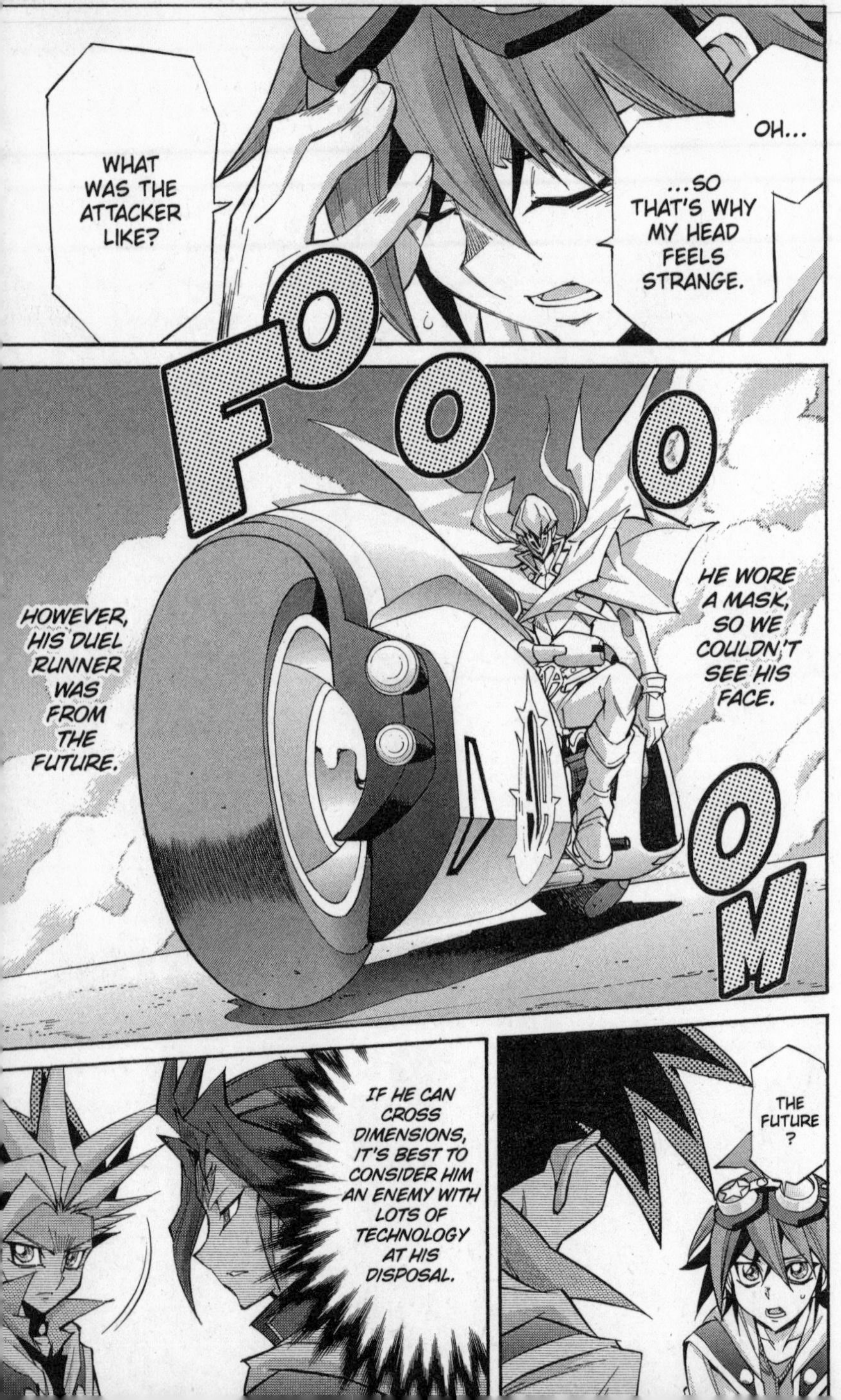
OH...
...SO THAT'S WHY MY HEAD FEELS STRANGE.
WHAT WAS THE ATTACKER LIKE?
FOOOOOM
HE WORE A MASK, SO WE COULDN'T SEE HIS FACE.
HOWEVER, HIS DUEL RUNNER WAS FROM THE FUTURE.
THE FUTURE?
IF HE CAN CROSS DIMENSIONS, IT'S BEST TO CONSIDER HIM AN ENEMY WITH LOTS OF TECHNOLOGY AT HIS DISPOSAL.

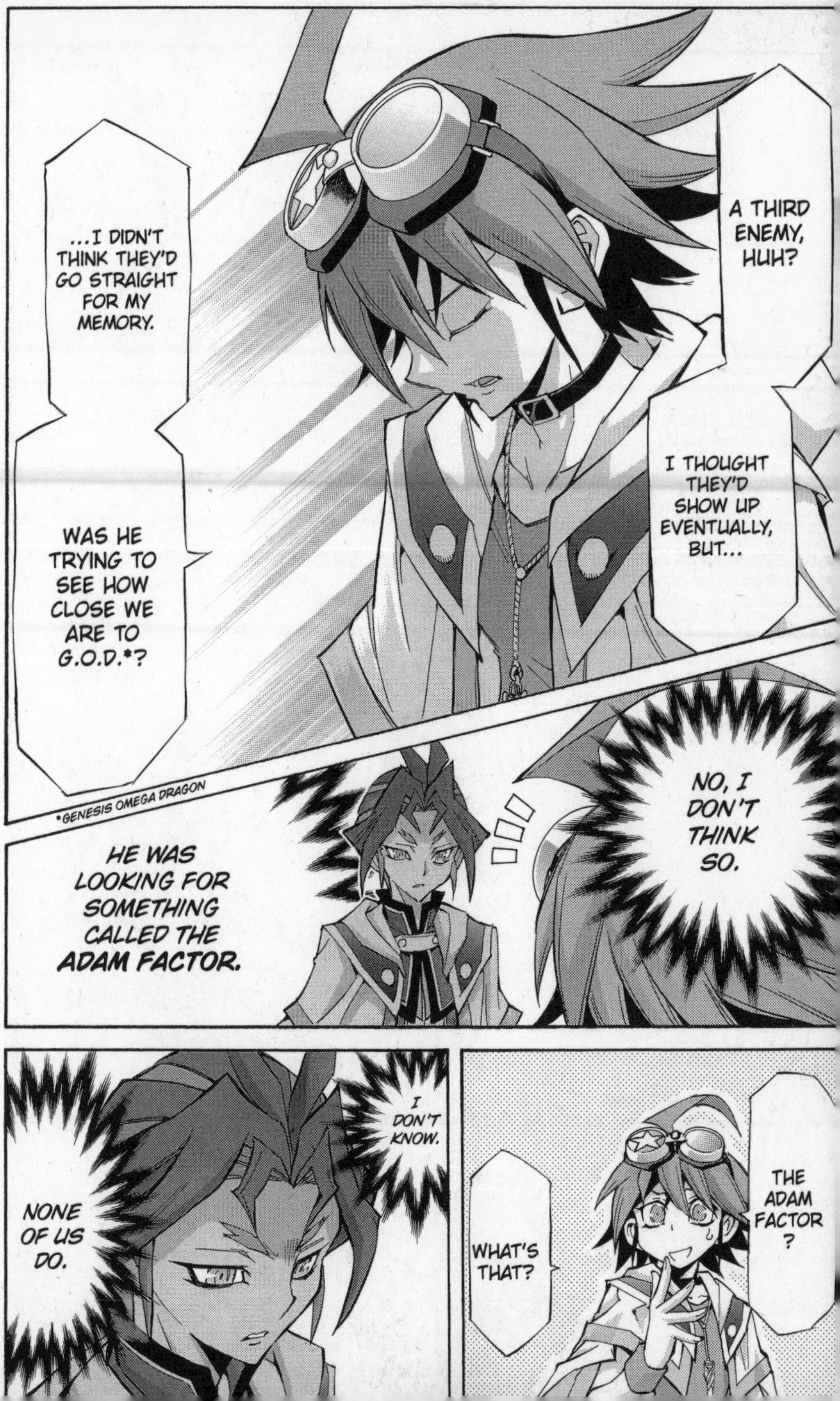
A THIRD ENEMY, HUH?
I THOUGHT THEY'D SHOW UP EVENTUALLY, BUT...
...I DIDN'T THINK THEY'D GO STRAIGHT FOR MY MEMORY.
WAS HE TRYING TO SEE HOW CLOSE WE ARE TO G.O.D.*?
*GENESIS OMEGA DRAGON
NO, I DON'T THINK SO.
HE WAS LOOKING FOR SOMETHING CALLED THE ADAM FACTOR.
THE ADAM FACTOR?
WHAT'S THAT?
I DON'T KNOW.
NONE OF US DO.

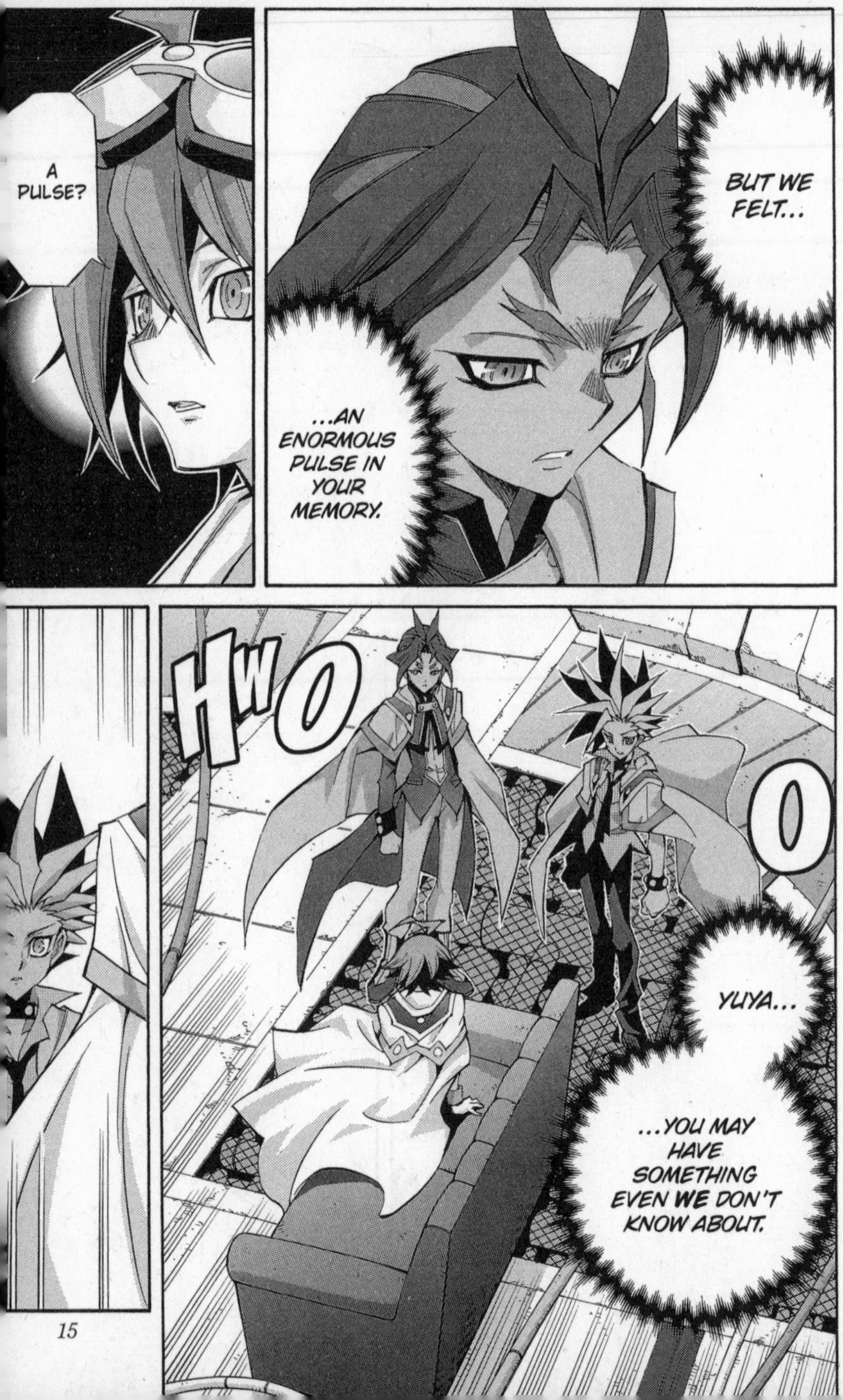
BUT WE FELT...
...AN ENORMOUS PULSE IN YOUR MEMORY.
A PULSE?
HWOO
YUYA...
...YOU MAY HAVE SOMETHING EVEN WE DON'T KNOW ABOUT.

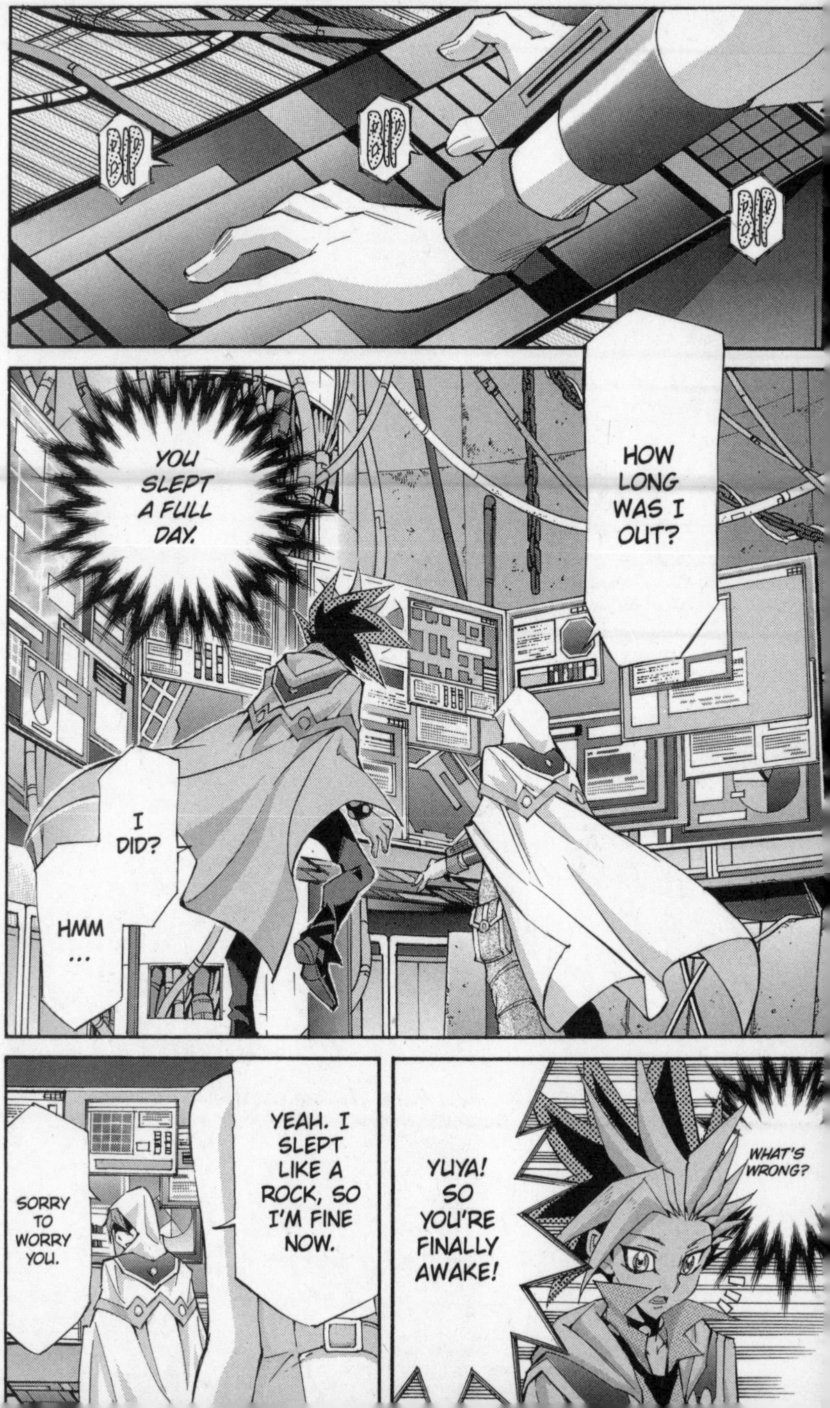
BIP
BIP
BIP
HOW LONG WAS I OUT?
YOU SLEPT A FULL DAY.
I DID?
HMM ...
WHAT'S WRONG?
YUYA! SO YOU'RE FINALLY AWAKE!
YEAH. I SLEPT LIKE A ROCK, SO I'M FINE NOW.
SORRY TO WORRY YOU.

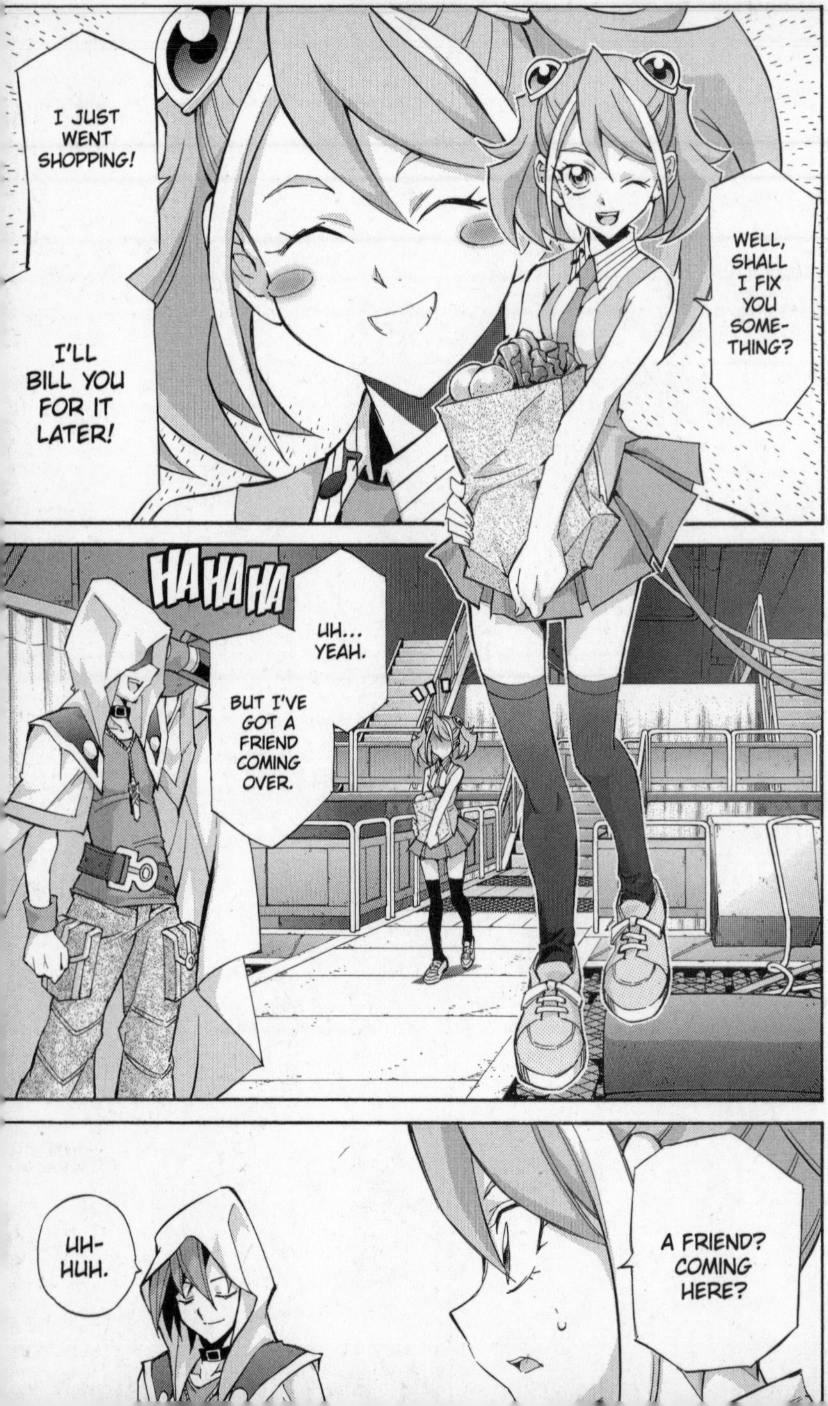
I JUST WENT SHOPPING!
WELL, SHALL I FIX YOU SOME-THING?
I'LL BILL YOU FOR IT LATER!
HA HA HA
UH... YEAH.
BUT I'VE GOT A FRIEND COMING OVER.
A FRIEND? COMING HERE?
UH-HUH.

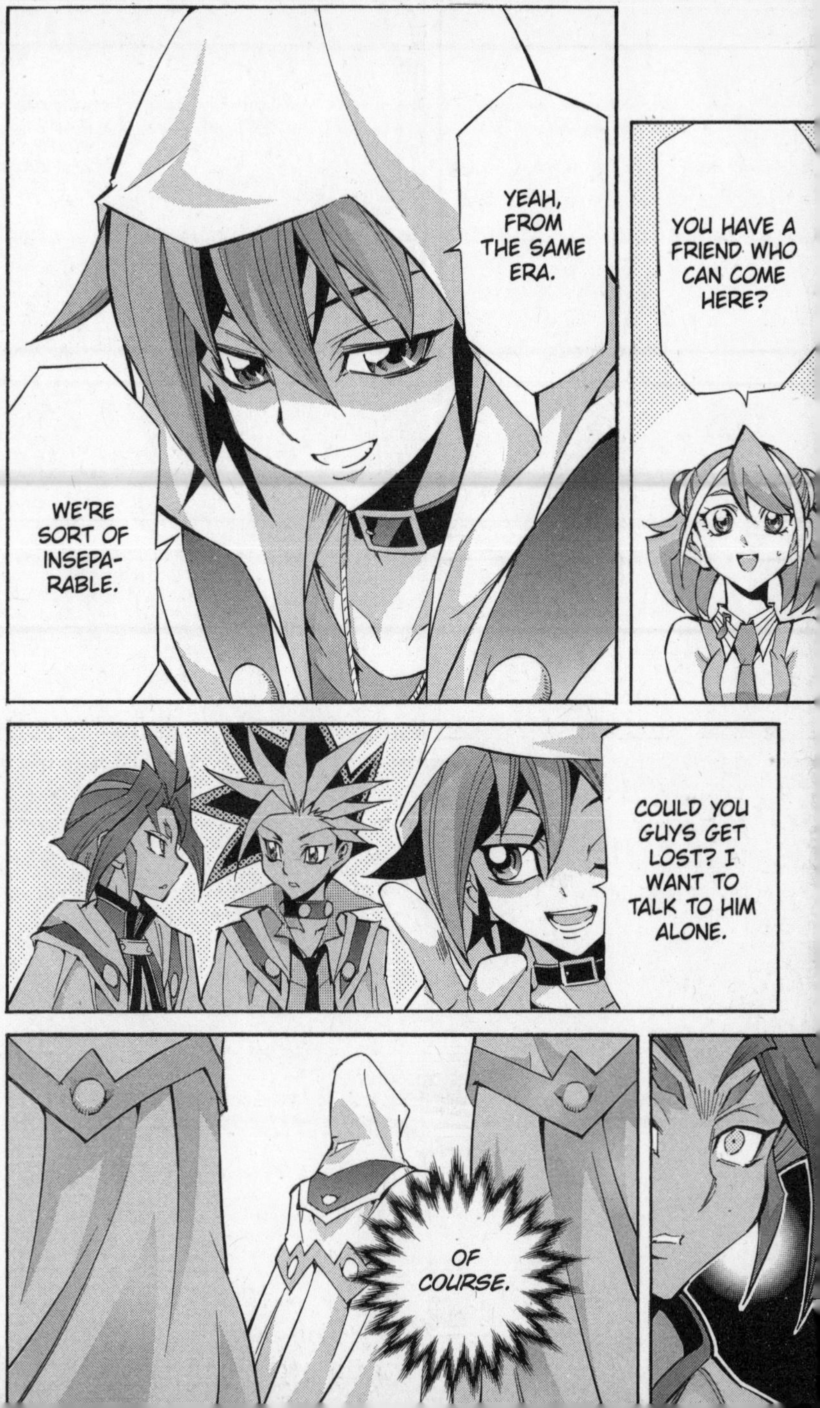
YOU HAVE A FRIEND WHO CAN COME HERE?
YEAH, FROM THE SAME ERA.
WE'RE SORT OF INSEPA-RABLE.
COULD YOU GUYS GET LOST? I WANT TO TALK TO HIM ALONE.
OF COURSE.

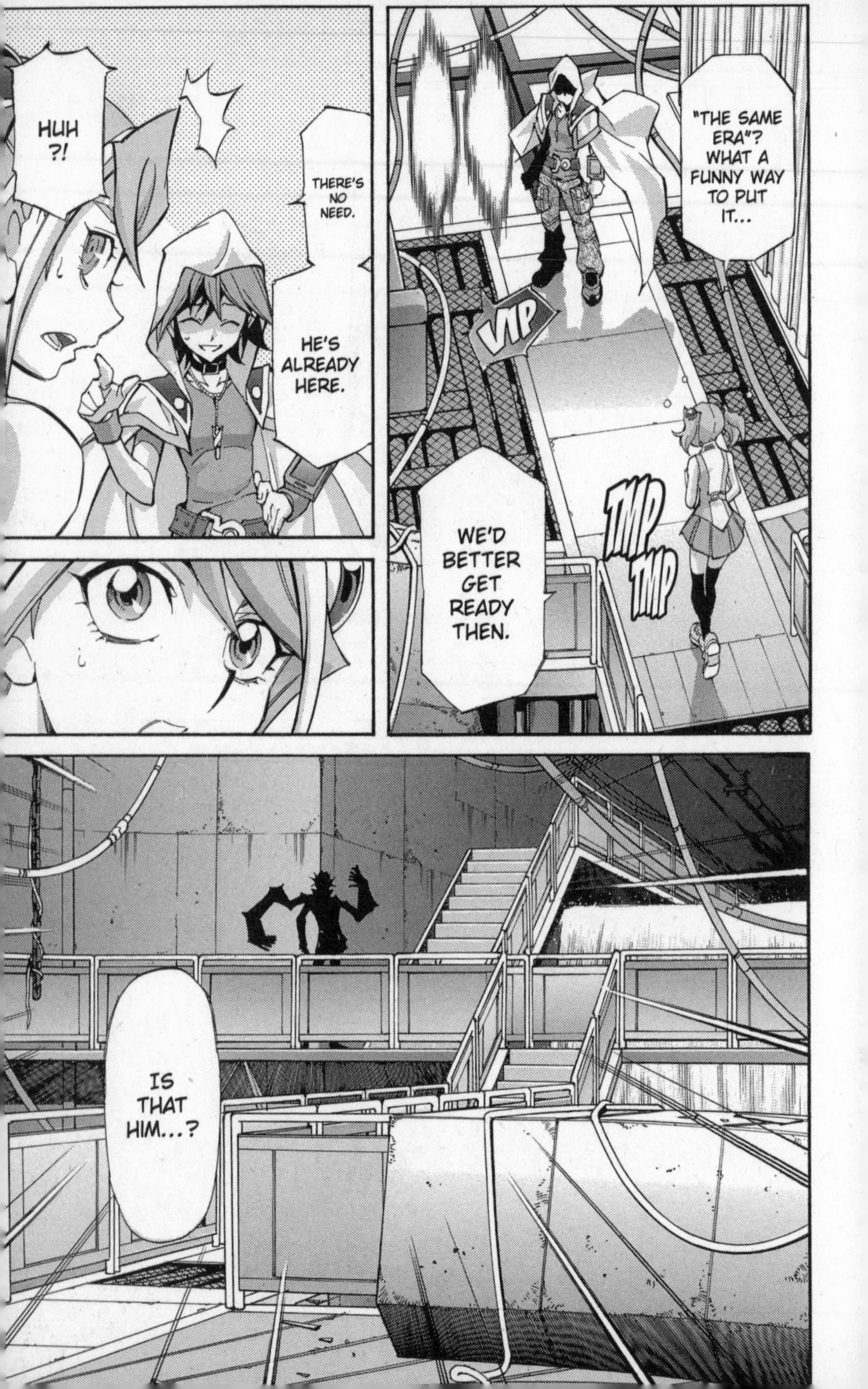
"THE SAME ERA"? WHAT A FUNNY WAY TO PUT IT...
VIP
WE'D BETTER GET READY THEN.
TMP TMP
THERE'S NO NEED.
HE'S ALREADY HERE.
HUH ?!
IS THAT HIM...?

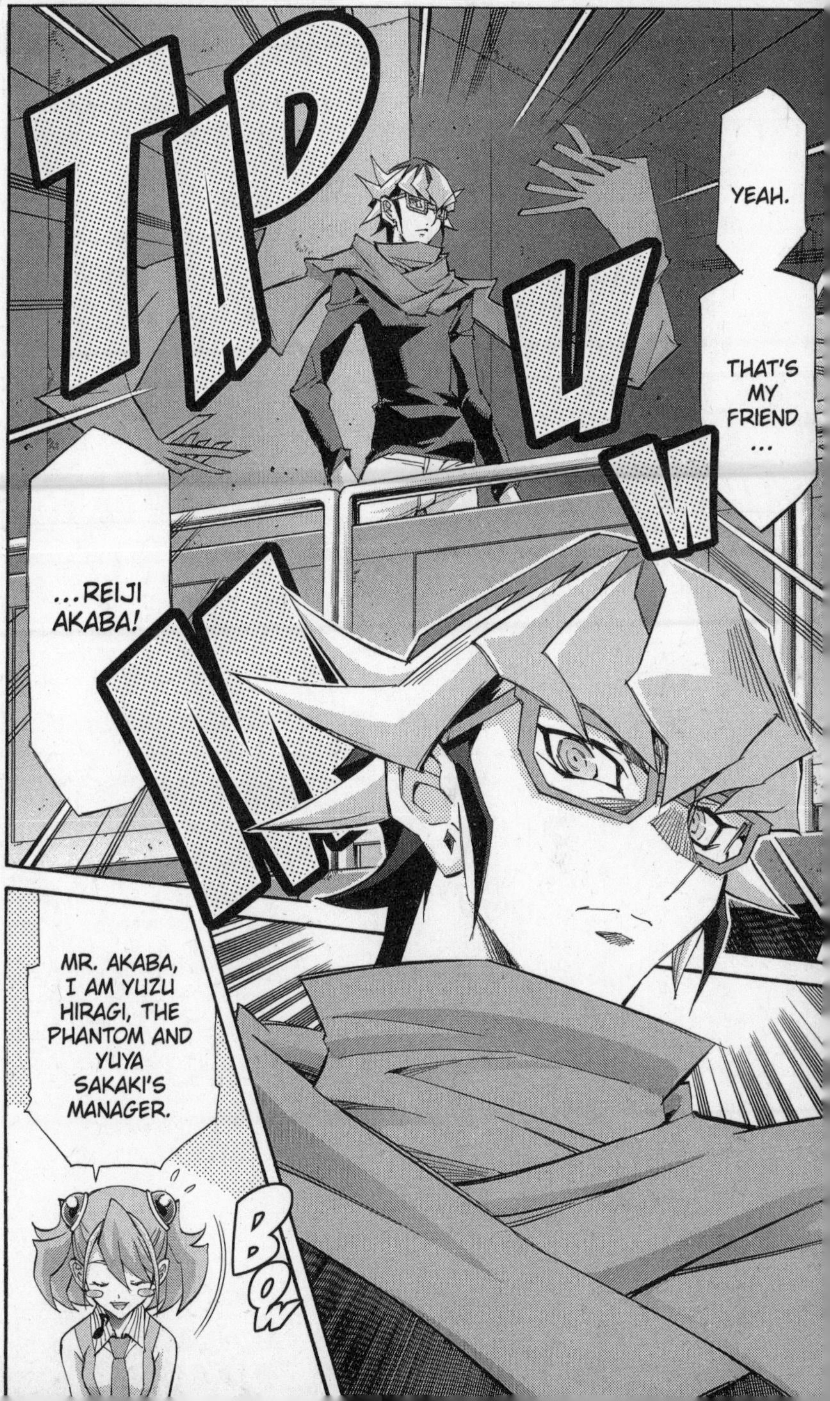
YEAH.
THAT'S MY FRIEND ...
TAP
...REIJI AKABA!
MR. AKABA, I AM YUZU HIRAGI, THE PHANTOM AND YUYA SAKAKI'S MANAGER.
BOW

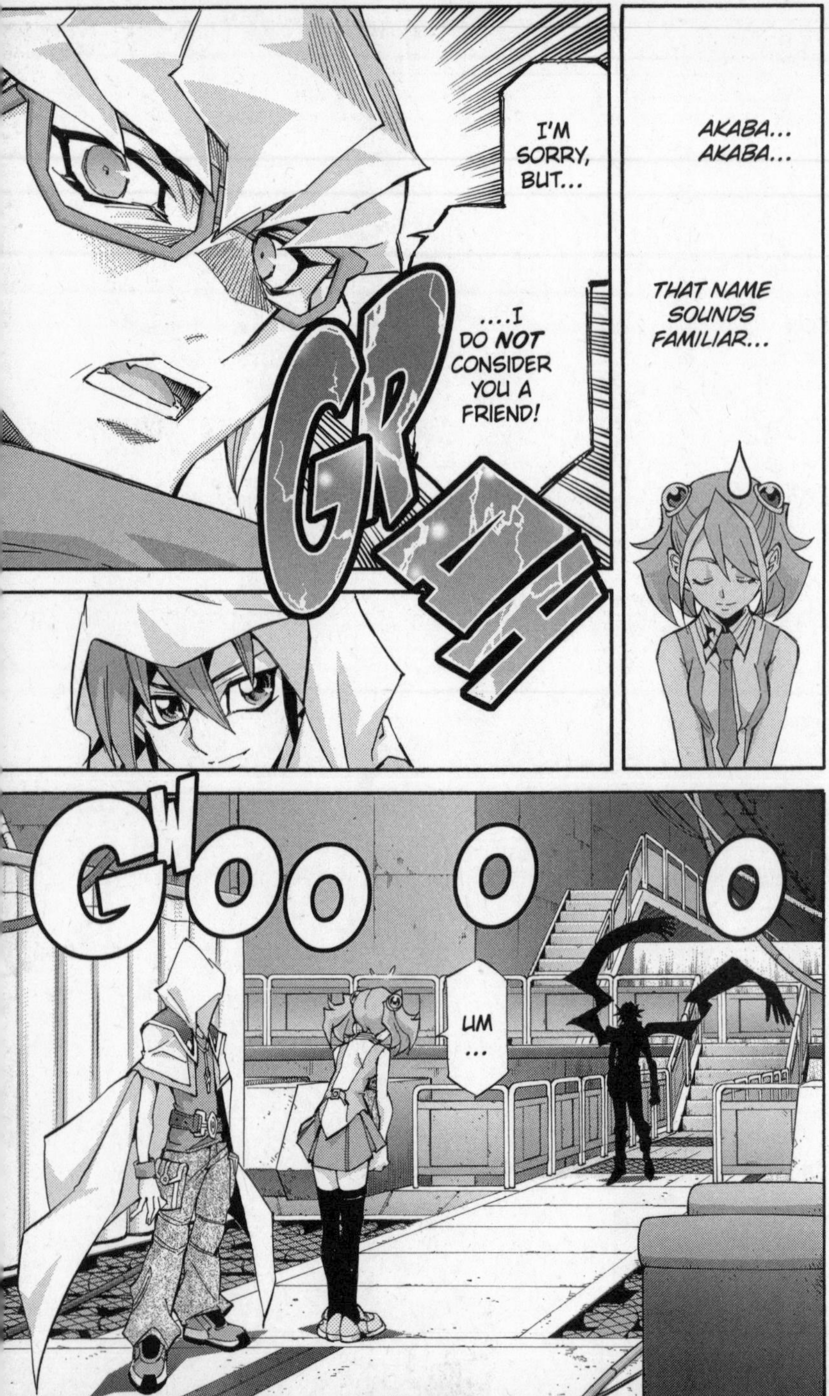
AKABA... AKABA...
THAT NAME SOUNDS FAMILIAR...
I'M SORRY, BUT...
....I DO NOT CONSIDER YOU A FRIEND!
GRAH
GWOOO O O
UM ...

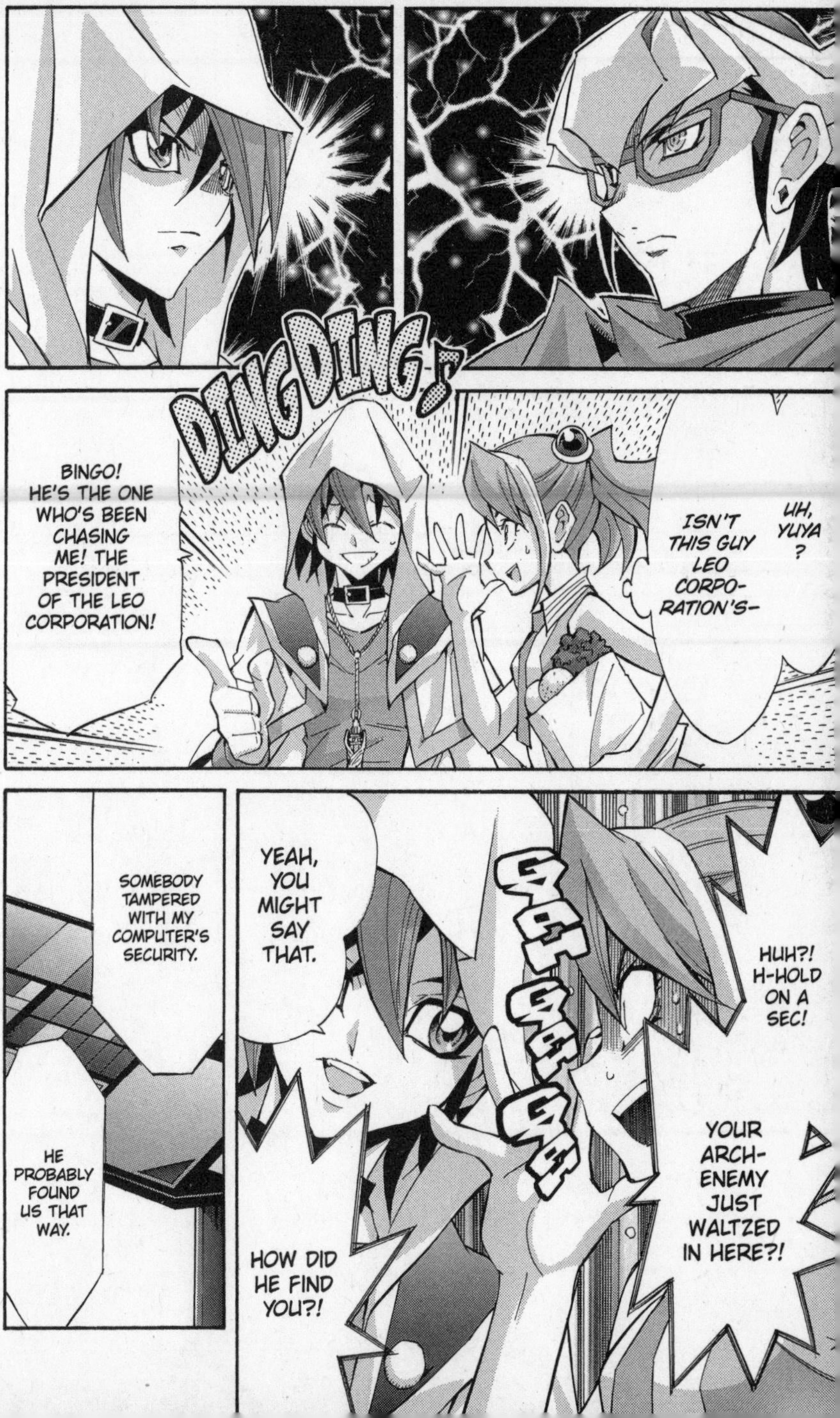
DING DING!
UH, YUYA?
ISN'T THIS GUY LEO CORPORATION'S-
BINGO! HE'S THE ONE WHO'S BEEN CHASING ME! THE PRESIDENT OF THE LEO CORPORATION!
HUH?! H-HOLD ON A SEC!
YOUR ARCH-ENEMY JUST WALTZED IN HERE?!
YEAH, YOU MIGHT SAY THAT.
HOW DID HE FIND YOU?!
SOMEBODY TAMPERED WITH MY COMPUTER'S SECURITY.
HE PROBABLY FOUND US THAT WAY.

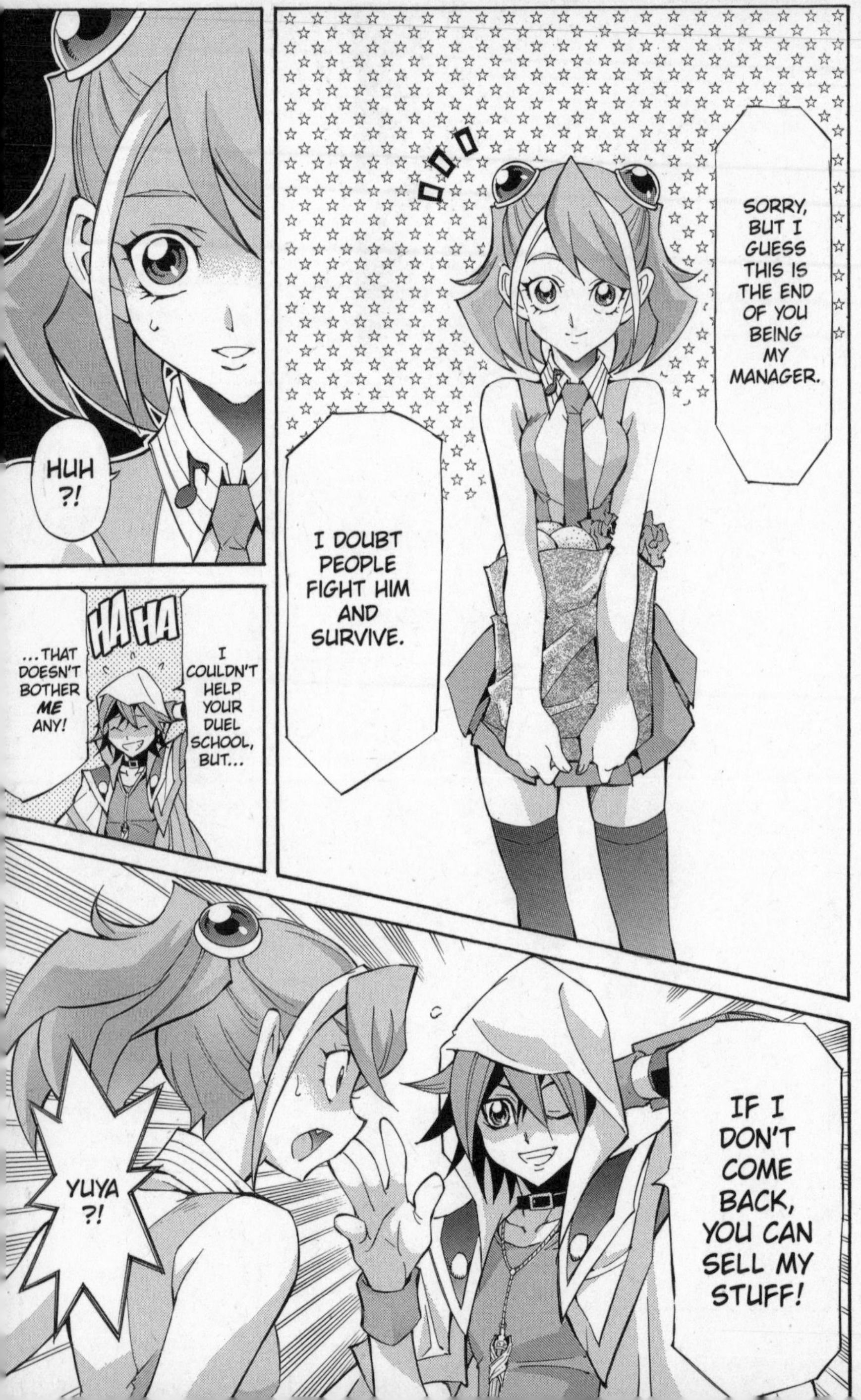
SORRY, BUT I GUESS THIS IS THE END OF YOU BEING MY MANAGER.
I DOUBT PEOPLE FIGHT HIM AND SURVIVE.
HUH?!
HA HA
I COULDN'T HELP YOUR DUEL SCHOOL, BUT...
...THAT DOESN'T BOTHER *ME* ANY!
IF I DON'T COME BACK, YOU CAN SELL MY STUFF!
YUYA?!

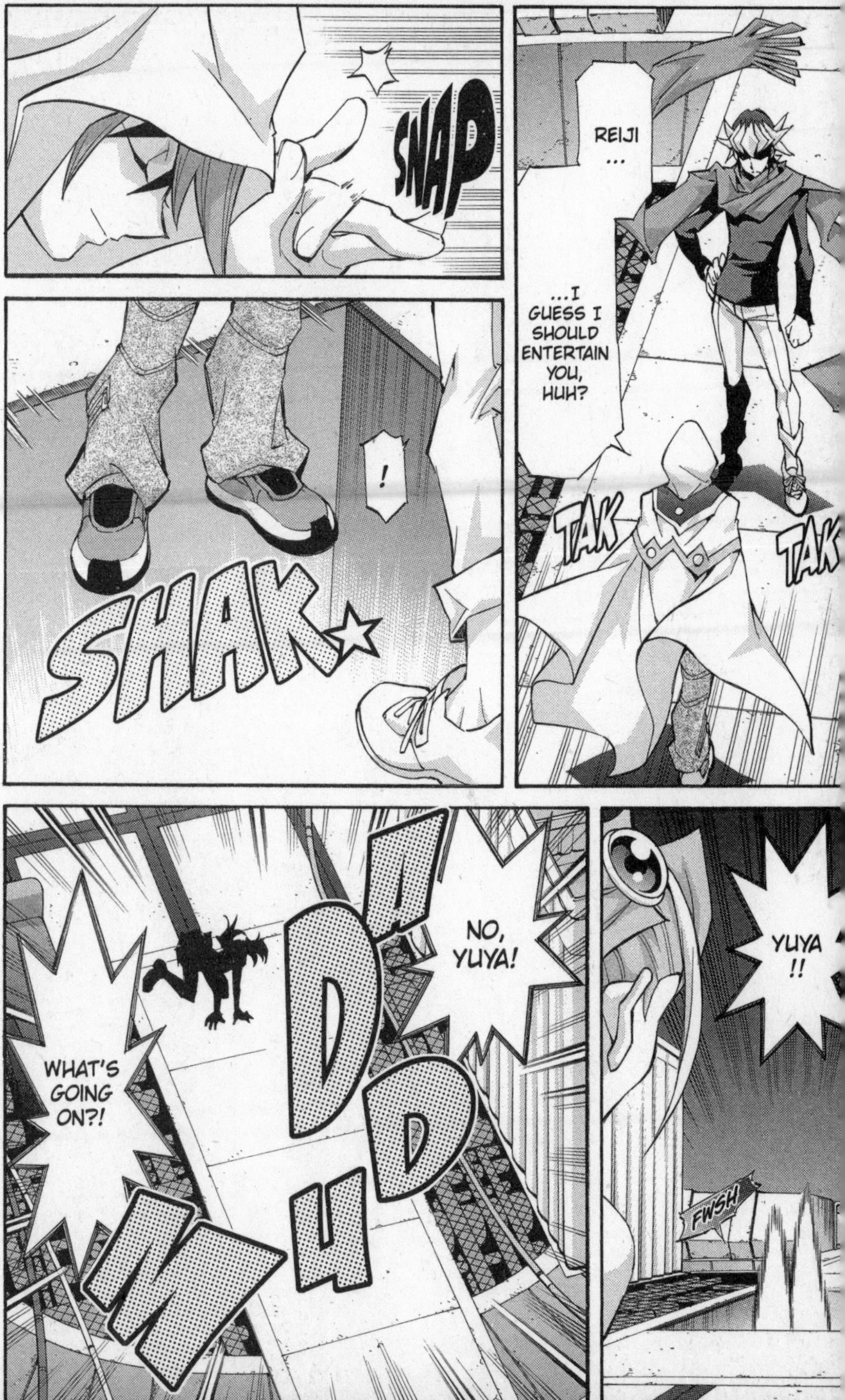
REIJI
...
...I GUESS I SHOULD ENTERTAIN YOU, HUH?
TAK
TAK
SNAP
!
SHAK
YUYA!!
FWSH
NO, YUYA!
DADUM
WHAT'S GOING ON?!

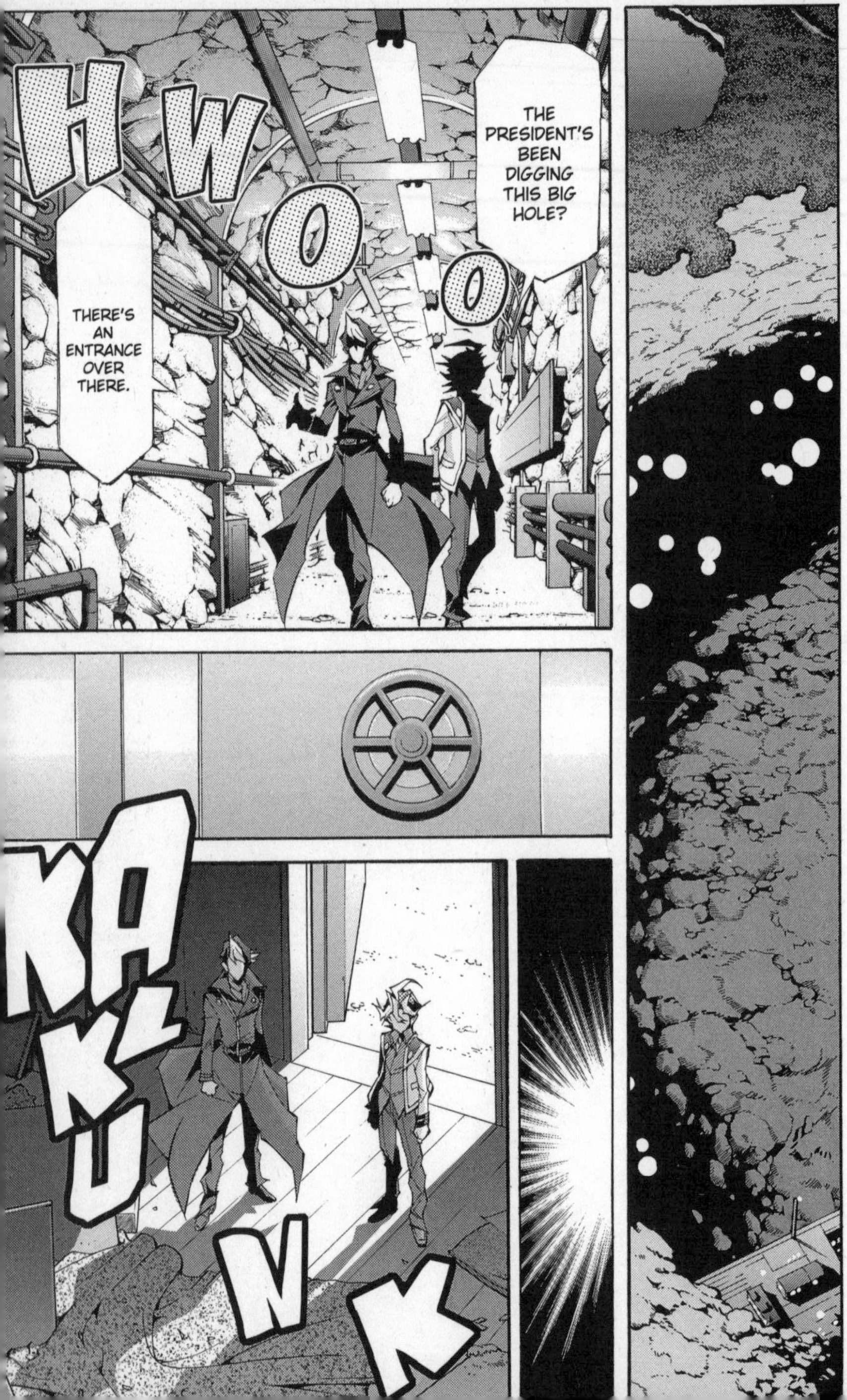
THE PRESIDENT'S BEEN DIGGING THIS BIG HOLE?
HWOO
THERE'S AN ENTRANCE OVER THERE.
KAKUNK

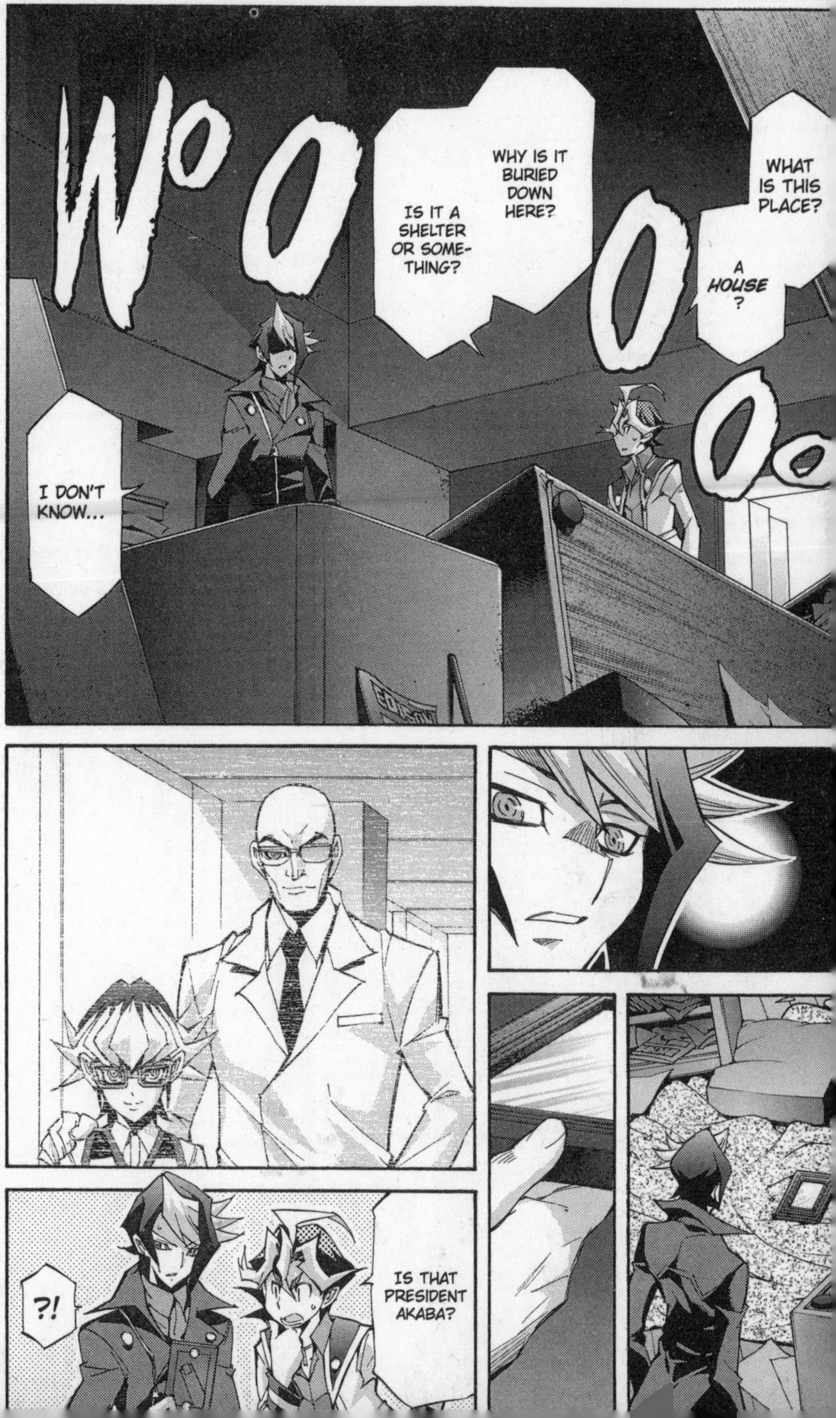
WoOOOOOo
WHAT IS THIS PLACE?
A HOUSE?
WHY IS IT BURIED DOWN HERE?
IS IT A SHELTER OR SOME-THING?
I DON'T KNOW...
IS THAT PRESIDENT AKABA?
?!

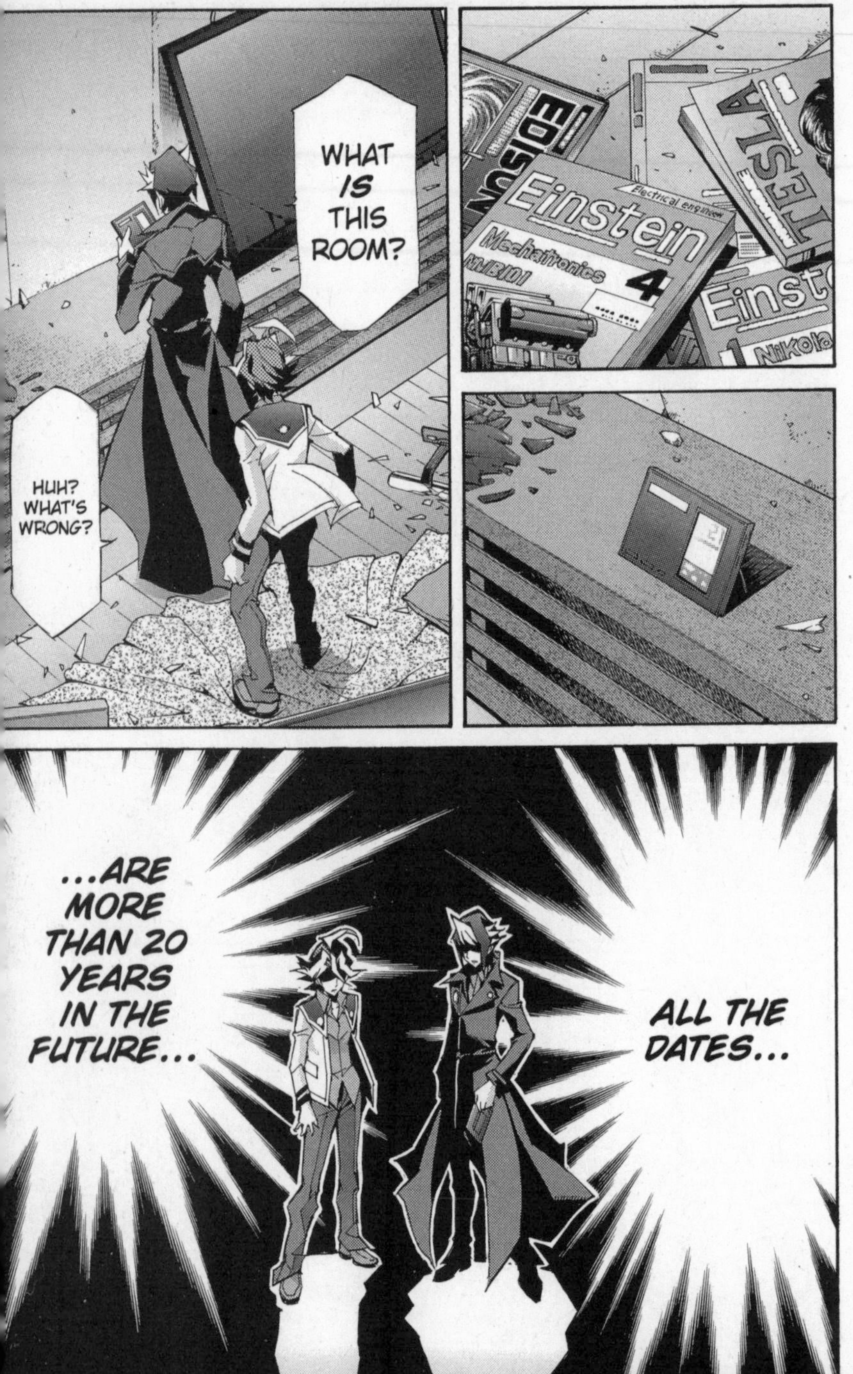
Einstein
Electrical engineer
Mechatronics
4
TESLA
WHAT *IS* THIS ROOM?
HUH? WHAT'S WRONG?
ALL THE DATES...
...ARE MORE THAN 20 YEARS IN THE FUTURE...

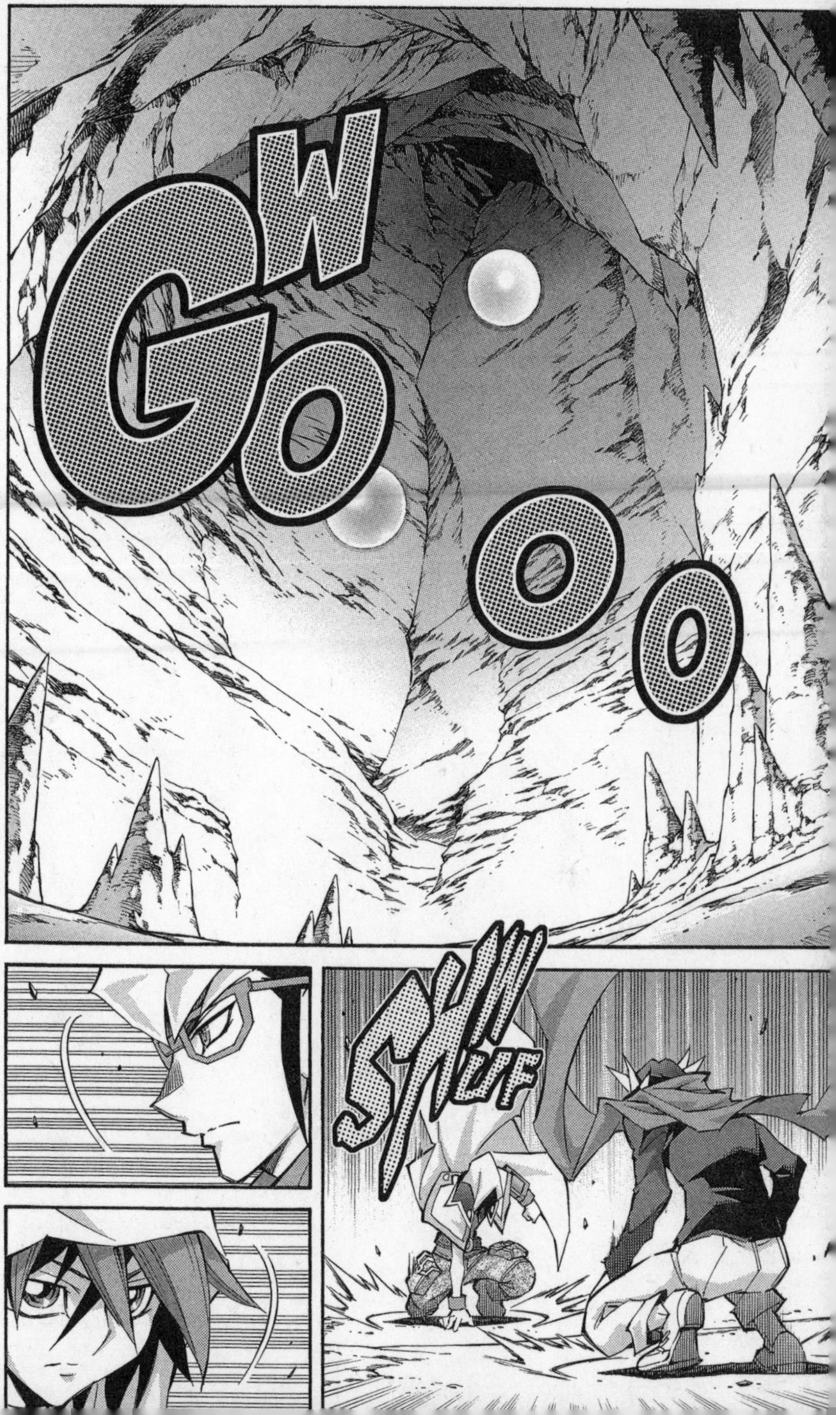
GWGOOOO
SHUF

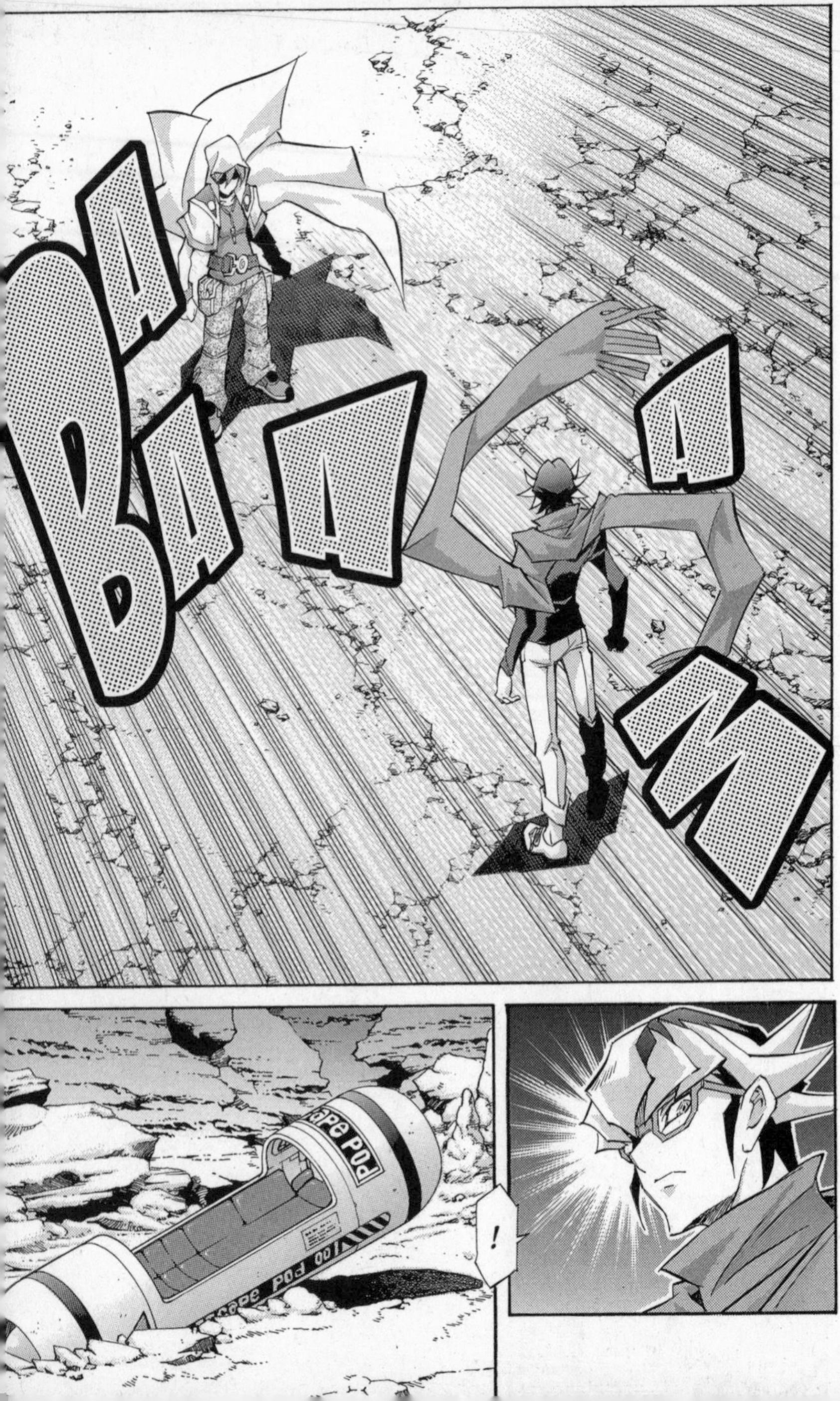
DABAAAM
!

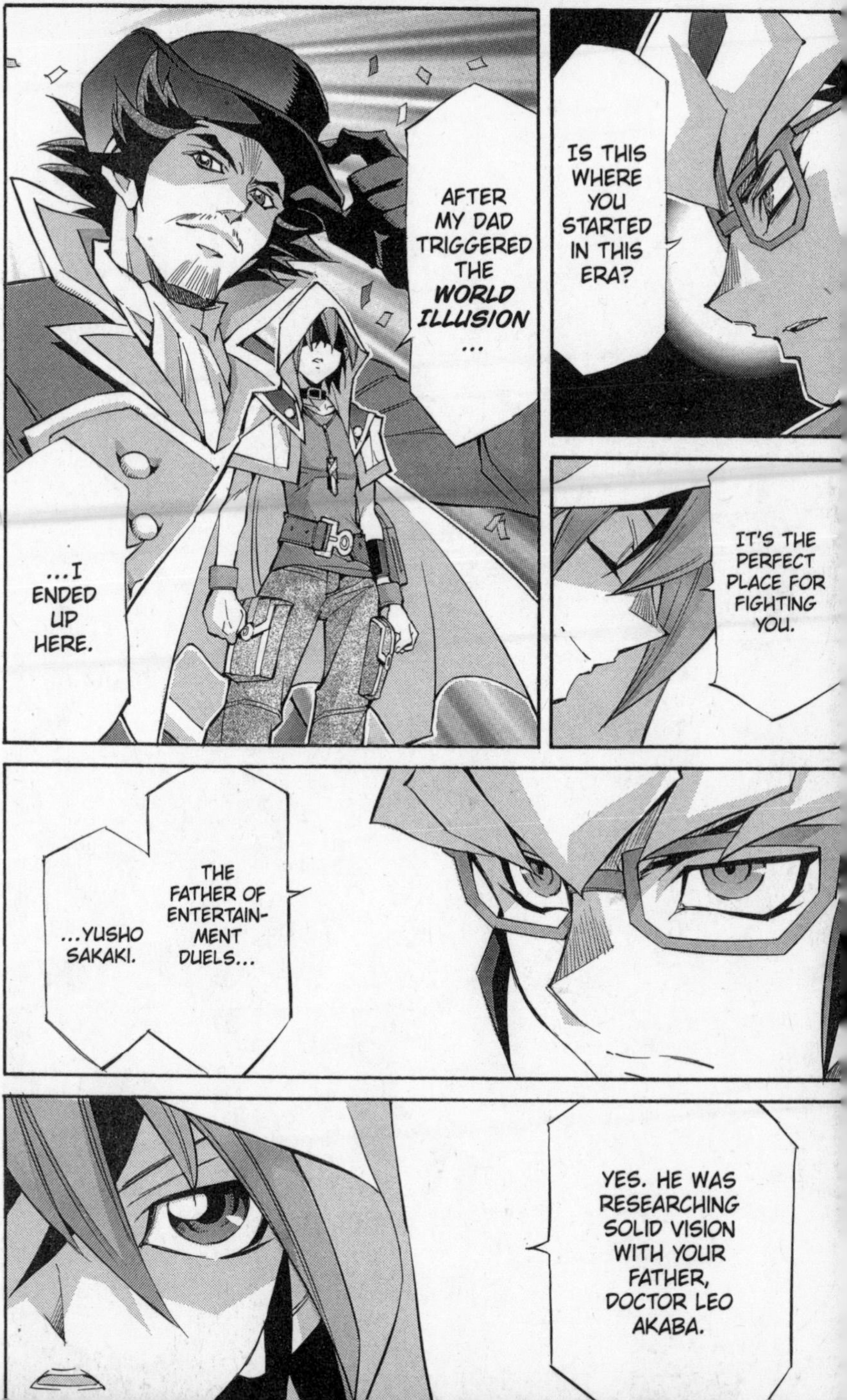
IS THIS WHERE YOU STARTED IN THIS ERA?
IT'S THE PERFECT PLACE FOR FIGHTING YOU.
AFTER MY DAD TRIGGERED THE *WORLD ILLUSION*...
...I ENDED UP HERE.
THE FATHER OF ENTERTAIN-MENT DUELS...
...YUSHO SAKAKI.
YES. HE WAS RESEARCHING SOLID VISION WITH YOUR FATHER, DOCTOR LEO AKABA.

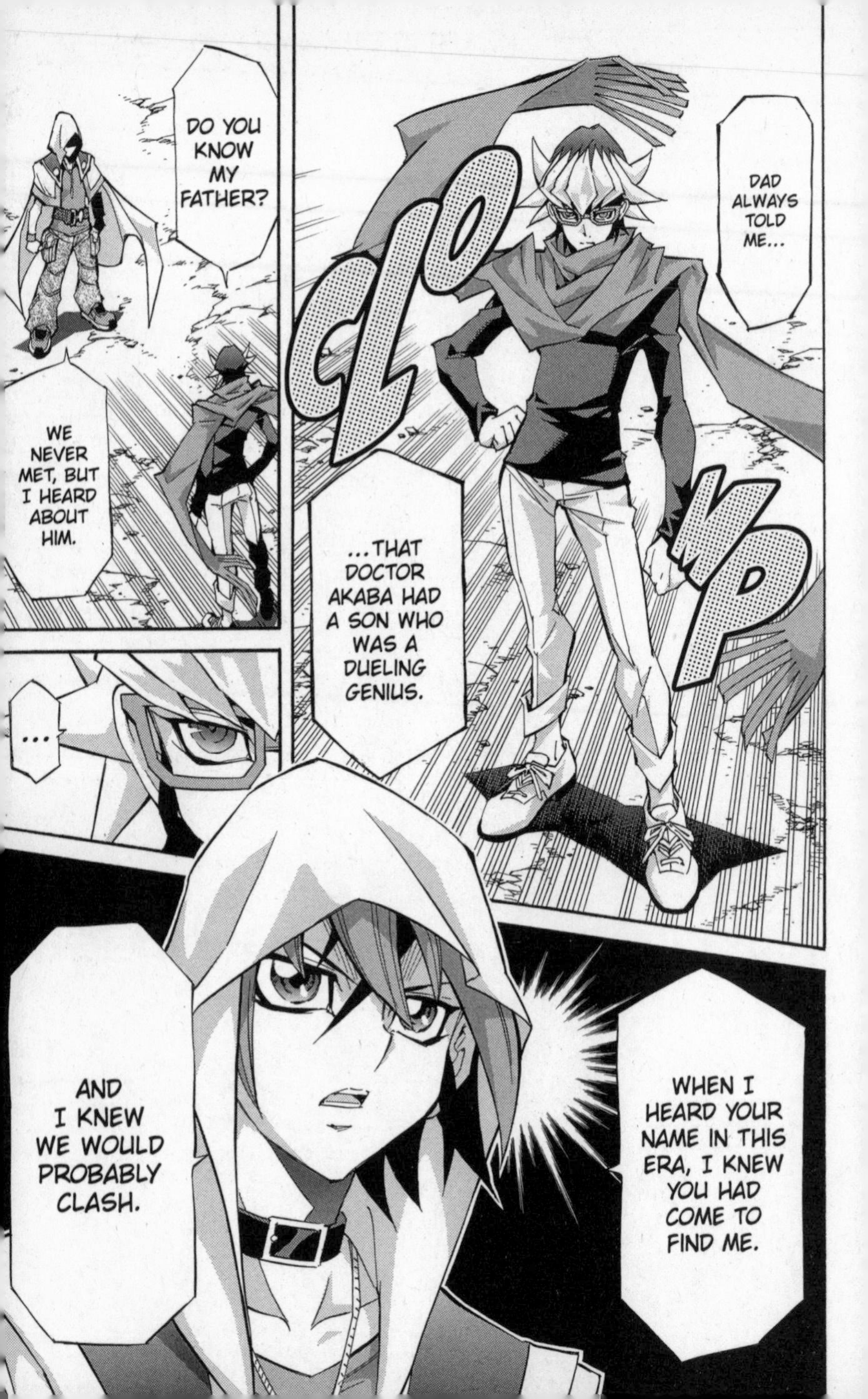
DAD ALWAYS TOLD ME...
...THAT DOCTOR AKABA HAD A SON WHO WAS A DUELING GENIUS.
DO YOU KNOW MY FATHER?
WE NEVER MET, BUT I HEARD ABOUT HIM.
...
WHEN I HEARD YOUR NAME IN THIS ERA, I KNEW YOU HAD COME TO FIND ME.
AND I KNEW WE WOULD PROBABLY CLASH.

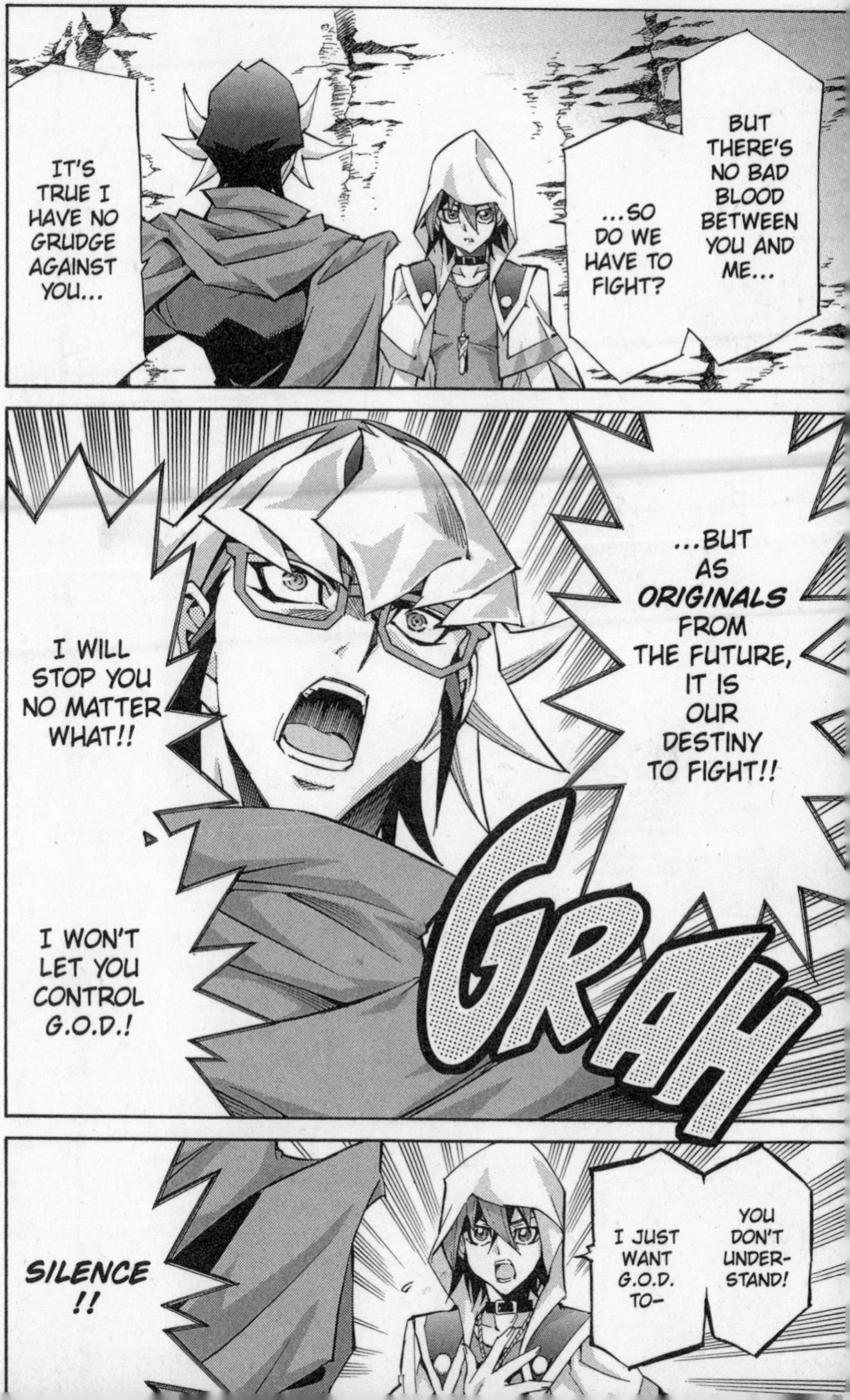

BUT THERE'S NO BAD BLOOD BETWEEN YOU AND ME...
...SO DO WE HAVE TO FIGHT?
IT'S TRUE I HAVE NO GRUDGE AGAINST YOU...
...BUT AS *ORIGINALS* FROM THE FUTURE, IT IS OUR DESTINY TO FIGHT!!
GRAH
I WILL STOP YOU NO MATTER WHAT!!
I WON'T LET YOU CONTROL G.O.D.!
YOU DON'T UNDER-STAND!
I JUST WANT G.O.D. TO-
SILENCE!!

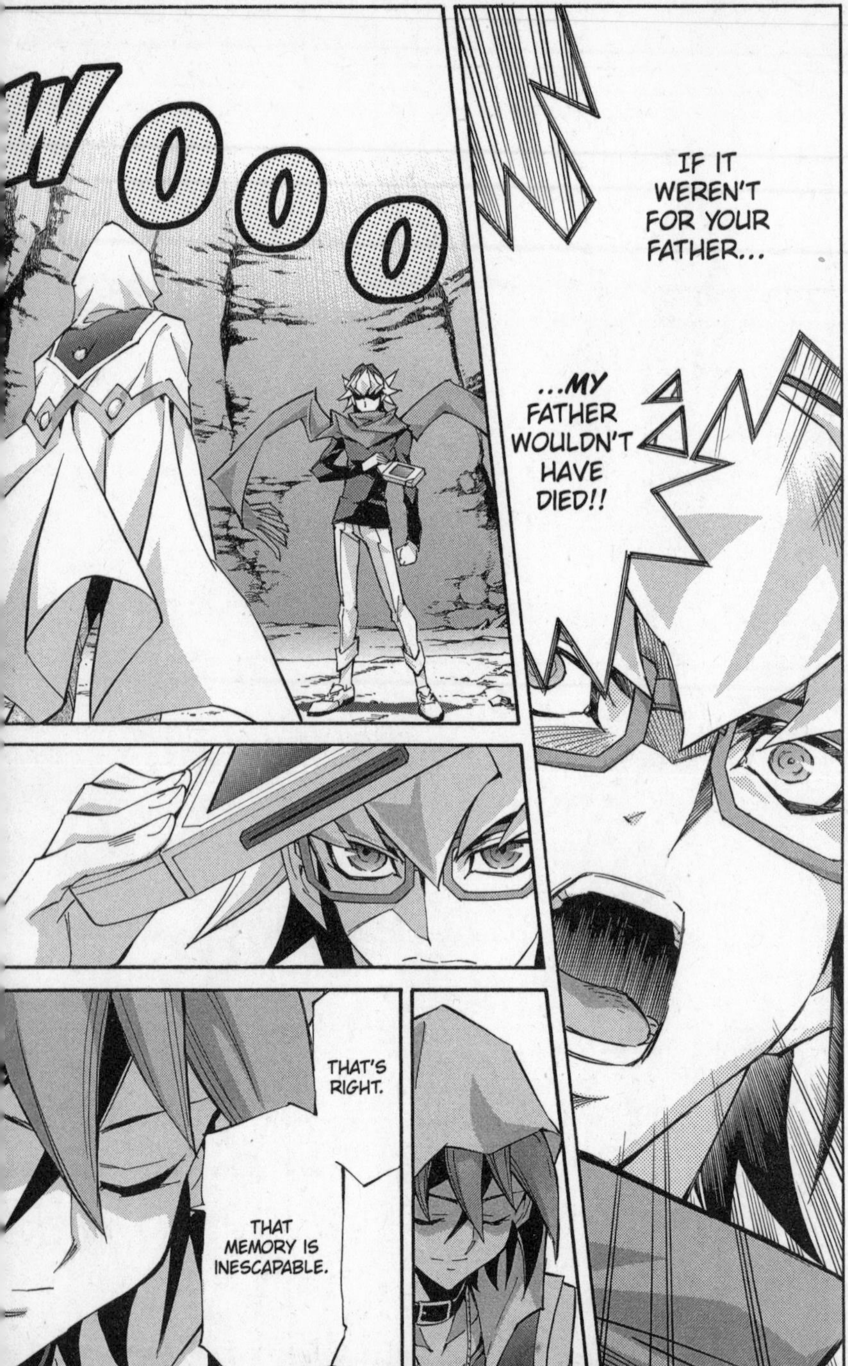
IF IT WEREN'T FOR YOUR FATHER...
...MY FATHER WOULDN'T HAVE DIED!!
WOOOO
THAT'S RIGHT.
THAT MEMORY IS INESCAPABLE.

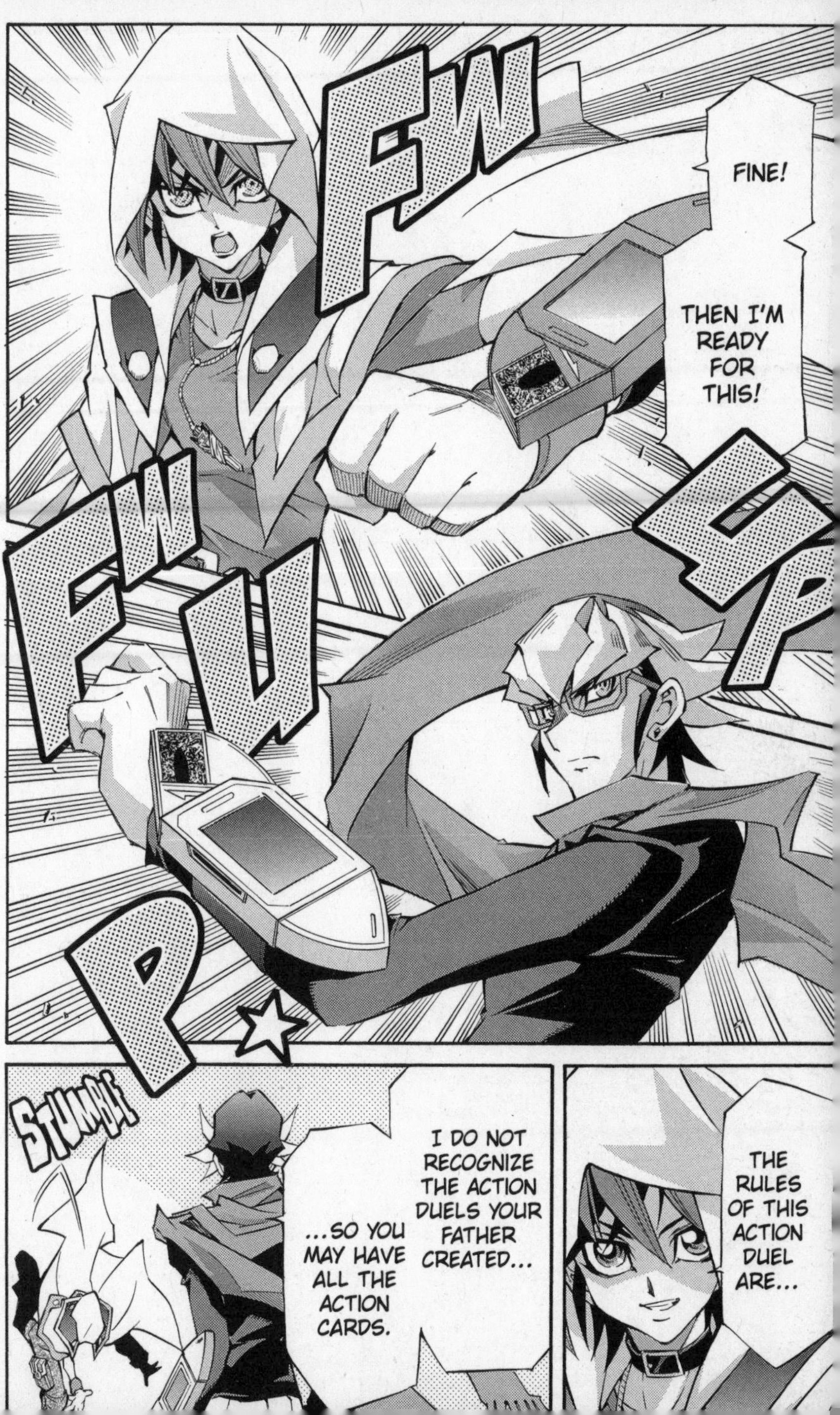
FINE!
THEN I'M READY FOR THIS!
THE RULES OF THIS ACTION DUEL ARE...
I DO NOT RECOGNIZE THE ACTION DUELS YOUR FATHER CREATED...
...SO YOU MAY HAVE ALL THE ACTION CARDS.
STUMBLE

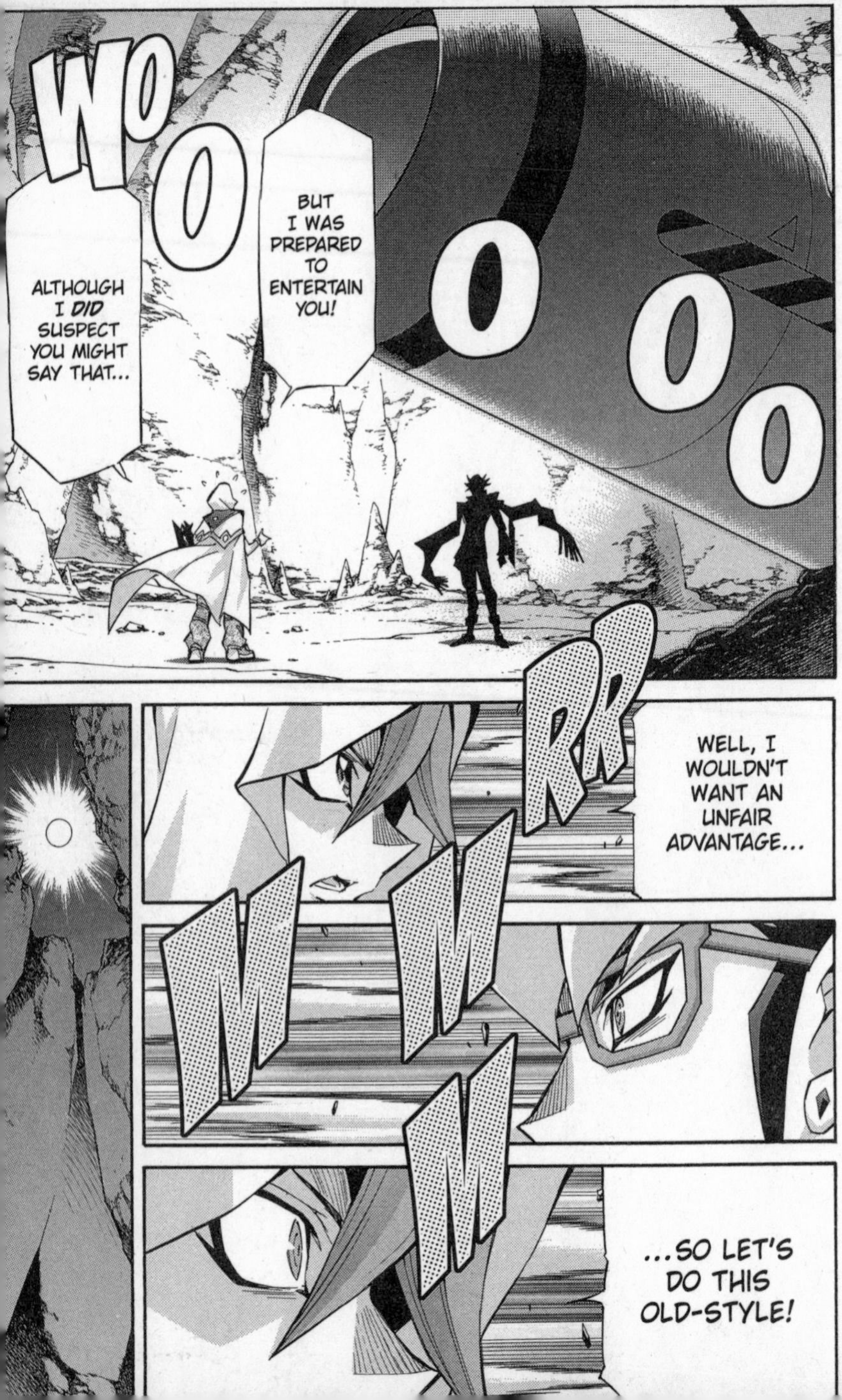
BUT I WAS PREPARED TO ENTERTAIN YOU!
ALTHOUGH I *DID* SUSPECT YOU MIGHT SAY THAT...
WOOOOOO
WELL, I WOULDN'T WANT AN UNFAIR ADVANTAGE...
RRMMM
...SO LET'S DO THIS OLD-STYLE!

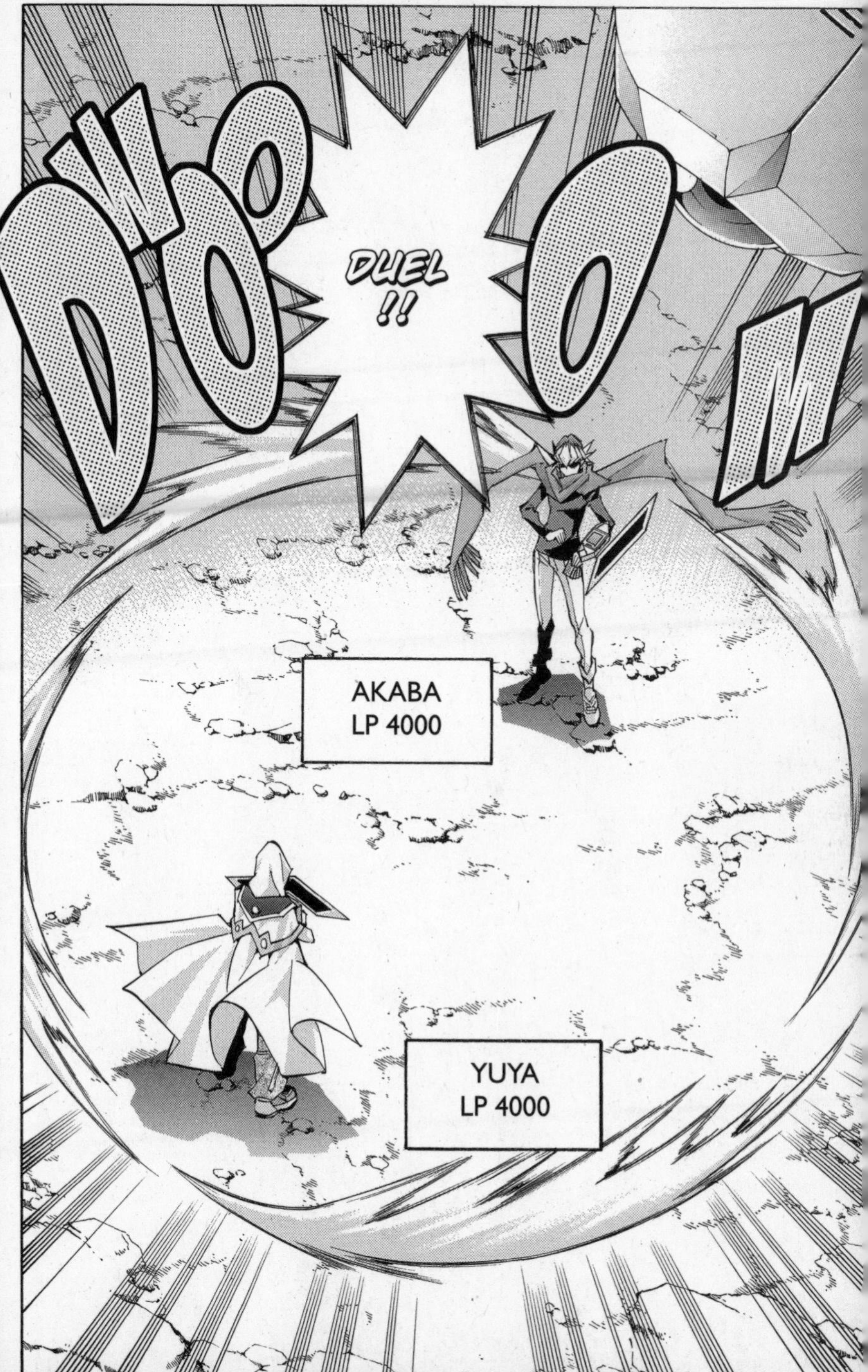
DOOOM
DUEL !!
AKABA
LP 4000
YUYA
LP 4000

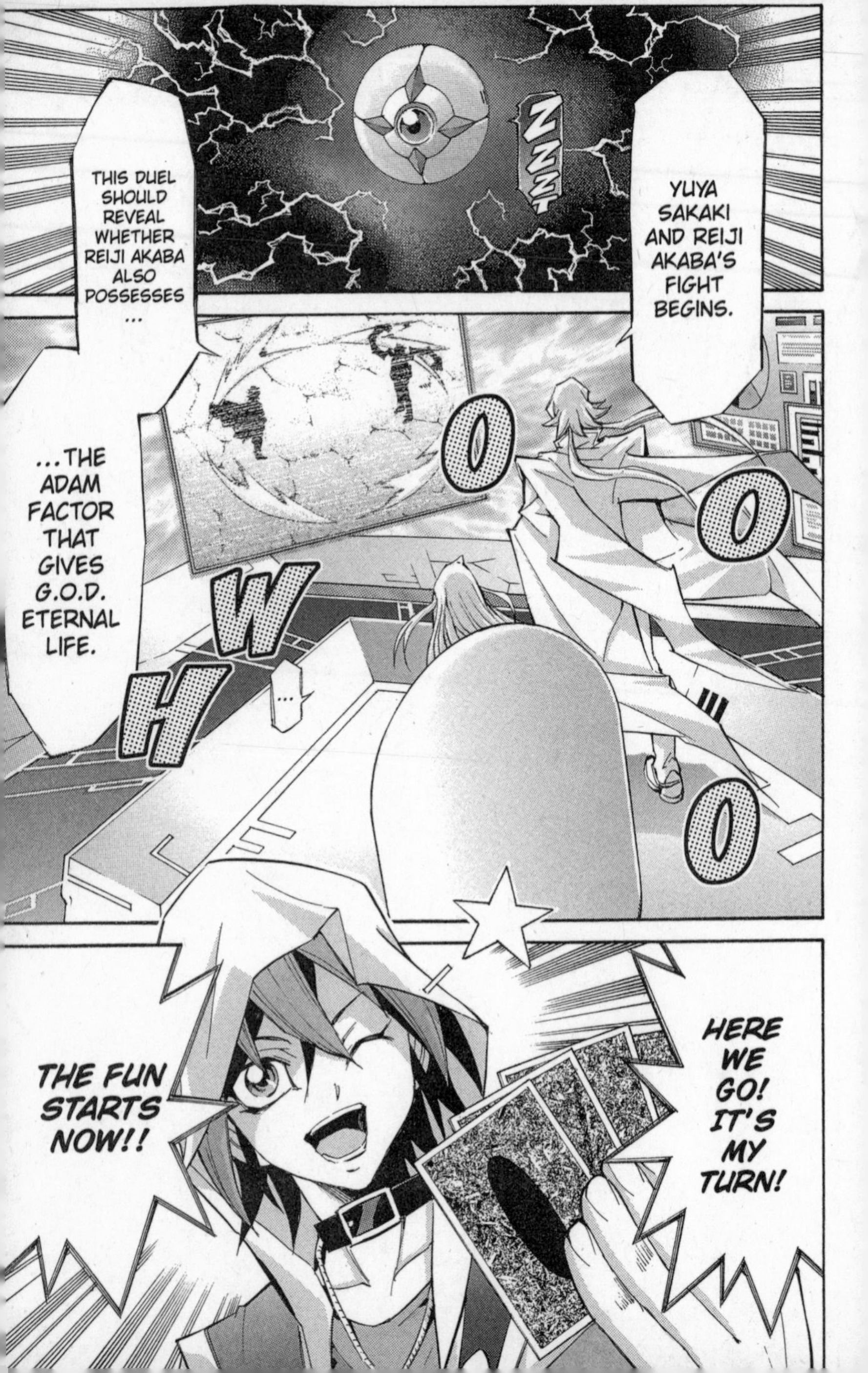
YUYA SAKAKI AND REIJI AKABA'S FIGHT BEGINS.
ZZZT
THIS DUEL SHOULD REVEAL WHETHER REIJI AKABA ALSO POSSESSES ...
...THE ADAM FACTOR THAT GIVES G.O.D. ETERNAL LIFE.
WHOOO
...
HERE WE GO! IT'S MY TURN!
THE FUN STARTS NOW!!

PRESENTING MIYOSHI SENSEI'S EARLY DESIGNS!

ARC-V CHARACTER SKETCHES

FUTOSHI

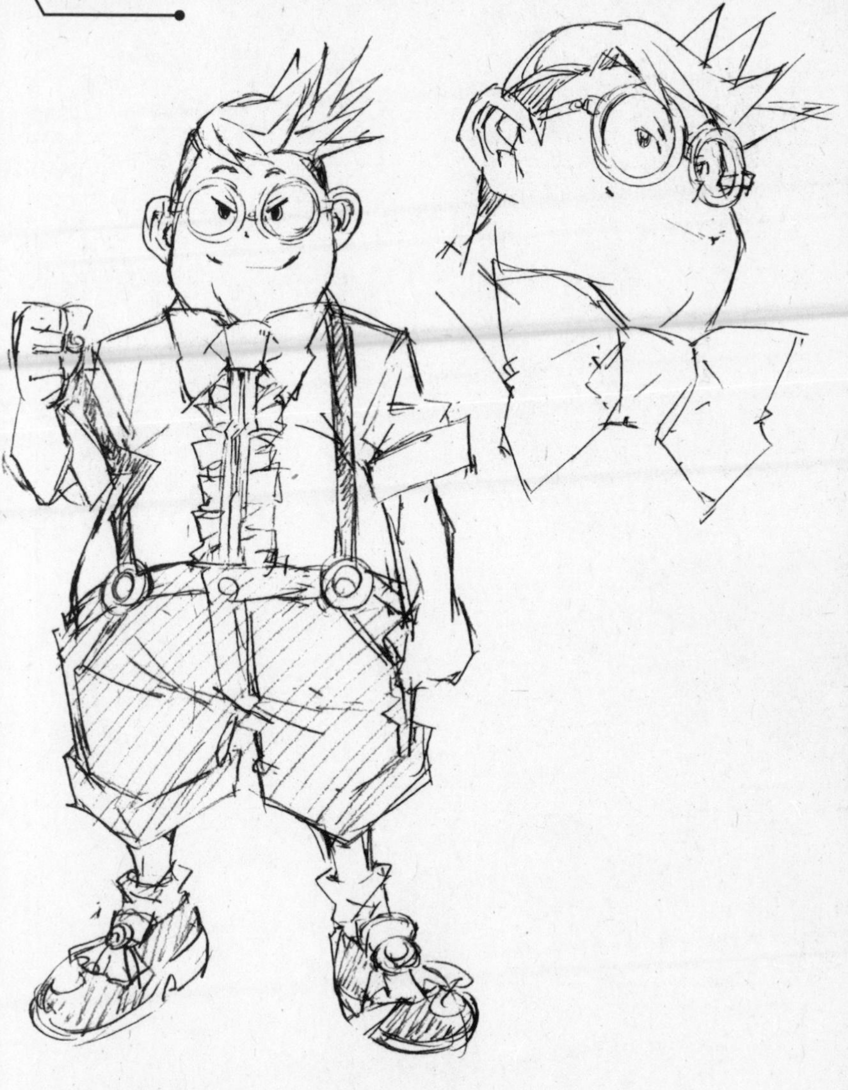

Futoshi hasn't shown up in the manga yet. In his early designs, he wore glasses. He looks like a rich kid from a good family!!

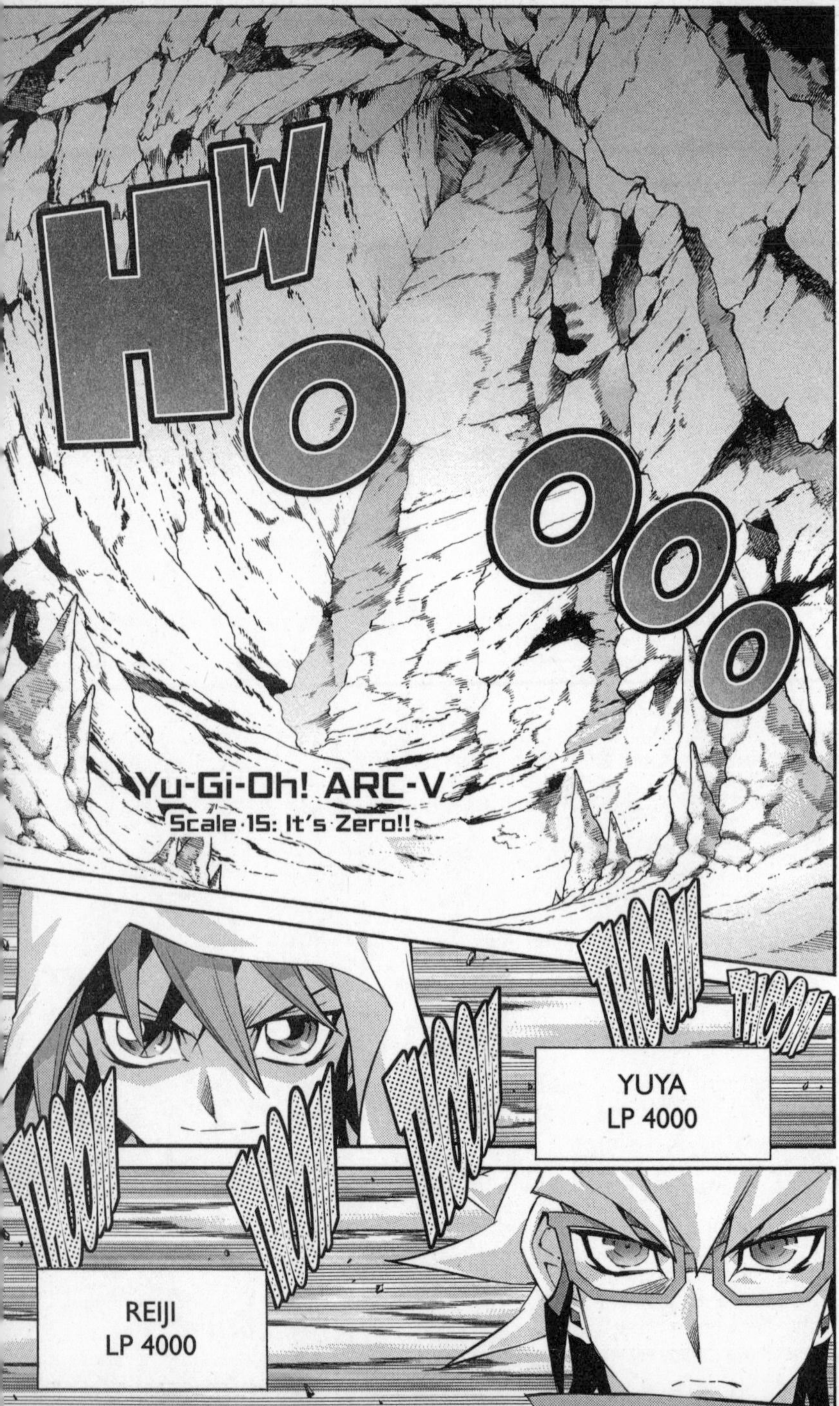
HWOOOO
Yu-Gi-Oh! ARC-V
Scale 15: It's Zero!!
THOOM
THOOM
YUYA
LP 4000
THOOM
THOOM
THOOM
REIJI
LP 4000

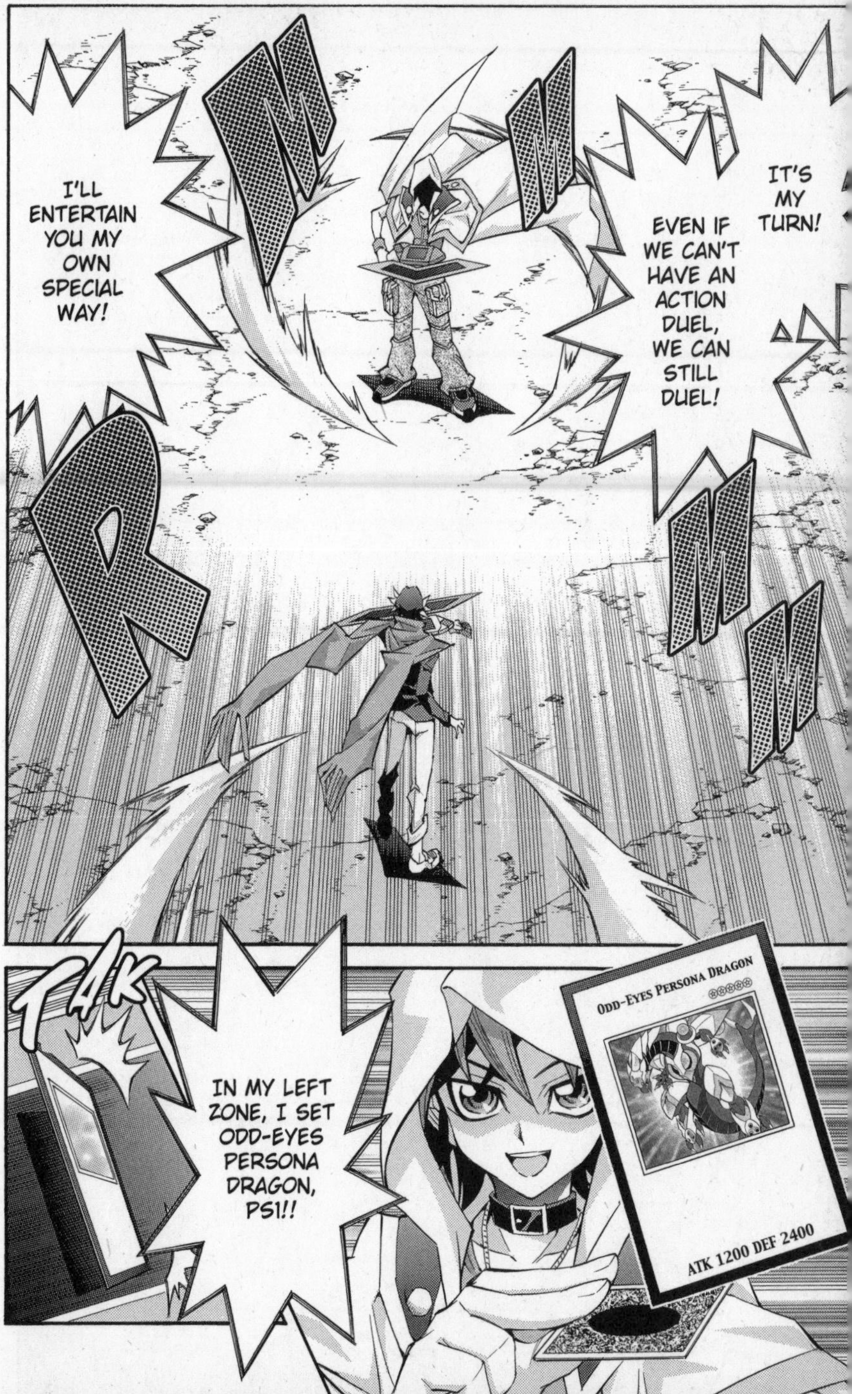
IT'S MY TURN!
EVEN IF WE CAN'T HAVE AN ACTION DUEL, WE CAN STILL DUEL!
I'LL ENTERTAIN YOU MY OWN SPECIAL WAY!
ODD-EYES PERSONA DRAGON
ATK 1200 DEF 2400
IN MY LEFT ZONE, I SET ODD-EYES PERSONA DRAGON, PS1!!
TAK

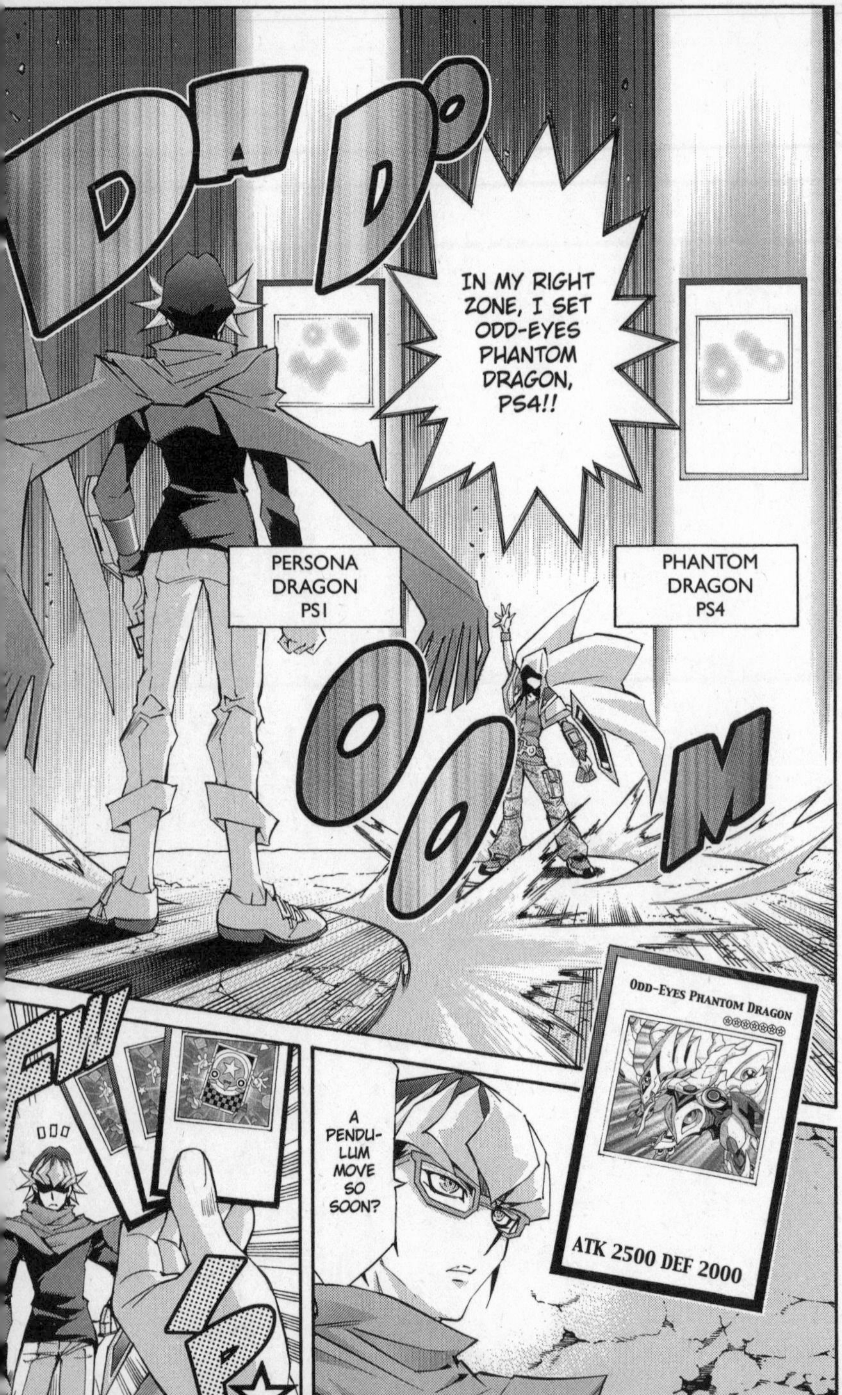
IN MY RIGHT ZONE, I SET ODD-EYES PHANTOM DRAGON, PS4!!
DADO
PHANTOM DRAGON PS4
PERSONA DRAGON PS1
OOOM
ODD-EYES PHANTOM DRAGON
ATK 2500 DEF 2000
A PENDULUM MOVE SO SOON?
...
PA

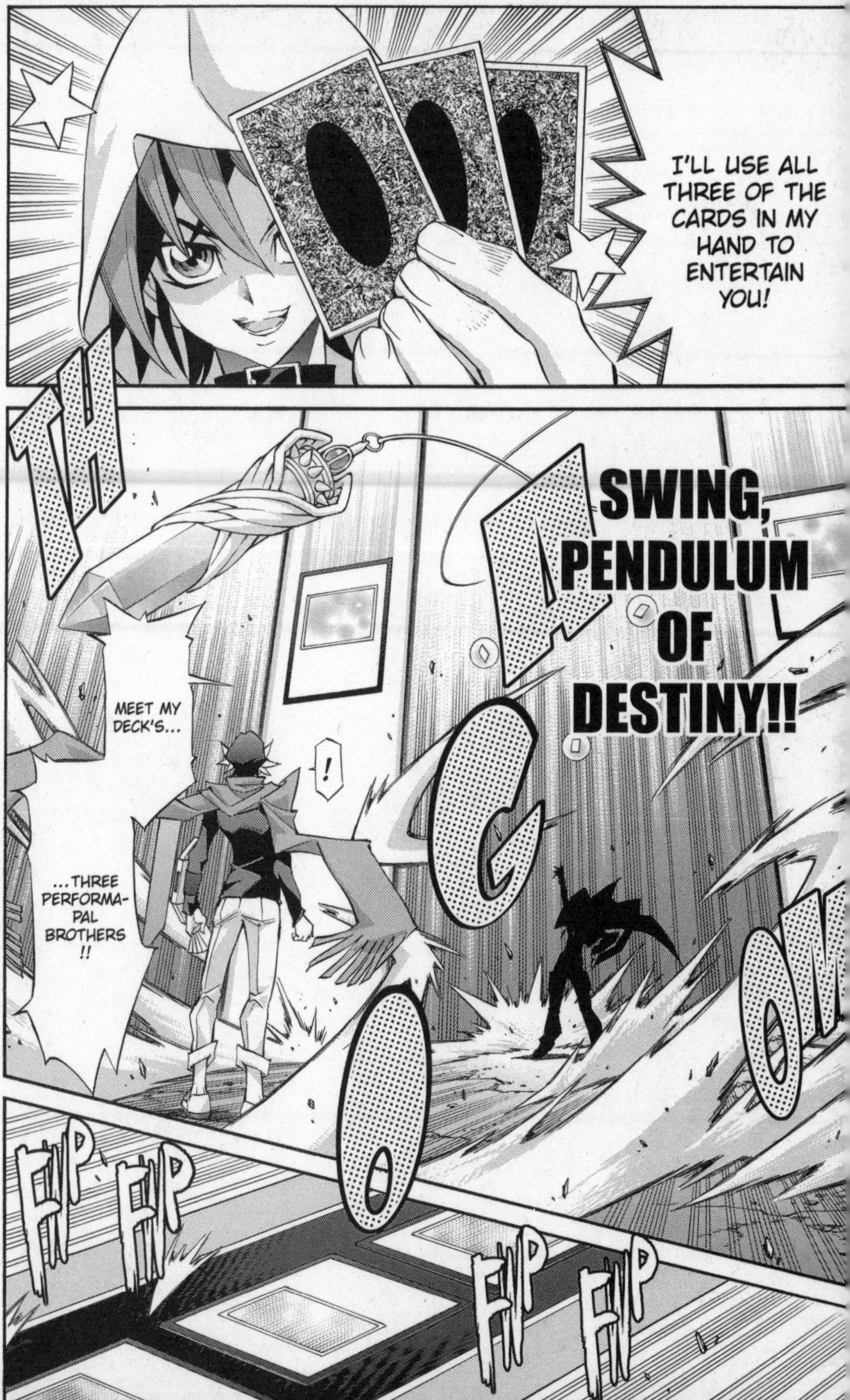
I'LL USE ALL THREE OF THE CARDS IN MY HAND TO ENTERTAIN YOU!
THAGOOM
SWING, PENDULUM OF DESTINY!!
!
MEET MY DECK'S...
...THREE PERFORMA-PAL BROTHERS!!
FLIP FLIP
FLIP FLIP

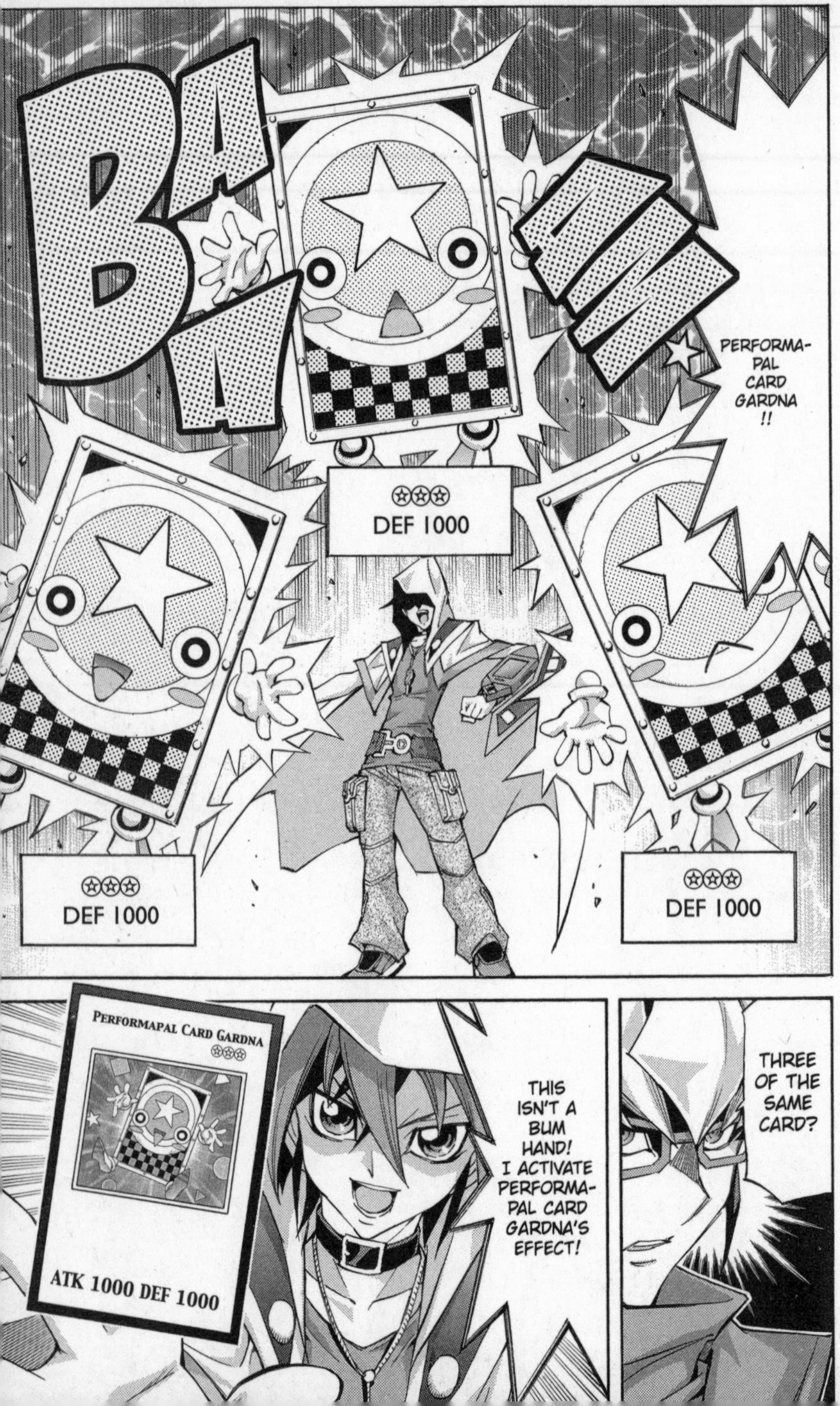
PERFORMA-PAL CARD GARDNA!!
DEF 1000
DEF 1000
DEF 1000
THREE OF THE SAME CARD?
THIS ISN'T A BUM HAND! I ACTIVATE PERFORMA-PAL CARD GARDNA'S EFFECT!
PERFORMAPAL CARD GARDNA
ATK 1000 DEF 1000

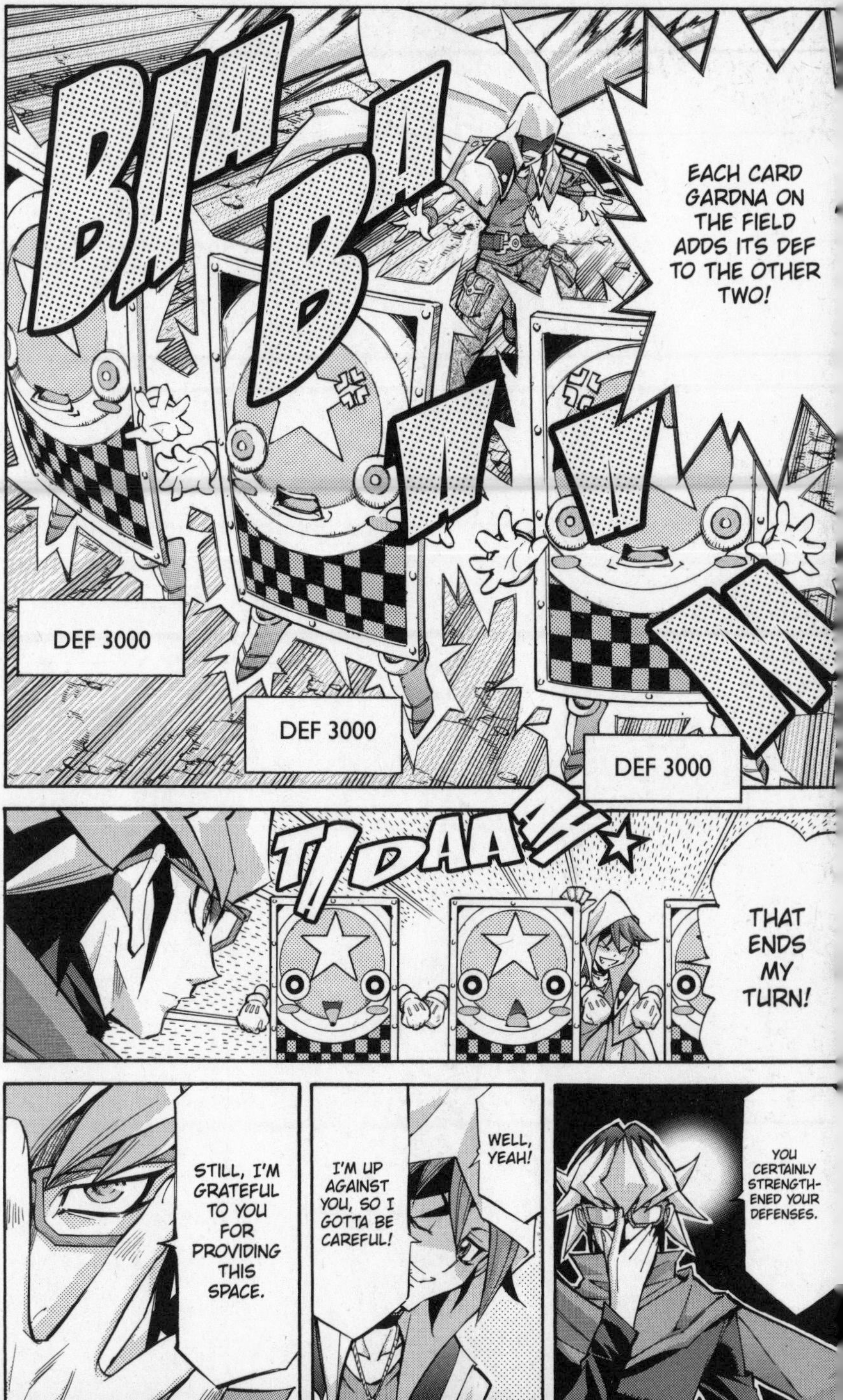
EACH CARD GARDNA ON THE FIELD ADDS ITS DEF TO THE OTHER TWO!
BABAAAMM
DEF 3000
DEF 3000
DEF 3000
THAT ENDS MY TURN!
TADAAAH!★
YOU CERTAINLY STRENGTH-ENED YOUR DEFENSES.
WELL, YEAH!
I'M UP AGAINST YOU, SO I GOTTA BE CAREFUL!
STILL, I'M GRATEFUL TO YOU FOR PROVIDING THIS SPACE.

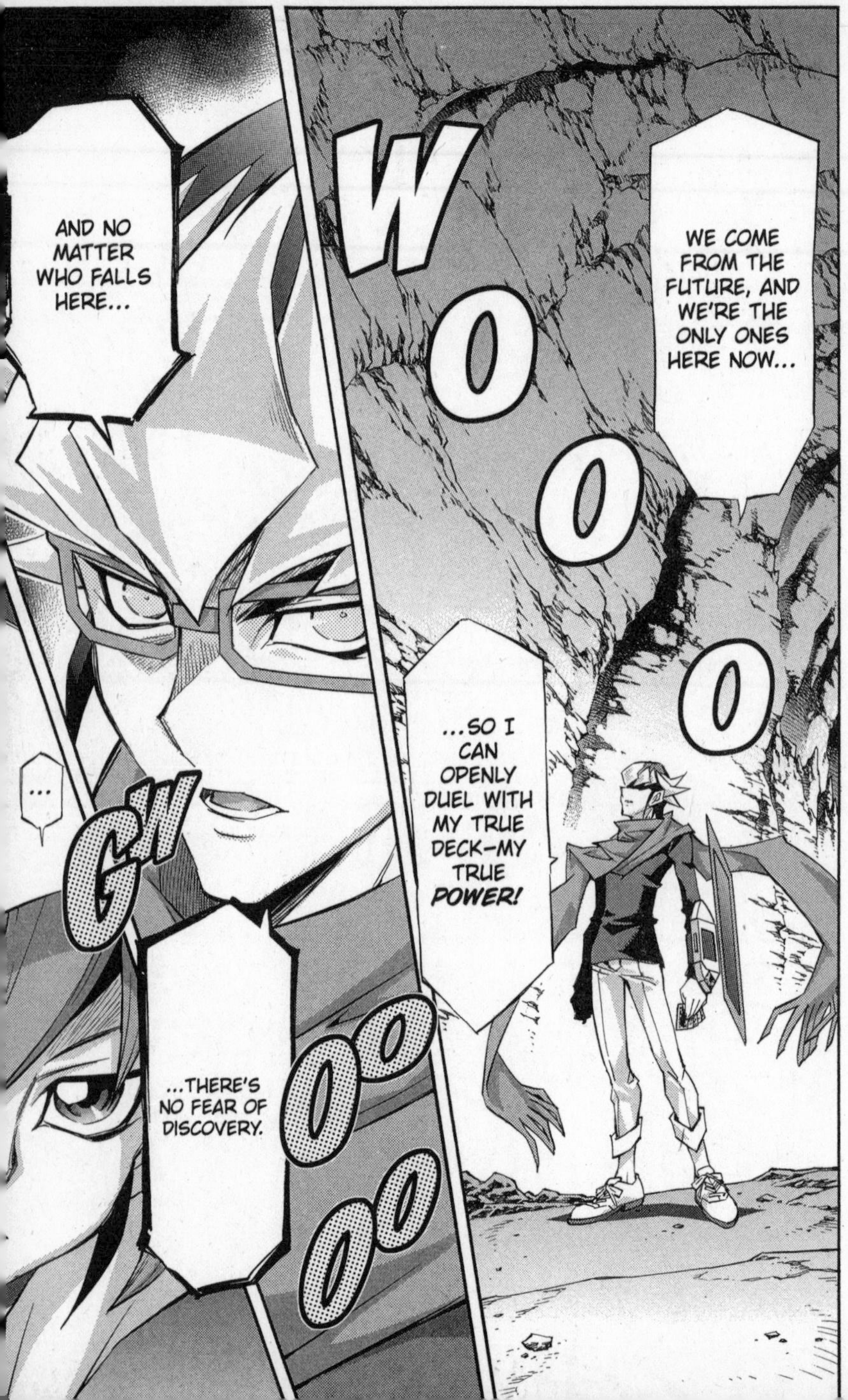
WE COME FROM THE FUTURE, AND WE'RE THE ONLY ONES HERE NOW...
WOOO
...SO I CAN OPENLY DUEL WITH MY TRUE DECK—MY TRUE *POWER!*
AND NO MATTER WHO FALLS HERE...
...
G'N
...THERE'S NO FEAR OF DISCOVERY.
OOOO

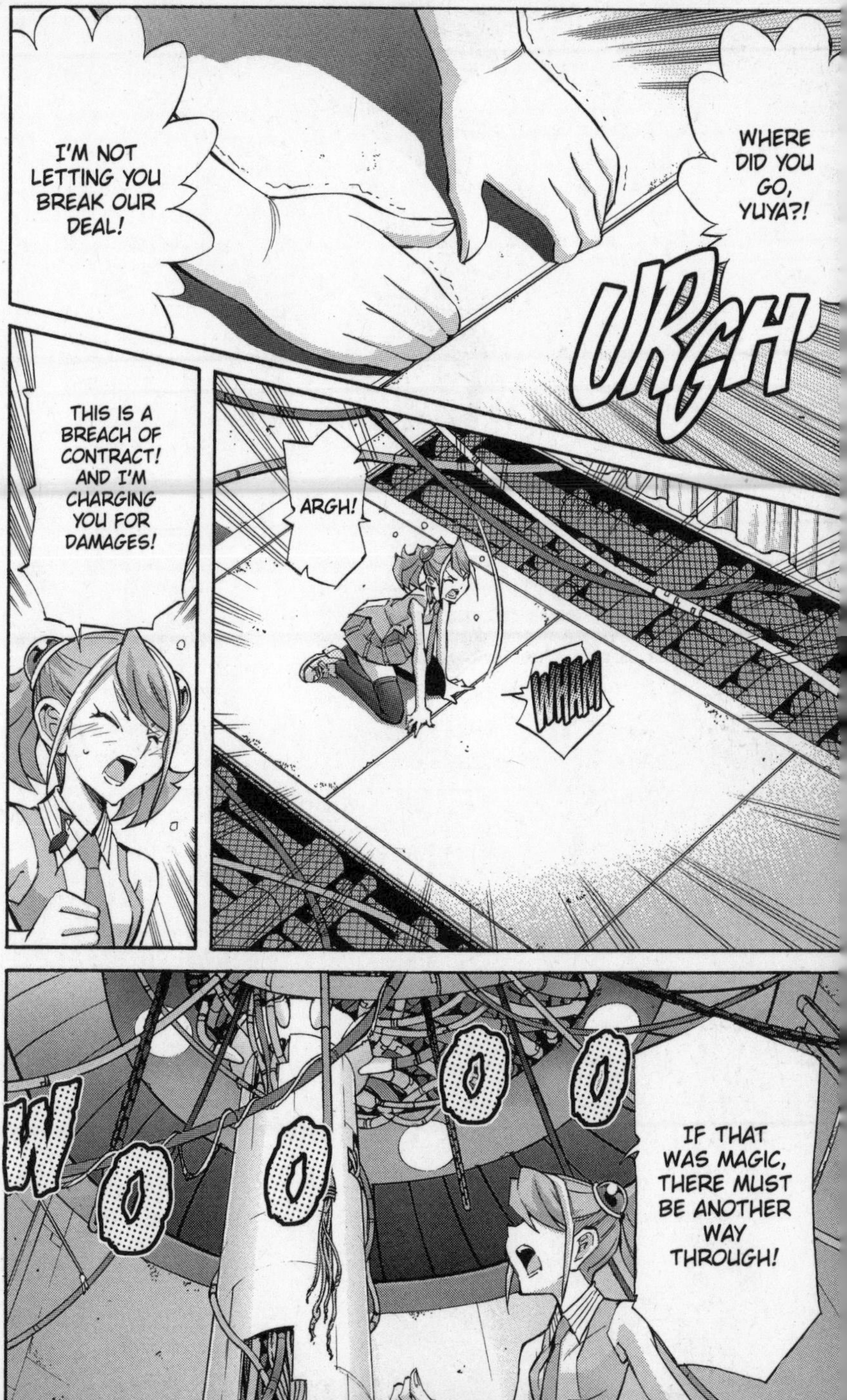
WHERE DID YOU GO, YUYA?!
URGH
I'M NOT LETTING YOU BREAK OUR DEAL!
ARGH!
WHAM
THIS IS A BREACH OF CONTRACT! AND I'M CHARGING YOU FOR DAMAGES!
IF THAT WAS MAGIC, THERE MUST BE ANOTHER WAY THROUGH!
WOOOOO

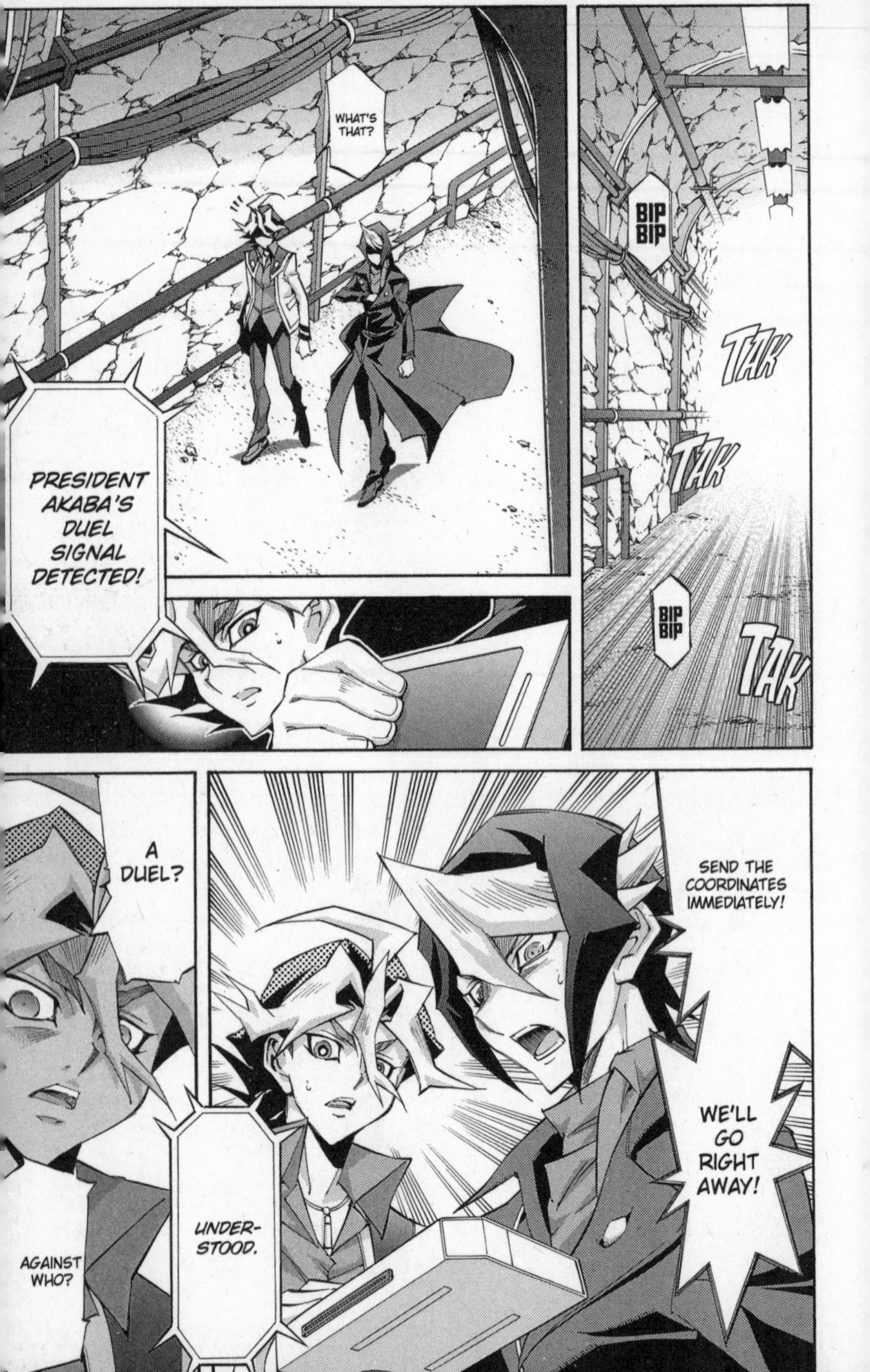
BIP BIP
TAK
TAK
BIP BIP
TAK
WHAT'S THAT?
PRESIDENT AKABA'S DUEL SIGNAL DETECTED!
SEND THE COORDINATES IMMEDIATELY!
WE'LL GO RIGHT AWAY!
UNDER-STOOD.
A DUEL?
AGAINST WHO?

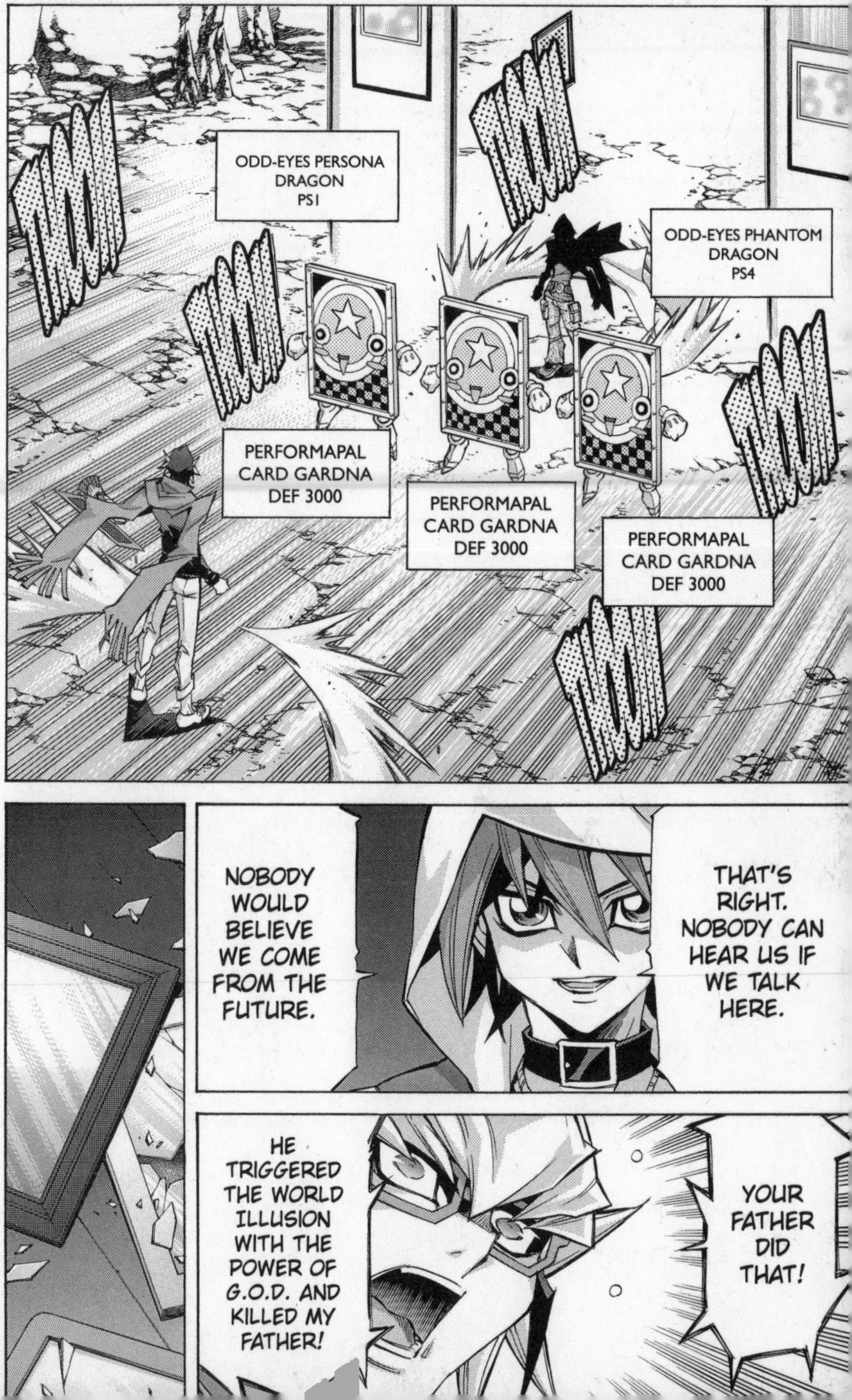
ODD-EYES PHANTOM DRAGON PS4
ODD-EYES PERSONA DRAGON PS1
THOOM
THOOM
THOOM
THOOM
THOOM
PERFORMAPAL CARD GARDNA DEF 3000
PERFORMAPAL CARD GARDNA DEF 3000
PERFORMAPAL CARD GARDNA DEF 3000
THAT'S RIGHT. NOBODY CAN HEAR US IF WE TALK HERE.
NOBODY WOULD BELIEVE WE COME FROM THE FUTURE.
YOUR FATHER DID THAT!
HE TRIGGERED THE WORLD ILLUSION WITH THE POWER OF G.O.D. AND KILLED MY FATHER!

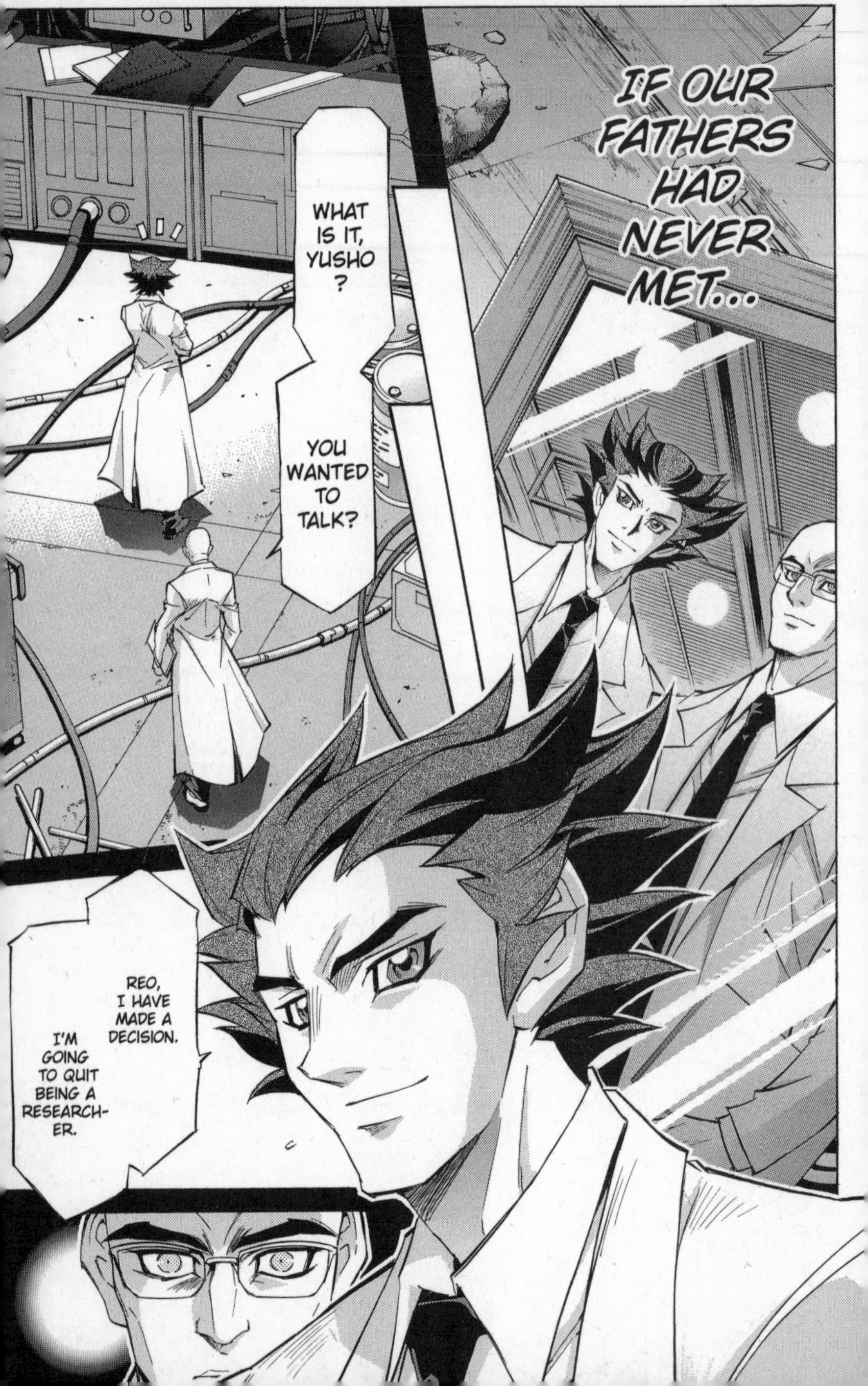
IF OUR FATHERS HAD NEVER MET...
WHAT IS IT, YUSHO?
YOU WANTED TO TALK?
REO, I HAVE MADE A DECISION.
I'M GOING TO QUIT BEING A RESEARCHER.

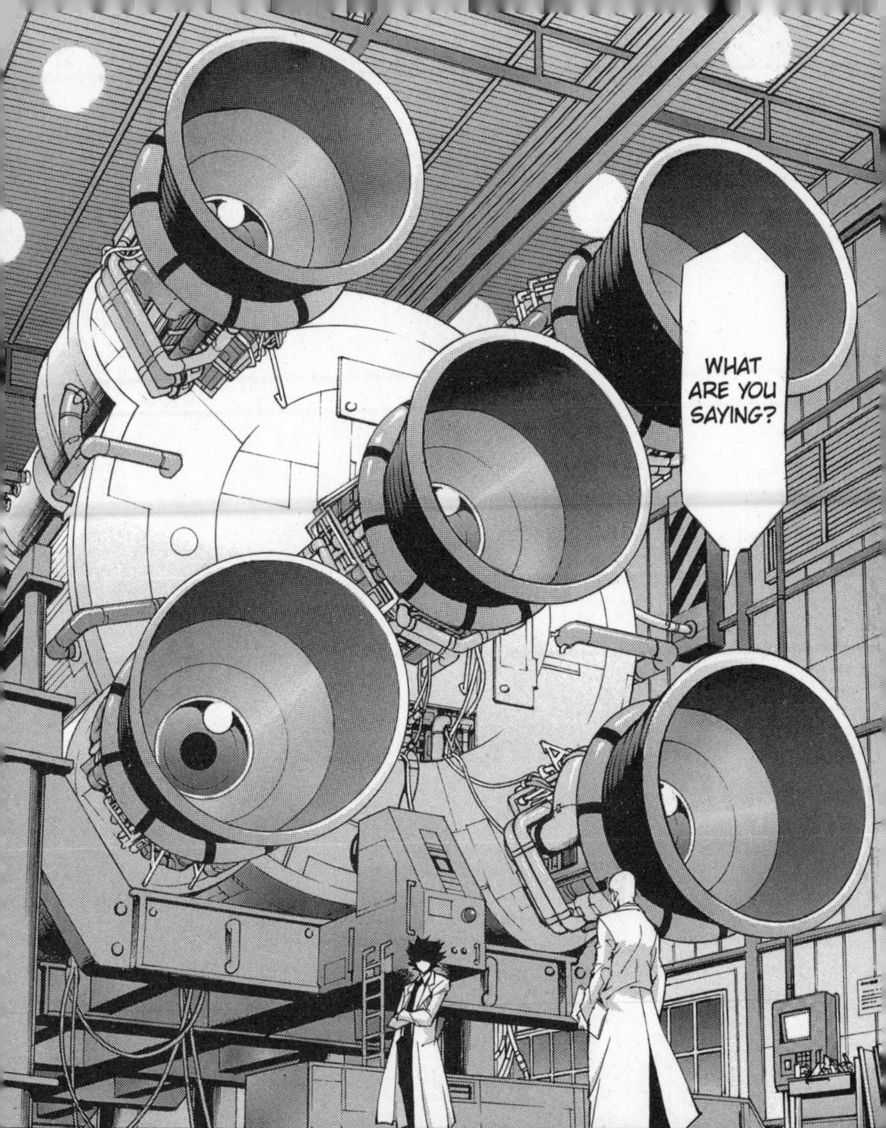
WHAT ARE YOU SAYING?
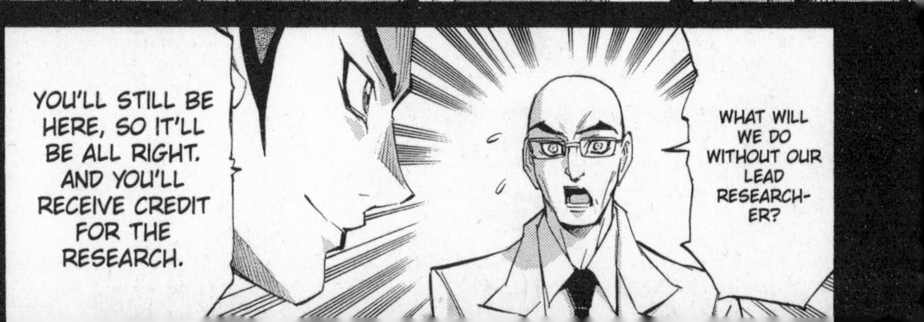
WHAT WILL WE DO WITHOUT OUR LEAD RESEARCH-ER?
YOU'LL STILL BE HERE, SO IT'LL BE ALL RIGHT. AND YOU'LL RECEIVE CREDIT FOR THE RESEARCH.

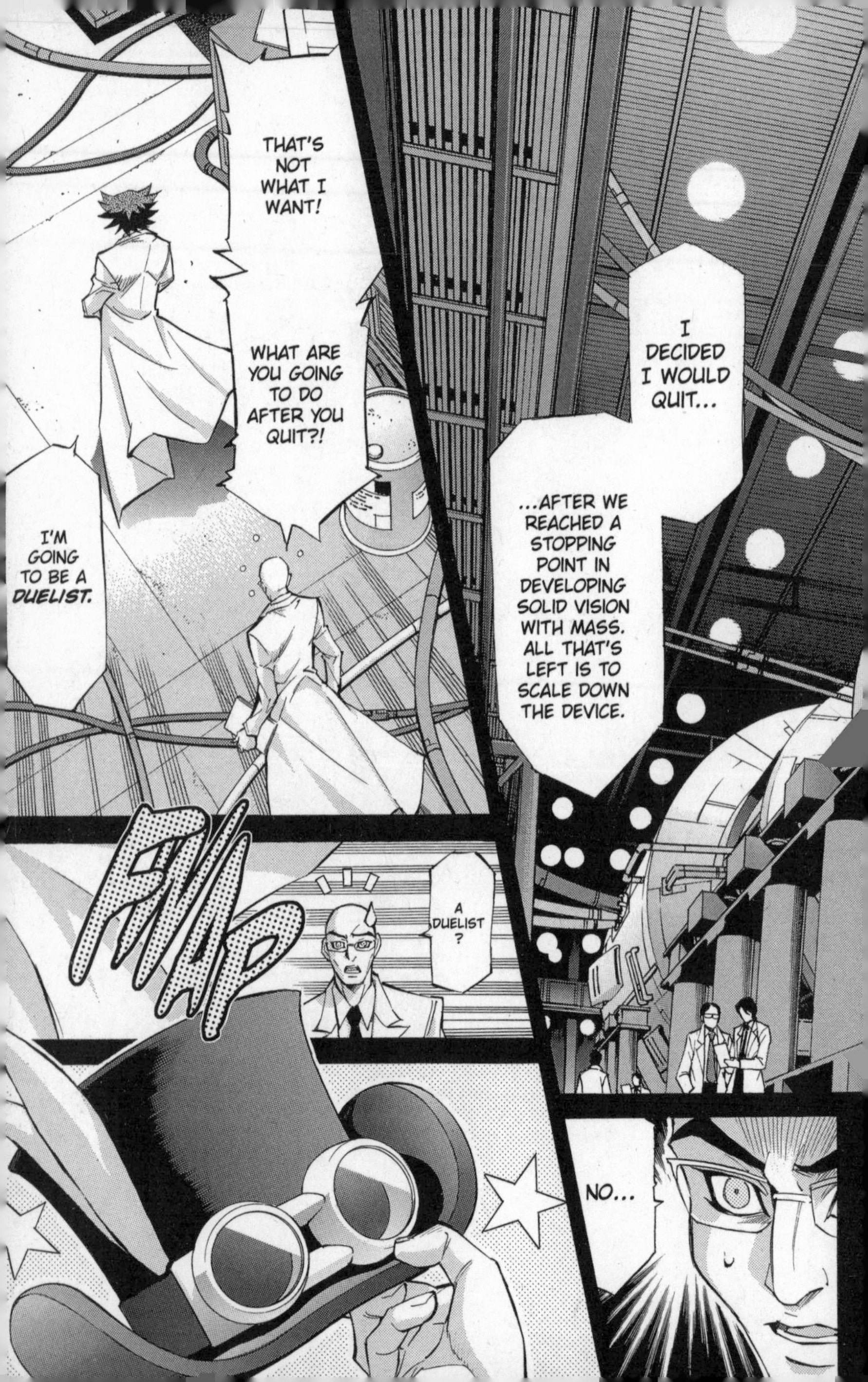
I DECIDED I WOULD QUIT...
...AFTER WE REACHED A STOPPING POINT IN DEVELOPING SOLID VISION WITH MASS. ALL THAT'S LEFT IS TO SCALE DOWN THE DEVICE.
THAT'S NOT WHAT I WANT!
WHAT ARE YOU GOING TO DO AFTER YOU QUIT?!
I'M GOING TO BE A *DUELIST.*
A DUELIST?
FWAP
NO...

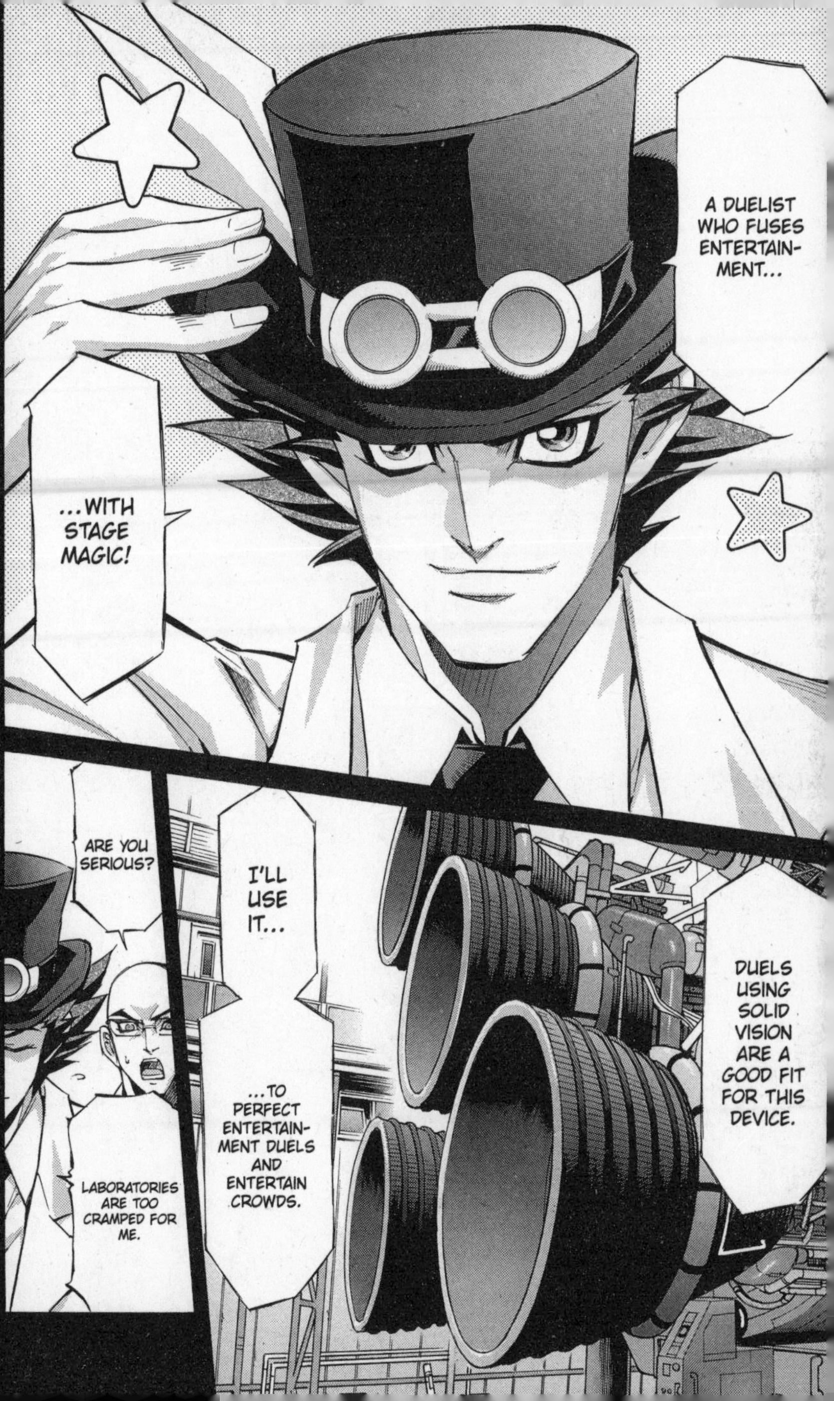
A DUELIST WHO FUSES ENTERTAIN-MENT...
...WITH STAGE MAGIC!
DUELS USING SOLID VISION ARE A GOOD FIT FOR THIS DEVICE.
I'LL USE IT...
...TO PERFECT ENTERTAIN-MENT DUELS AND ENTERTAIN CROWDS.
ARE YOU SERIOUS?
LABORATORIES ARE TOO CRAMPED FOR ME.

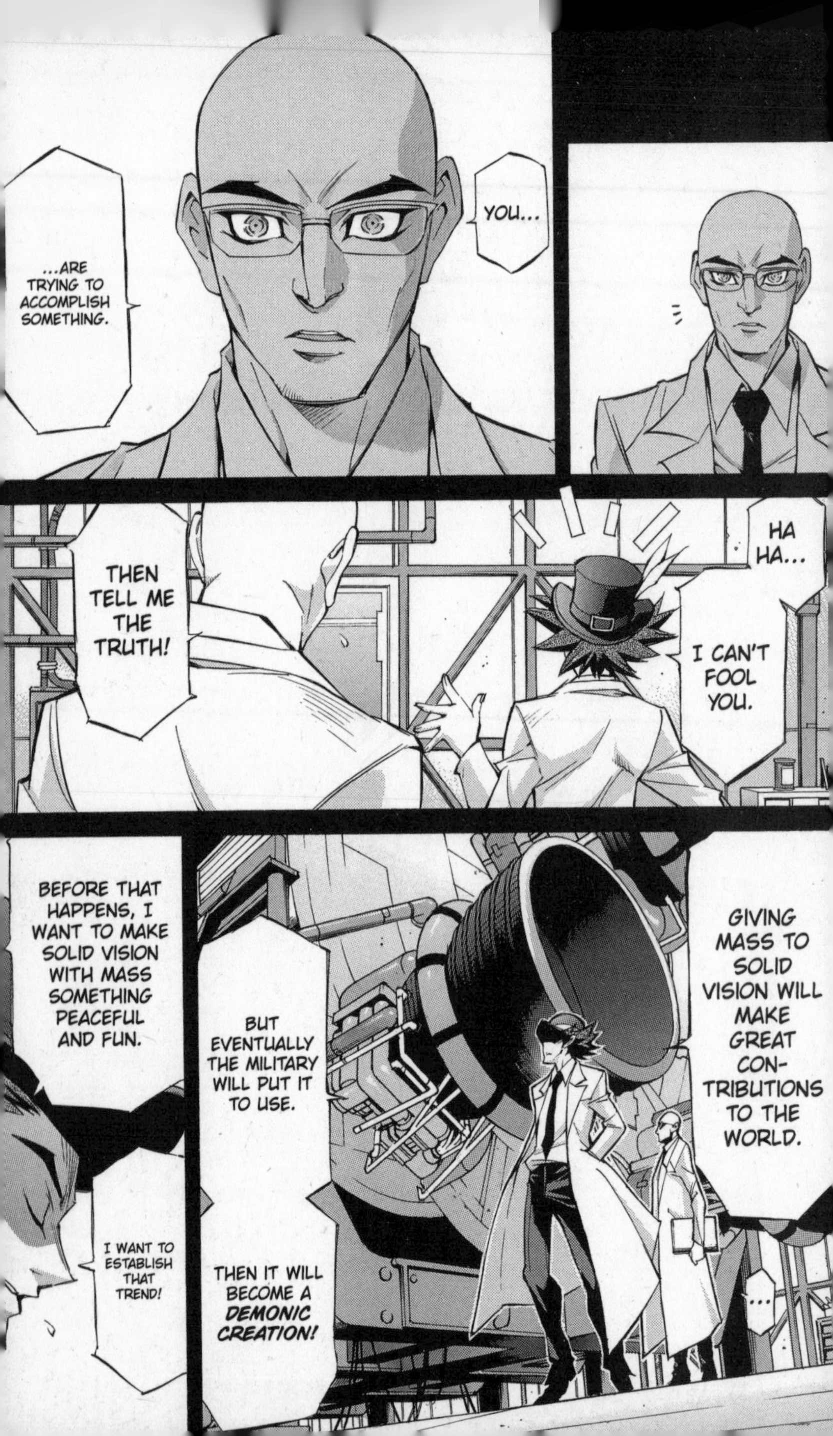
YOU...
...ARE TRYING TO ACCOMPLISH SOMETHING.
HA HA...
I CAN'T FOOL YOU.
THEN TELL ME THE TRUTH!
GIVING MASS TO SOLID VISION WILL MAKE GREAT CON-TRIBUTIONS TO THE WORLD.
BUT EVENTUALLY THE MILITARY WILL PUT IT TO USE.
...
THEN IT WILL BECOME A *DEMONIC CREATION!*
BEFORE THAT HAPPENS, I WANT TO MAKE SOLID VISION WITH MASS SOMETHING PEACEFUL AND FUN.
I WANT TO ESTABLISH THAT TREND!

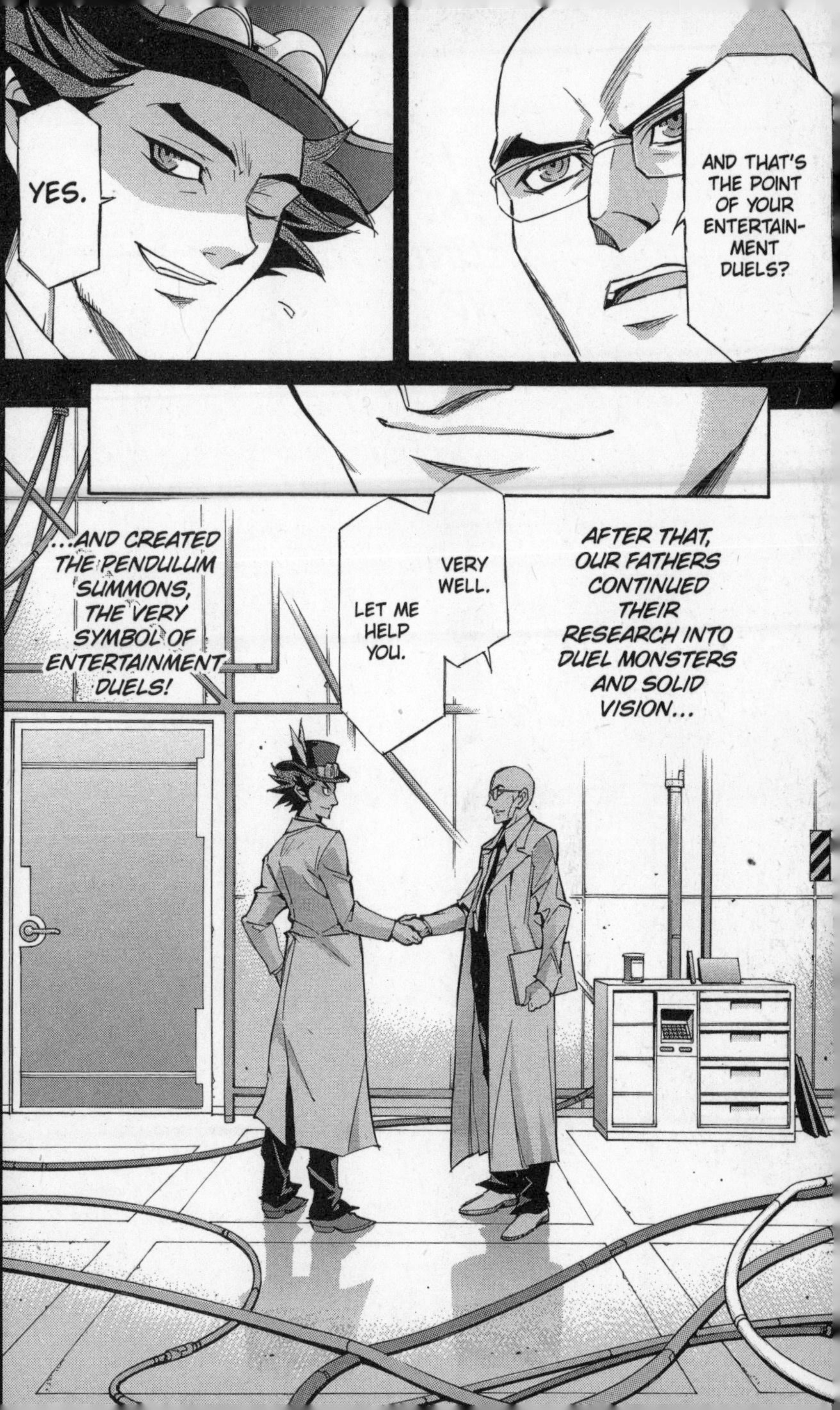
AND THAT'S THE POINT OF YOUR ENTERTAINMENT DUELS?
YES.
VERY WELL.
LET ME HELP YOU.
AFTER THAT, OUR FATHERS CONTINUED THEIR RESEARCH INTO DUEL MONSTERS AND SOLID VISION...
...AND CREATED THE PENDULUM SUMMONS, THE VERY SYMBOL OF ENTERTAINMENT DUELS!

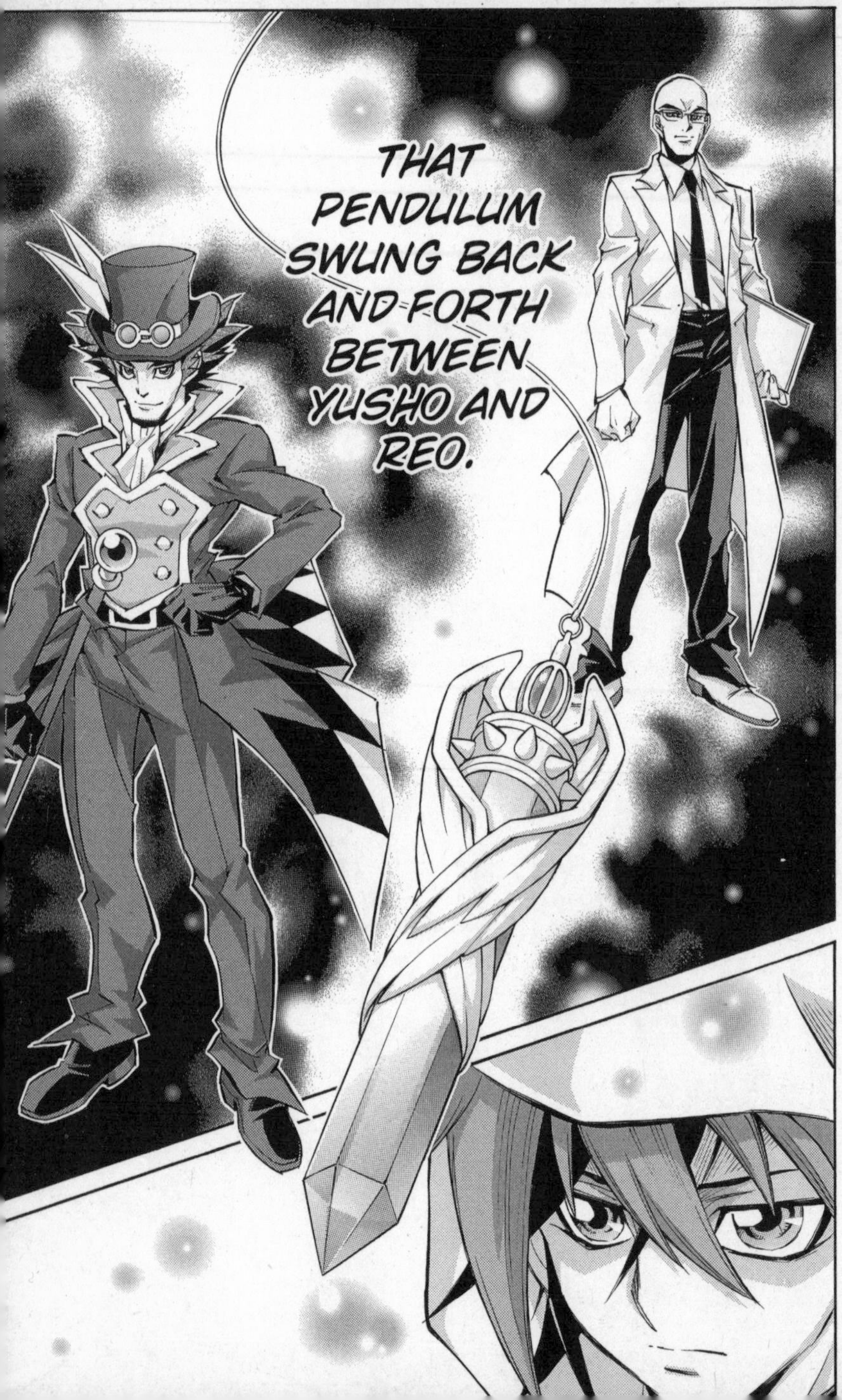
THAT PENDULUM SWUNG BACK AND FORTH BETWEEN YUSHO AND REO.

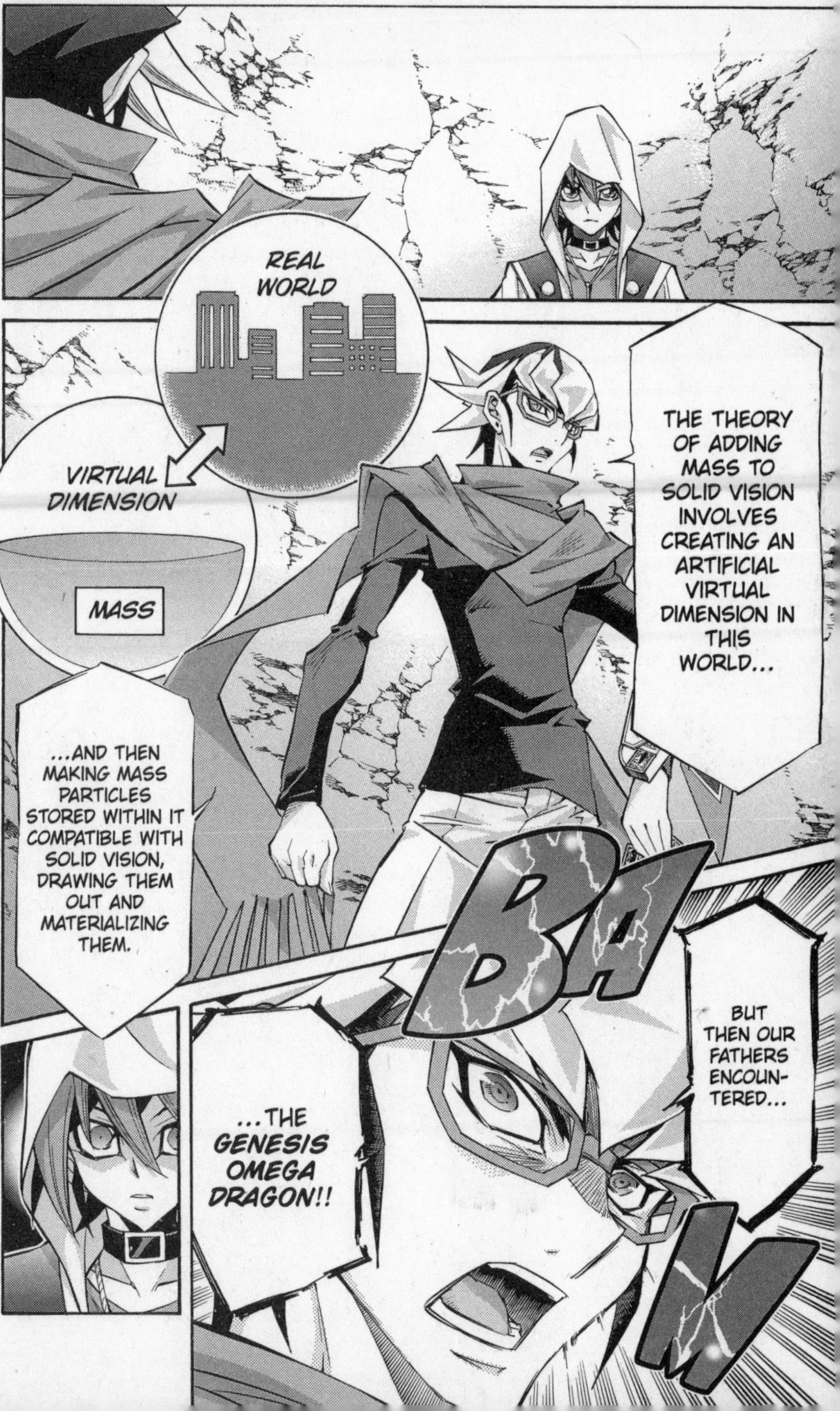
THE THEORY OF ADDING MASS TO SOLID VISION INVOLVES CREATING AN ARTIFICIAL VIRTUAL DIMENSION IN THIS WORLD...
REAL WORLD
VIRTUAL DIMENSION
MASS
...AND THEN MAKING MASS PARTICLES STORED WITHIN IT COMPATIBLE WITH SOLID VISION, DRAWING THEM OUT AND MATERIALIZING THEM.
BUT THEN OUR FATHERS ENCOUN-TERED...
BAN
...THE GENESIS OMEGA DRAGON!!

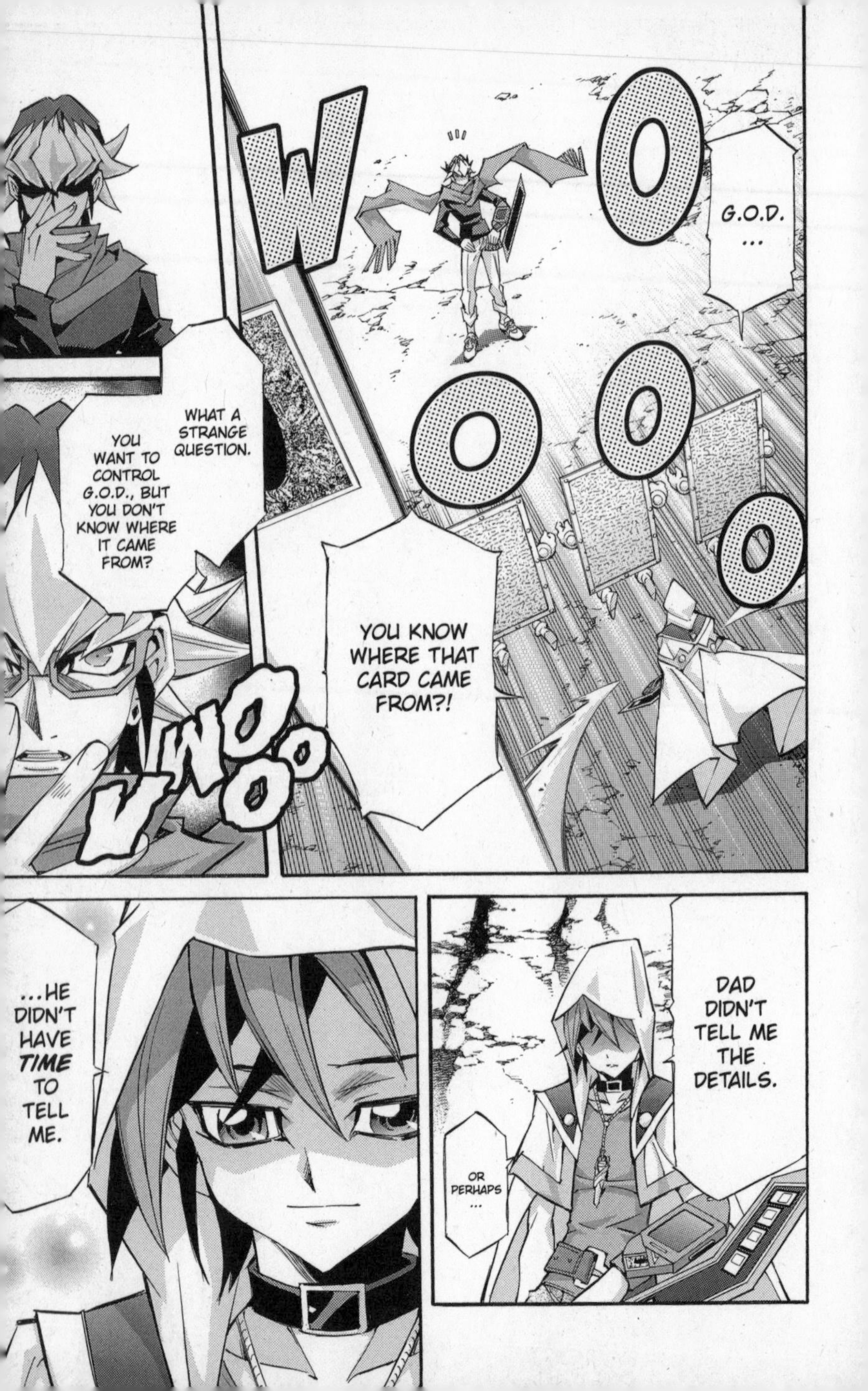
WOOOOO
G.O.D. ...
YOU KNOW WHERE THAT CARD CAME FROM?!
WHAT A STRANGE QUESTION.
YOU WANT TO CONTROL G.O.D., BUT YOU DON'T KNOW WHERE IT CAME FROM?
WOOOO
DAD DIDN'T TELL ME THE DETAILS.
OR PERHAPS ...
...HE DIDN'T HAVE *TIME* TO TELL ME.

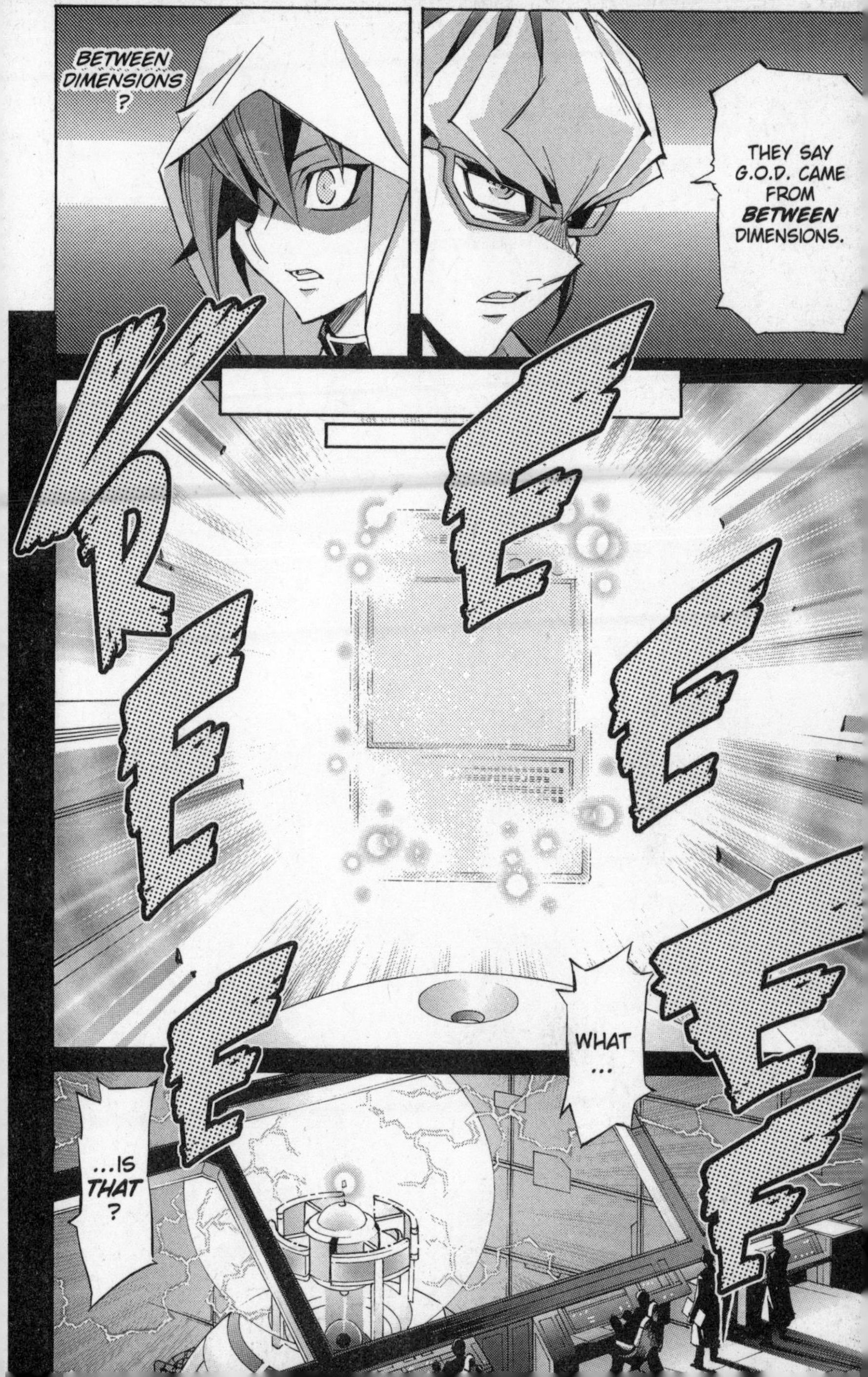
THEY SAY G.O.D. CAME FROM BETWEEN DIMENSIONS.
BETWEEN DIMENSIONS?
VREEEEEE
WHAT...
...IS THAT?

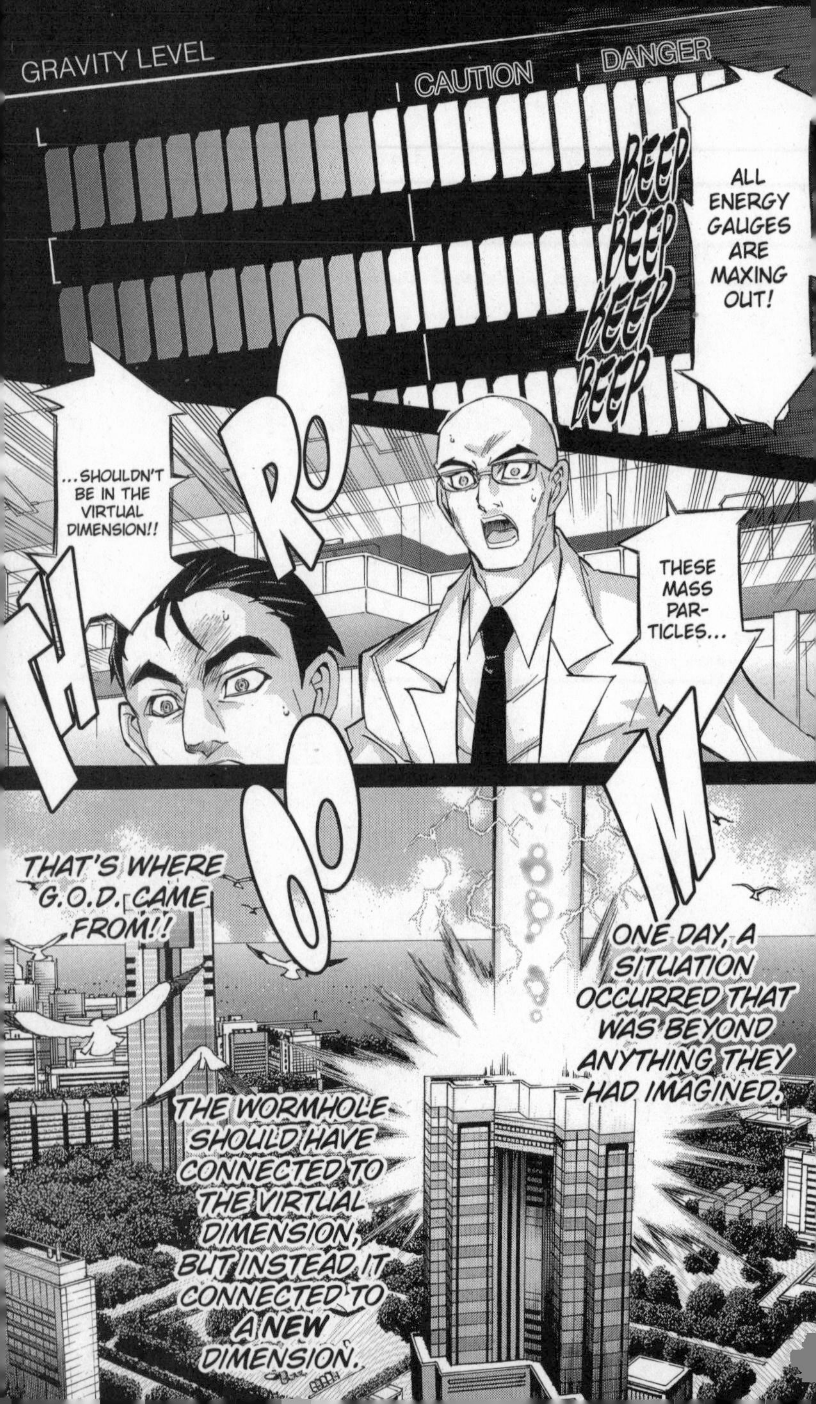
ALL ENERGY GAUGES ARE MAXING OUT!
BEEP BEEP BEEP BEEP
DANGER
CAUTION
GRAVITY LEVEL
THESE MASS PAR-TICLES...
...SHOULDN'T BE IN THE VIRTUAL DIMENSION!!
THROOOM
ONE DAY, A SITUATION OCCURRED THAT WAS BEYOND ANYTHING THEY HAD IMAGINED.
THE WORMHOLE SHOULD HAVE CONNECTED TO THE VIRTUAL DIMENSION, BUT INSTEAD IT CONNECTED TO A NEW DIMENSION.
THAT'S WHERE G.O.D. CAME FROM!!

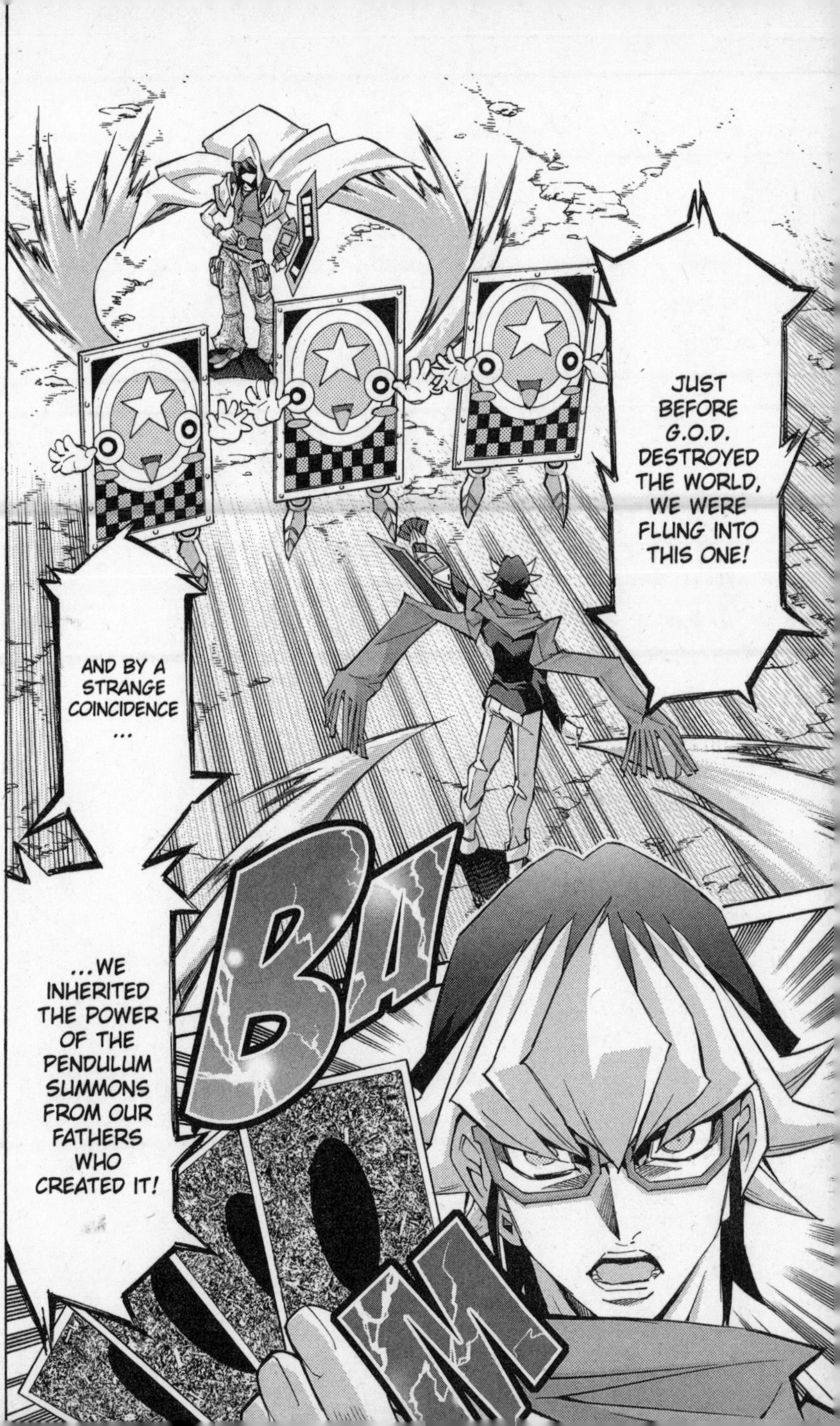
JUST BEFORE G.O.D. DESTROYED THE WORLD, WE WERE FLUNG INTO THIS ONE!
AND BY A STRANGE COINCIDENCE ...
...WE INHERITED THE POWER OF THE PENDULUM SUMMONS FROM OUR FATHERS WHO CREATED IT!

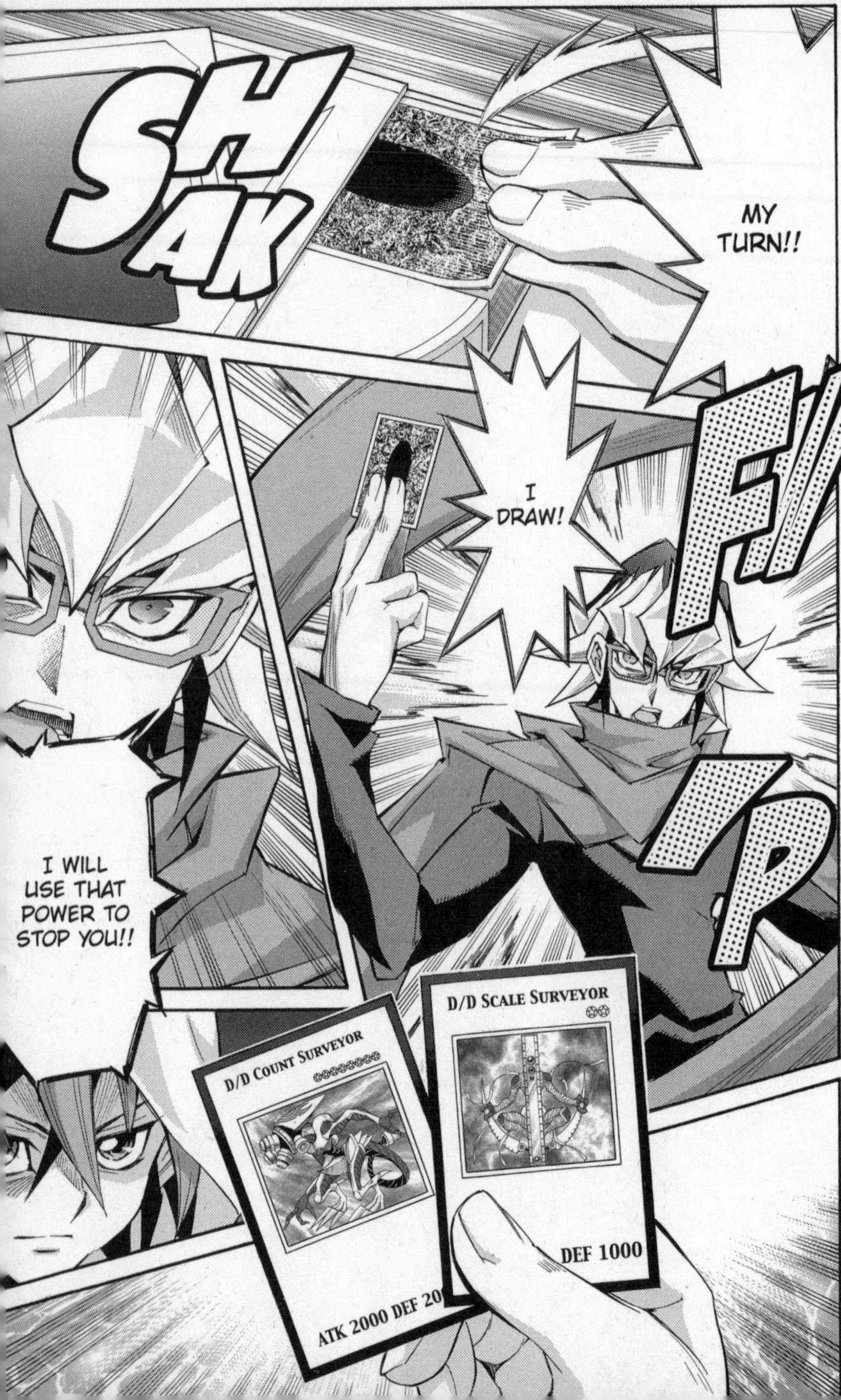
SHAK
MY TURN!!
I DRAW!
FWIP
I WILL USE THAT POWER TO STOP YOU!!
D/D SCALE SURVEYOR
DEF 1000
D/D COUNT SURVEYOR
ATK 2000 DEF 20

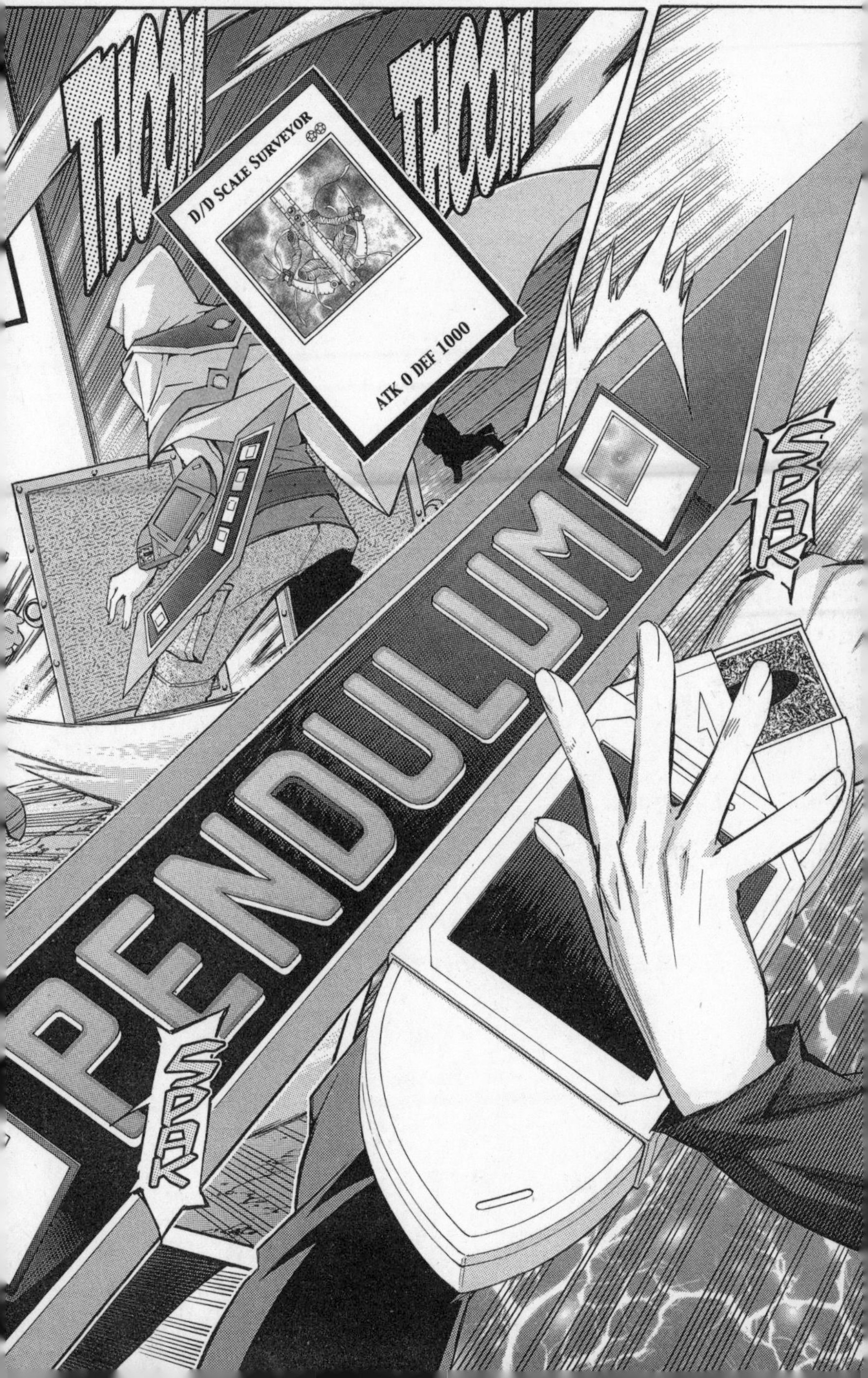
THOOM
THOOM
D/D SCALE SURVEYOR
ATK 0 DEF 1000
SPARK
PENDULUM
SPARK

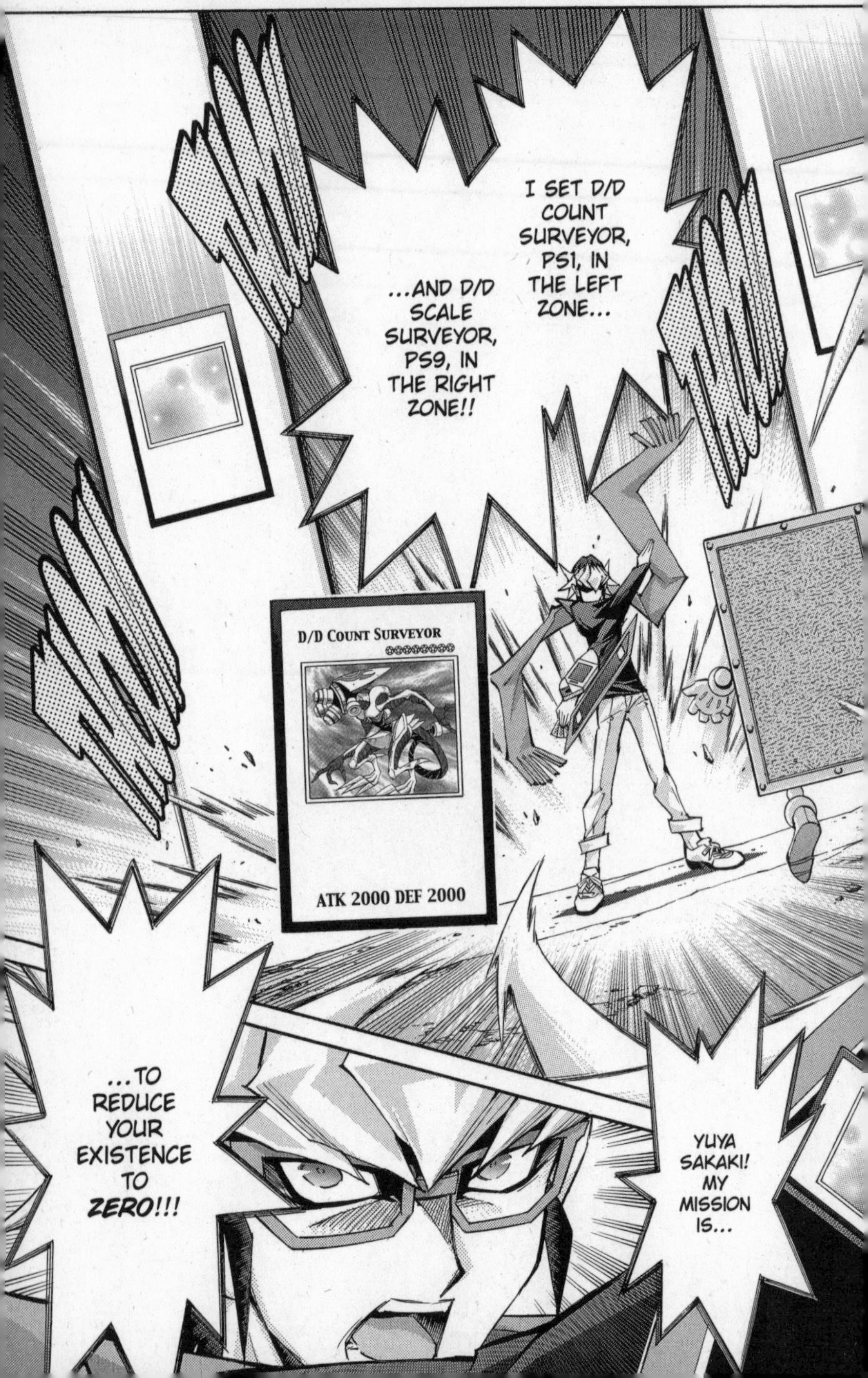
I SET D/D COUNT SURVEYOR, PS1, IN THE LEFT ZONE...
...AND D/D SCALE SURVEYOR, PS9, IN THE RIGHT ZONE!!
D/D COUNT SURVEYOR
ATK 2000 DEF 2000
YUYA SAKAKI! MY MISSION IS...
...TO REDUCE YOUR EXISTENCE TO ZERO!!!

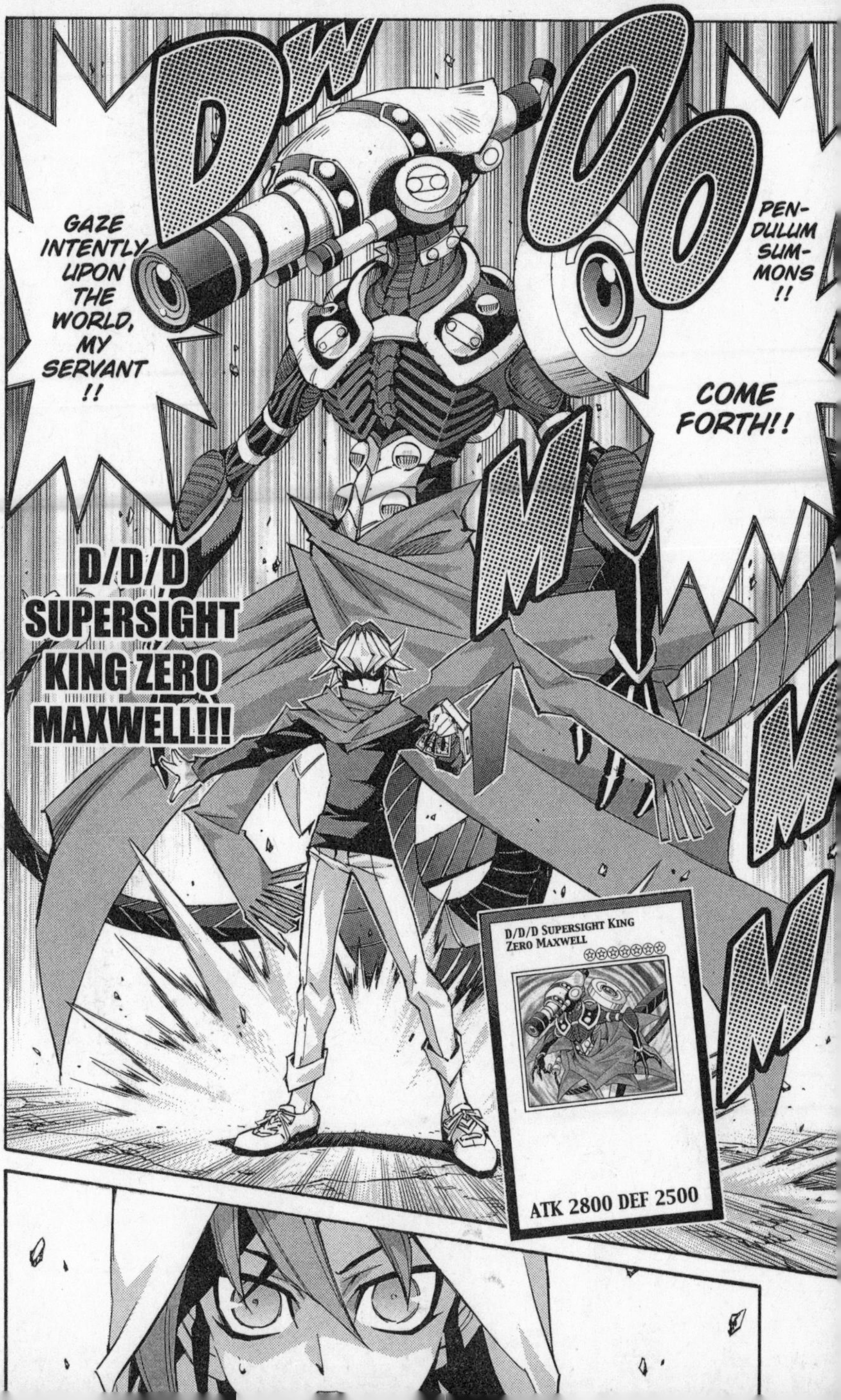
PEN-DULUM SUM-MONS!!
COME FORTH!!
GAZE INTENTLY UPON THE WORLD, MY SERVANT!!
DWOOMMMM
D/D/D SUPERSIGHT KING ZERO MAXWELL!!!
D/D/D SUPERSIGHT KING ZERO MAXWELL
ATK 2800 DEF 2500

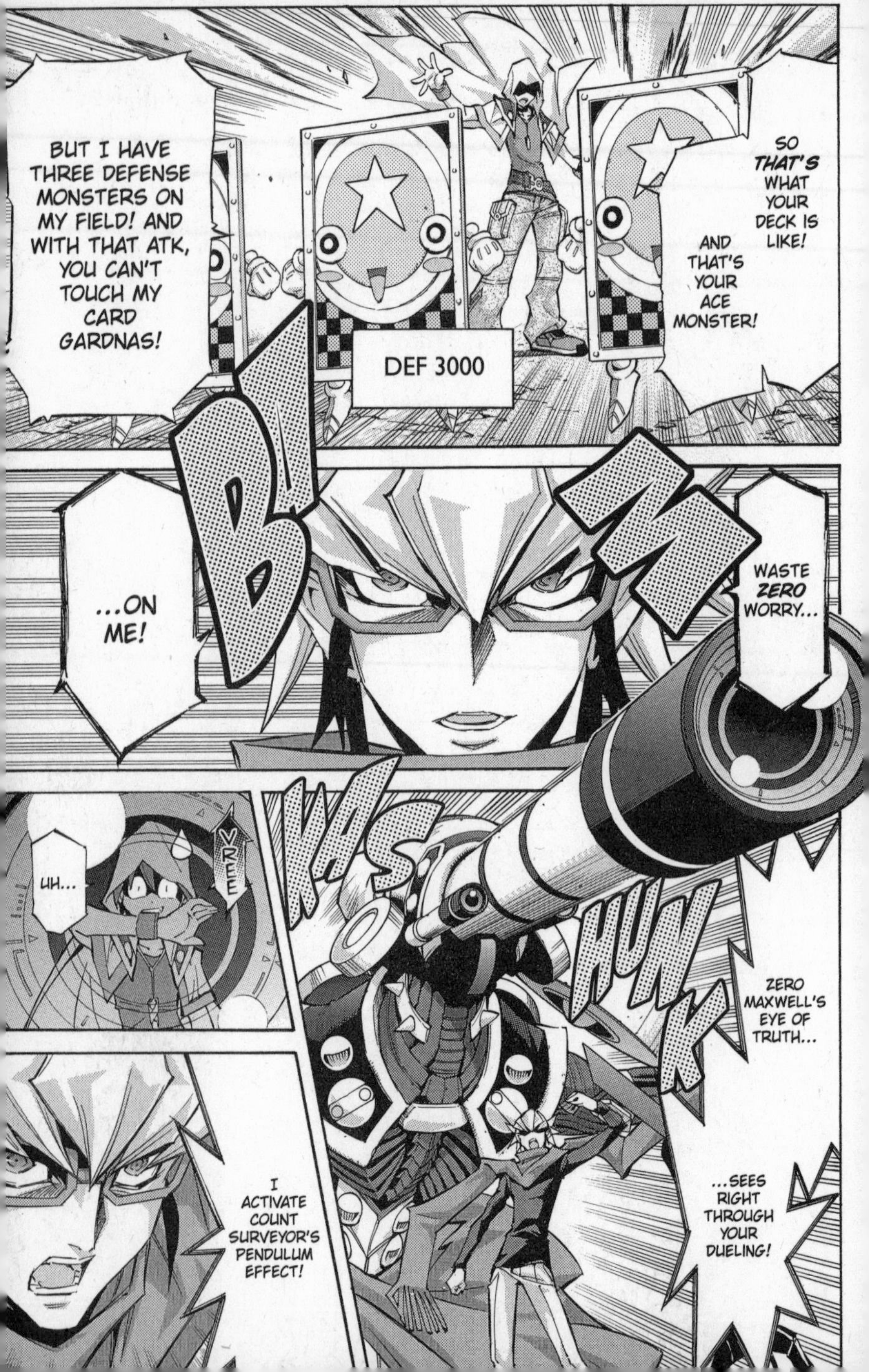

SO THAT'S WHAT YOUR DECK IS LIKE!
AND THAT'S YOUR ACE MONSTER!
BUT I HAVE THREE DEFENSE MONSTERS ON MY FIELD! AND WITH THAT ATK, YOU CAN'T TOUCH MY CARD GARDNAS!
DEF 3000
WASTE ZERO WORRY...
...ON ME!
ZERO MAXWELL'S EYE OF TRUTH...
...SEES RIGHT THROUGH YOUR DUELING!
VREE
UH...
I ACTIVATE COUNT SURVEYOR'S PENDULUM EFFECT!

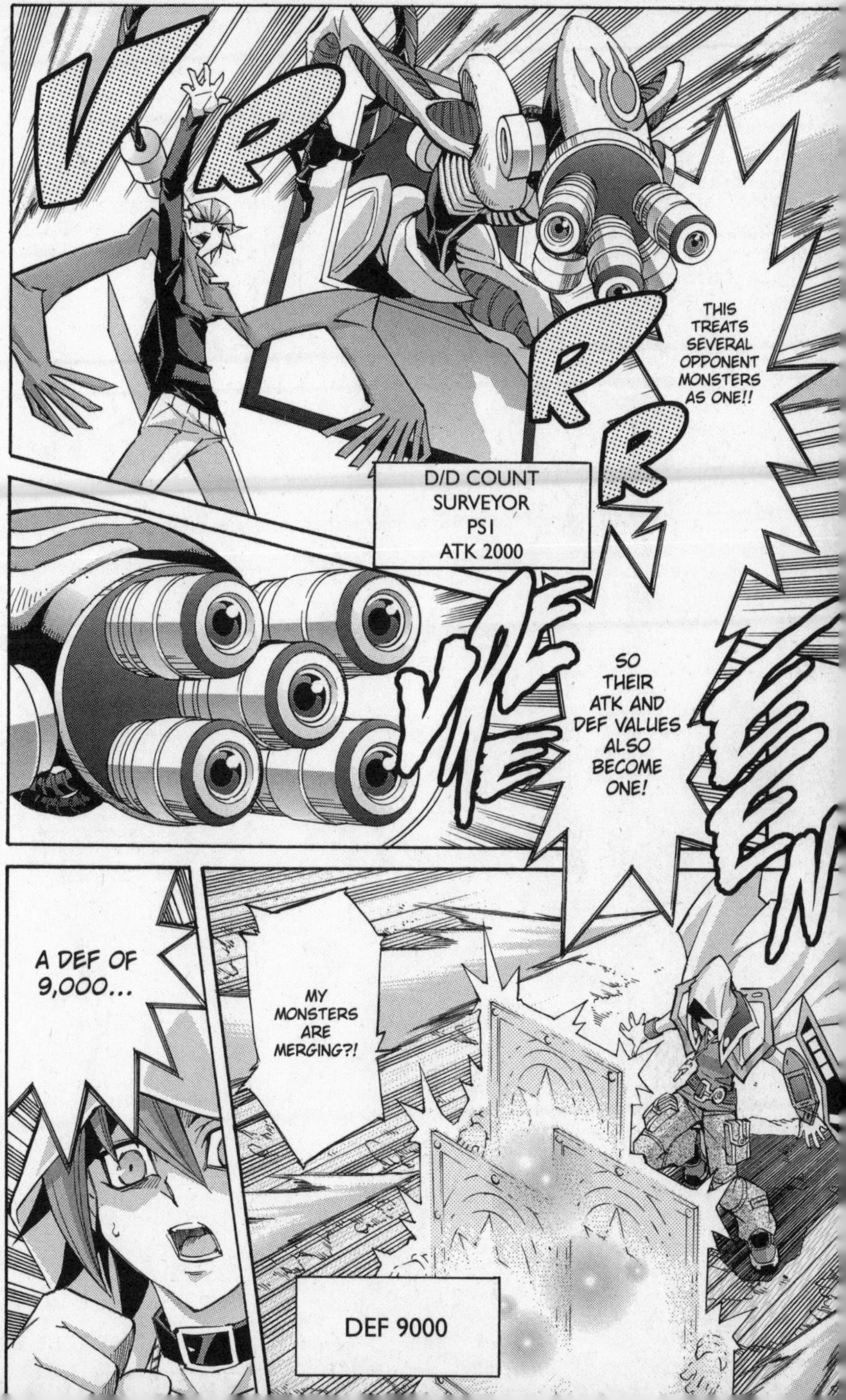
VRRR
THIS TREATS SEVERAL OPPONENT MONSTERS AS ONE!!
D/D COUNT SURVEYOR PS1 ATK 2000
SO THEIR ATK AND DEF VALUES ALSO BECOME ONE!
MY MONSTERS ARE MERGING?!
A DEF OF 9,000...
DEF 9000

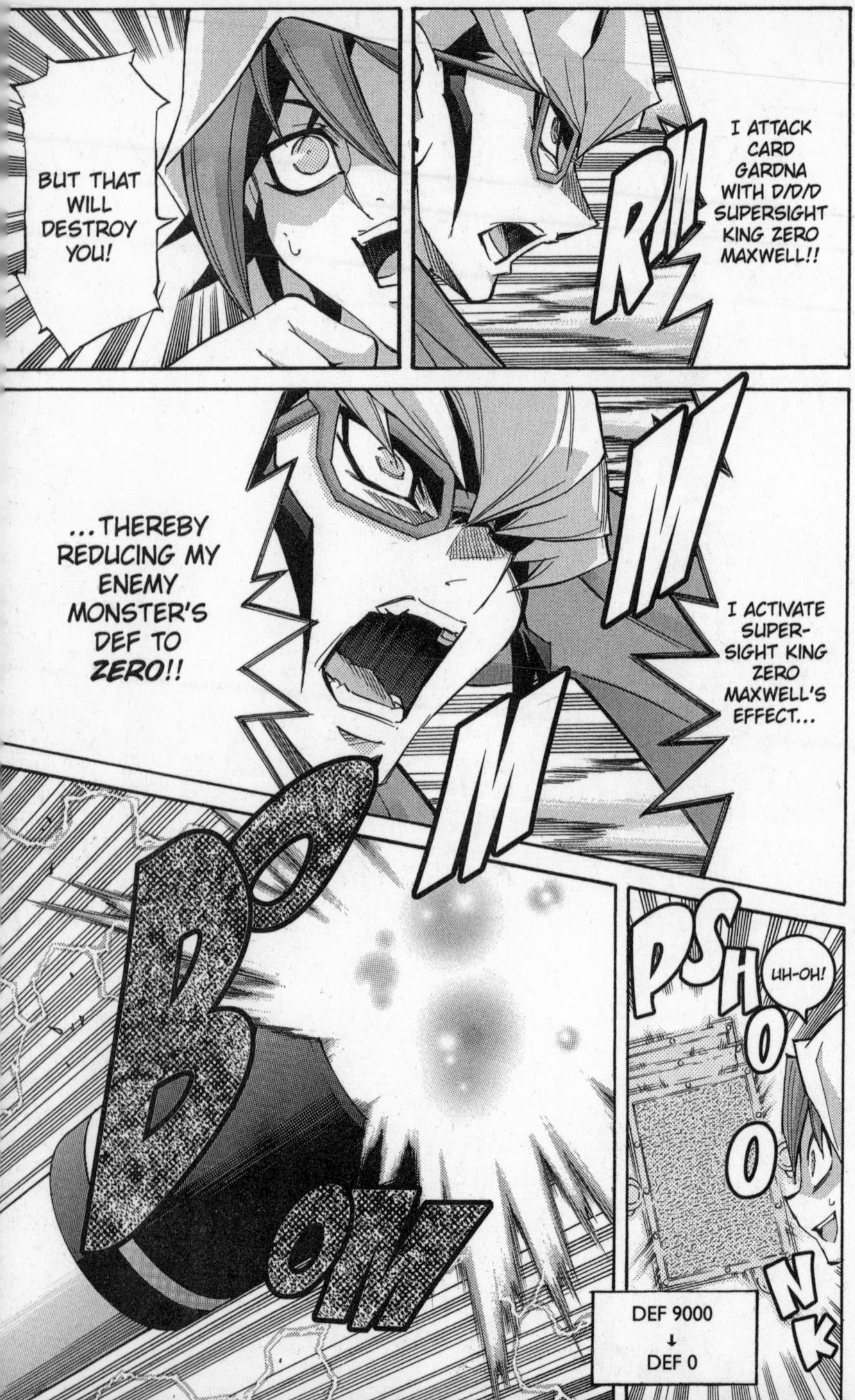

I ATTACK CARD GARDNA WITH D/D/D SUPERSIGHT KING ZERO MAXWELL!!
BUT THAT WILL DESTROY YOU!
I ACTIVATE SUPER-SIGHT KING ZERO MAXWELL'S EFFECT...
...THEREBY REDUCING MY ENEMY MONSTER'S DEF TO ZERO!!
PSHOOONK
UH-OH!
DEF 9000
↓
DEF 0
BOOM

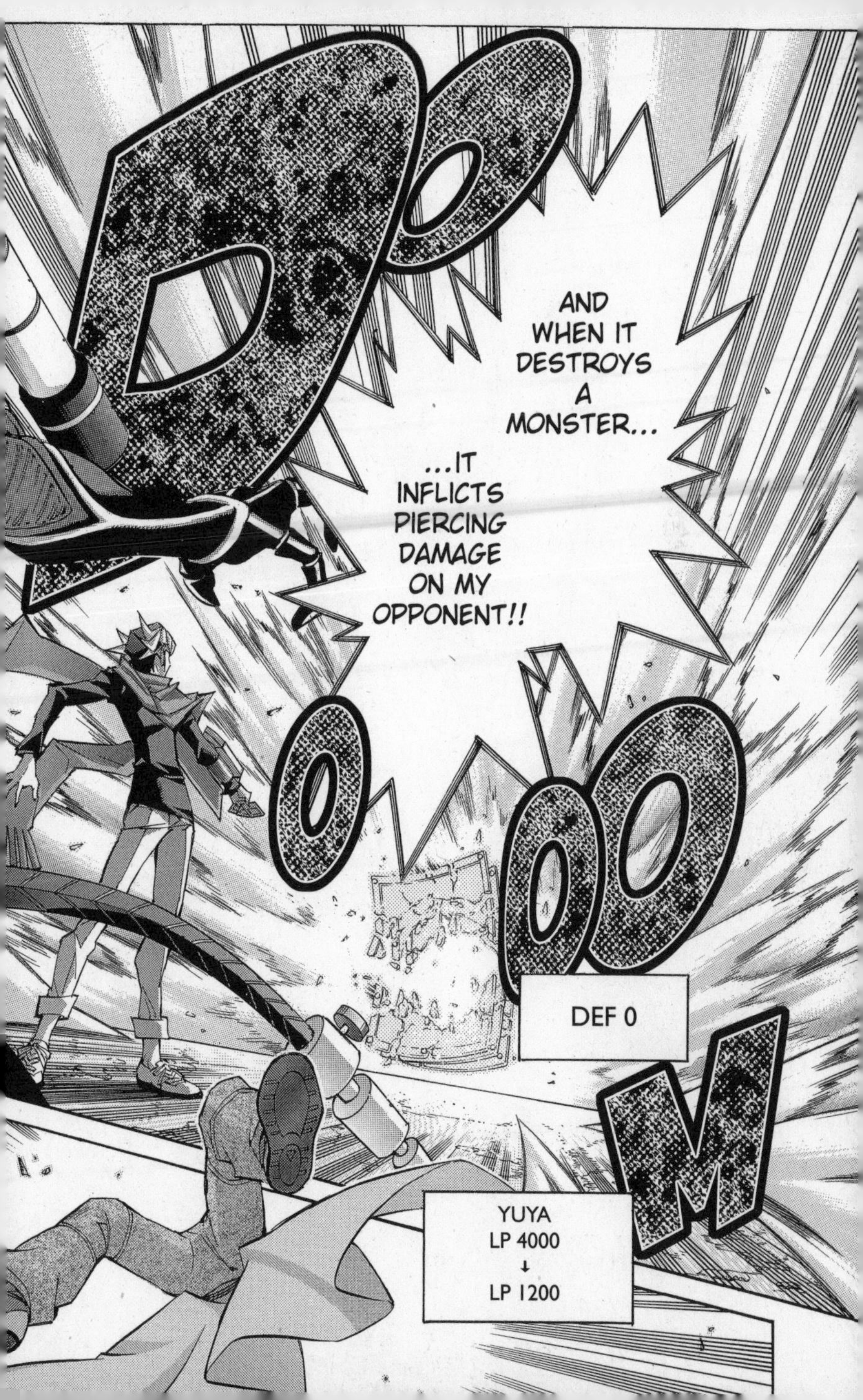
DOOOM
AND WHEN IT DESTROYS A MONSTER...
...IT INFLICTS PIERCING DAMAGE ON MY OPPONENT!!
DEF 0
YUYA
LP 4000
↓
LP 1200

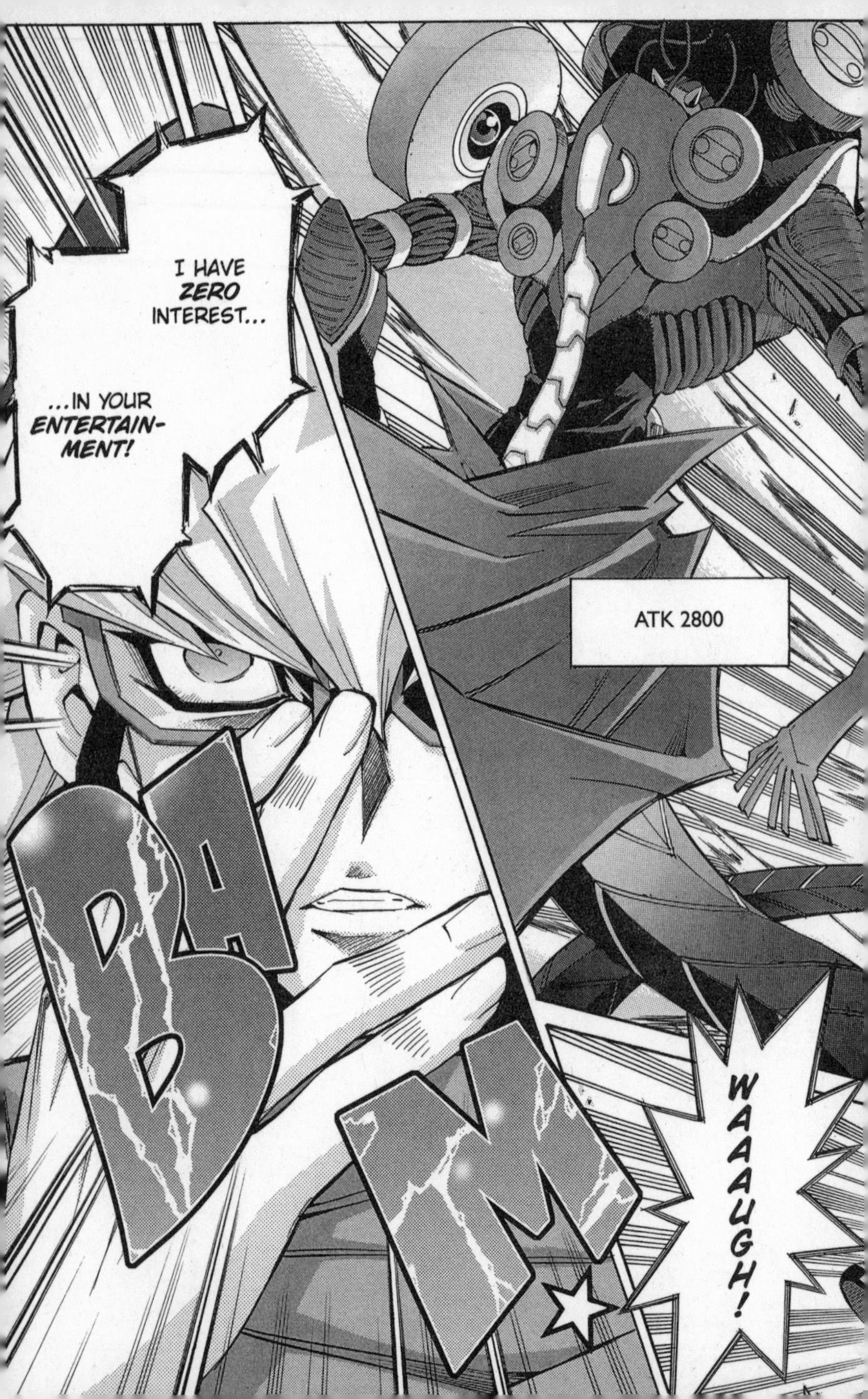
ATK 2800
I HAVE *ZERO* INTEREST...
...IN YOUR *ENTERTAINMENT!*
BAM
WAAAAUGH!

PRESENTING MIYOSHI SENSEI'S EARLY DESIGNS!

ARC-V CHARACTER SKETCHES

AYU

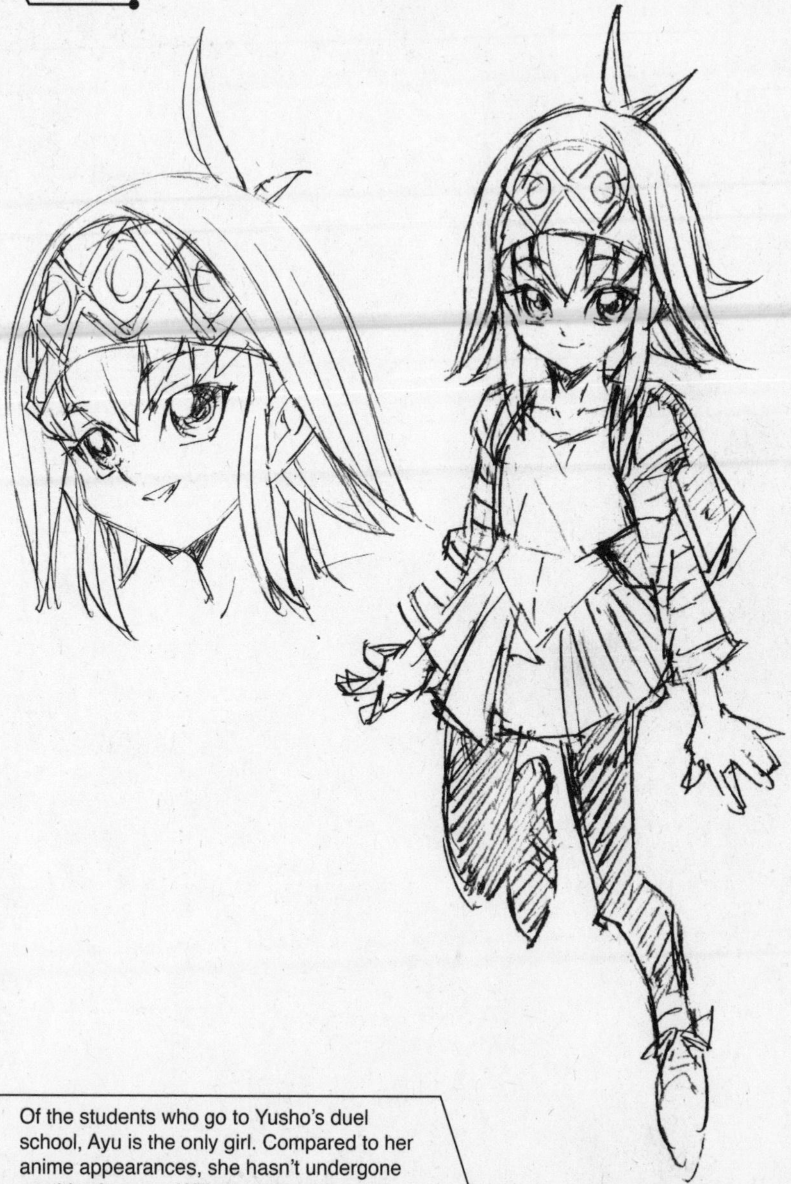

Of the students who go to Yusho's duel school, Ayu is the only girl. Compared to her anime appearances, she hasn't undergone any big changes. Will she play a big role in the manga?

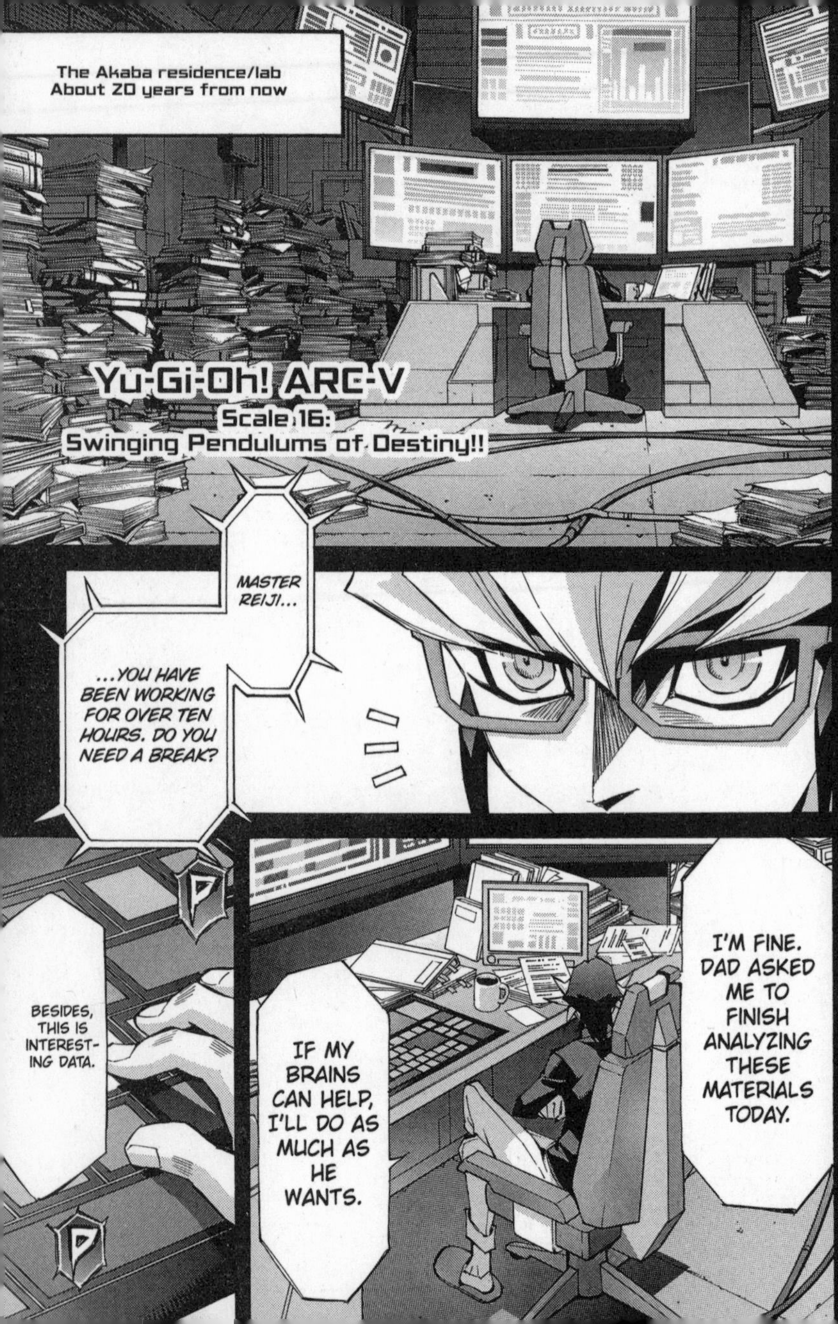
The Akaba residence/lab
About 20 years from now
Yu-Gi-Oh! ARC-V
Scale 16:
Swinging Pendulums of Destiny!!
MASTER REIJI...
...YOU HAVE BEEN WORKING FOR OVER TEN HOURS. DO YOU NEED A BREAK?
I'M FINE. DAD ASKED ME TO FINISH ANALYZING THESE MATERIALS TODAY.
IF MY BRAINS CAN HELP, I'LL DO AS MUCH AS HE WANTS.
BESIDES, THIS IS INTERESTING DATA.

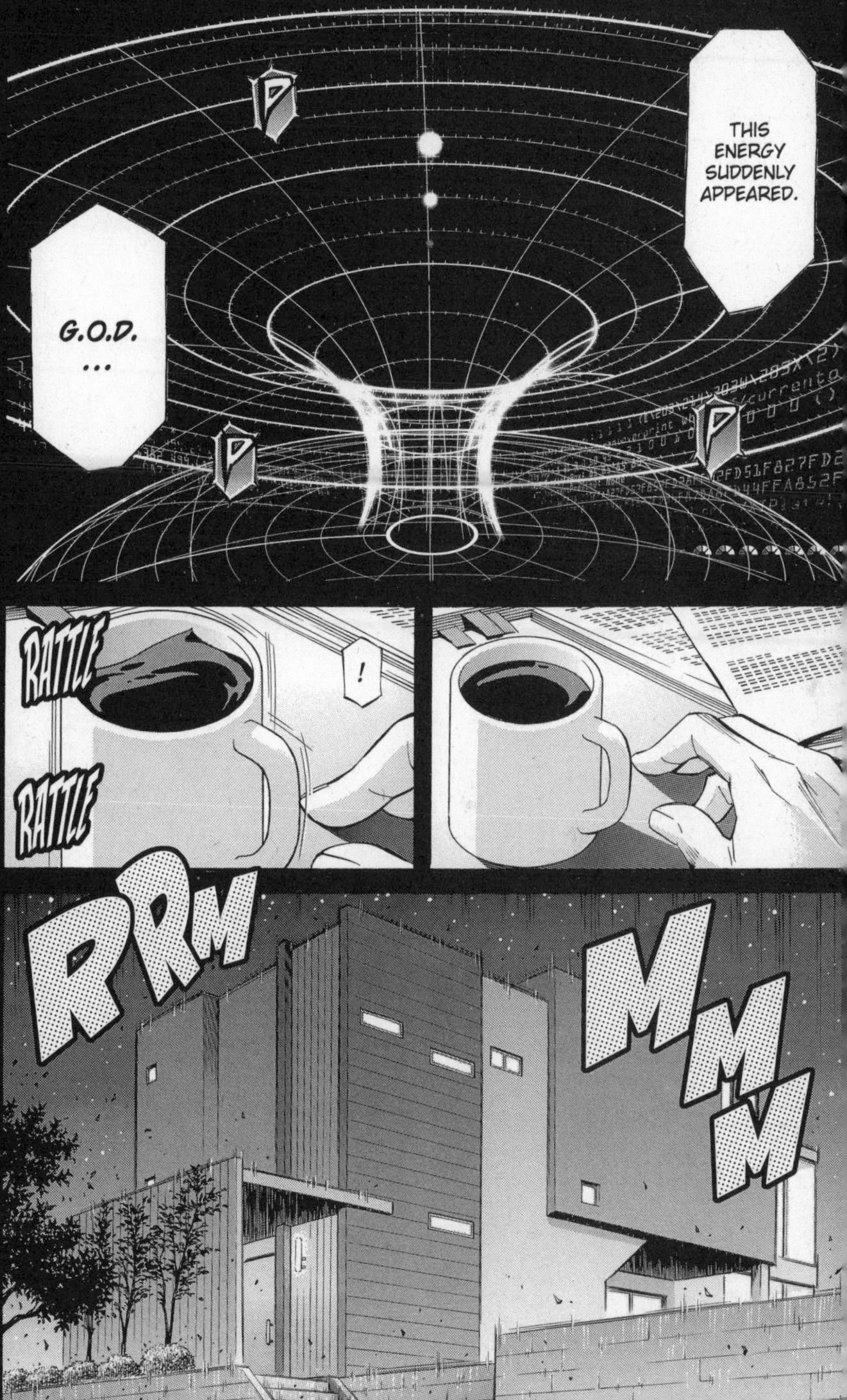
THIS ENERGY SUDDENLY APPEARED.
G.O.D. ...
!
RATTLE
RATTLE
RRM
MMMM

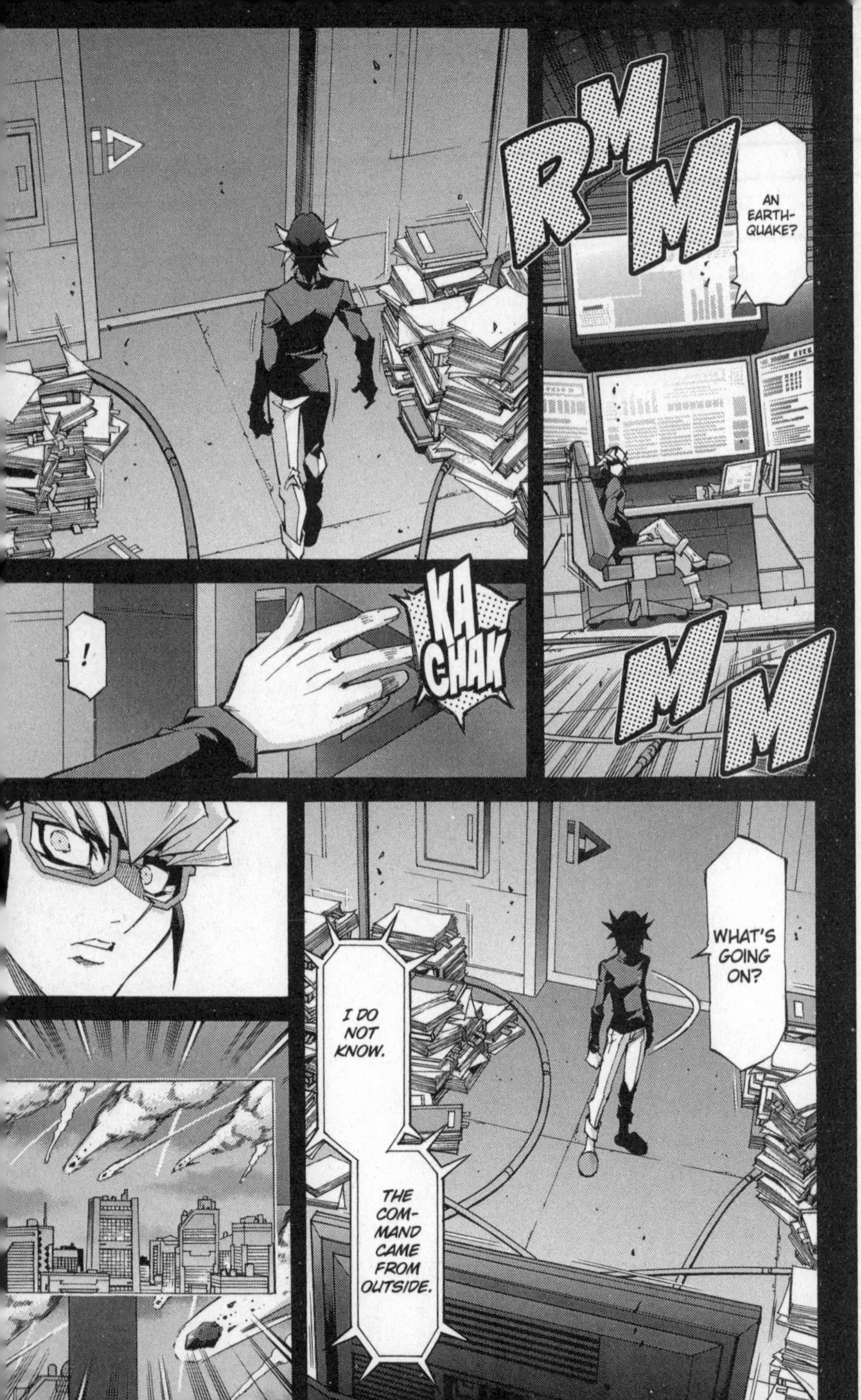
RMM
AN EARTHQUAKE?
MM
!
KA CHAK
WHAT'S GOING ON?
I DO NOT KNOW.
THE COMMAND CAME FROM OUTSIDE.

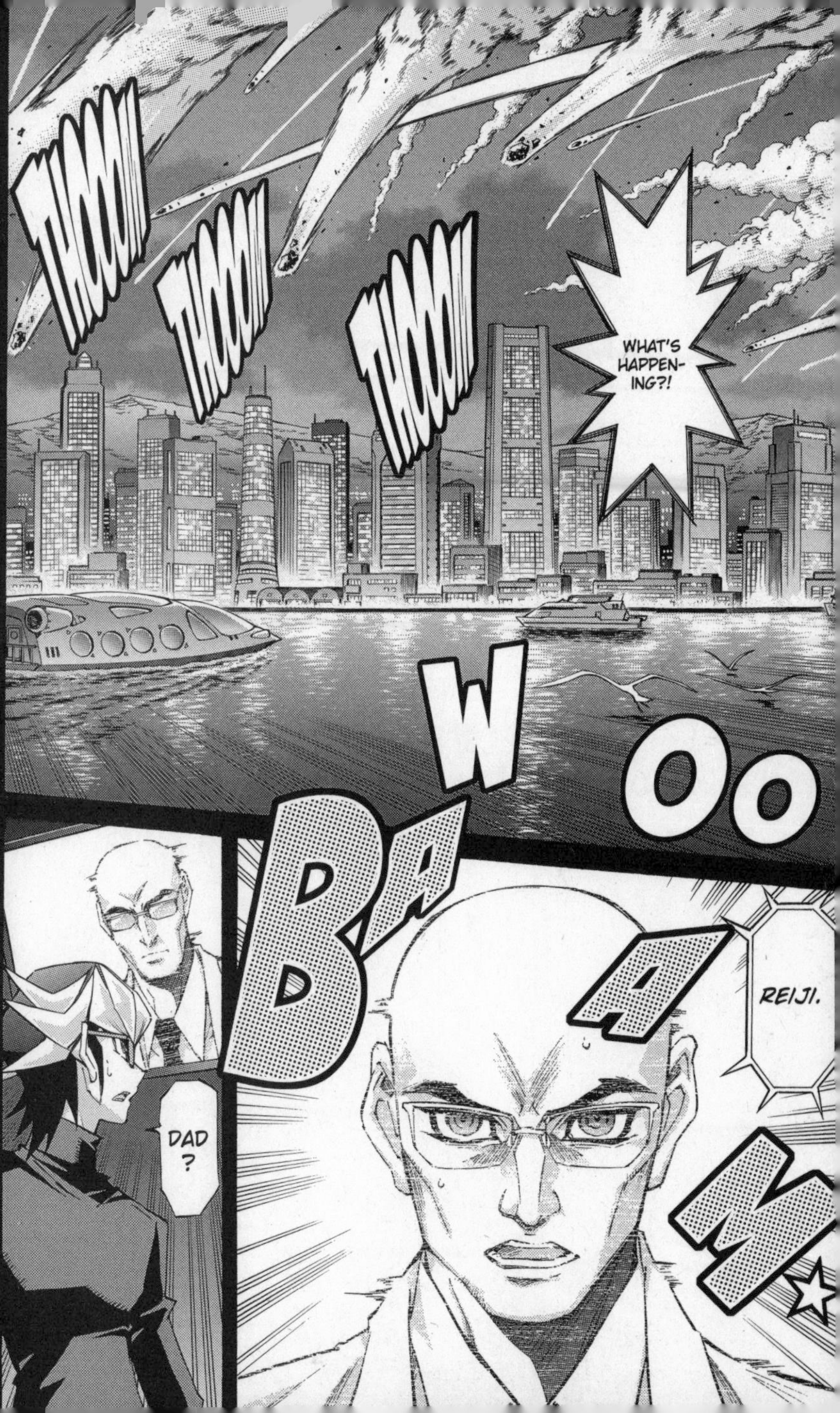

WHAT'S HAPPEN-ING?!
THOOOM
THOOOM
THOOOM
WOOO
BAAAM☆
REIJI.
DAD?

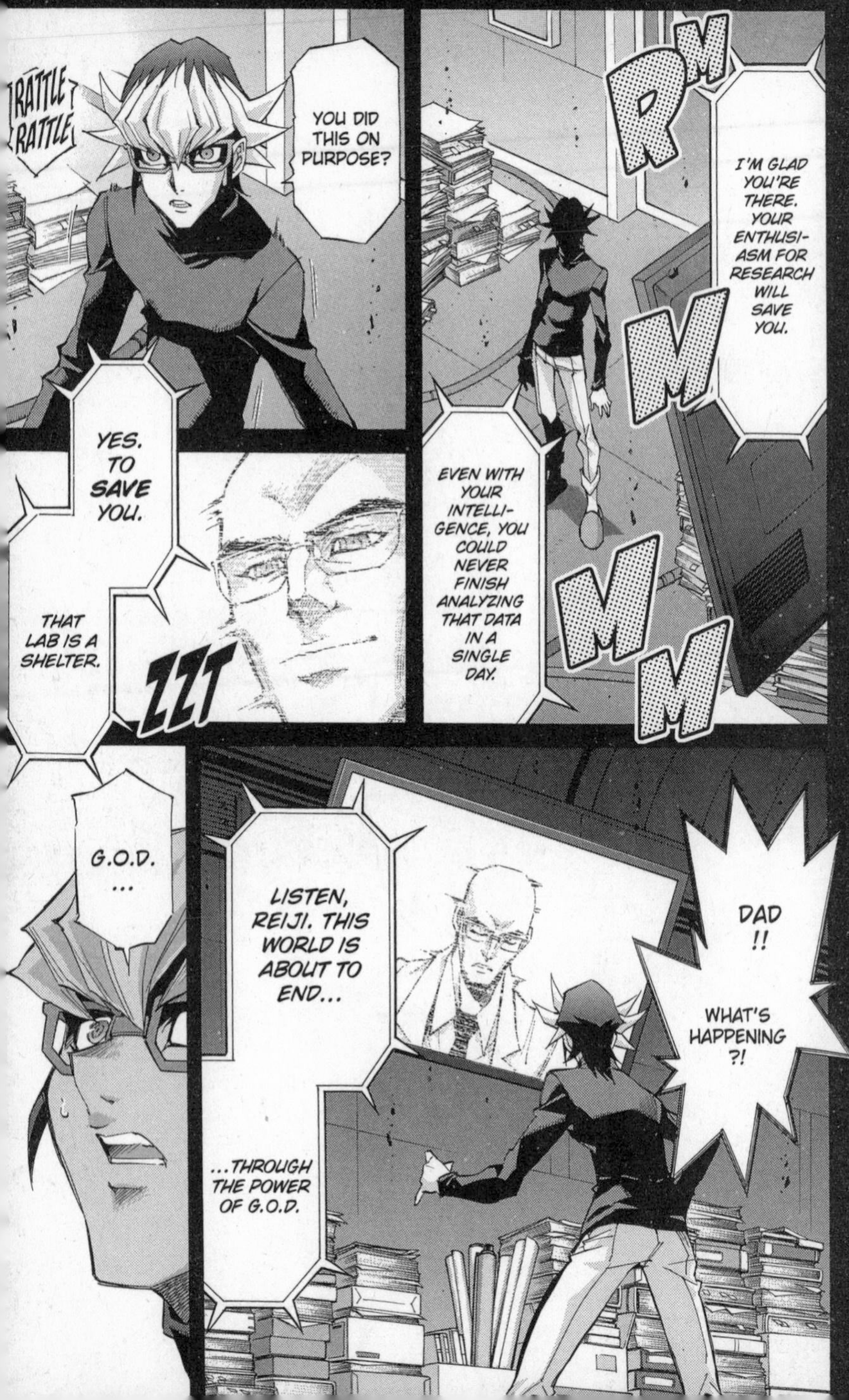
RMMMM
I'M GLAD YOU'RE THERE. YOUR ENTHUSIASM FOR RESEARCH WILL SAVE YOU.
EVEN WITH YOUR INTELLIGENCE, YOU COULD NEVER FINISH ANALYZING THAT DATA IN A SINGLE DAY.
RATTLE RATTLE
YOU DID THIS ON PURPOSE?
YES. TO SAVE YOU.
THAT LAB IS A SHELTER.
ZZT
DAD!!
WHAT'S HAPPENING?!
LISTEN, REIJI. THIS WORLD IS ABOUT TO END...
...THROUGH THE POWER OF G.O.D.
G.O.D. ...

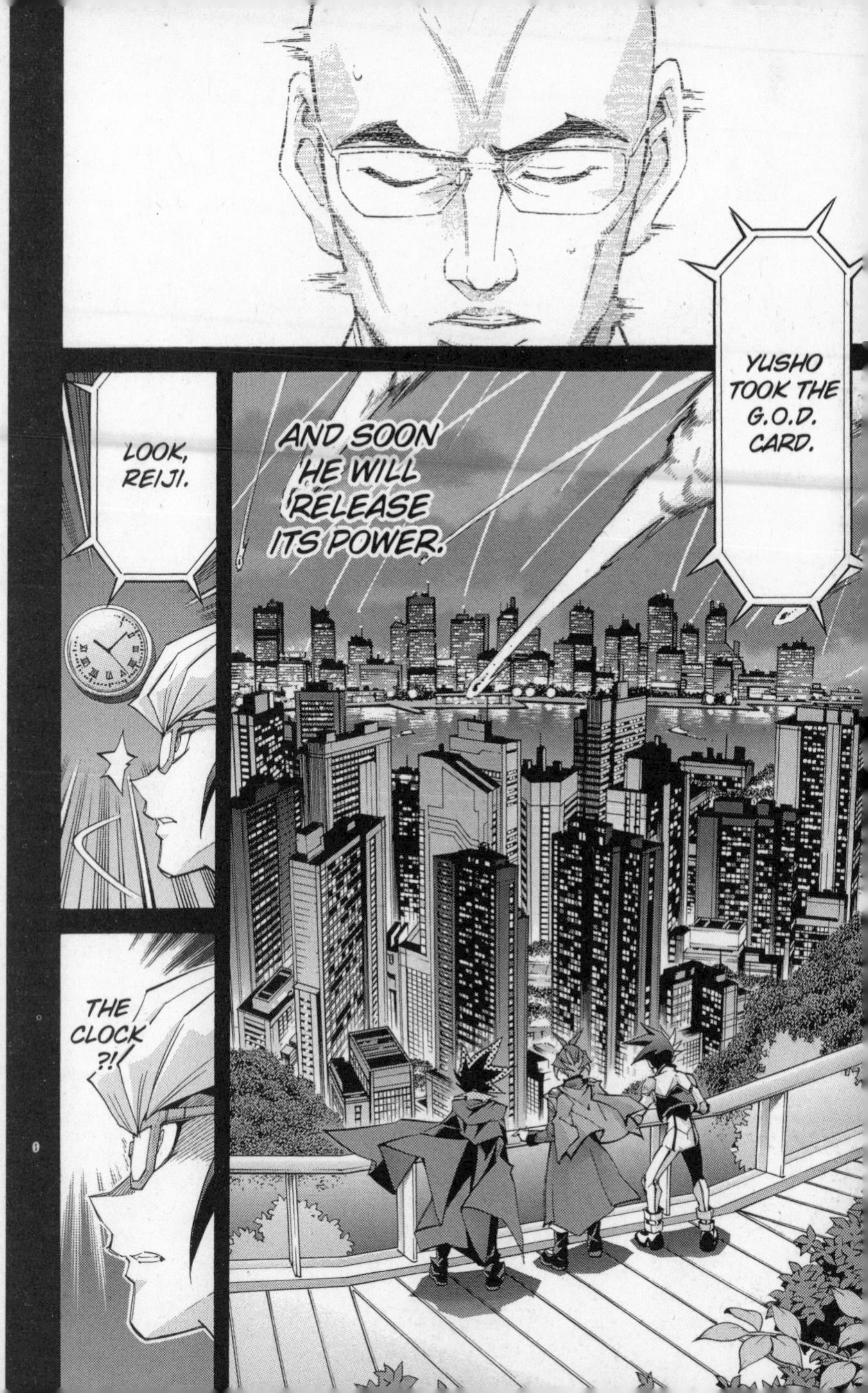
YUSHO TOOK THE G.O.D. CARD.
AND SOON HE WILL RELEASE ITS POWER.
LOOK, REIJI.
THE CLOCK ?!

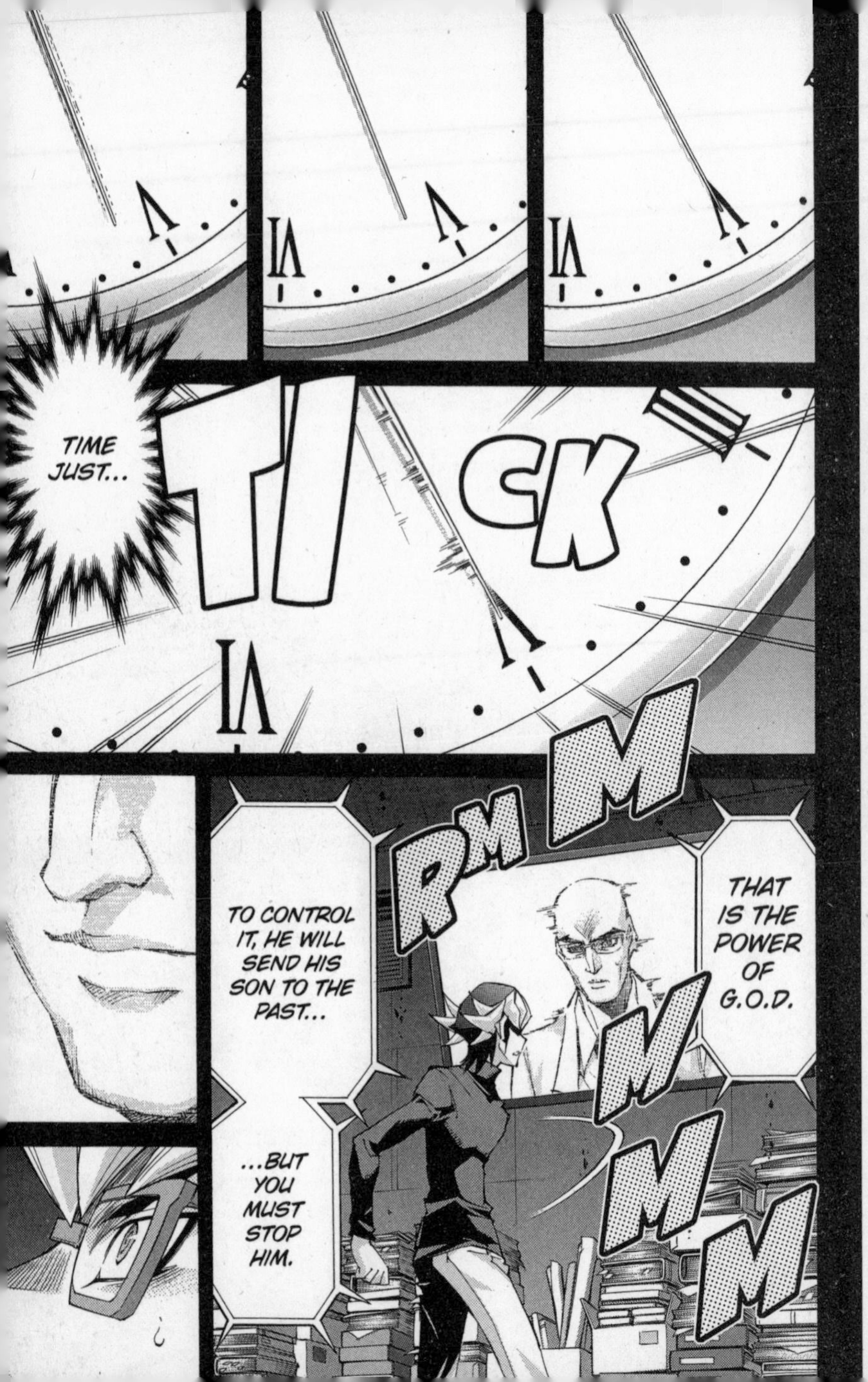
TIME JUST...
TICK
THAT IS THE POWER OF G.O.D.
RMMMMMM
TO CONTROL IT, HE WILL SEND HIS SON TO THE PAST...
...BUT YOU MUST STOP HIM.

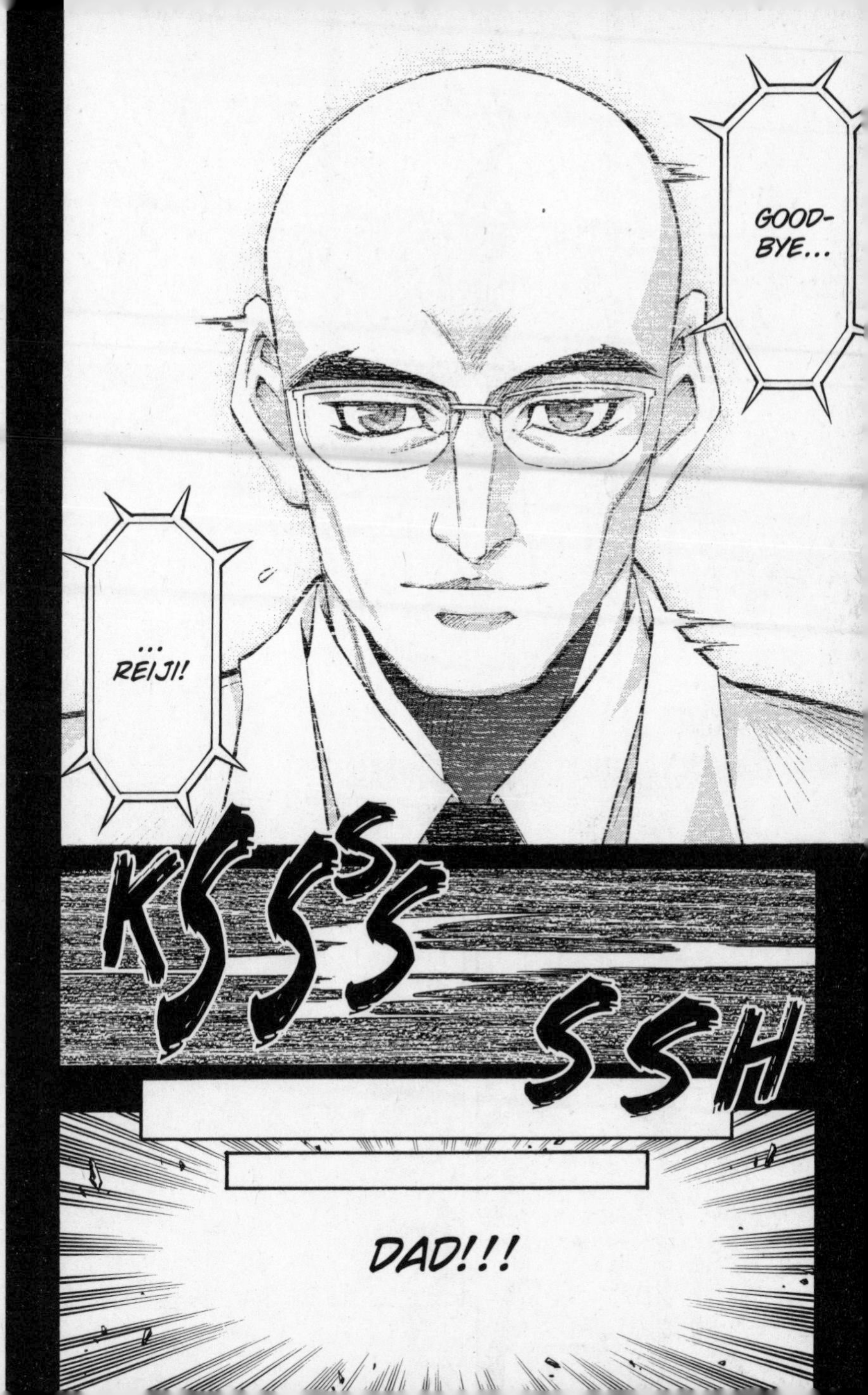
GOOD-BYE...
...REIJI!
KSSSS SSH
DAD!!!

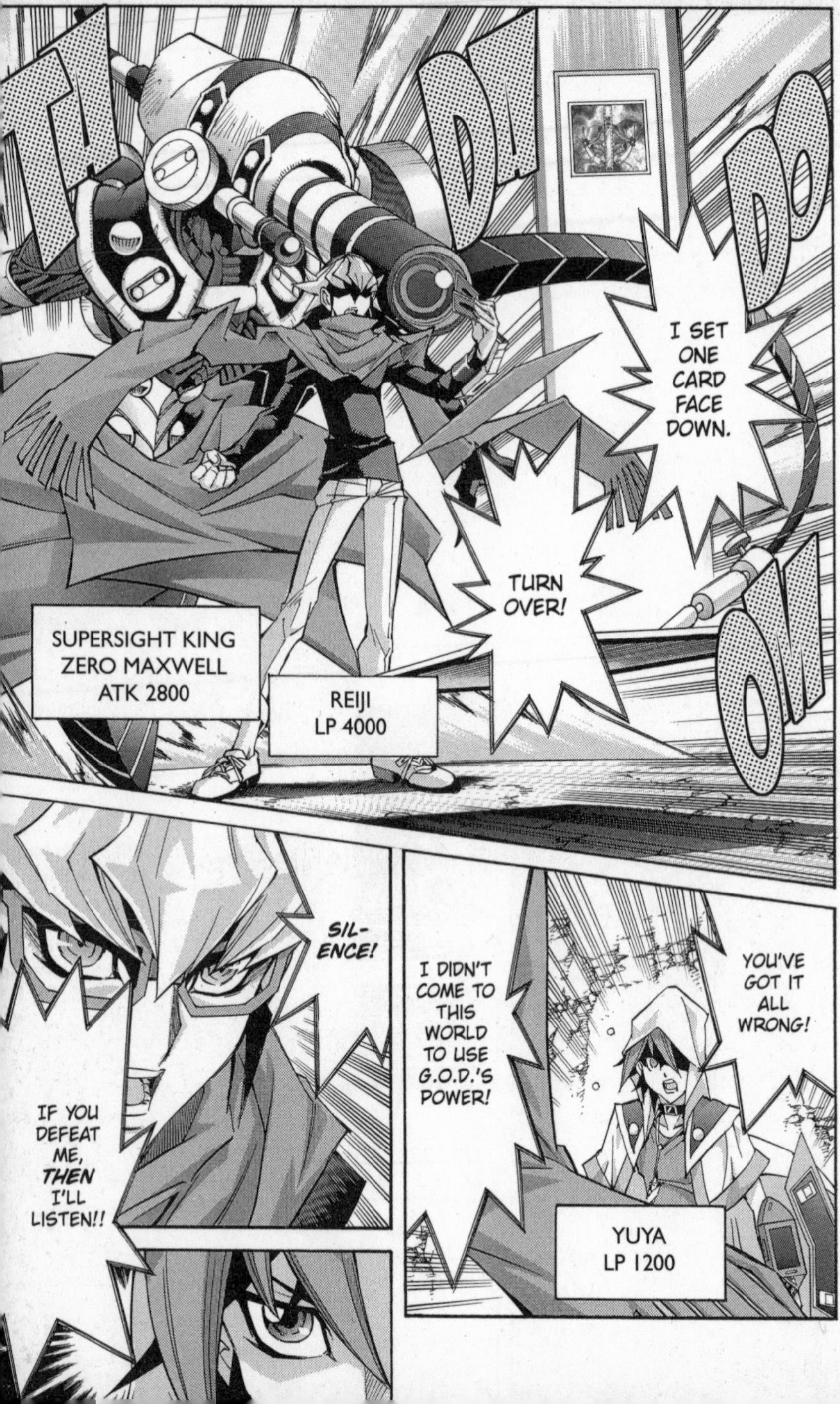
THA
DA
DO
OM
I SET ONE CARD FACE DOWN.
TURN OVER!
REIJI LP 4000
SUPERSIGHT KING ZERO MAXWELL ATK 2800
YOU'VE GOT IT ALL WRONG!
I DIDN'T COME TO THIS WORLD TO USE G.O.D.'S POWER!
YUYA LP 1200
SIL-ENCE!
IF YOU DEFEAT ME, *THEN* I'LL LISTEN!!

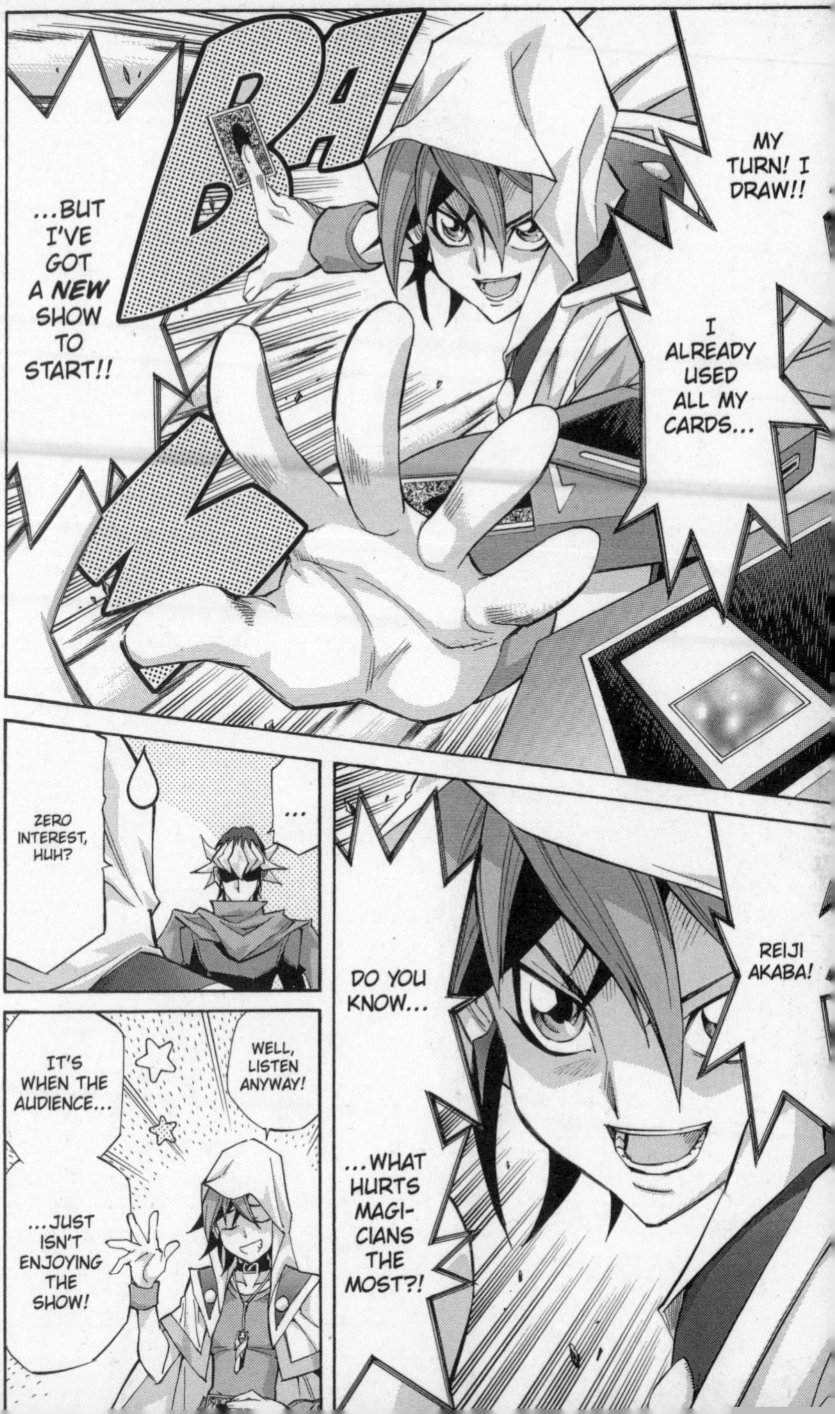
MY TURN! I DRAW!!
I ALREADY USED ALL MY CARDS...
...BUT I'VE GOT A **NEW** SHOW TO START!!
REIJI AKABA!
DO YOU KNOW...
...WHAT HURTS MAGI-CIANS THE MOST?!
...
ZERO INTEREST, HUH?
WELL, LISTEN ANYWAY!
IT'S WHEN THE AUDIENCE...
...JUST ISN'T ENJOYING THE SHOW!

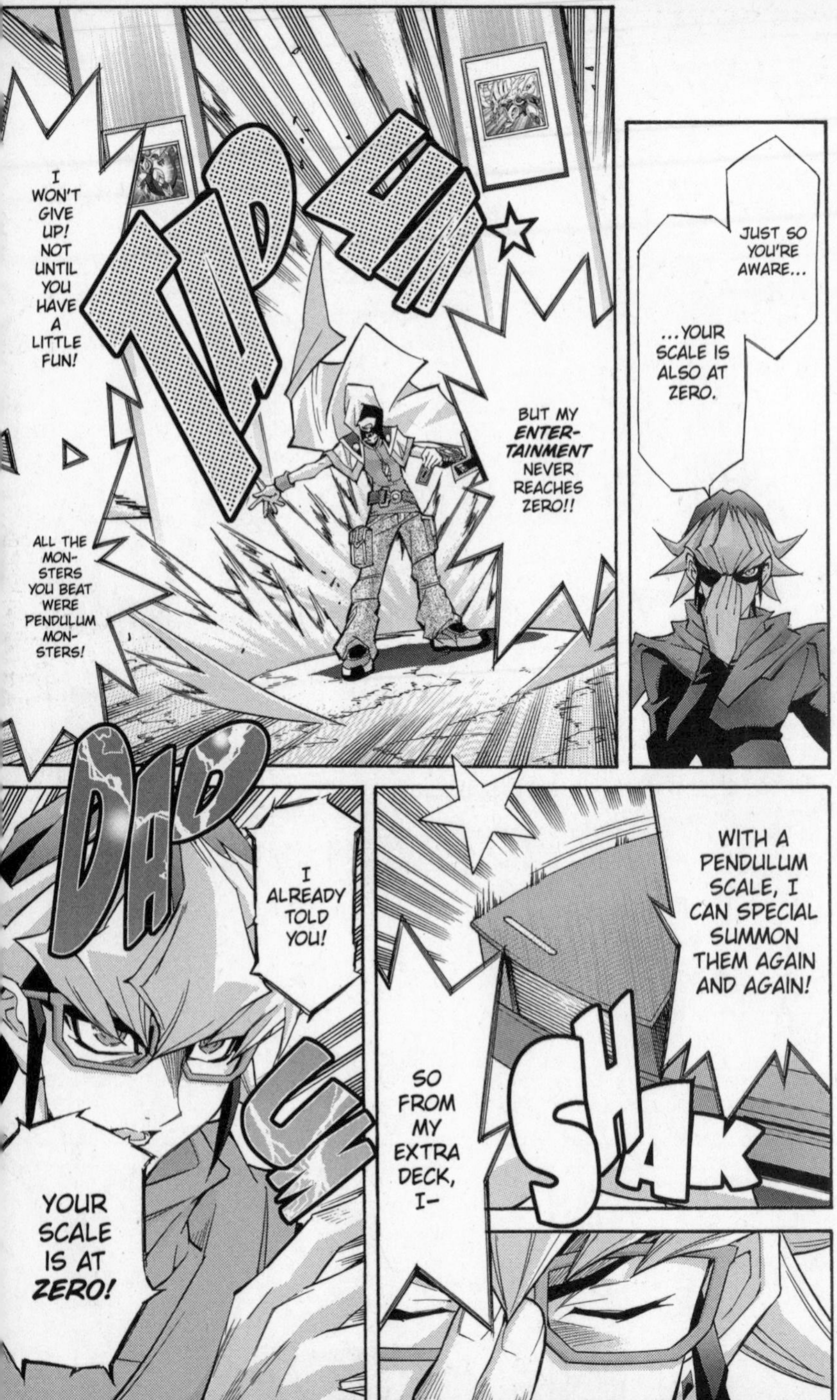
JUST SO YOU'RE AWARE...
...YOUR SCALE IS ALSO AT ZERO.
BUT MY *ENTERTAINMENT* NEVER REACHES ZERO!!
I WON'T GIVE UP! NOT UNTIL YOU HAVE A LITTLE FUN!
ALL THE MONSTERS YOU BEAT WERE PENDULUM MONSTERS!
WITH A PENDULUM SCALE, I CAN SPECIAL SUMMON THEM AGAIN AND AGAIN!
SO FROM MY EXTRA DECK, I-
SHAK
I ALREADY TOLD YOU!
YOUR SCALE IS AT *ZERO!*

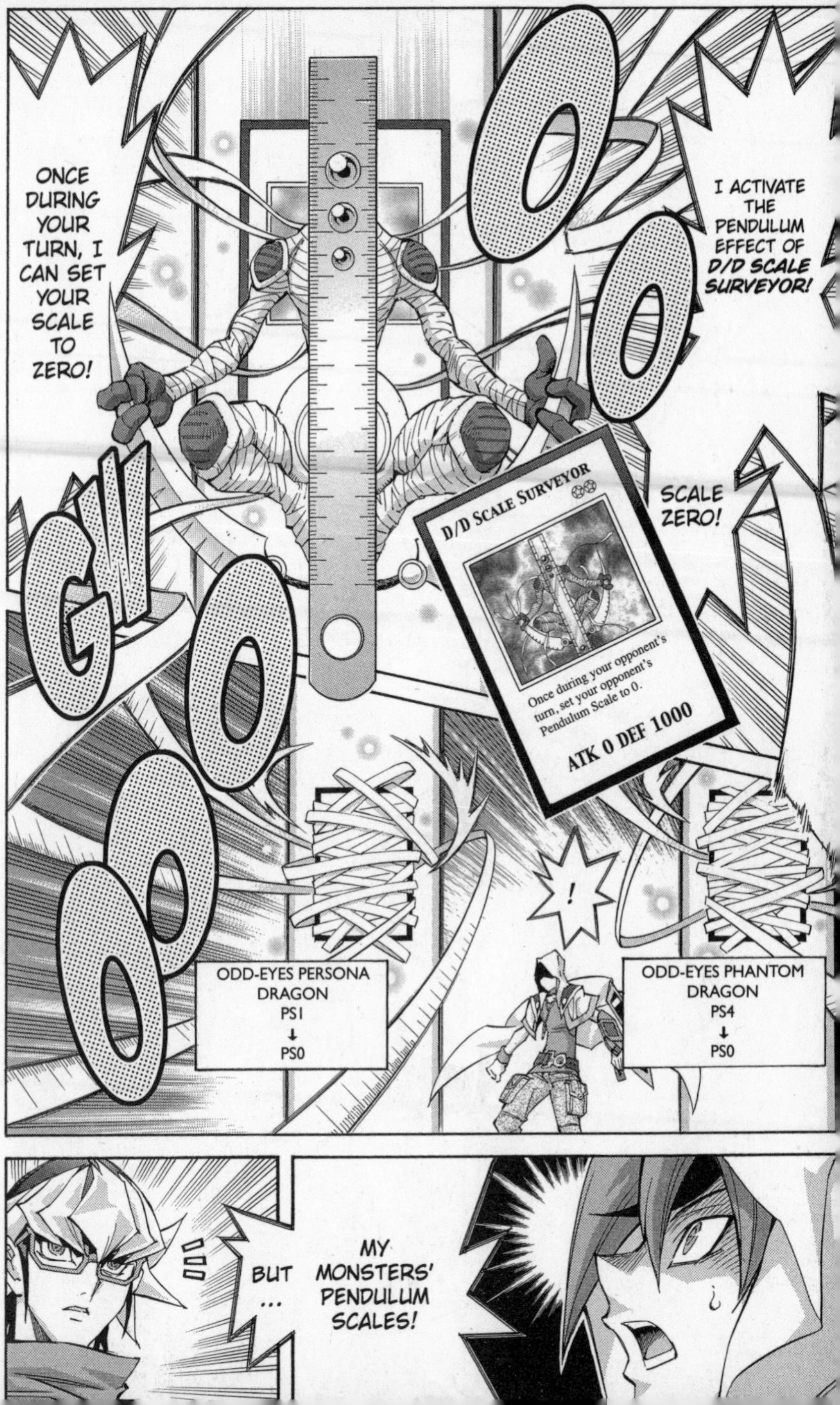
I ACTIVATE THE PENDULUM EFFECT OF D/D SCALE SURVEYOR!
ONCE DURING YOUR TURN, I CAN SET YOUR SCALE TO ZERO!
GWOOOOOO
SCALE ZERO!
D/D SCALE SURVEYOR
Once during your opponent's turn, set your opponent's Pendulum Scale to 0.
ATK 0 DEF 1000
!
ODD-EYES PHANTOM DRAGON PS4 ↓ PS0
ODD-EYES PERSONA DRAGON PS1 ↓ PS0
MY MONSTERS' PENDULUM SCALES!
BUT ...

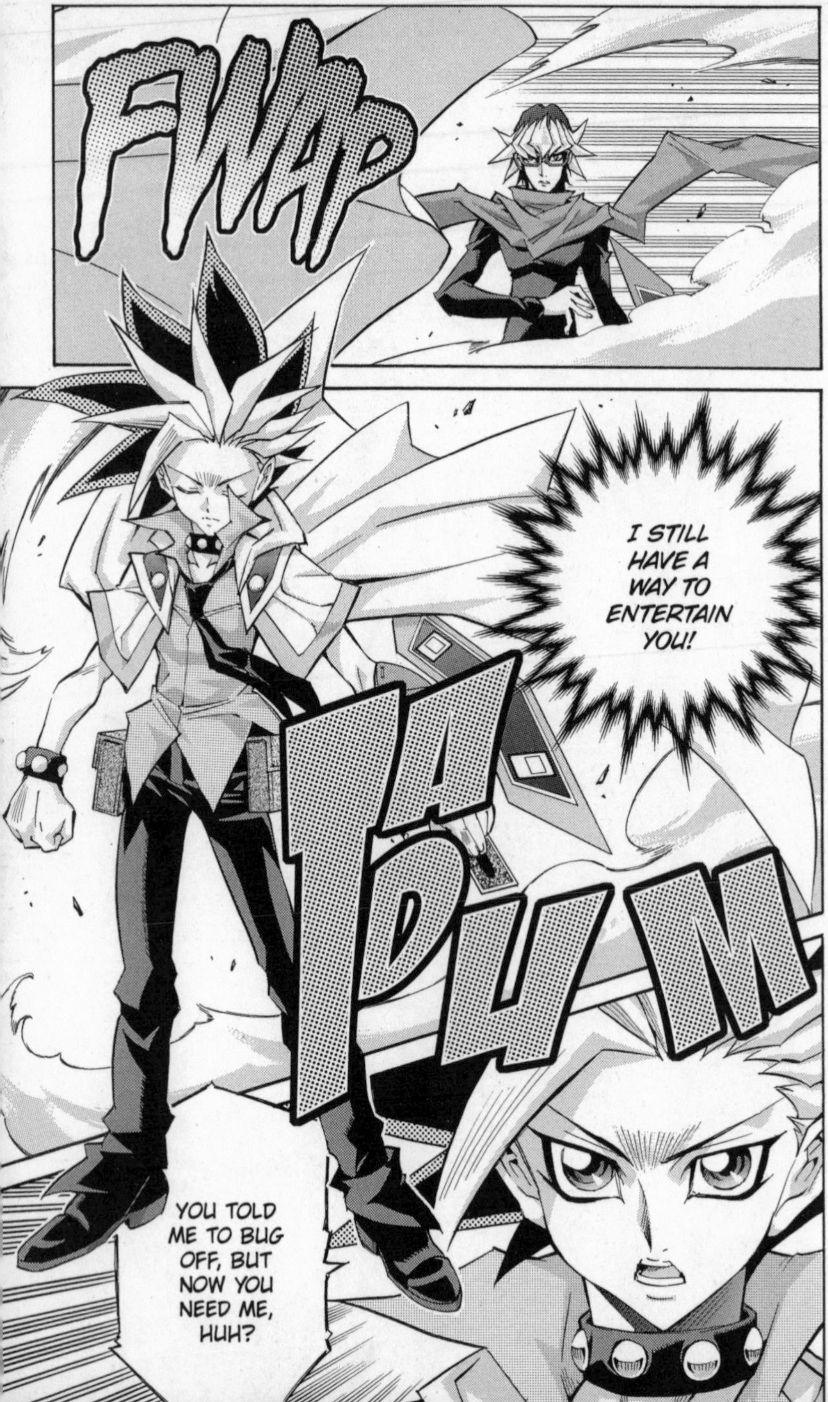
FWAP
I STILL HAVE A WAY TO ENTERTAIN YOU!
TA DUM
YOU TOLD ME TO BUG OFF, BUT NOW YOU NEED ME, HUH?

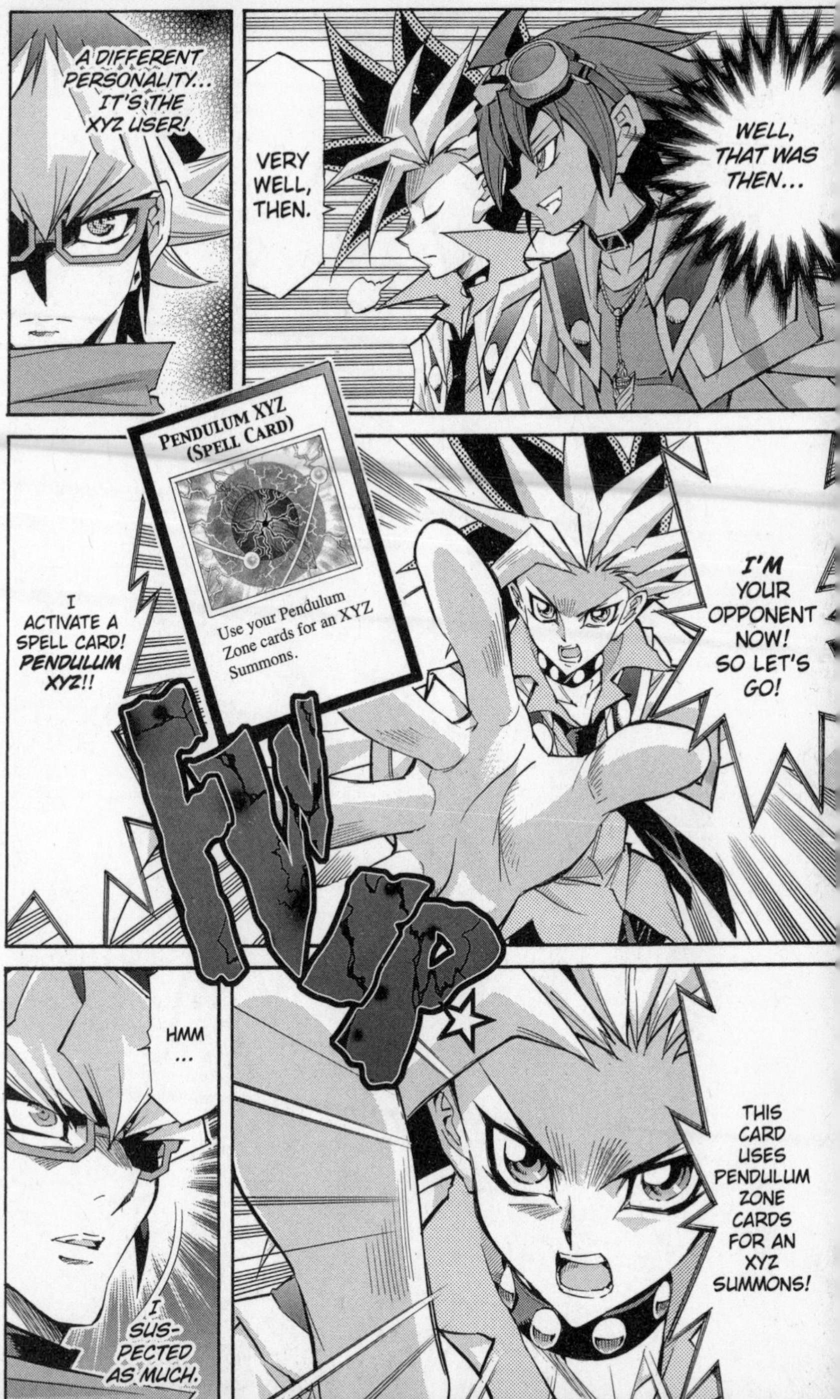
WELL, THAT WAS THEN...
VERY WELL, THEN.
A DIFFERENT PERSONALITY... IT'S THE XYZ USER!
I'M YOUR OPPONENT NOW! SO LET'S GO!
PENDULUM XYZ (SPELL CARD)
Use your Pendulum Zone cards for an XYZ Summons.
I ACTIVATE A SPELL CARD! PENDULUM XYZ!!
FLIP
THIS CARD USES PENDULUM ZONE CARDS FOR AN XYZ SUMMONS!
HMM...
I SUS-PECTED AS MUCH.

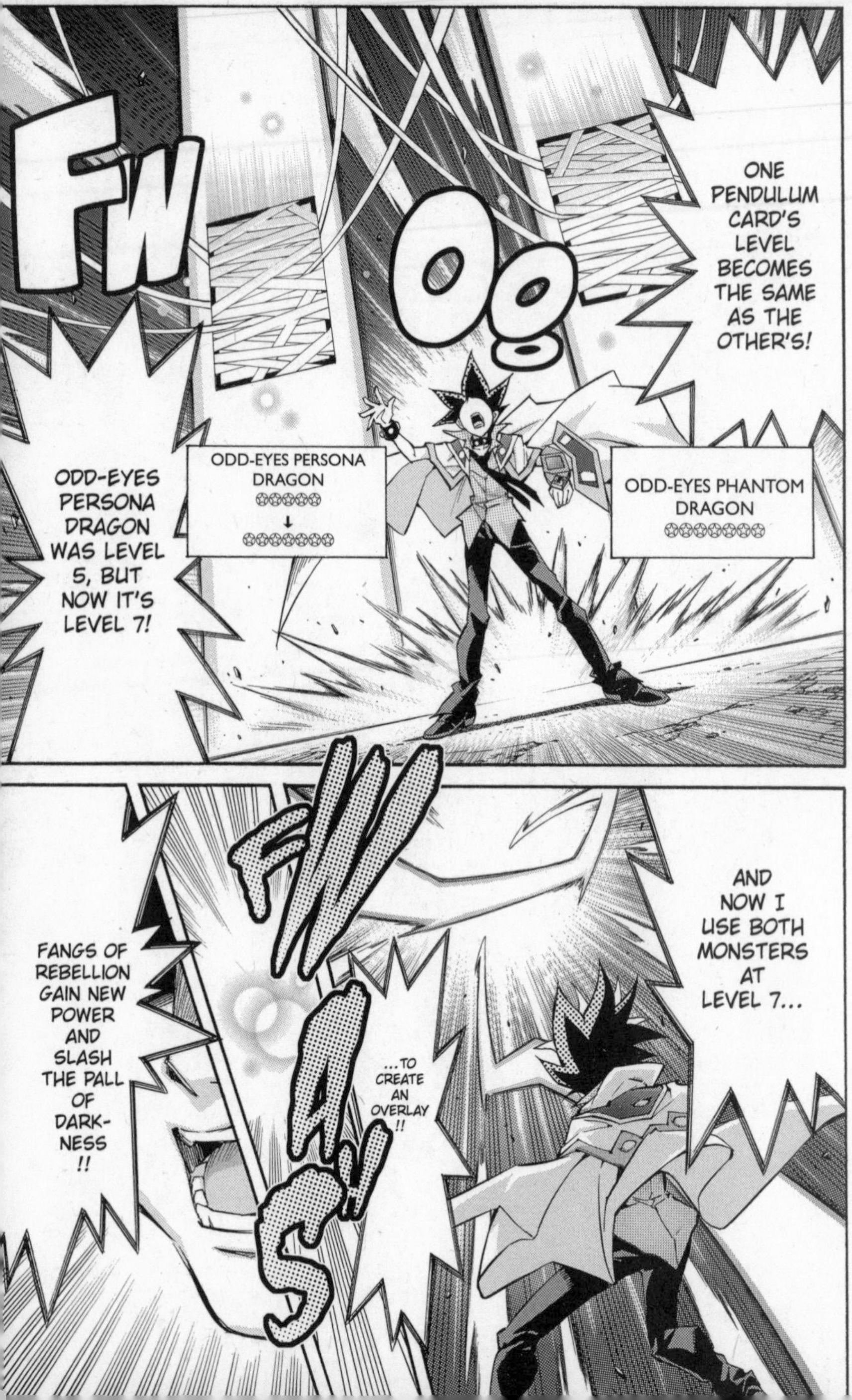
ONE PENDULUM CARD'S LEVEL BECOMES THE SAME AS THE OTHER'S!
FWOOO
ODD-EYES PHANTOM DRAGON
ODD-EYES PERSONA DRAGON
ODD-EYES PERSONA DRAGON WAS LEVEL 5, BUT NOW IT'S LEVEL 7!
AND NOW I USE BOTH MONSTERS AT LEVEL 7...
...TO CREATE AN OVERLAY!!
FWASH!
FANGS OF REBELLION GAIN NEW POWER AND SLASH THE PALL OF DARK-NESS!!

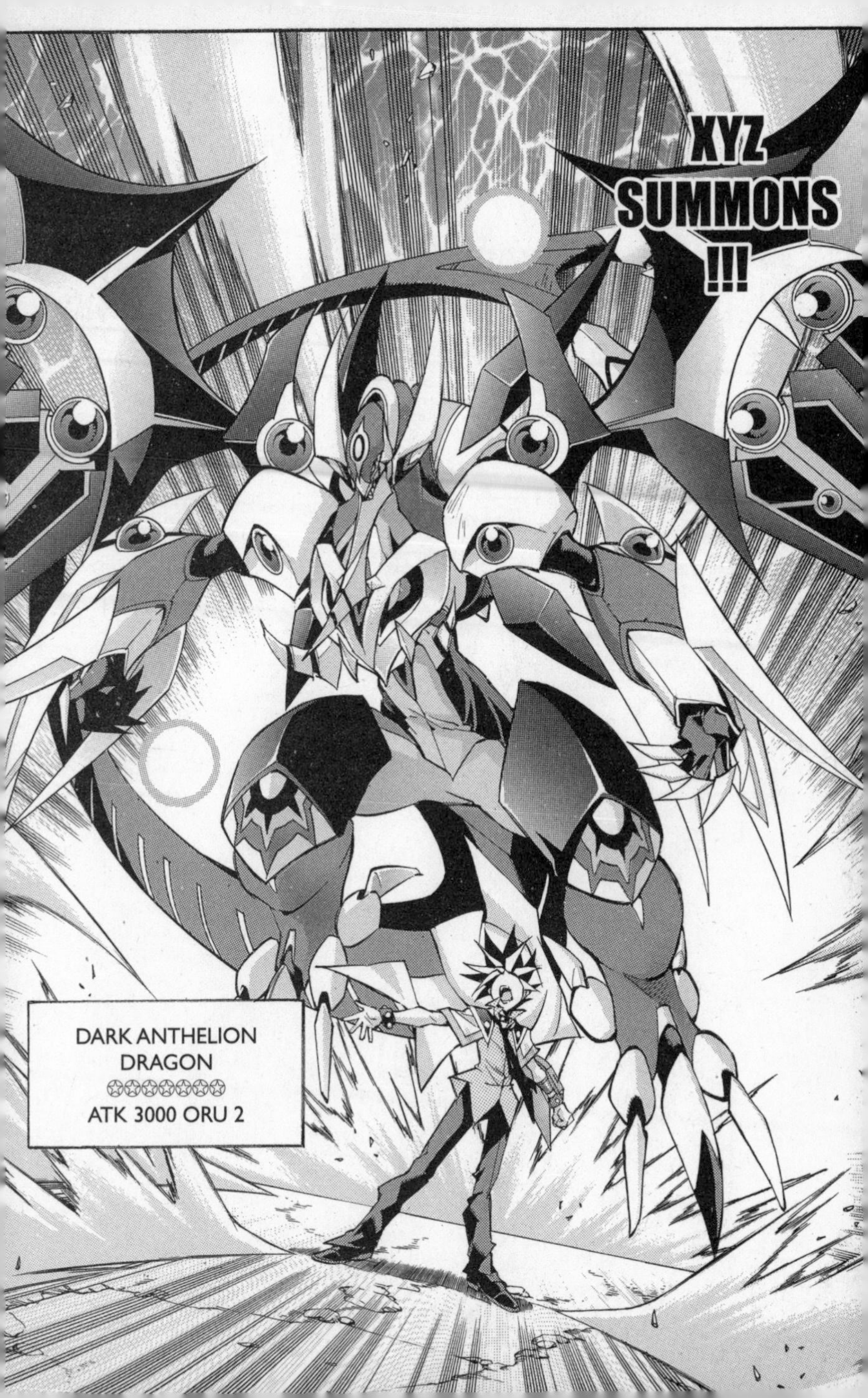
XYZ SUMMONS !!!
DARK ANTHELION DRAGON
ATK 3000 ORU 2

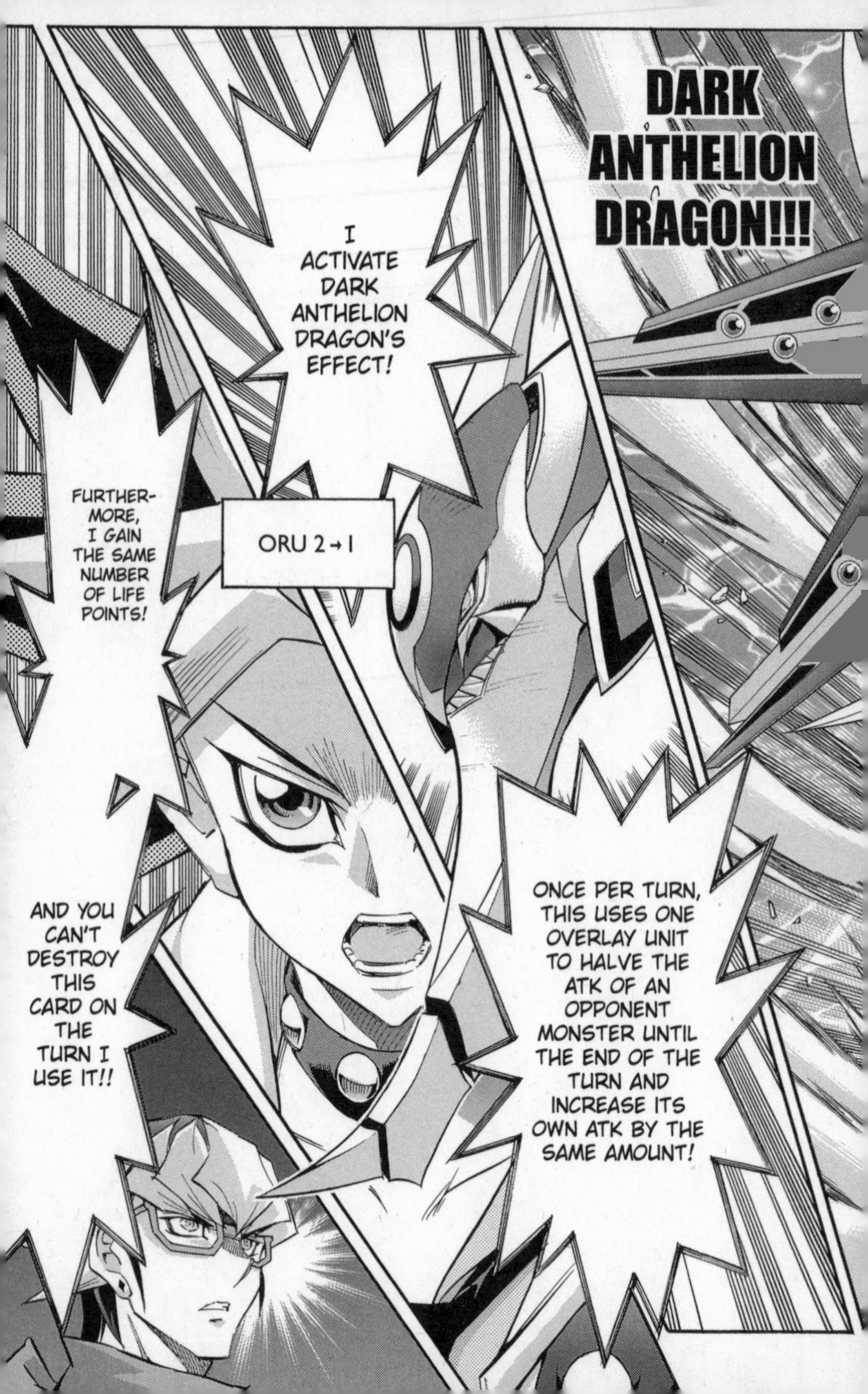
DARK ANTHELION DRAGON!!!
I ACTIVATE DARK ANTHELION DRAGON'S EFFECT!
ORU 2→1
ONCE PER TURN, THIS USES ONE OVERLAY UNIT TO HALVE THE ATK OF AN OPPONENT MONSTER UNTIL THE END OF THE TURN AND INCREASE ITS OWN ATK BY THE SAME AMOUNT!
FURTHER-MORE, I GAIN THE SAME NUMBER OF LIFE POINTS!
AND YOU CAN'T DESTROY THIS CARD ON THE TURN I USE IT!!

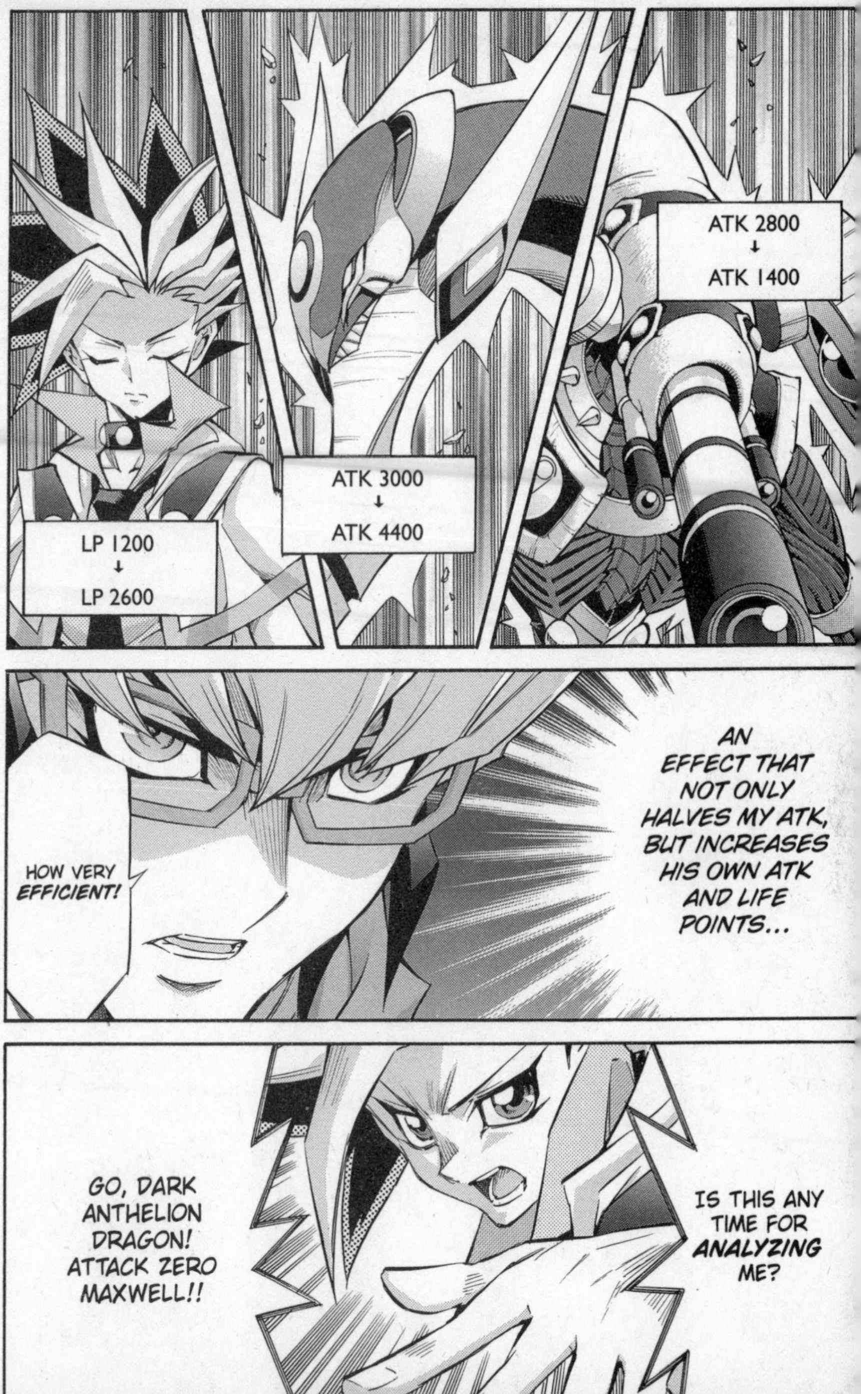
ATK 2800 ↓ ATK 1400
ATK 3000 ↓ ATK 4400
LP 1200 ↓ LP 2600
AN EFFECT THAT NOT ONLY HALVES MY ATK, BUT INCREASES HIS OWN ATK AND LIFE POINTS...
HOW VERY EFFICIENT!
IS THIS ANY TIME FOR ANALYZING ME?
GO, DARK ANTHELION DRAGON! ATTACK ZERO MAXWELL!!

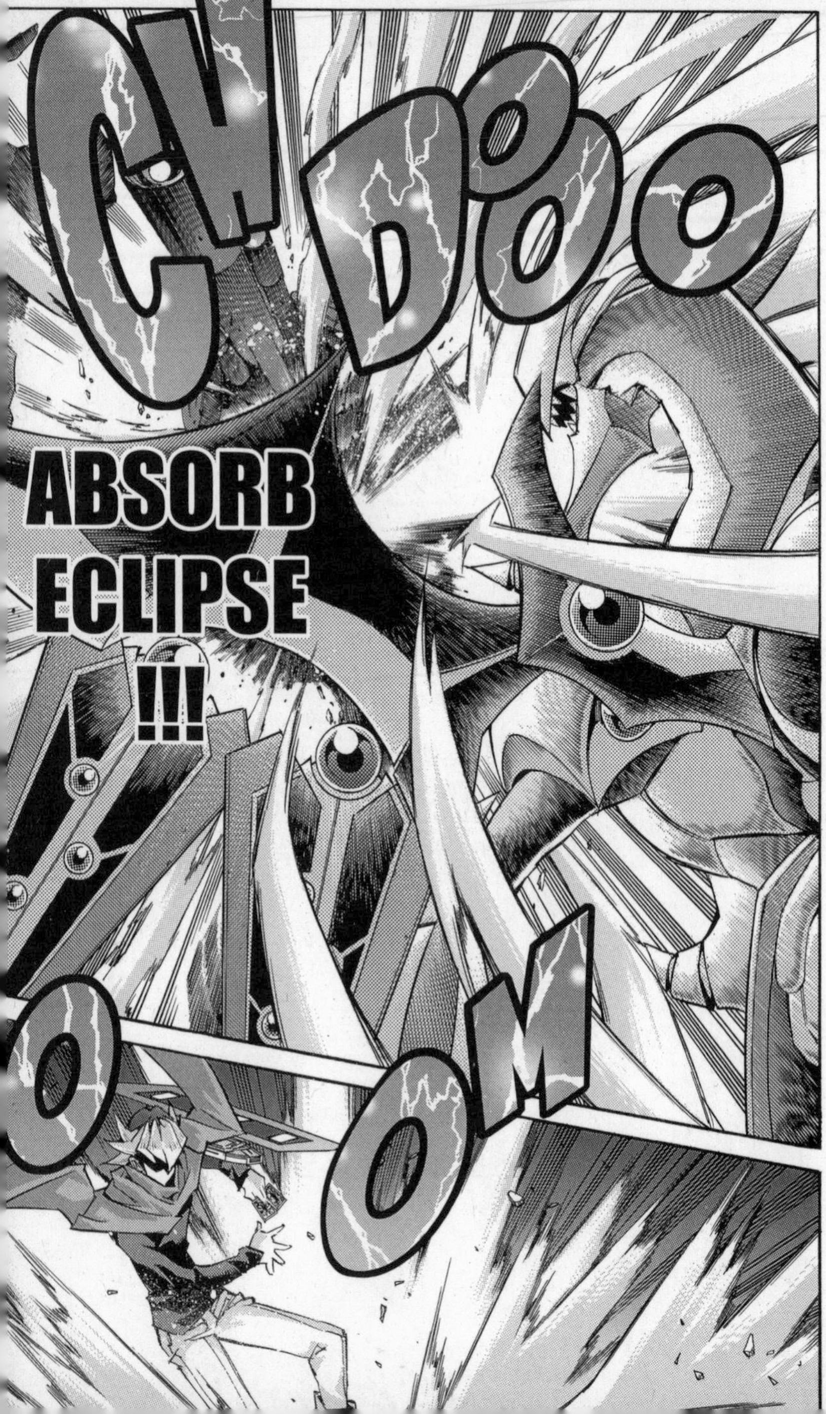
CHDOOO
ABSORB ECLIPSE !!!
OOM

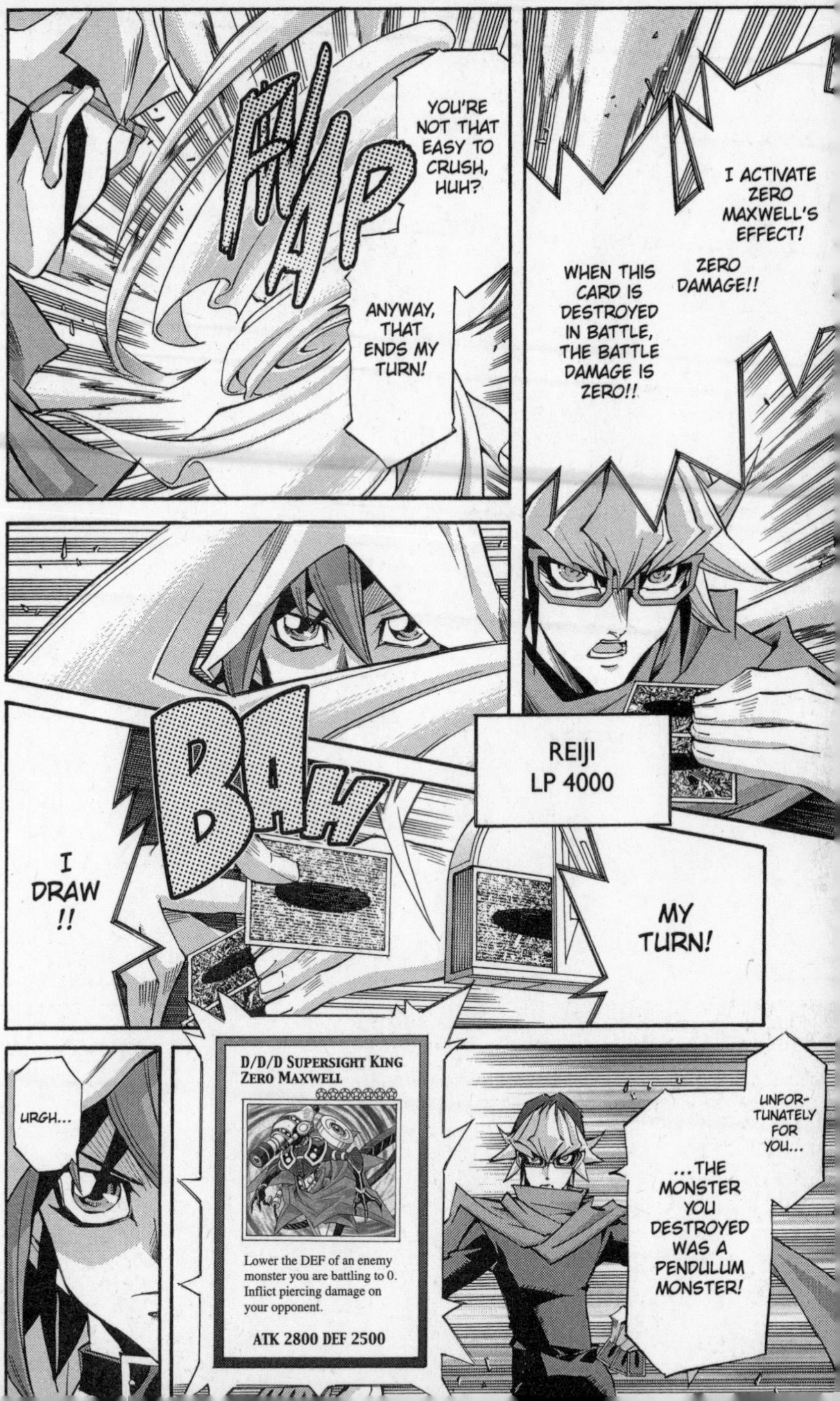

I ACTIVATE ZERO MAXWELL'S EFFECT!
ZERO DAMAGE!!
WHEN THIS CARD IS DESTROYED IN BATTLE, THE BATTLE DAMAGE IS ZERO!!
YOU'RE NOT THAT EASY TO CRUSH, HUH?
FWAP
ANYWAY, THAT ENDS MY TURN!
REIJI LP 4000
MY TURN!
BAH
I DRAW !!
UNFORTUNATELY FOR YOU...
...THE MONSTER YOU DESTROYED WAS A PENDULUM MONSTER!
D/D/D SUPERSIGHT KING ZERO MAXWELL
Lower the DEF of an enemy monster you are battling to 0. Inflict piercing damage on your opponent.
ATK 2800 DEF 2500
URGH...

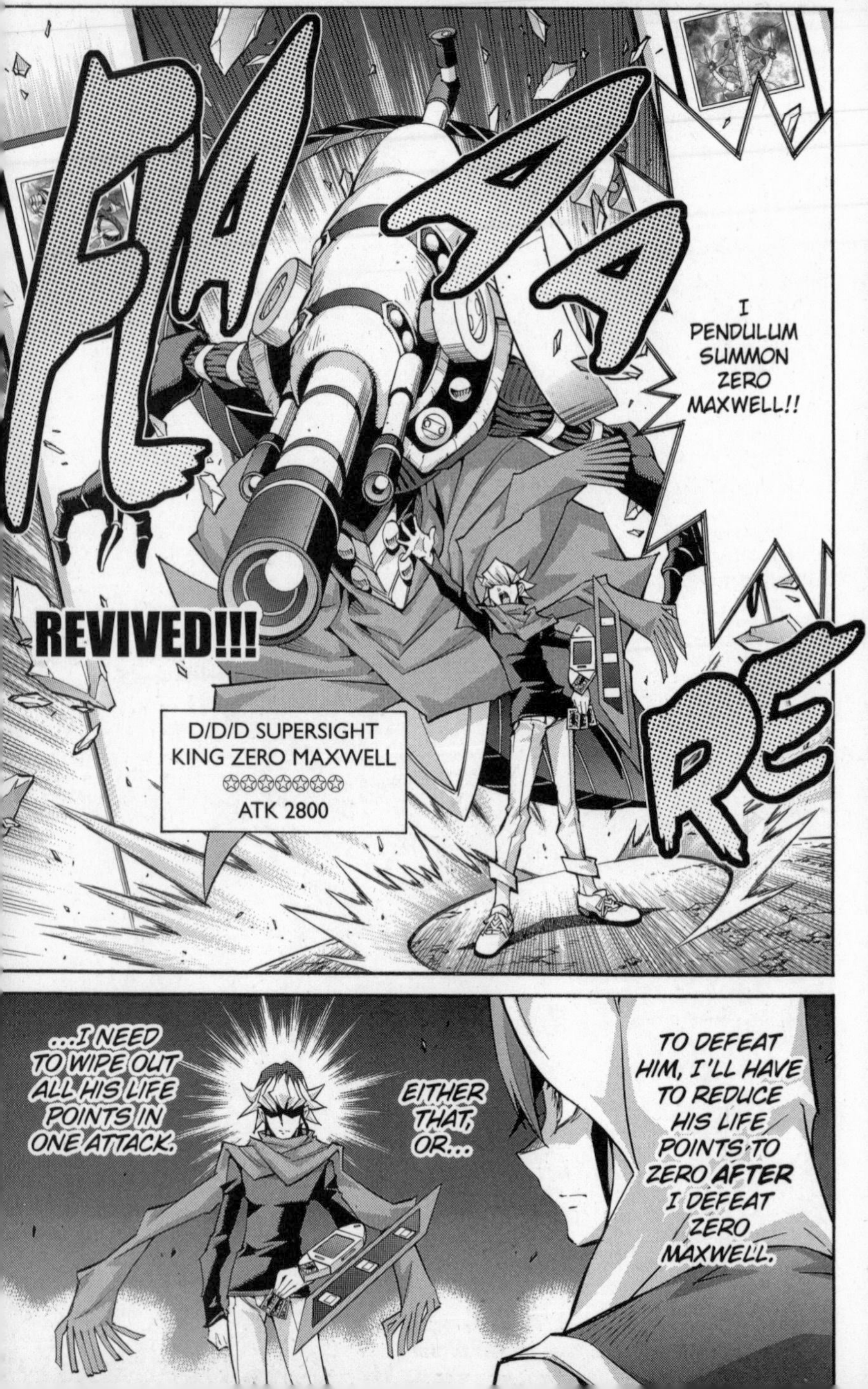
I PENDULUM SUMMON ZERO MAXWELL!!
D/D/D SUPERSIGHT KING ZERO MAXWELL
✪✪✪✪✪✪✪
ATK 2800
REVIVED!!!
TO DEFEAT HIM, I'LL HAVE TO REDUCE HIS LIFE POINTS TO ZERO **AFTER** I DEFEAT ZERO MAXWELL.
EITHER THAT, OR...
...I NEED TO WIPE OUT ALL HIS LIFE POINTS IN ONE ATTACK.

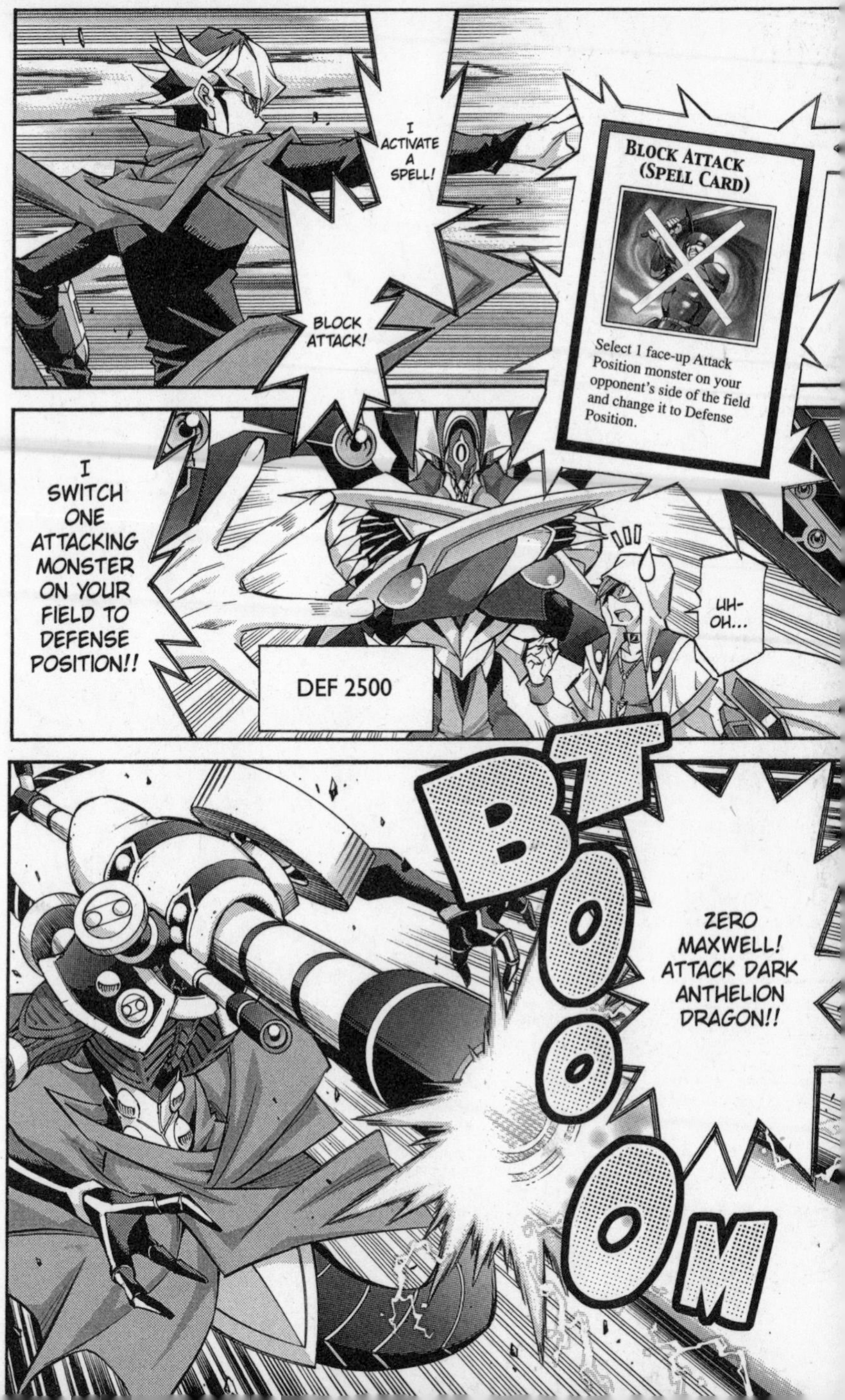
I ACTIVATE A SPELL!
BLOCK ATTACK!
BLOCK ATTACK (SPELL CARD)
Select 1 face-up Attack Position monster on your opponent's side of the field and change it to Defense Position.
UH-OH...
I SWITCH ONE ATTACKING MONSTER ON YOUR FIELD TO DEFENSE POSITION!!
DEF 2500
ZERO MAXWELL! ATTACK DARK ANTHELION DRAGON!!
BOOOOOM

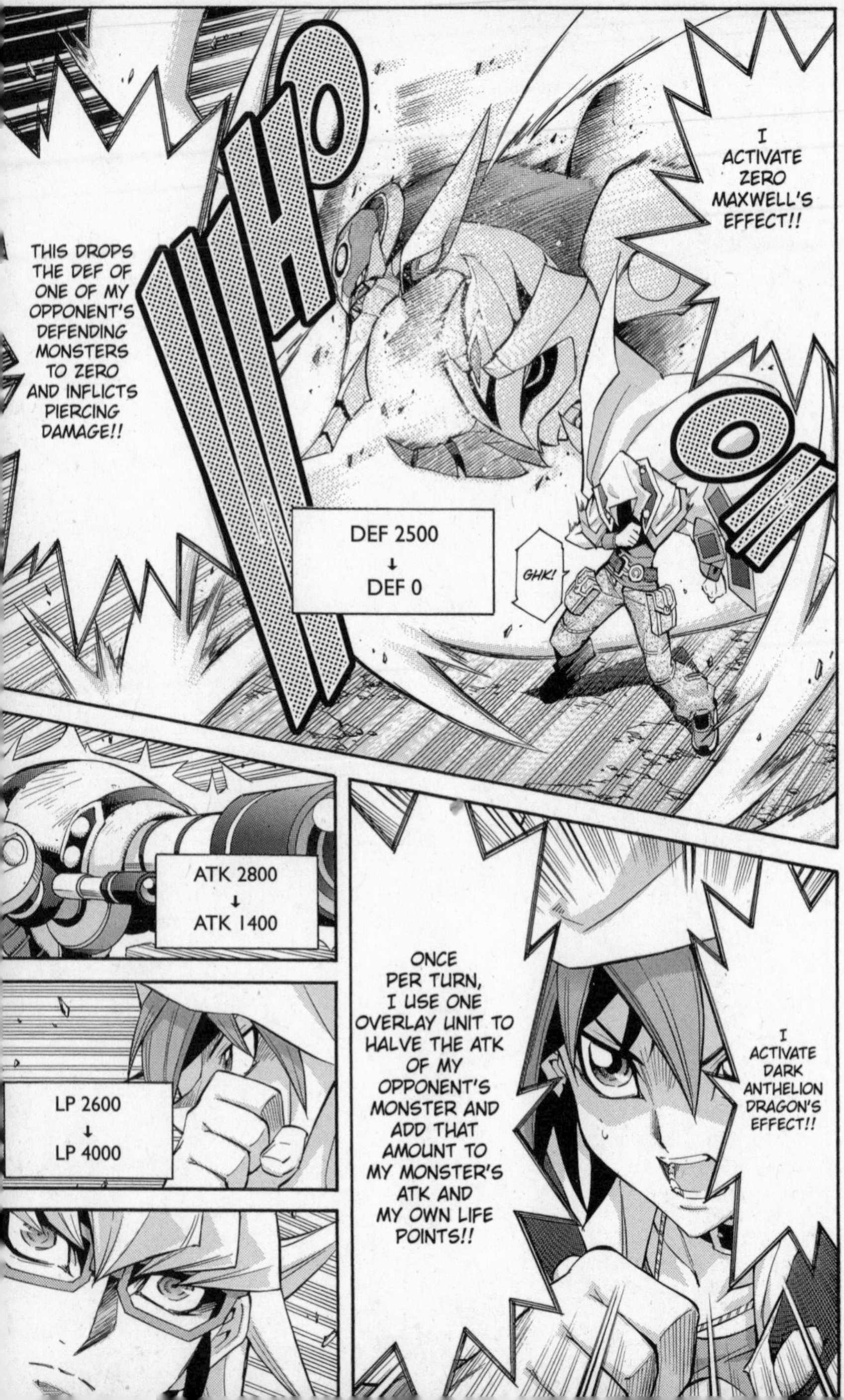
I ACTIVATE ZERO MAXWELL'S EFFECT!!
THIS DROPS THE DEF OF ONE OF MY OPPONENT'S DEFENDING MONSTERS TO ZERO AND INFLICTS PIERCING DAMAGE!!
DEF 2500 ↓ DEF 0
GHK!
I ACTIVATE DARK ANTHELION DRAGON'S EFFECT!!
ONCE PER TURN, I USE ONE OVERLAY UNIT TO HALVE THE ATK OF MY OPPONENT'S MONSTER AND ADD THAT AMOUNT TO MY MONSTER'S ATK AND MY OWN LIFE POINTS!!
ATK 2800 ↓ ATK 1400
LP 2600 ↓ LP 4000

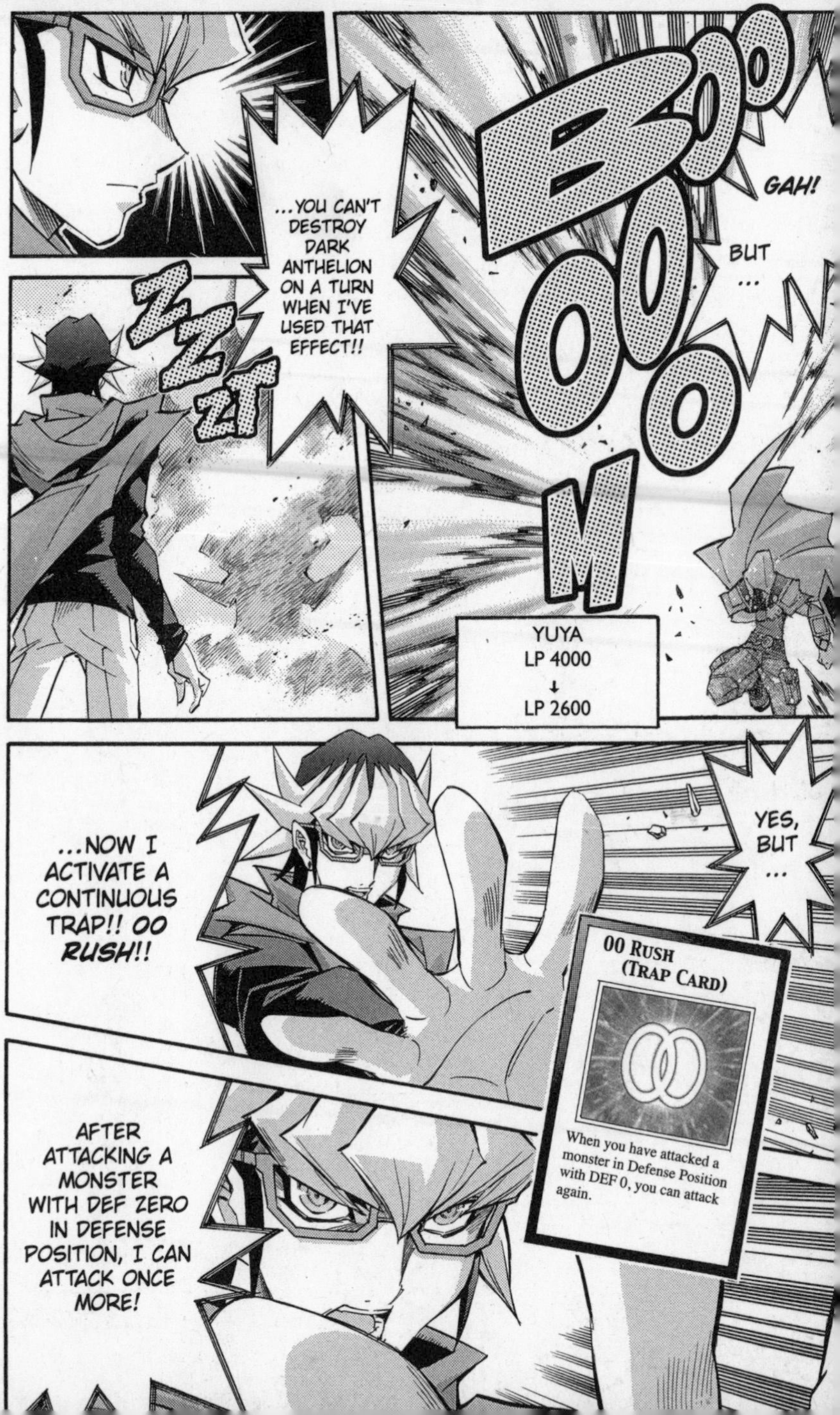
GAH!
BOOOOOOM
BUT ...
YUYA
LP 4000
↓
LP 2600
...YOU CAN'T DESTROY DARK ANTHELION ON A TURN WHEN I'VE USED THAT EFFECT!!
ZZZT
YES, BUT ...
...NOW I ACTIVATE A CONTINUOUS TRAP!! 00 RUSH!!
00 RUSH
(TRAP CARD)
When you have attacked a monster in Defense Position with DEF 0, you can attack again.
AFTER ATTACKING A MONSTER WITH DEF ZERO IN DEFENSE POSITION, I CAN ATTACK ONCE MORE!

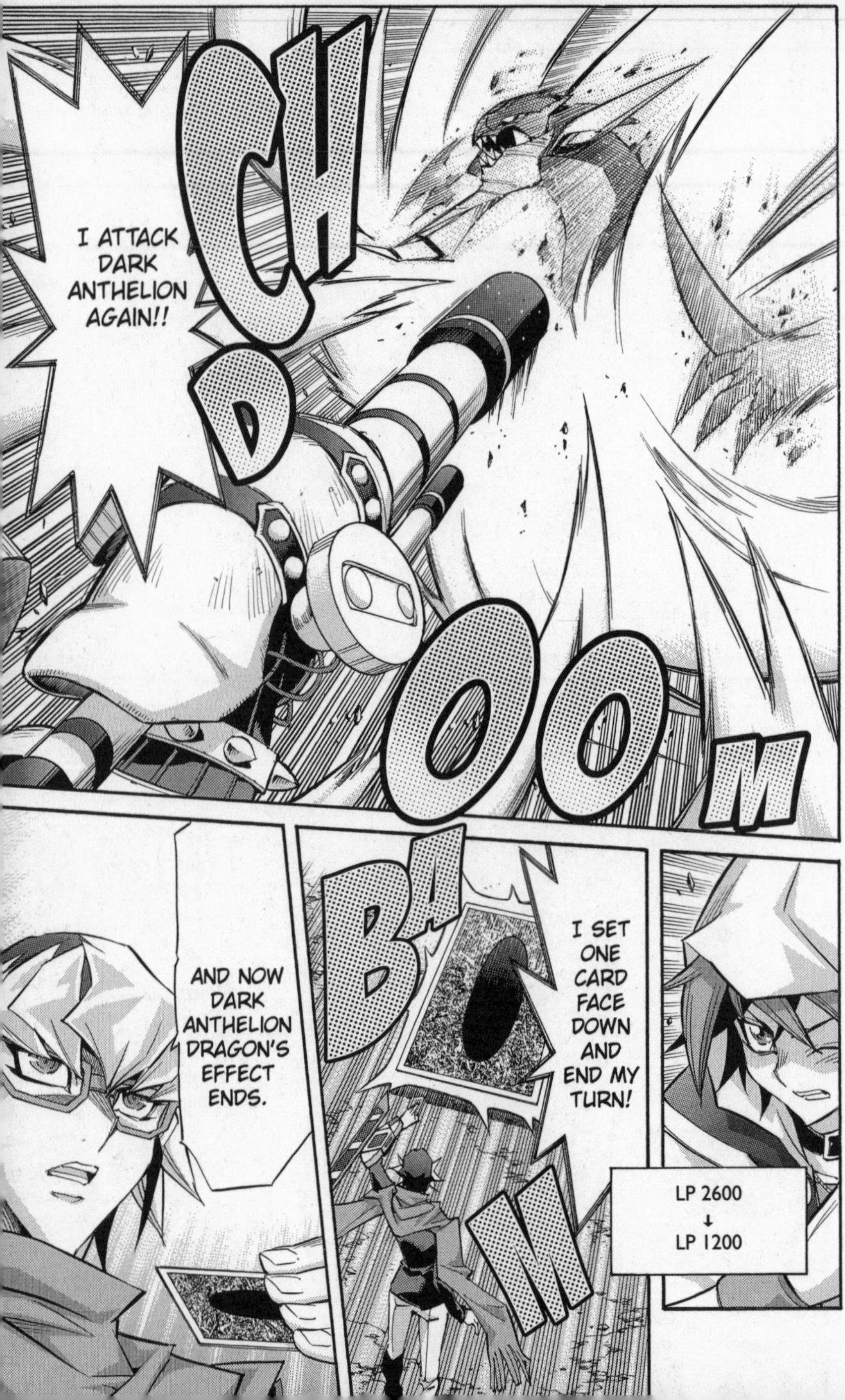
CHDOOM
I ATTACK DARK ANTHELION AGAIN!!
LP 2600 ↓ LP 1200
I SET ONE CARD FACE DOWN AND END MY TURN!
BAM
AND NOW DARK ANTHELION DRAGON'S EFFECT ENDS.

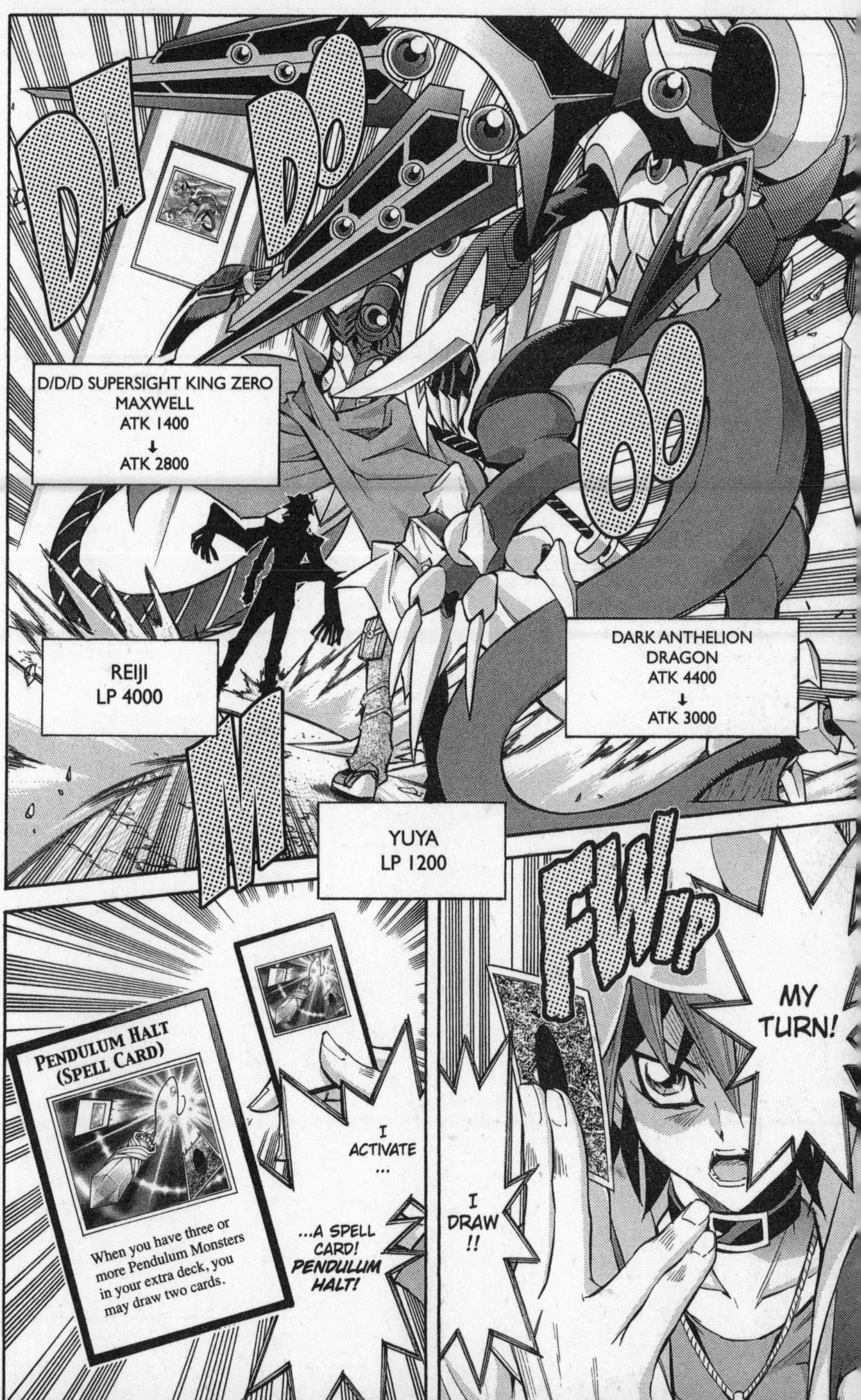

D/D/D SUPERSIGHT KING ZERO MAXWELL ATK 1400 ↓ ATK 2800
DARK ANTHELION DRAGON ATK 4400 ↓ ATK 3000
REIJI LP 4000
YUYA LP 1200
FWIP
MY TURN!
I DRAW!!
I ACTIVATE...
...A SPELL CARD! PENDULUM HALT!
PENDULUM HALT (SPELL CARD)
When you have three or more Pendulum Monsters in your extra deck, you may draw two cards.

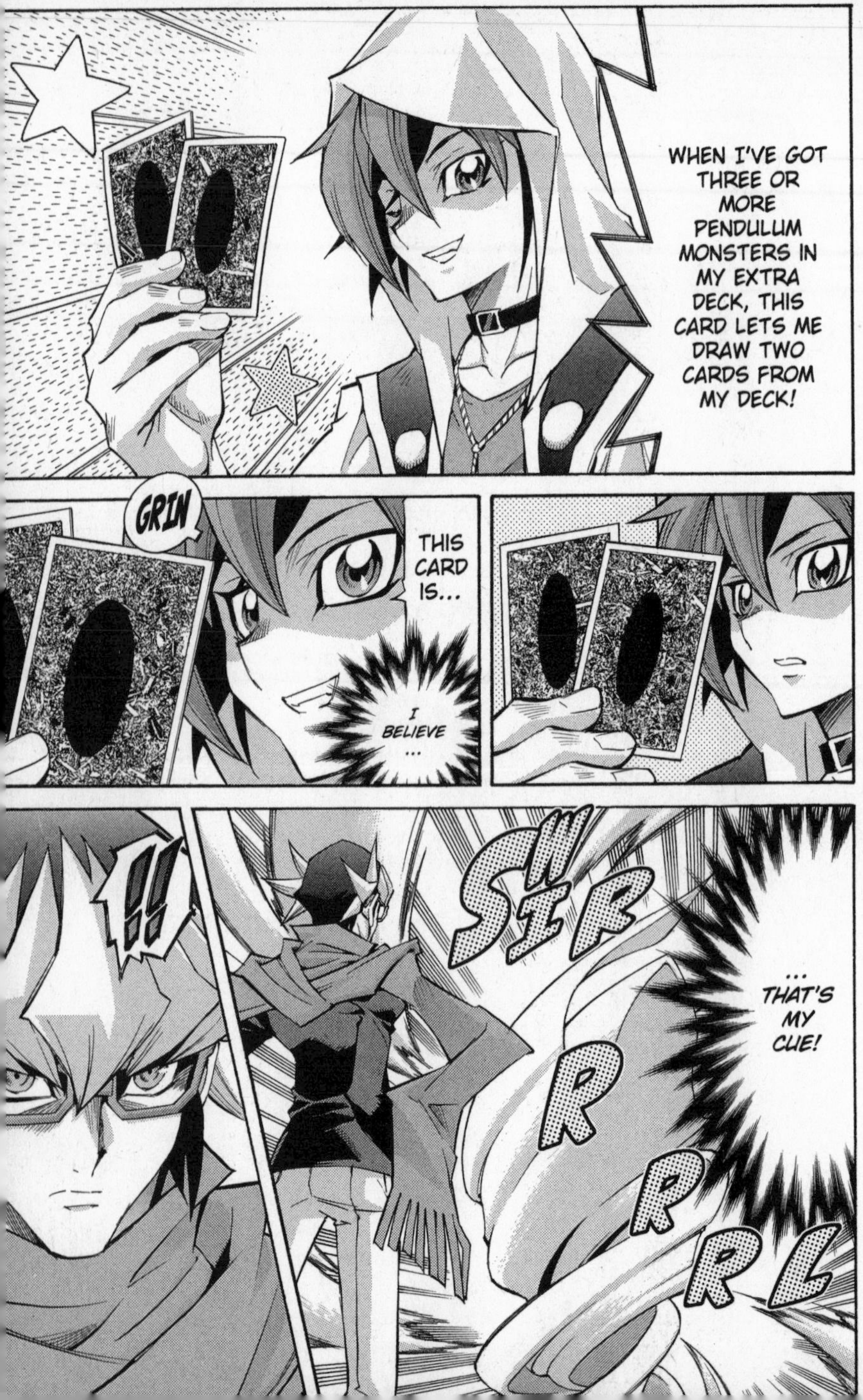
WHEN I'VE GOT THREE OR MORE PENDULUM MONSTERS IN MY EXTRA DECK, THIS CARD LETS ME DRAW TWO CARDS FROM MY DECK!
GRIN
THIS CARD IS...
I BELIEVE ...
SHRRRRL
... THAT'S MY CUE!
!!

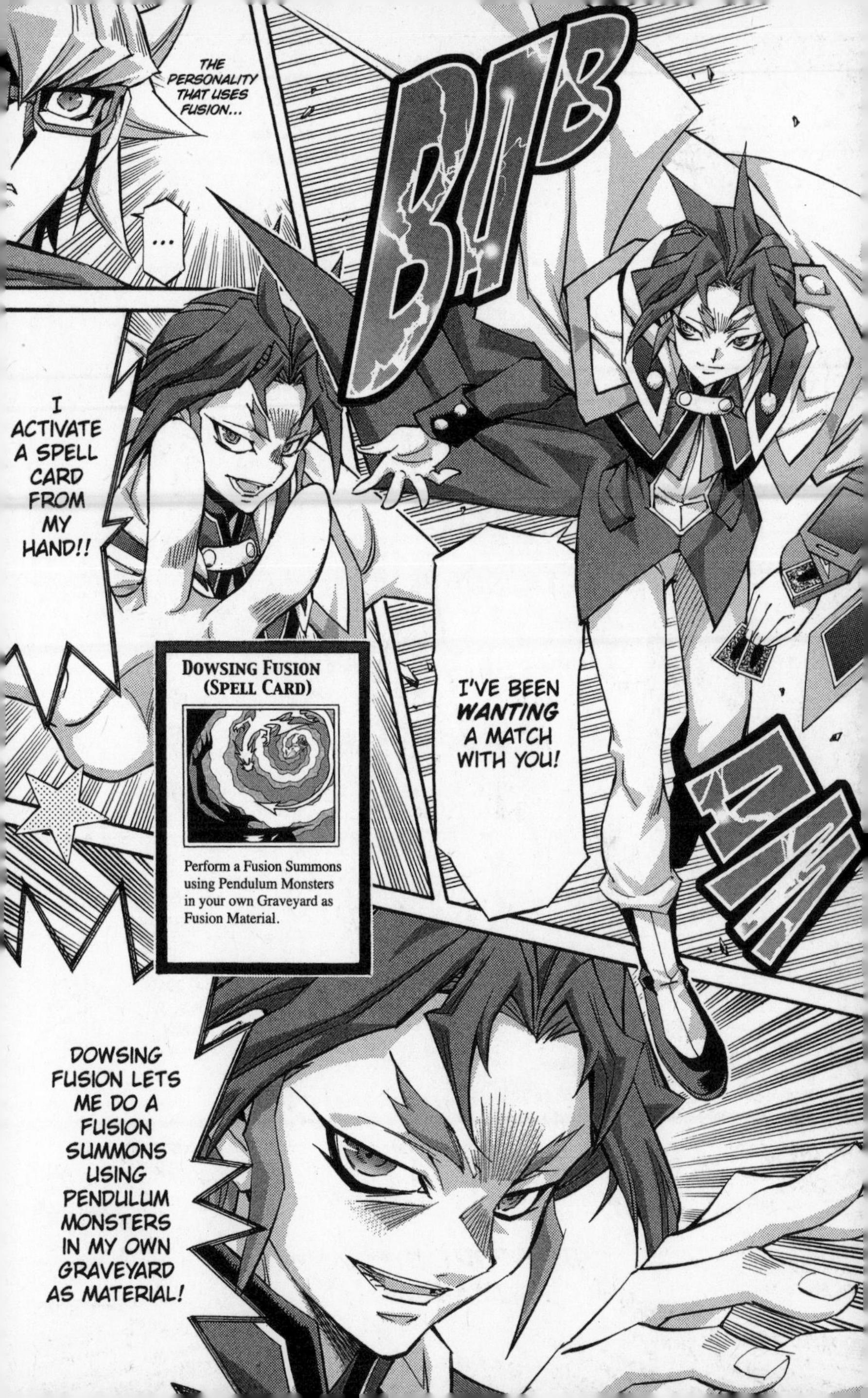
I'VE BEEN WANTING A MATCH WITH YOU!
THE PERSONALITY THAT USES FUSION...
...
I ACTIVATE A SPELL CARD FROM MY HAND!!
DOWSING FUSION (SPELL CARD)
Perform a Fusion Summons using Pendulum Monsters in your own Graveyard as Fusion Material.
DOWSING FUSION LETS ME DO A FUSION SUMMONS USING PENDULUM MONSTERS IN MY OWN GRAVEYARD AS MATERIAL!

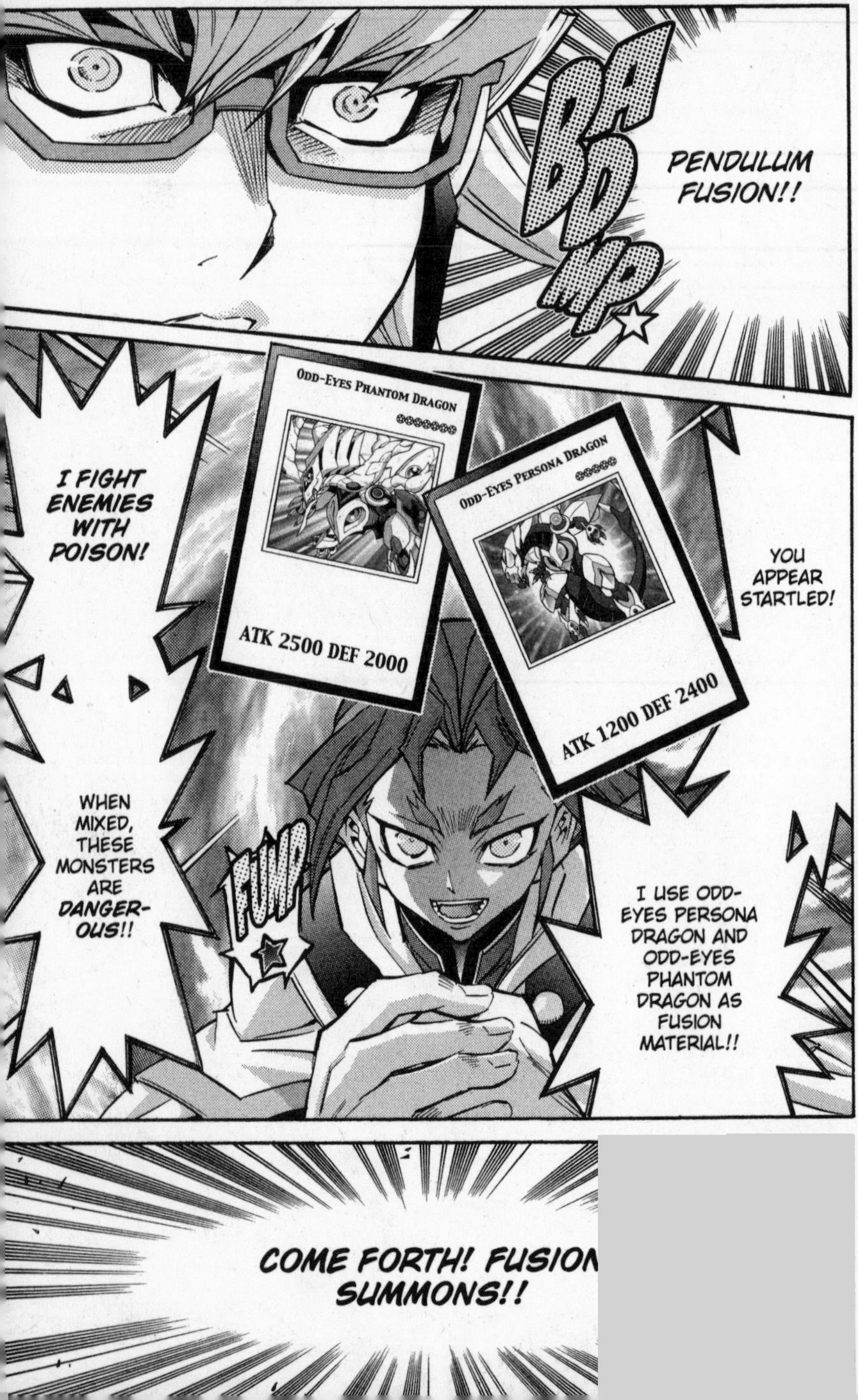
BA-DUMP
PENDULUM FUSION!!
YOU APPEAR STARTLED!
ODD-EYES PHANTOM DRAGON
ATK 2500 DEF 2000
ODD-EYES PERSONA DRAGON
ATK 1200 DEF 2400
I FIGHT ENEMIES WITH POISON!
WHEN MIXED, THESE MONSTERS ARE DANGER-OUS!!
FUMP
I USE ODD-EYES PERSONA DRAGON AND ODD-EYES PHANTOM DRAGON AS FUSION MATERIAL!!
COME FORTH! FUSION SUMMONS!!

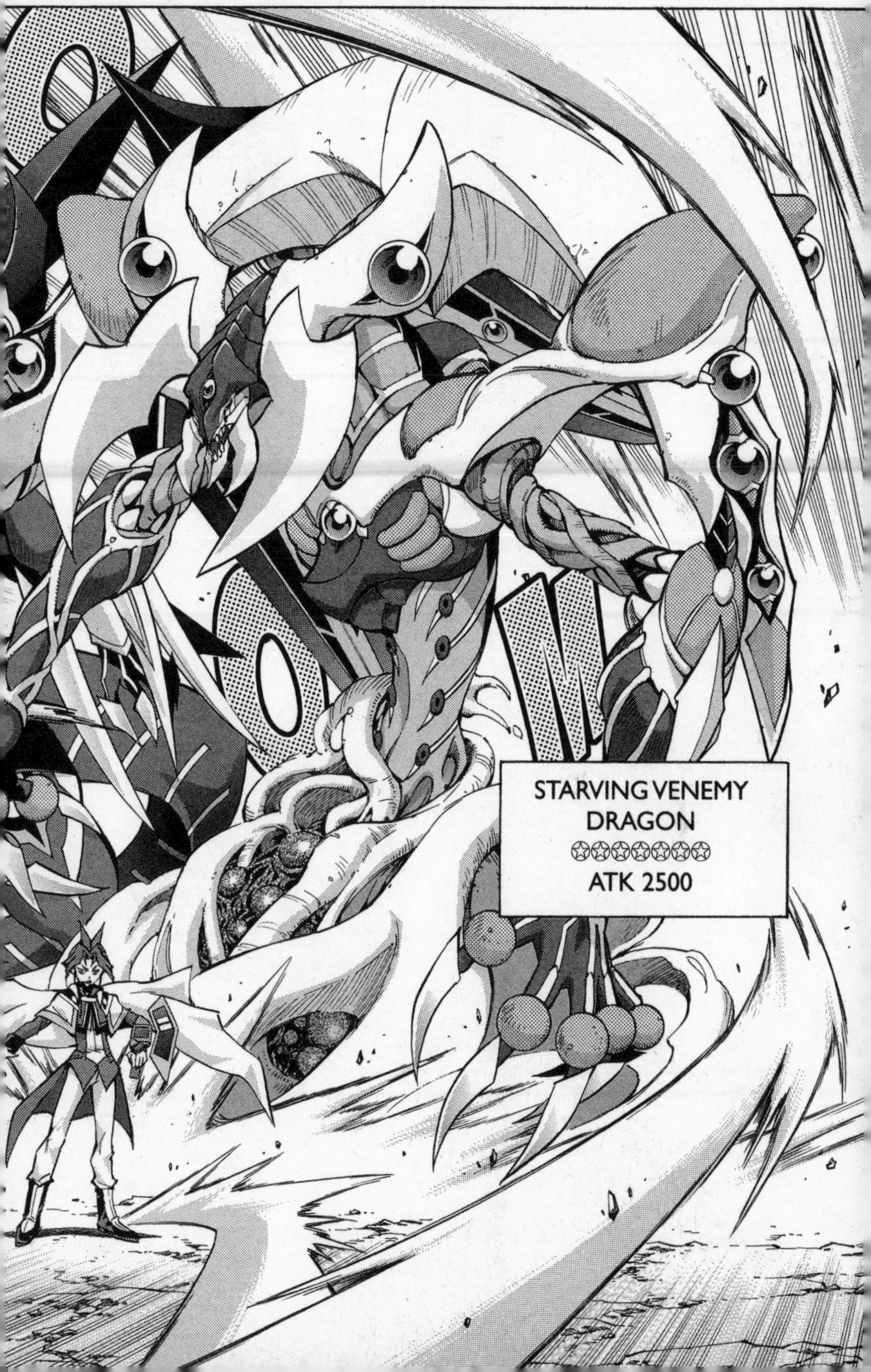
STARVING VENEMY DRAGON
ATK 2500

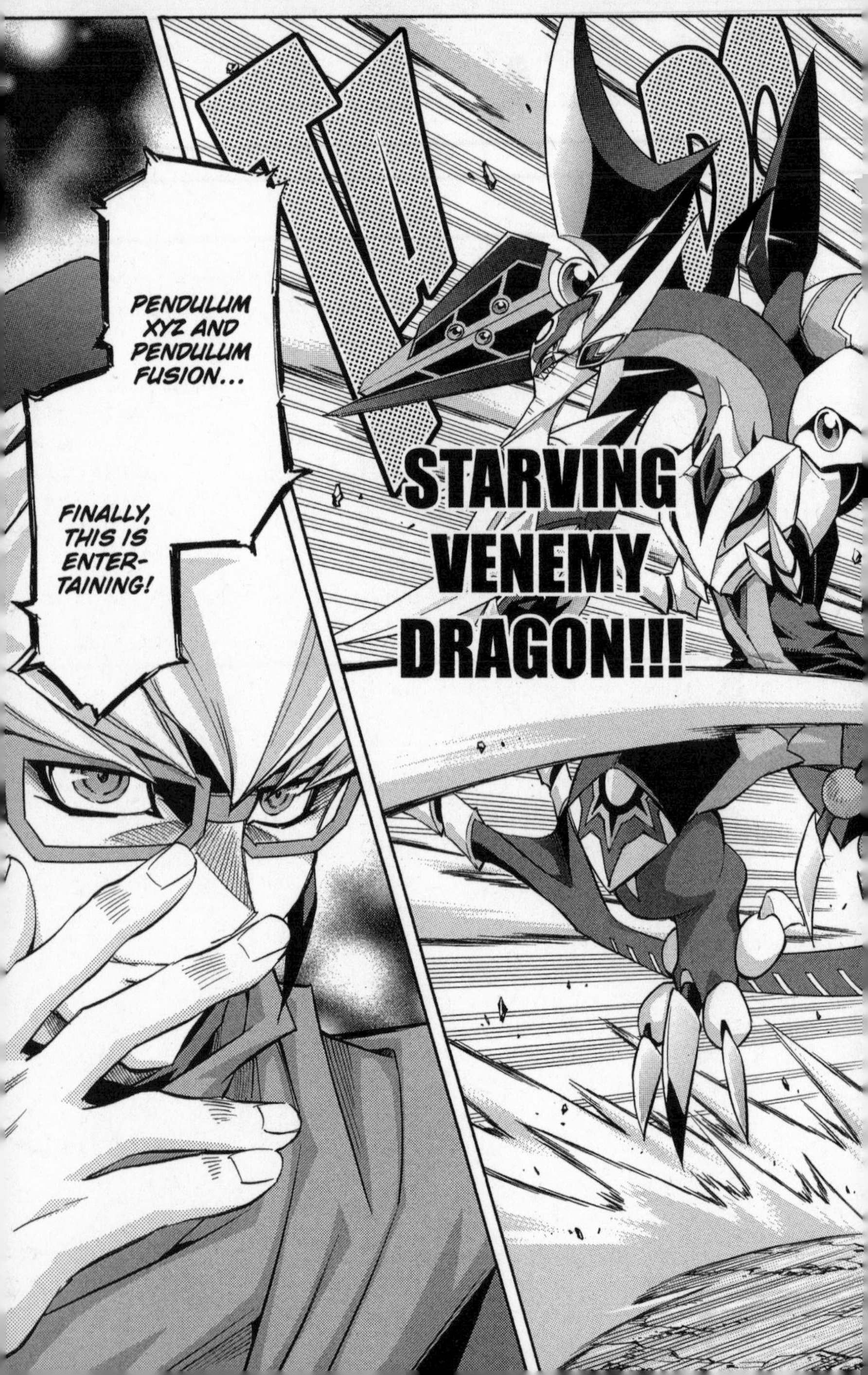
STARVING VENEMY DRAGON!!!
PENDULUM XYZ AND PENDULUM FUSION...
FINALLY, THIS IS ENTER-TAINING!

PRESENTING MIYOSHI SENSEI'S EARLY DESIGNS!

ARC-V CHARACTER SKETCHES

TATSUYA

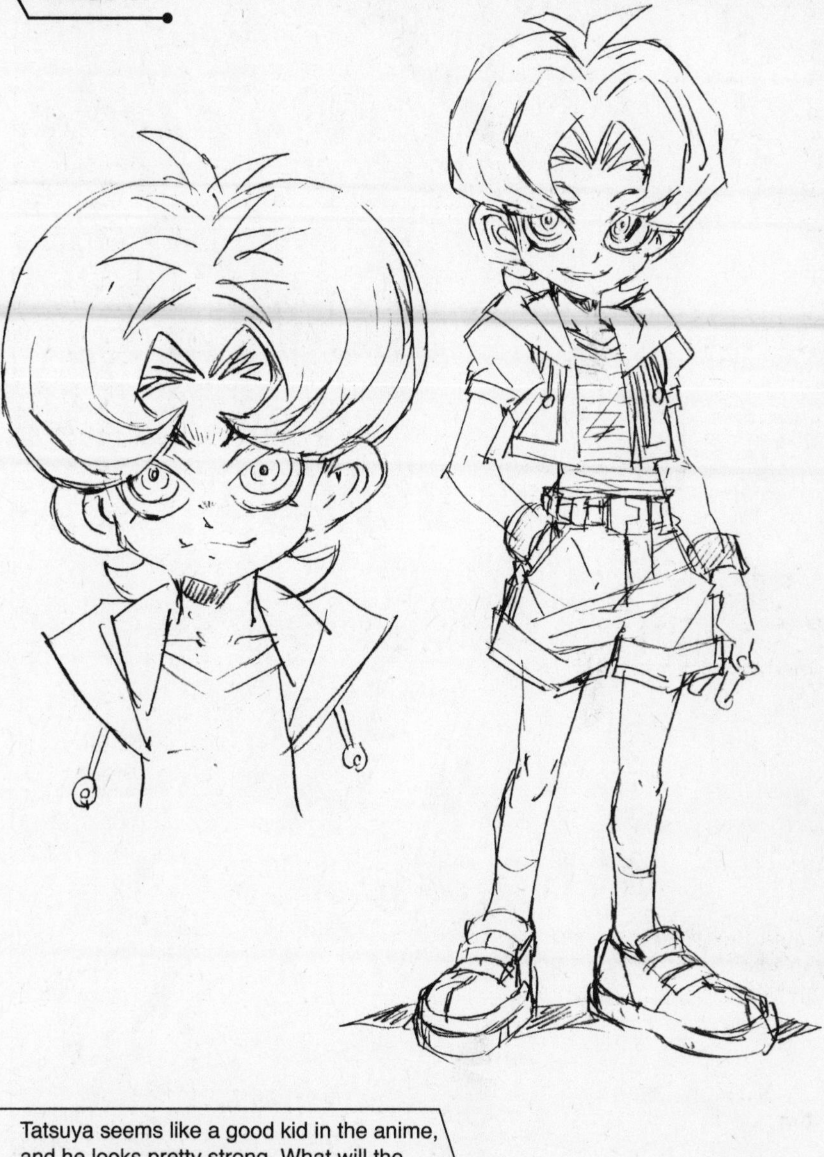

Tatsuya seems like a good kid in the anime, and he looks pretty strong. What will the three of them talk about?

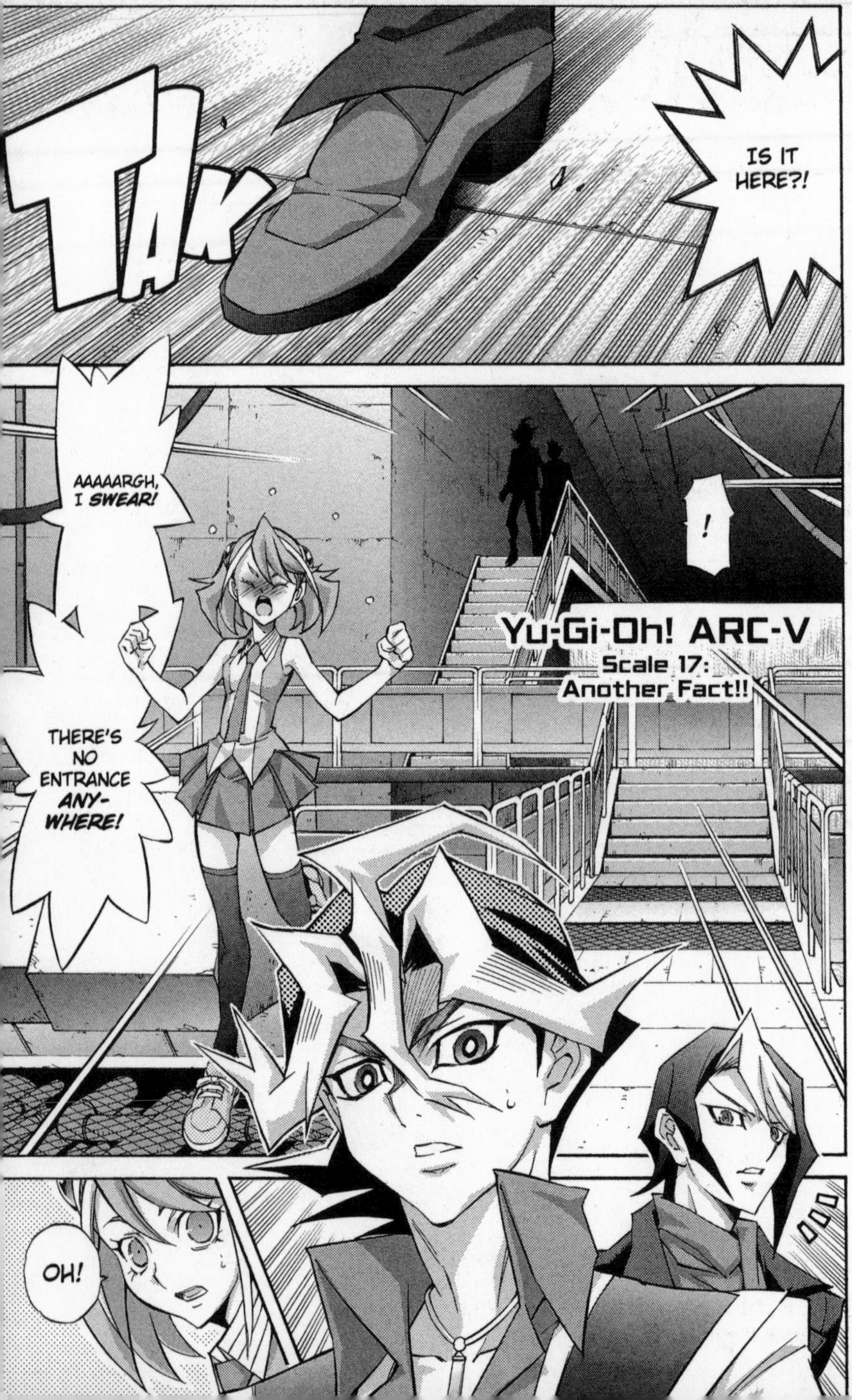
IS IT HERE?!
TAK
!
Yu-Gi-Oh! ARC-V
Scale 17: Another Fact!!
AAAAARGH, I SWEAR!
THERE'S NO ENTRANCE ANYWHERE!
OH!

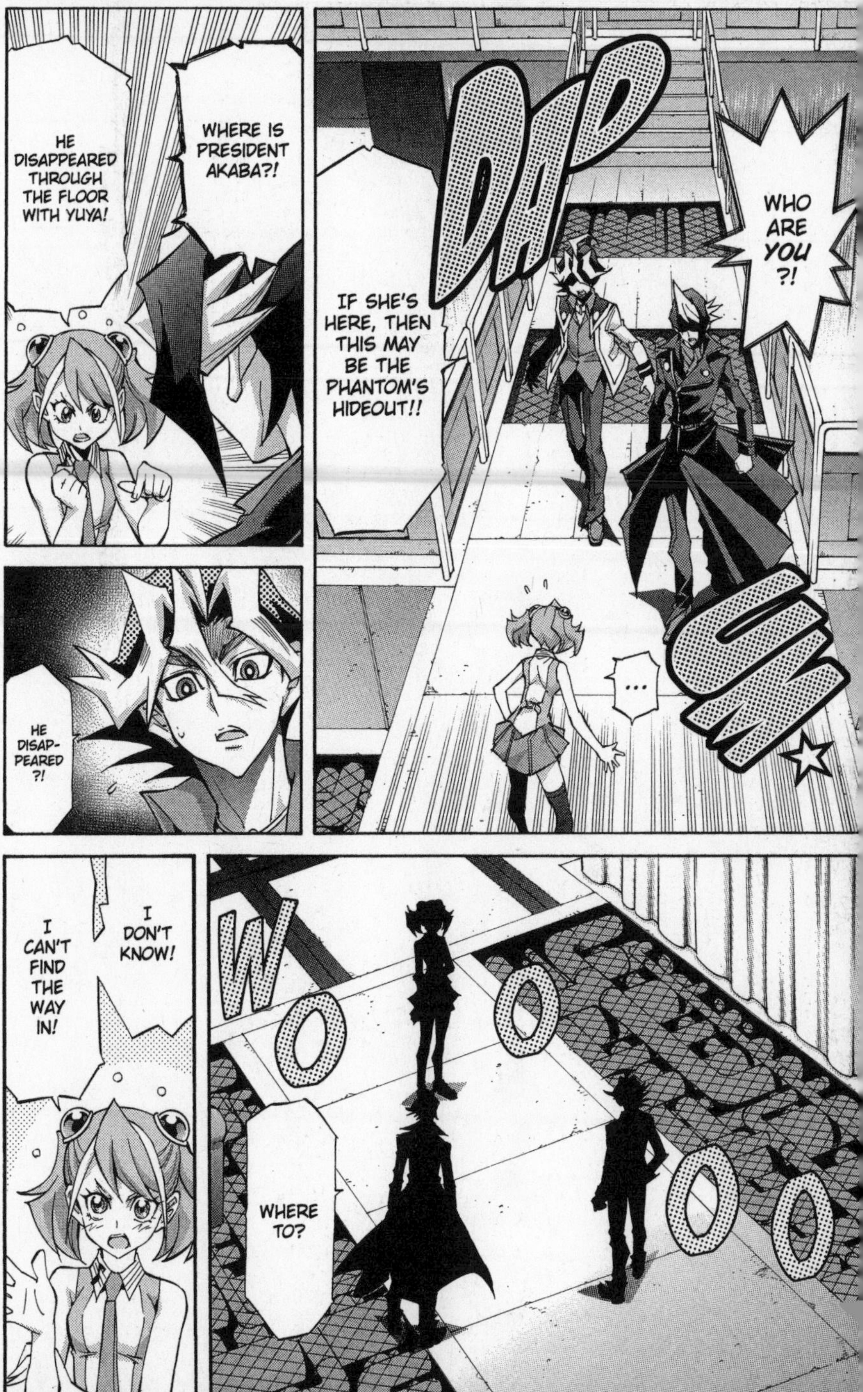
WHO ARE YOU?!
DAP
IF SHE'S HERE, THEN THIS MAY BE THE PHANTOM'S HIDEOUT!!
...
WHERE IS PRESIDENT AKABA?!
HE DISAPPEARED THROUGH THE FLOOR WITH YUYA!
HE DISAPPEARED?!
WOOOOO
WHERE TO?
I DON'T KNOW!
I CAN'T FIND THE WAY IN!

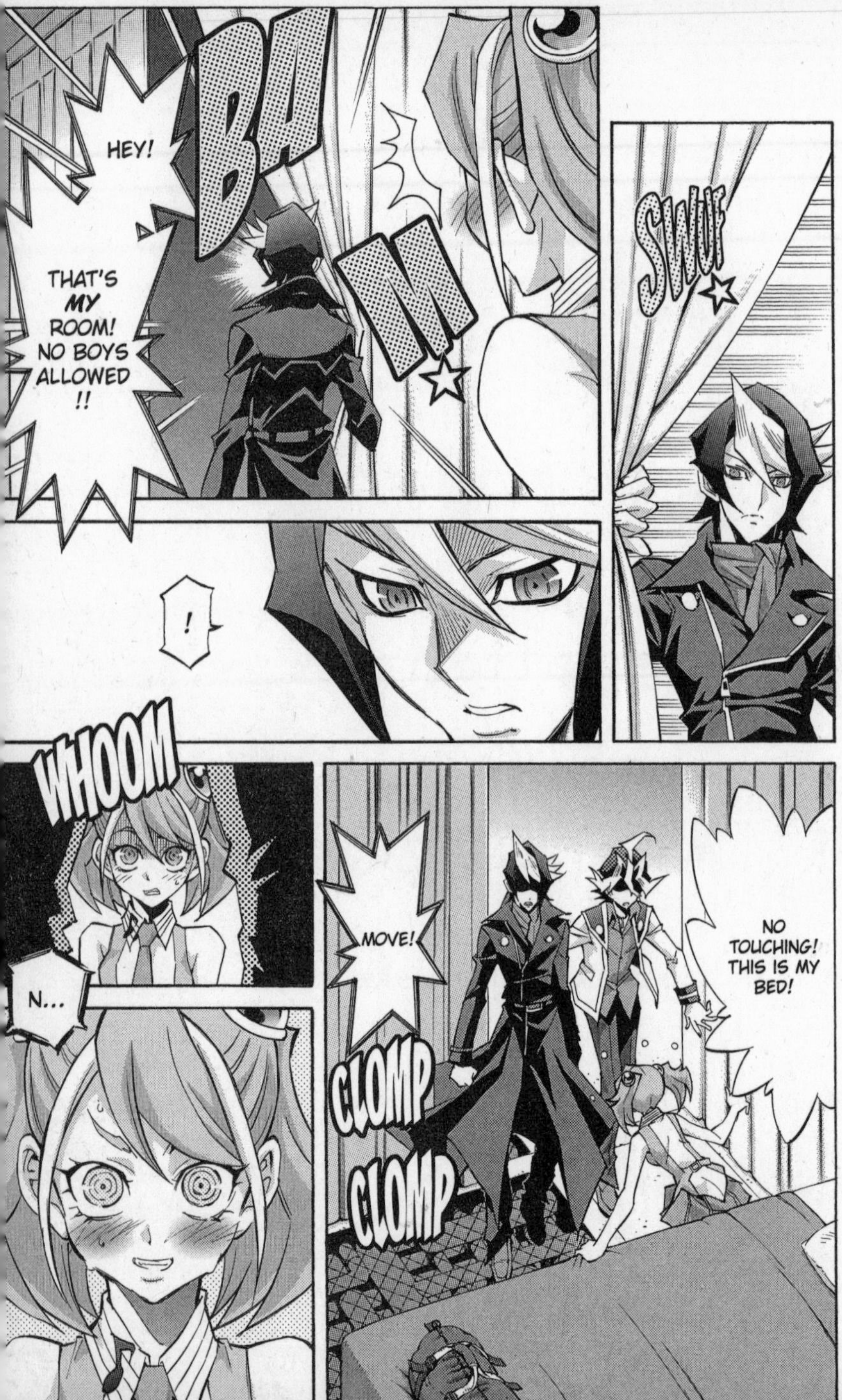
SWUF
BAM
HEY!
THAT'S *MY* ROOM! NO BOYS ALLOWED !!
!
NO TOUCHING! THIS IS MY BED!
MOVE!
CLOMP
CLOMP
WHOOM
N...

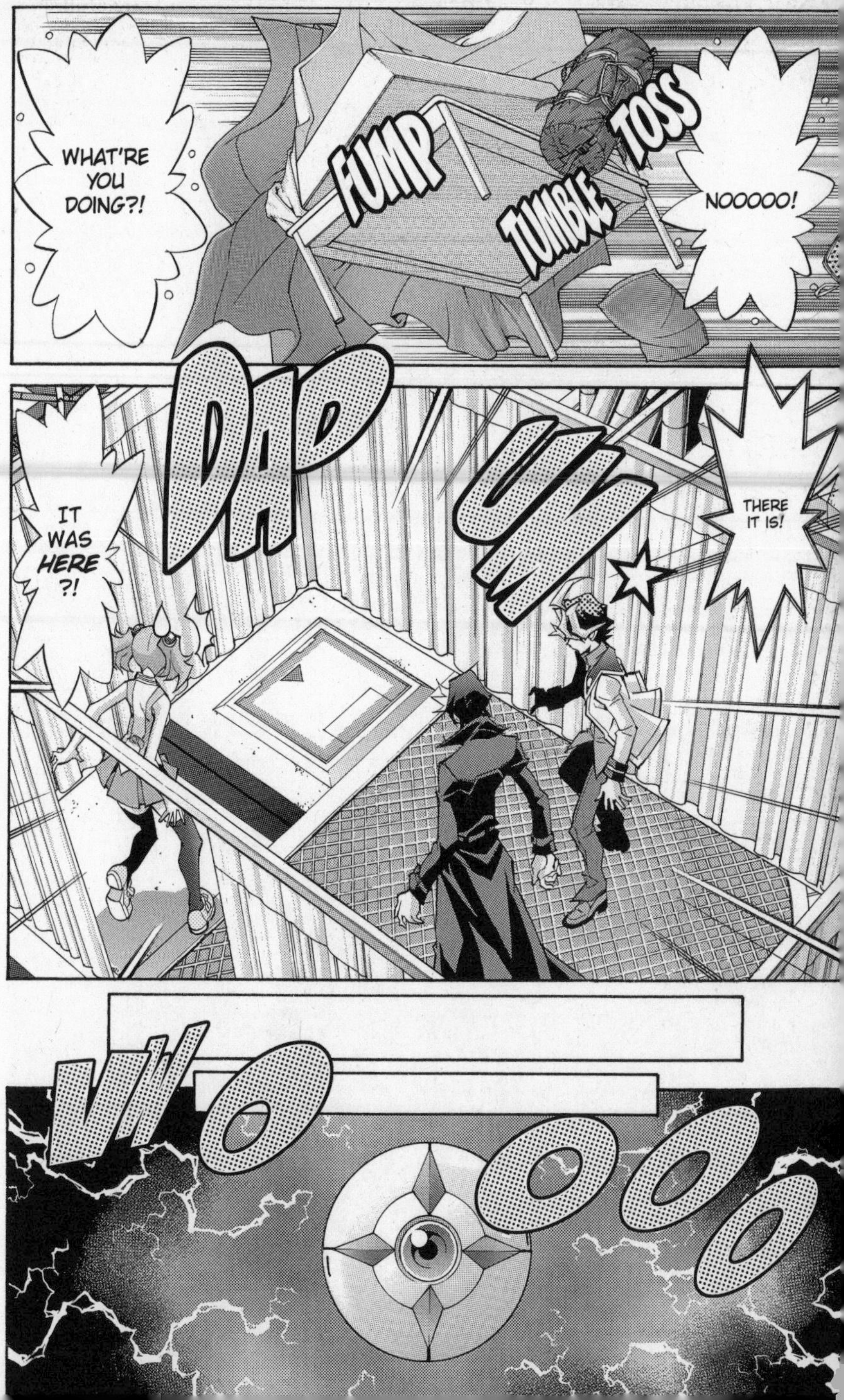

NOOOOO!
TOSS
TUMBLE
FUMP
WHAT'RE YOU DOING?!
THERE IT IS!
UN
DAP
IT WAS *HERE* ?!
VWOOOOO

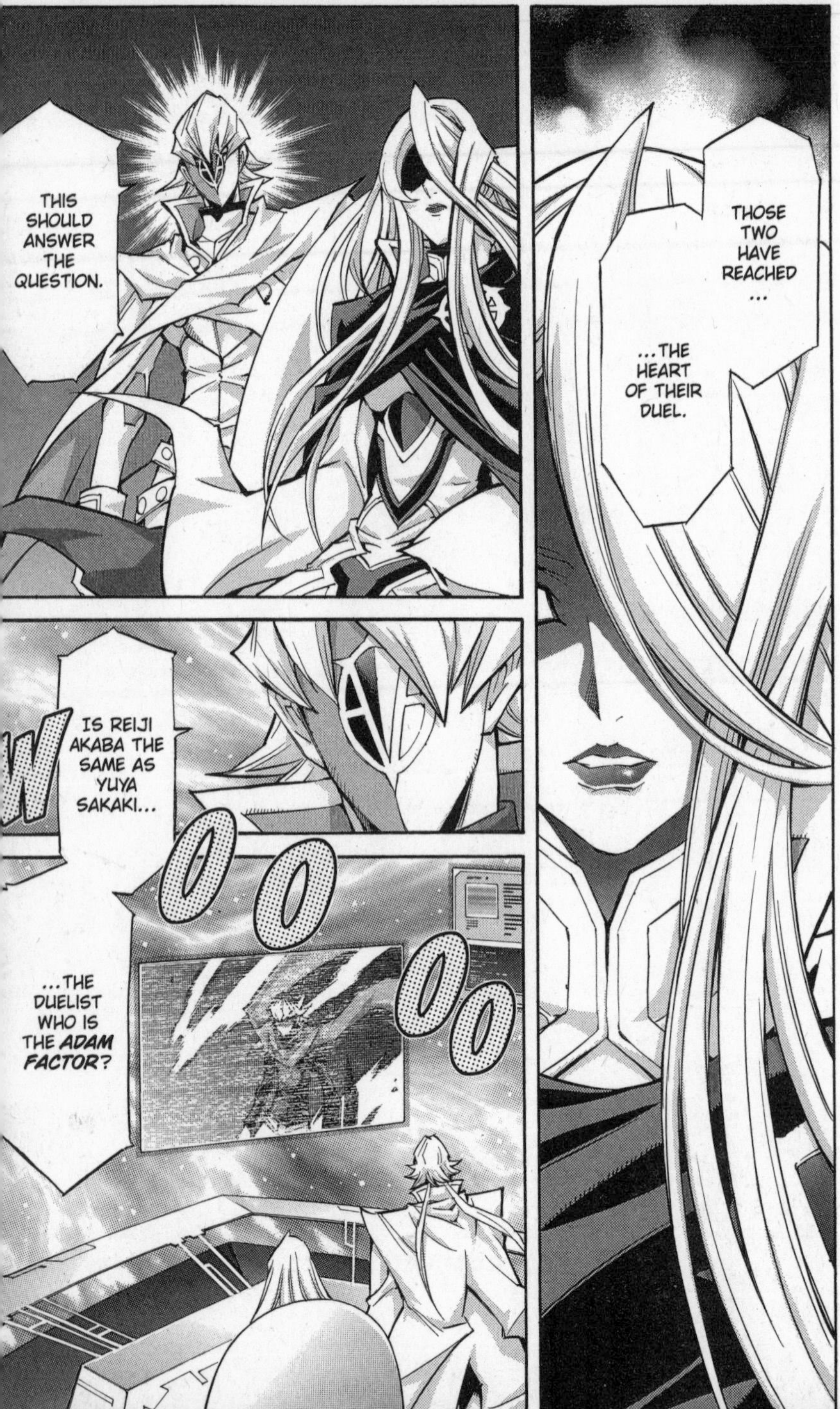
THOSE TWO HAVE REACHED ...
...THE HEART OF THEIR DUEL.
THIS SHOULD ANSWER THE QUESTION.
IS REIJI AKABA THE SAME AS YUYA SAKAKI...
WOOOO
...THE DUELIST WHO IS THE *ADAM FACTOR*?

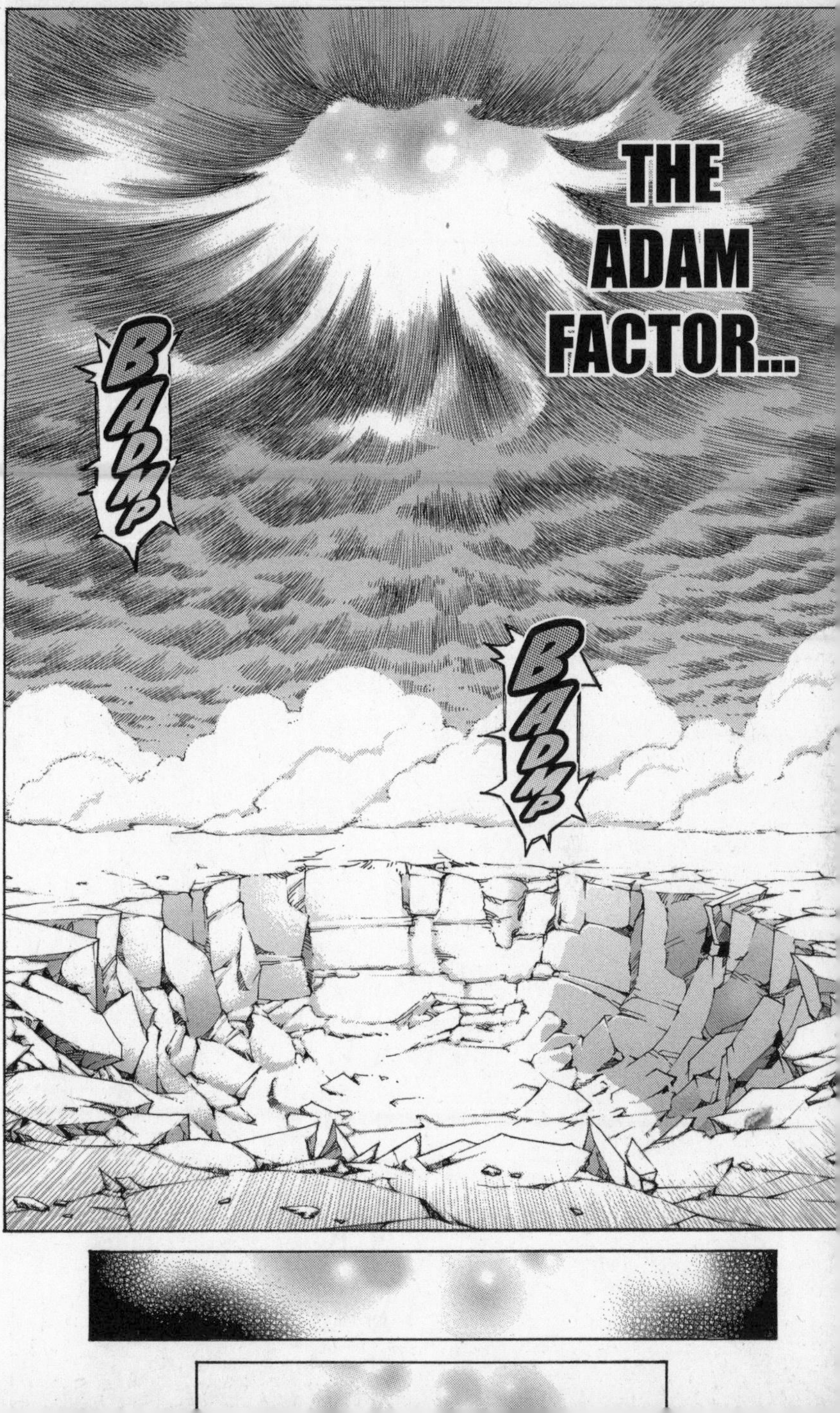
THE ADAM FACTOR...
BADMP
BADMP

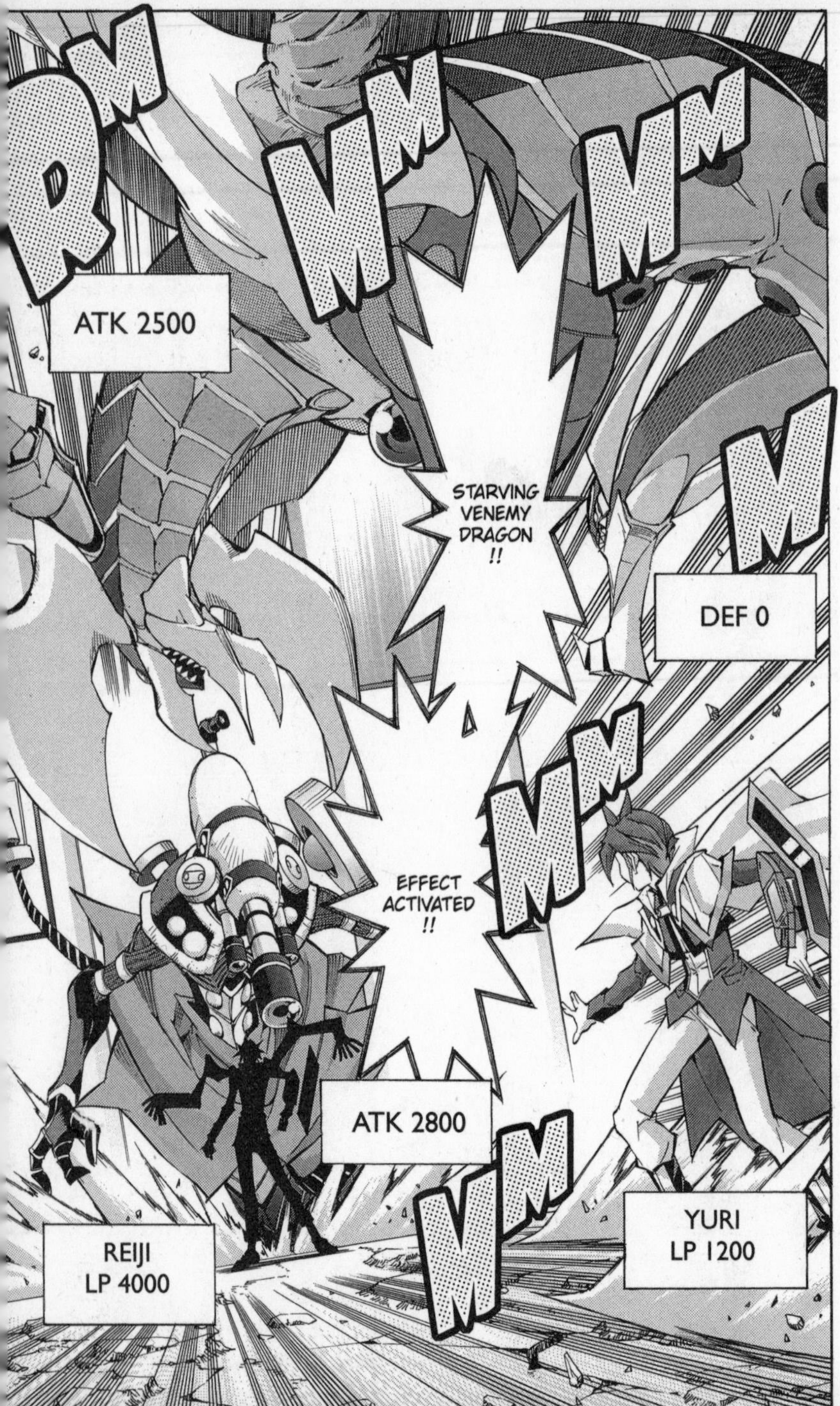
RM
MM
MMM
M
MMM
MMM
STARVING VENEMY DRAGON !!
DEF 0
ATK 2500
EFFECT ACTIVATED !!
ATK 2800
YURI
LP 1200
REIJI
LP 4000

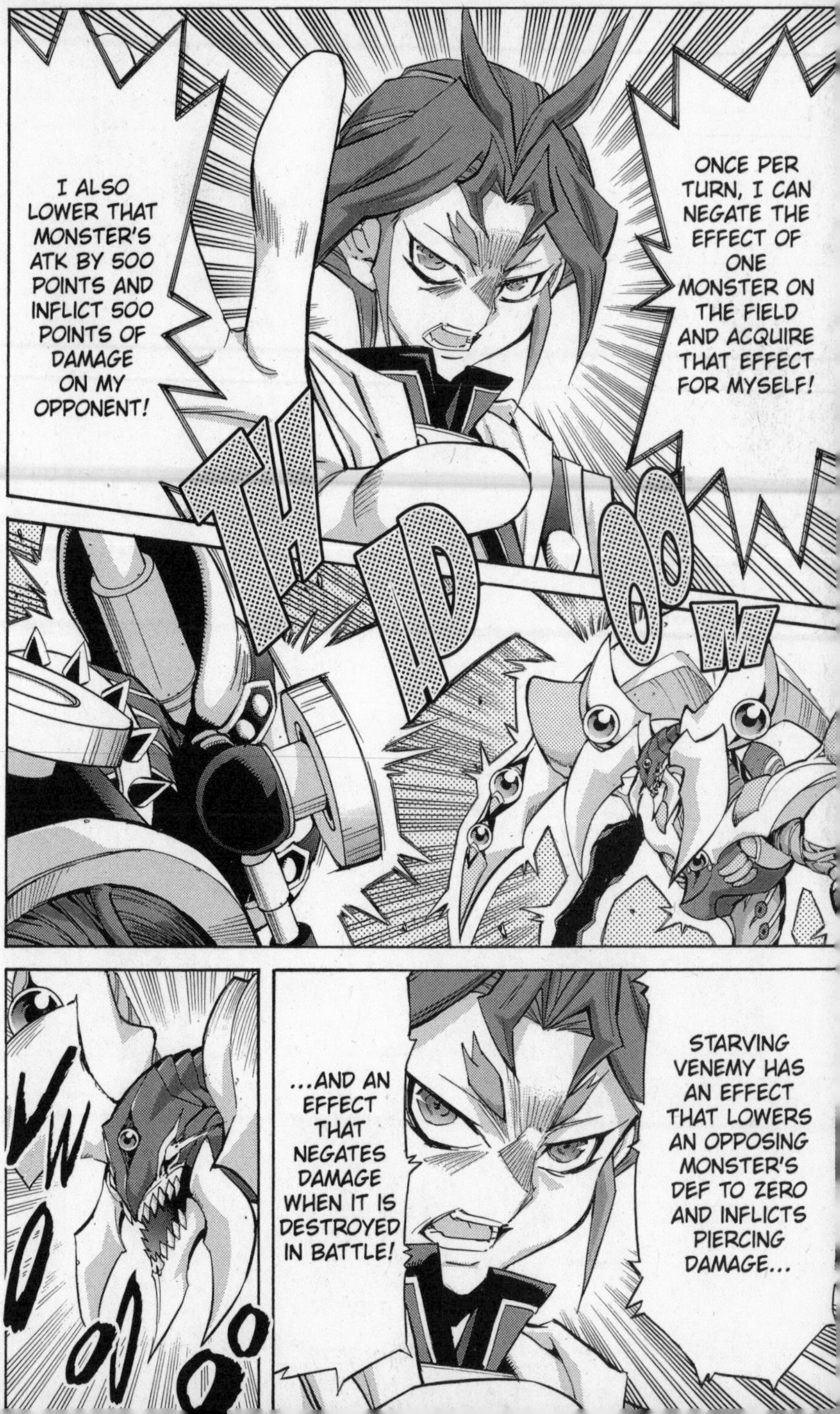
ONCE PER TURN, I CAN NEGATE THE EFFECT OF ONE MONSTER ON THE FIELD AND ACQUIRE THAT EFFECT FOR MYSELF!
I ALSO LOWER THAT MONSTER'S ATK BY 500 POINTS AND INFLICT 500 POINTS OF DAMAGE ON MY OPPONENT!
STARVING VENEMY HAS AN EFFECT THAT LOWERS AN OPPOSING MONSTER'S DEF TO ZERO AND INFLICTS PIERCING DAMAGE...
...AND AN EFFECT THAT NEGATES DAMAGE WHEN IT IS DESTROYED IN BATTLE!

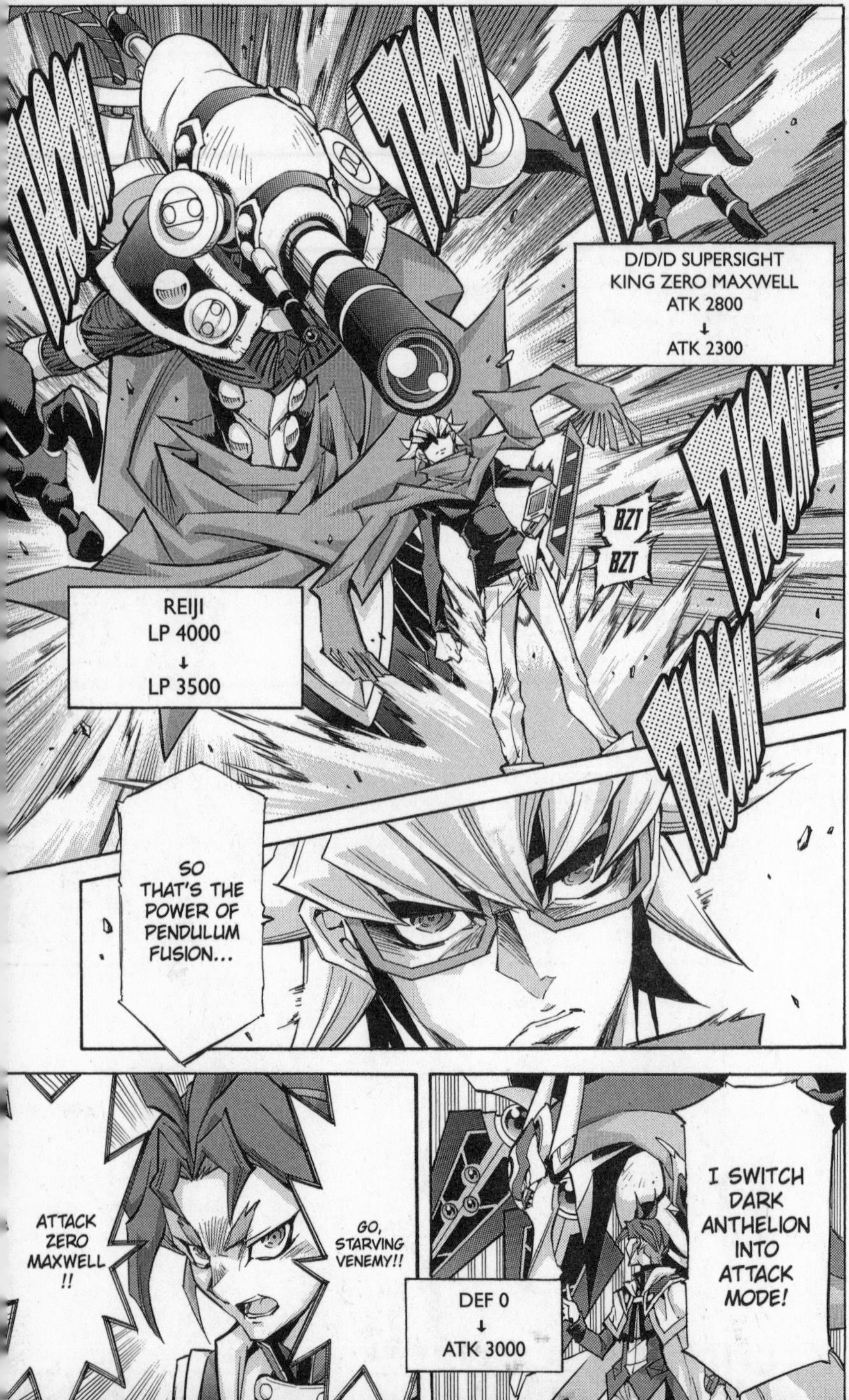
THOOM
THOOM
THOOM
D/D/D SUPERSIGHT KING ZERO MAXWELL ATK 2800 ↓ ATK 2300
THOOM
BZT BZT
THOOM
REIJI LP 4000 ↓ LP 3500
SO THAT'S THE POWER OF PENDULUM FUSION...
I SWITCH DARK ANTHELION INTO ATTACK MODE!
DEF 0 ↓ ATK 3000
GO, STARVING VENEMY!!
ATTACK ZERO MAXWELL!!

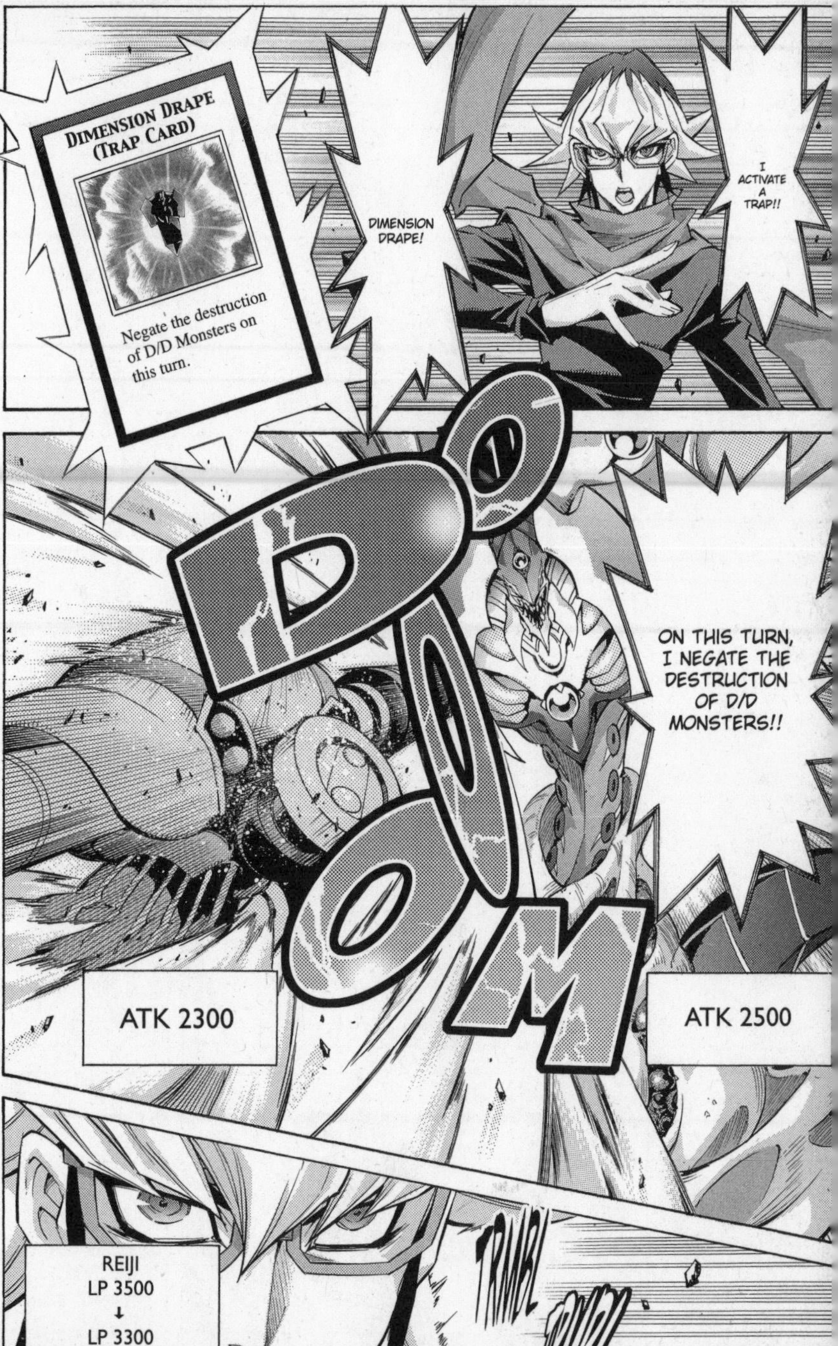
I ACTIVATE A TRAP!!
DIMENSION DRAPE!
DIMENSION DRAPE (TRAP CARD)
Negate the destruction of D/D Monsters on this turn.
DOOOM
ON THIS TURN, I NEGATE THE DESTRUCTION OF D/D MONSTERS!!
ATK 2500
ATK 2300
REIJI
LP 3500
↓
LP 3300

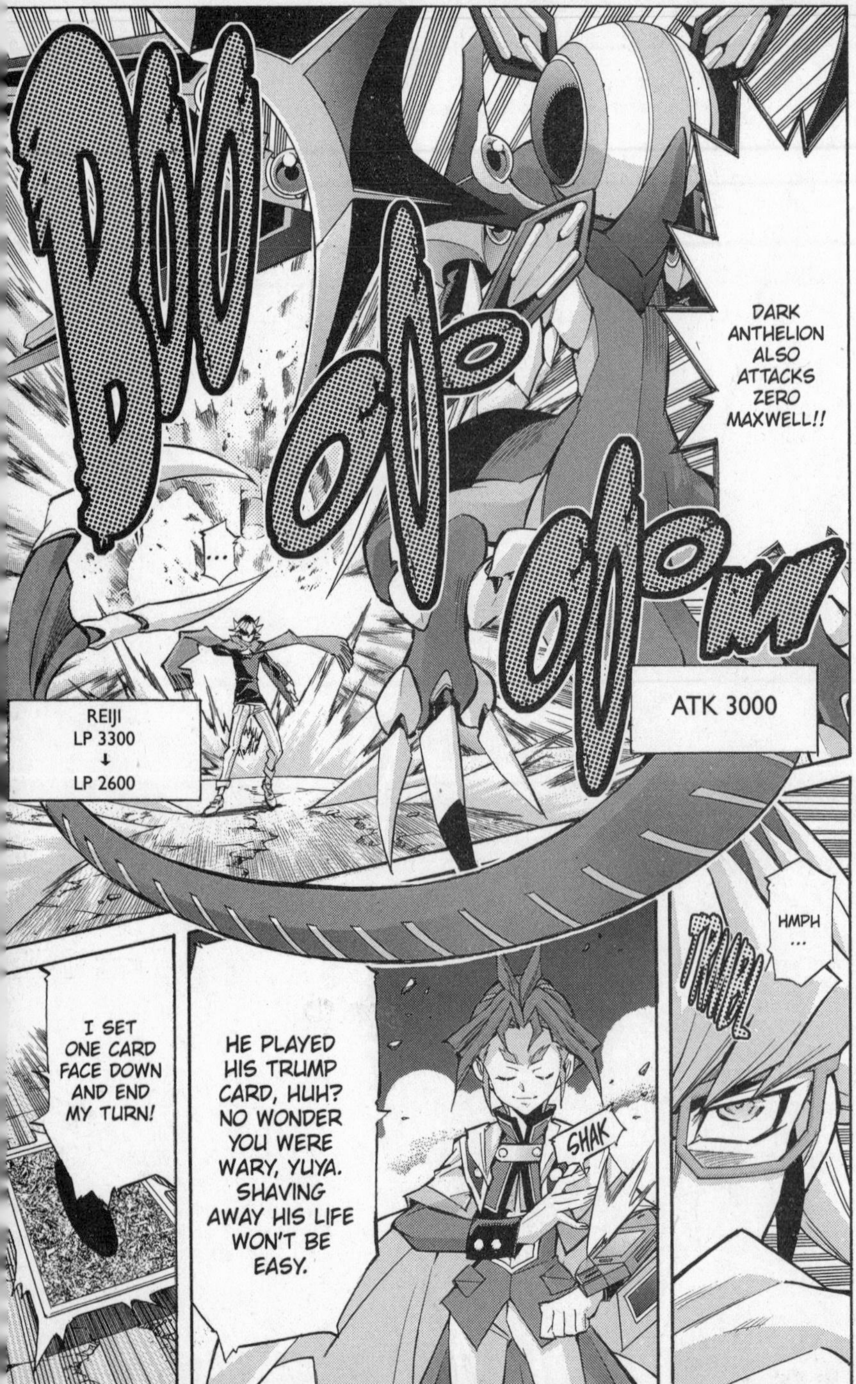
DARK ANTHELION ALSO ATTACKS ZERO MAXWELL!!
ATK 3000
...
REIJI LP 3300 ↓ LP 2600
HMPH ...
SHAK
HE PLAYED HIS TRUMP CARD, HUH? NO WONDER YOU WERE WARY, YUYA. SHAVING AWAY HIS LIFE WON'T BE EASY.
I SET ONE CARD FACE DOWN AND END MY TURN!

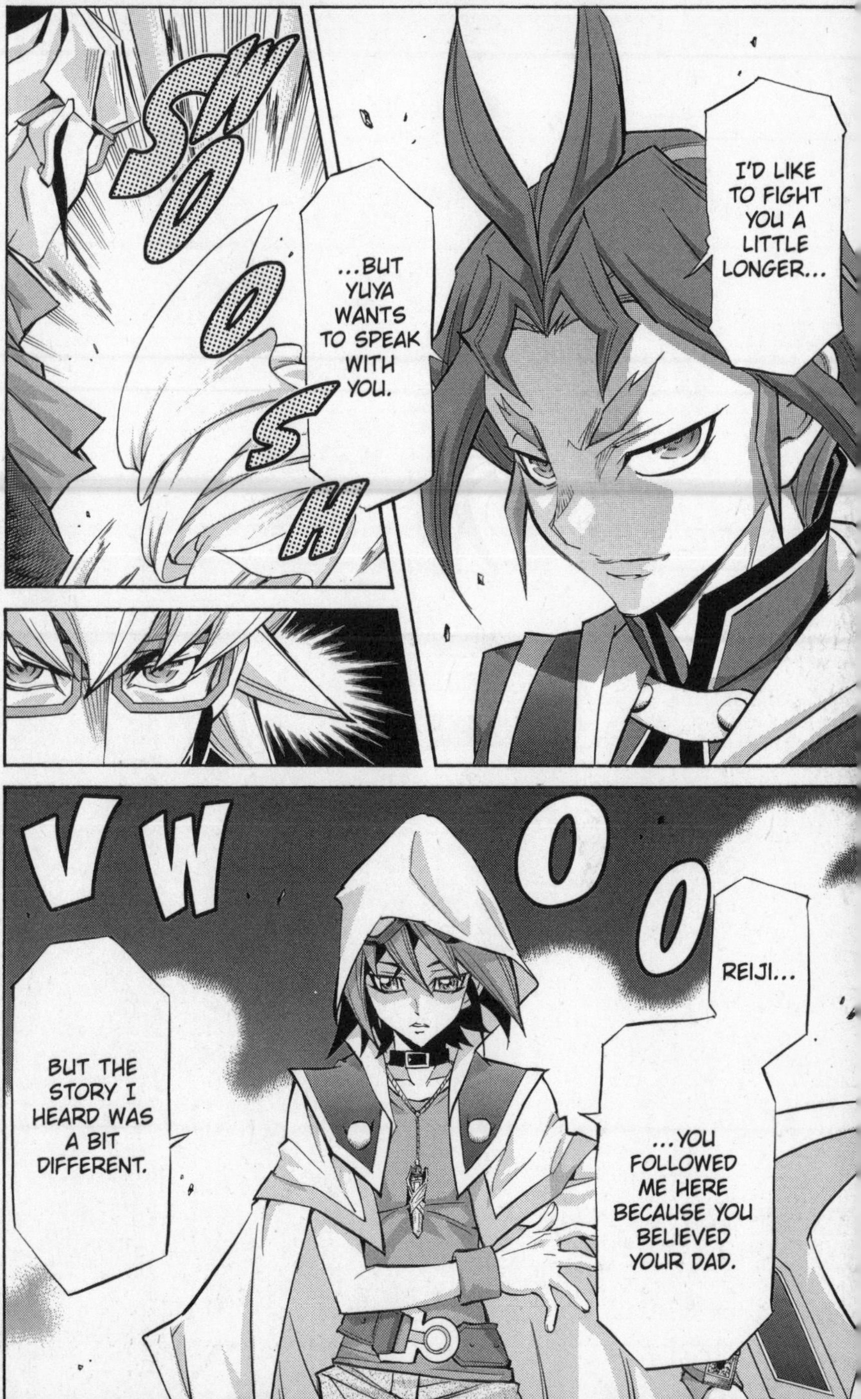
I'D LIKE TO FIGHT YOU A LITTLE LONGER...
...BUT YUYA WANTS TO SPEAK WITH YOU.
SHOOOSH
VWOO
REIJI...
...YOU FOLLOWED ME HERE BECAUSE YOU BELIEVED YOUR DAD.
BUT THE STORY I HEARD WAS A BIT DIFFERENT.

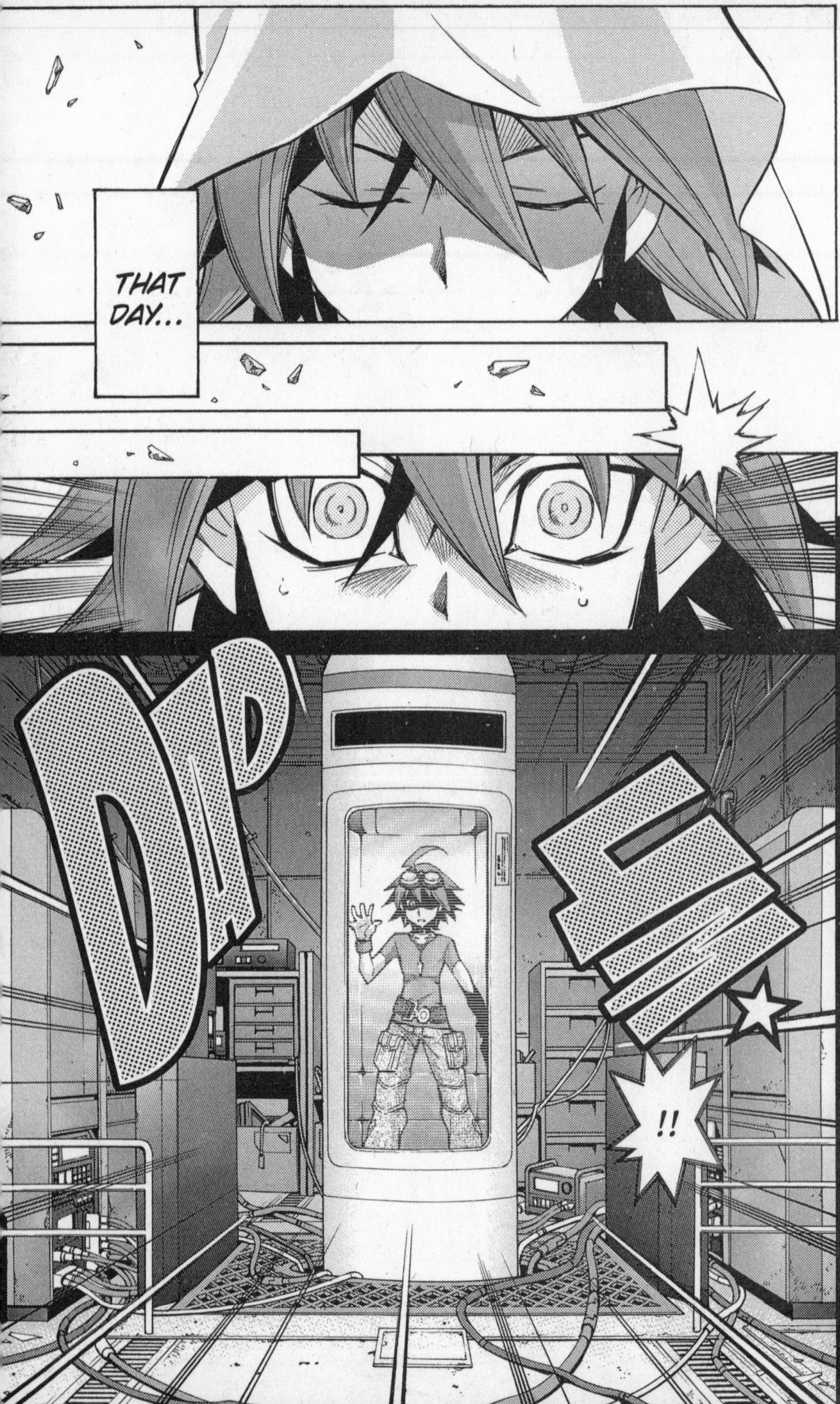
THAT DAY...
!!
DAP

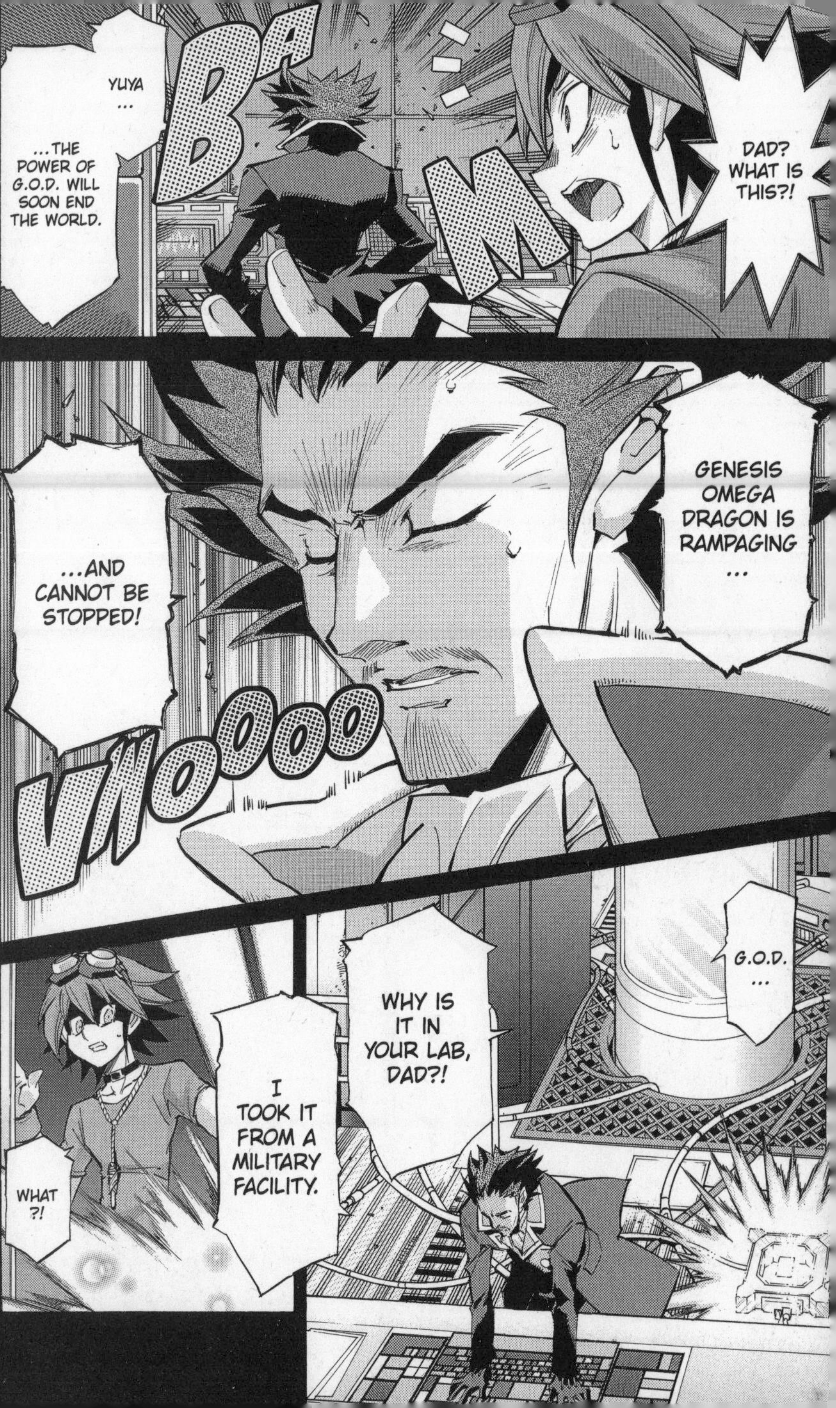
DAD? WHAT IS THIS?!
BAM
YUYA ...
...THE POWER OF G.O.D. WILL SOON END THE WORLD.
GENESIS OMEGA DRAGON IS RAMPAGING ...
...AND CANNOT BE STOPPED!
VHOOOO
G.O.D. ...
WHY IS IT IN YOUR LAB, DAD?!
I TOOK IT FROM A MILITARY FACILITY.
WHAT ?!

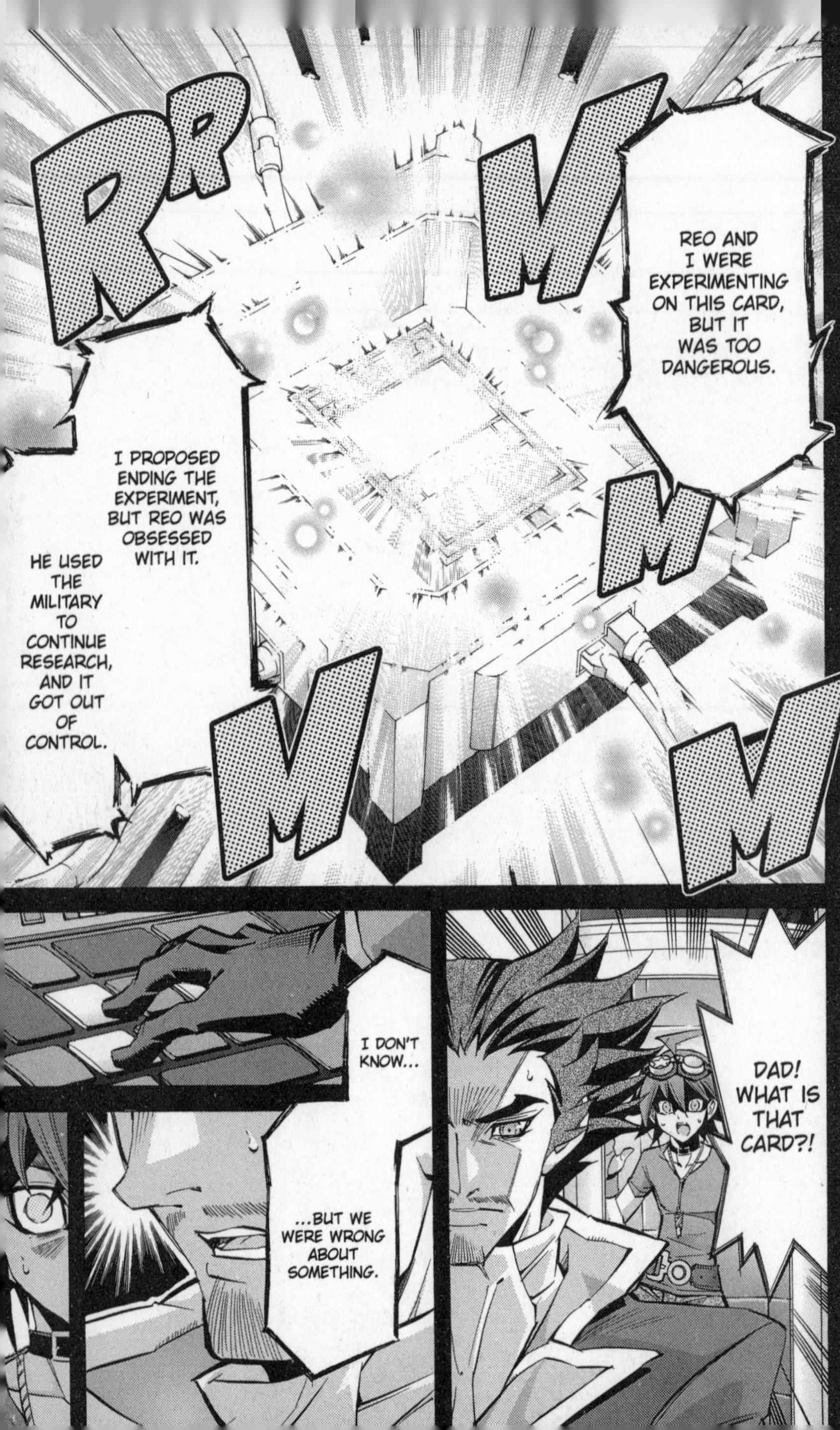

RRMMMM
REO AND I WERE EXPERIMENTING ON THIS CARD, BUT IT WAS TOO DANGEROUS.
I PROPOSED ENDING THE EXPERIMENT, BUT REO WAS OBSESSED WITH IT.
HE USED THE MILITARY TO CONTINUE RESEARCH, AND IT GOT OUT OF CONTROL.
DAD! WHAT IS THAT CARD?!
I DON'T KNOW...
...BUT WE WERE WRONG ABOUT SOMETHING.

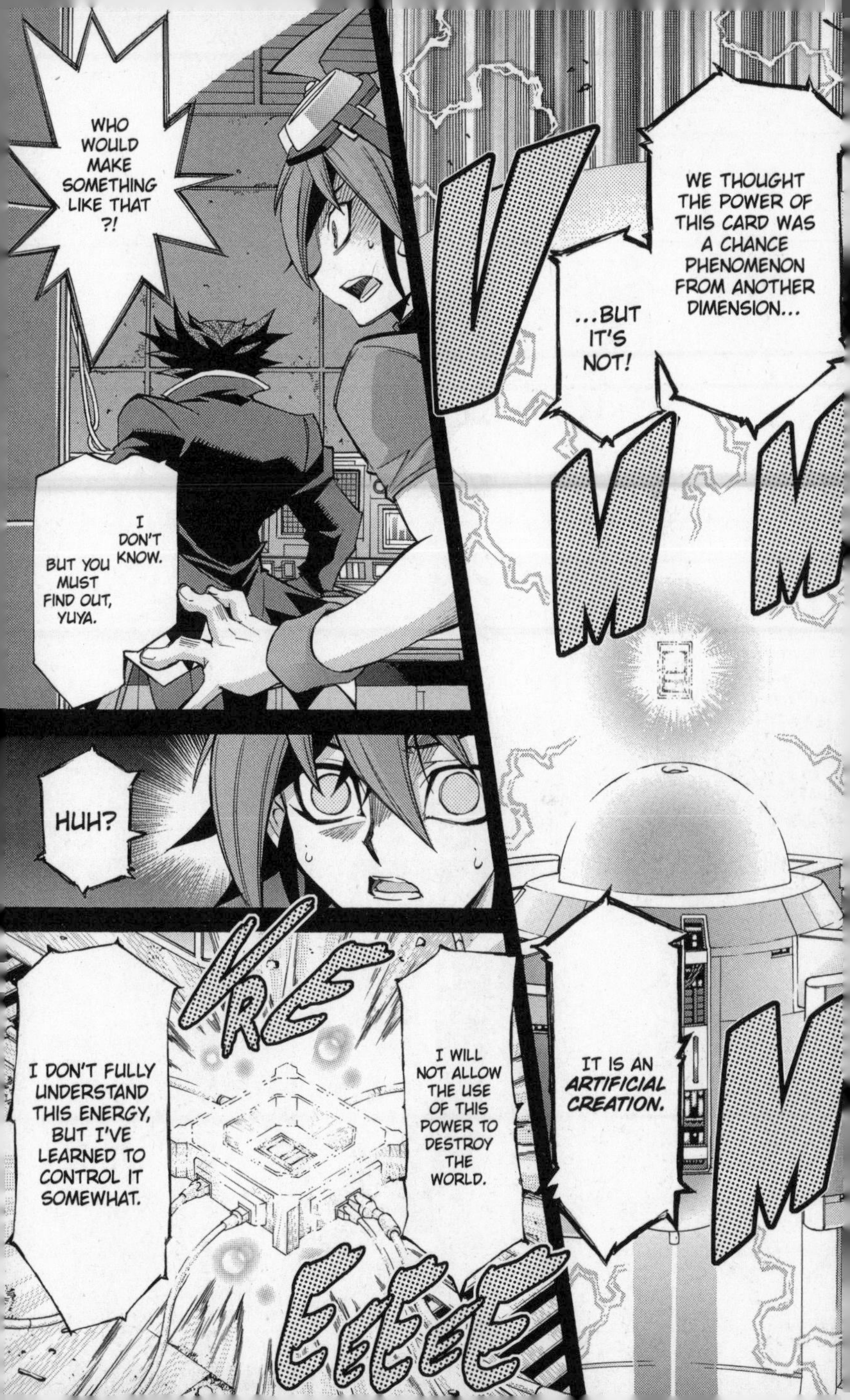
WE THOUGHT THE POWER OF THIS CARD WAS A CHANCE PHENOMENON FROM ANOTHER DIMENSION...
...BUT IT'S NOT!
VMMMM
IT IS AN *ARTIFICIAL CREATION.*
WHO WOULD MAKE SOMETHING LIKE THAT?!
I DON'T KNOW.
BUT YOU MUST FIND OUT, YUYA.
HUH?
I WILL NOT ALLOW THE USE OF THIS POWER TO DESTROY THE WORLD.
I DON'T FULLY UNDERSTAND THIS ENERGY, BUT I'VE LEARNED TO CONTROL IT SOMEWHAT.
VREEEEE

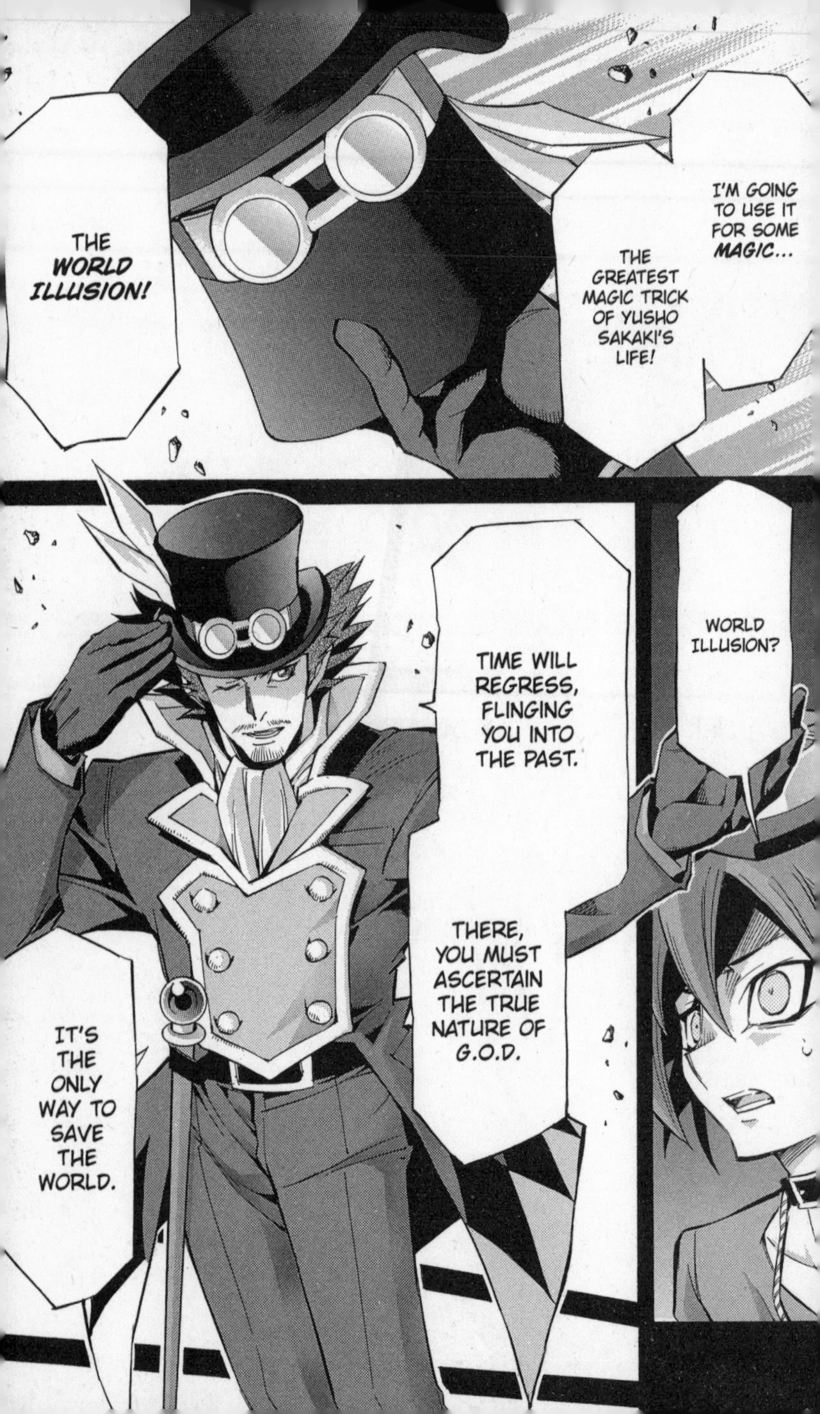
I'M GOING TO USE IT FOR SOME MAGIC...
THE GREATEST MAGIC TRICK OF YUSHO SAKAKI'S LIFE!
THE WORLD ILLUSION!
WORLD ILLUSION?
TIME WILL REGRESS, FLINGING YOU INTO THE PAST.
THERE, YOU MUST ASCERTAIN THE TRUE NATURE OF G.O.D.
IT'S THE ONLY WAY TO SAVE THE WORLD.

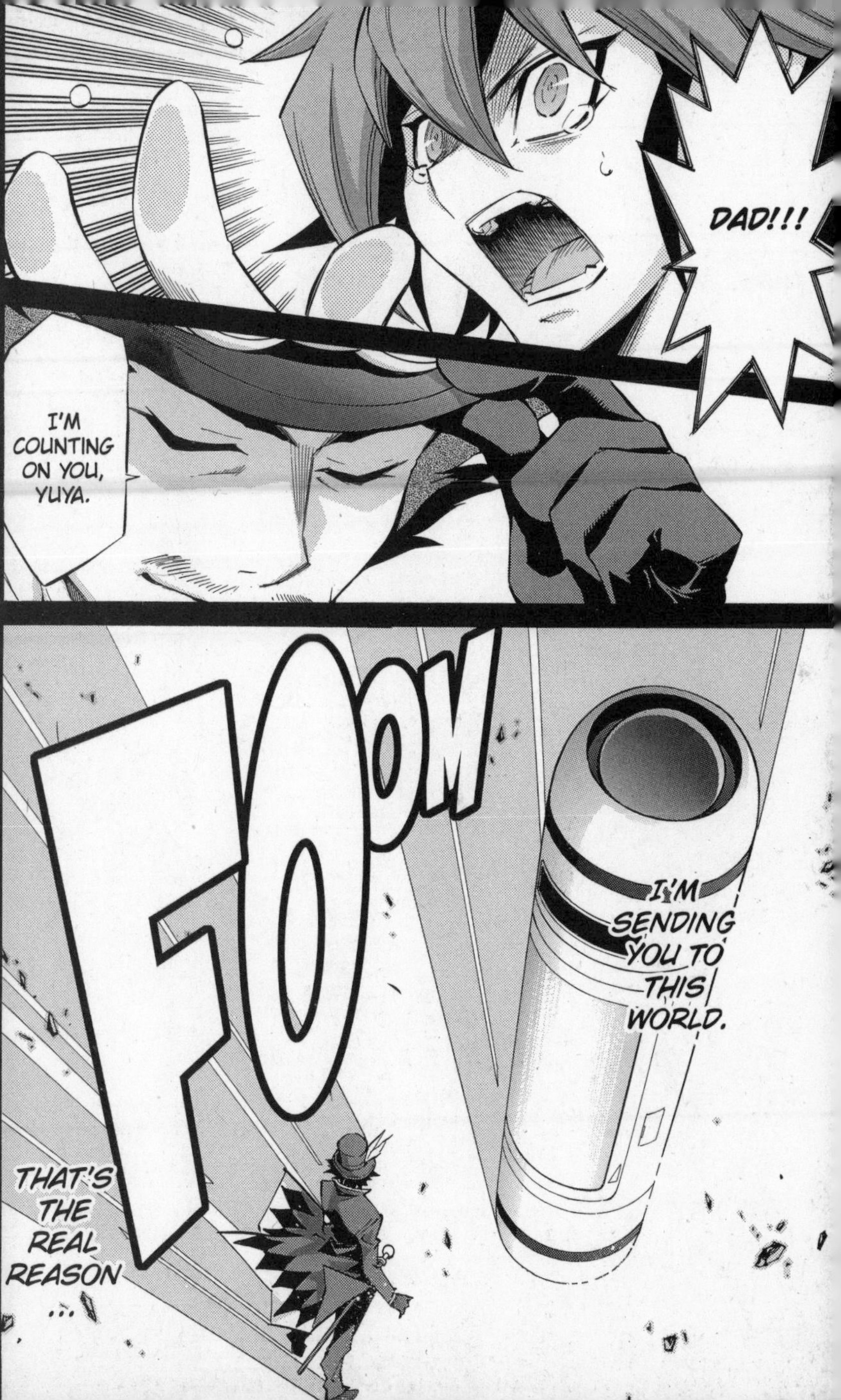
DAD!!!
I'M COUNTING ON YOU, YUYA.
FOOM
I'M SENDING YOU TO THIS WORLD.
THAT'S THE REAL REASON ...

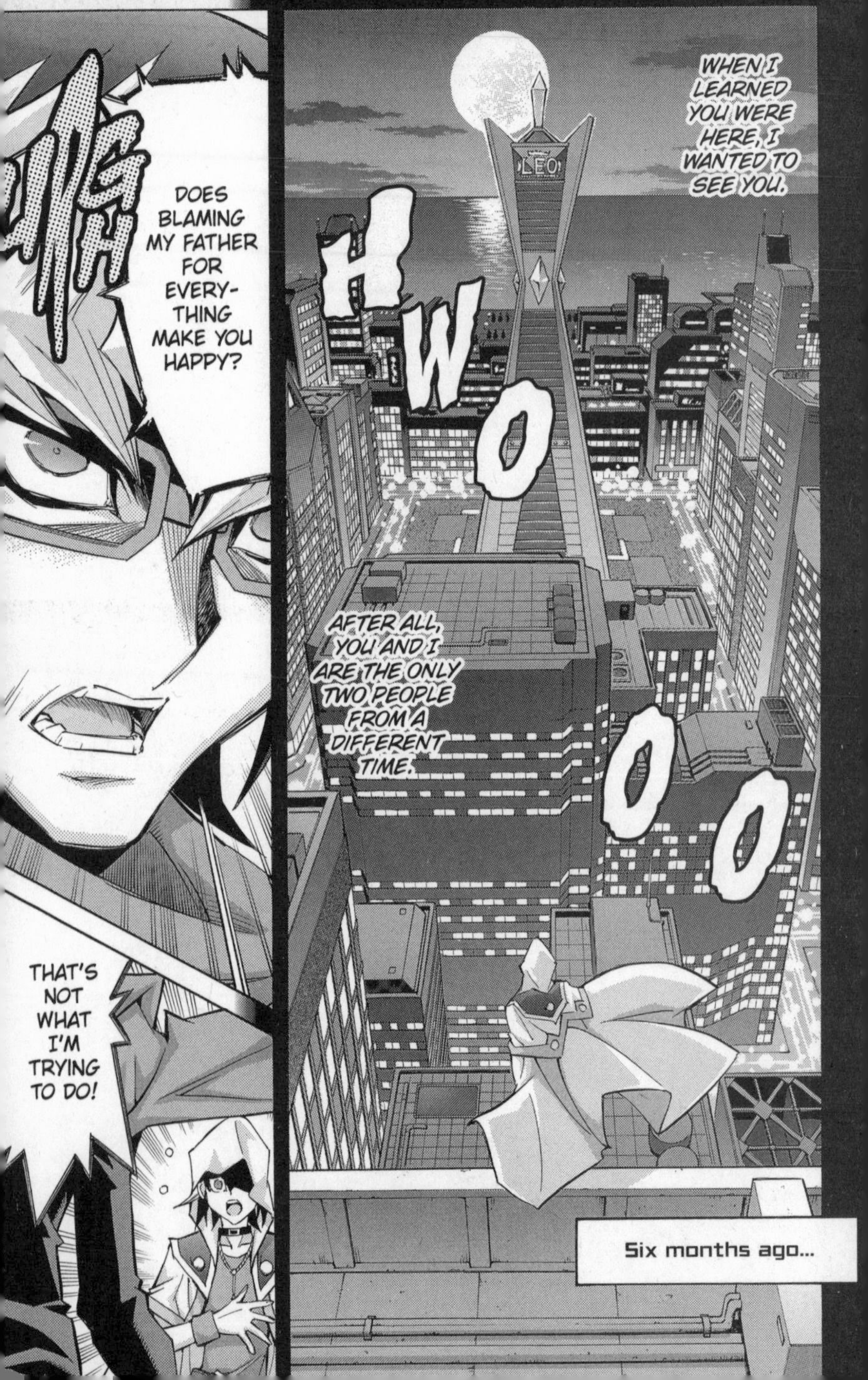

WHEN I LEARNED YOU WERE HERE, I WANTED TO SEE YOU.
HWOOOO
AFTER ALL, YOU AND I ARE THE ONLY TWO PEOPLE FROM A DIFFERENT TIME.
Six months ago...
DOES BLAMING MY FATHER FOR EVERY-THING MAKE YOU HAPPY?
THAT'S NOT WHAT I'M TRYING TO DO!

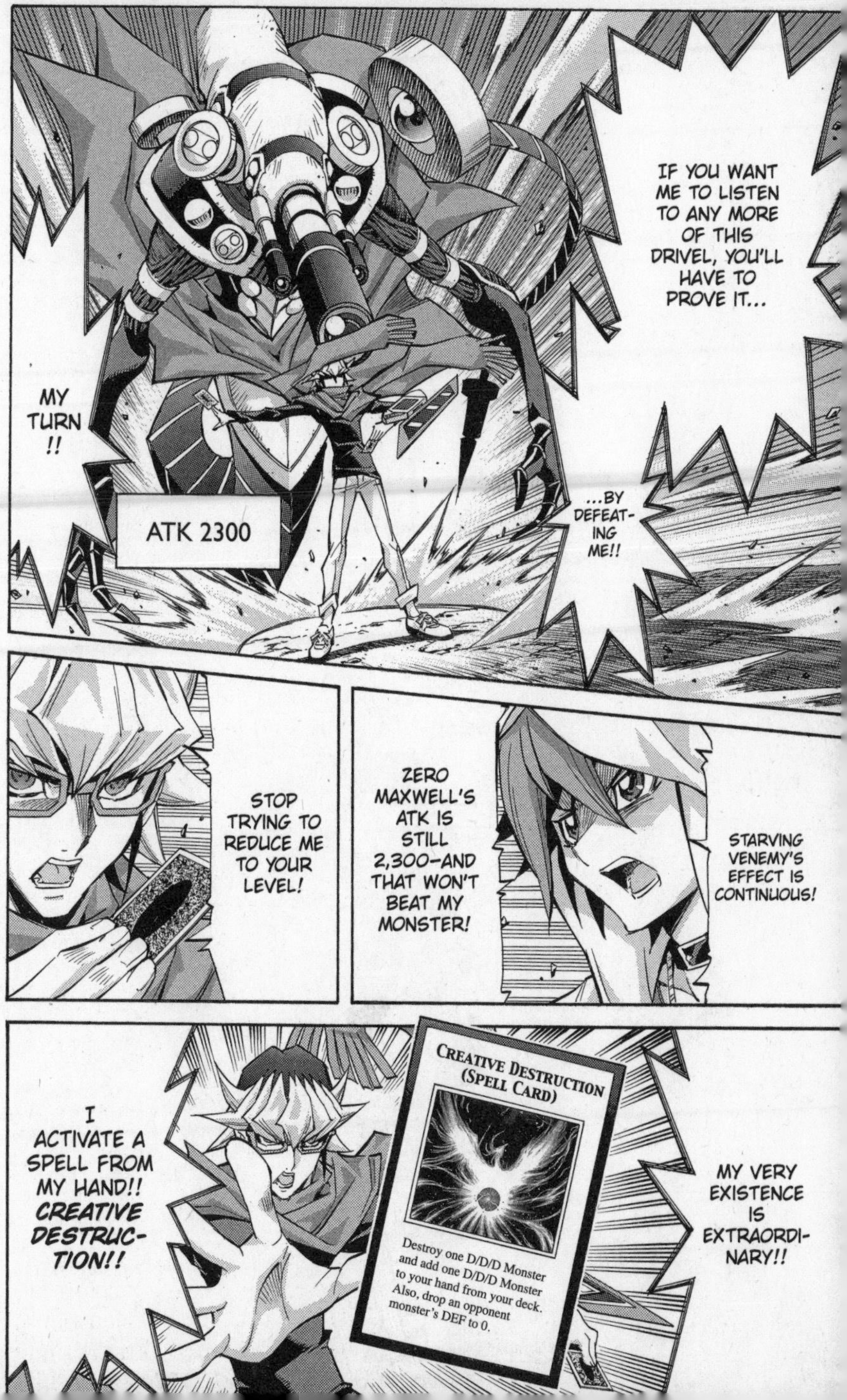
IF YOU WANT ME TO LISTEN TO ANY MORE OF THIS DRIVEL, YOU'LL HAVE TO PROVE IT...
...BY DEFEATING ME!!
MY TURN!!
ATK 2300
STARVING VENEMY'S EFFECT IS CONTINUOUS!
ZERO MAXWELL'S ATK IS STILL 2,300—AND THAT WON'T BEAT MY MONSTER!
STOP TRYING TO REDUCE ME TO YOUR LEVEL!
MY VERY EXISTENCE IS EXTRAORDINARY!!
CREATIVE DESTRUCTION (SPELL CARD)
Destroy one D/D/D Monster and add one D/D/D Monster to your hand from your deck. Also, drop an opponent monster's DEF to 0.
I ACTIVATE A SPELL FROM MY HAND!! CREATIVE DESTRUCTION!!

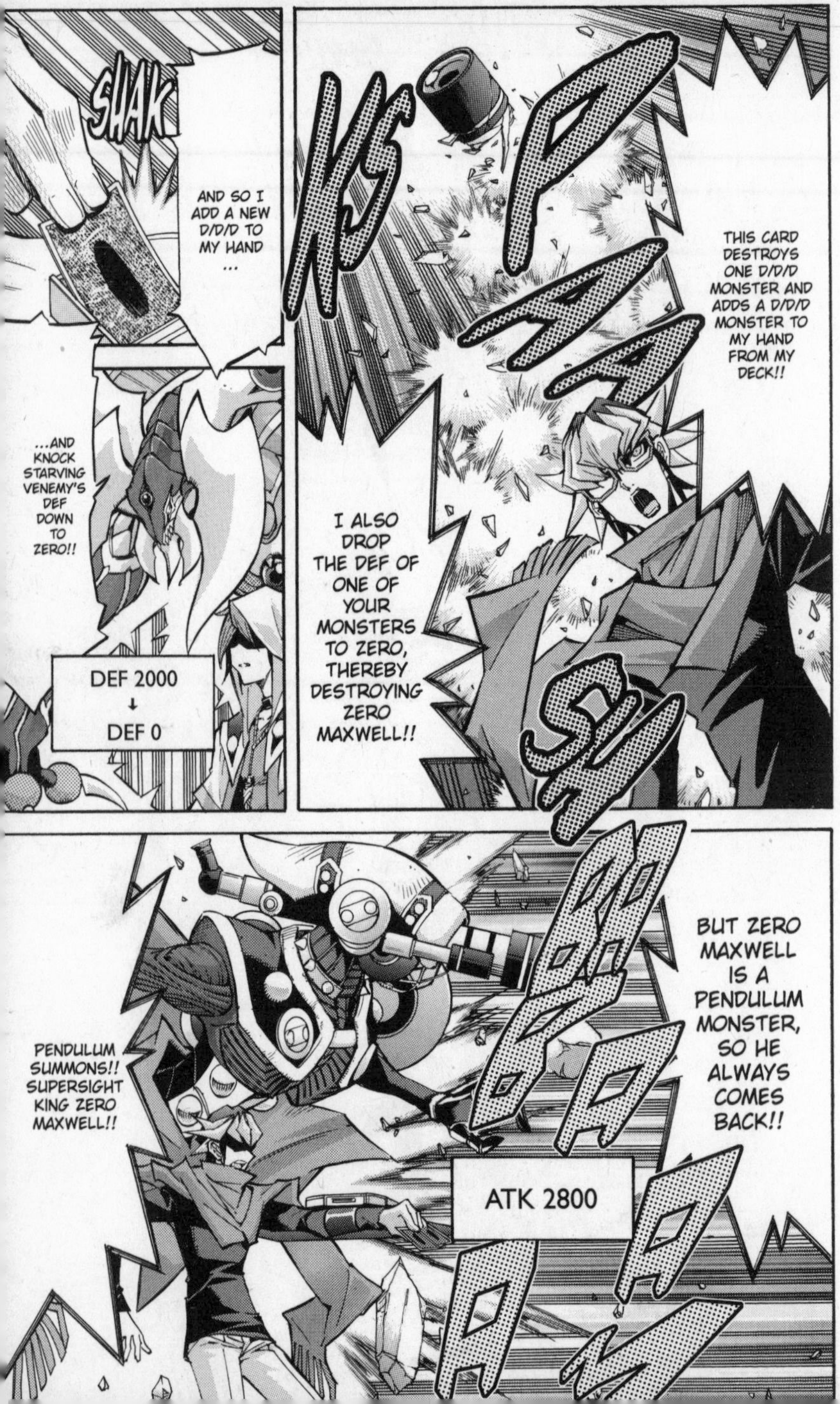
THIS CARD DESTROYS ONE D/D/D MONSTER AND ADDS A D/D/D MONSTER TO MY HAND FROM MY DECK!!
I ALSO DROP THE DEF OF ONE OF YOUR MONSTERS TO ZERO, THEREBY DESTROYING ZERO MAXWELL!!
SHAK
AND SO I ADD A NEW D/D/D TO MY HAND ...
...AND KNOCK STARVING VENEMY'S DEF DOWN TO ZERO!!
DEF 2000
↓
DEF 0
BUT ZERO MAXWELL IS A PENDULUM MONSTER, SO HE ALWAYS COMES BACK!!
ATK 2800
PENDULUM SUMMONS!! SUPERSIGHT KING ZERO MAXWELL!!

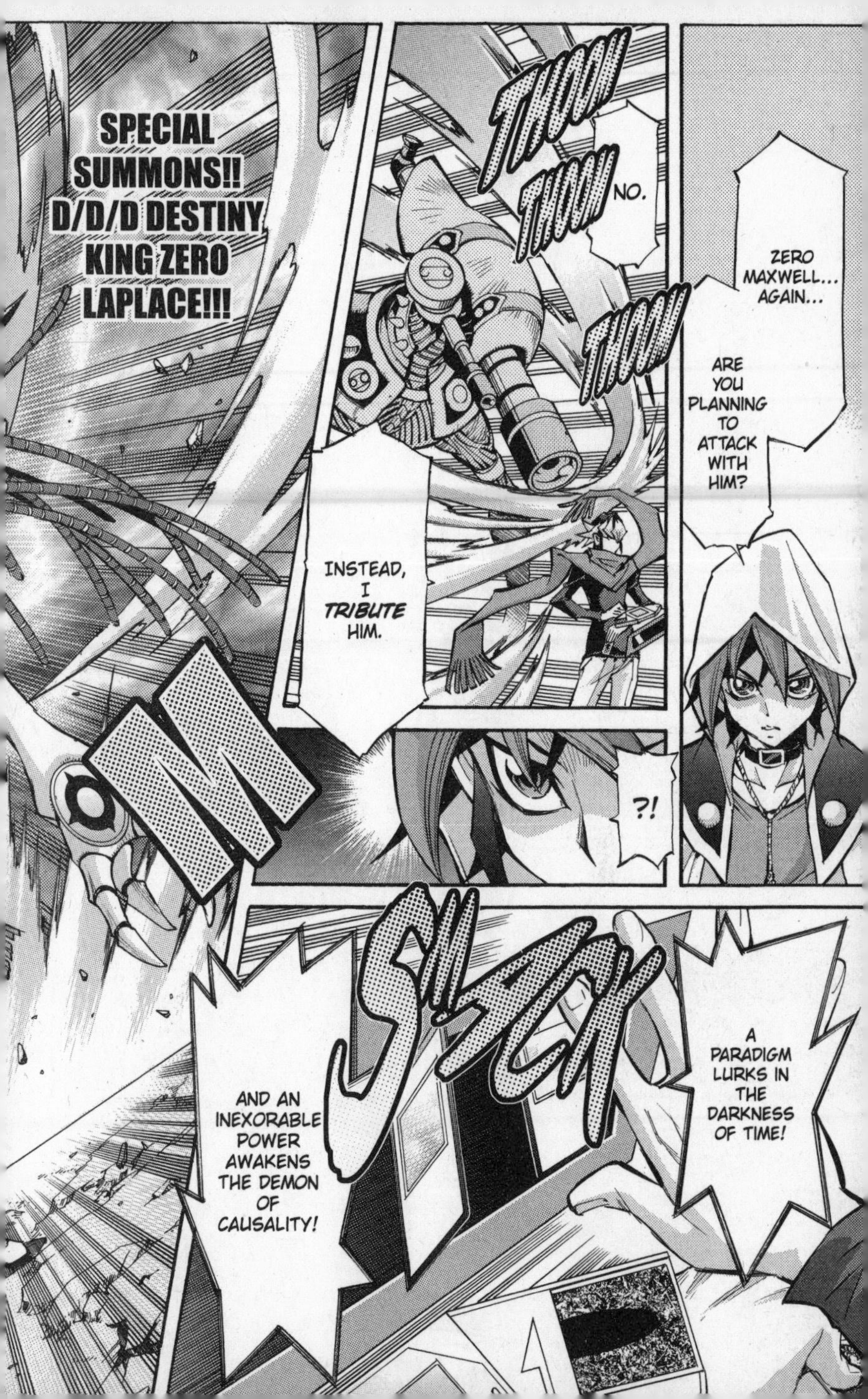
ZERO MAXWELL... AGAIN...
ARE YOU PLANNING TO ATTACK WITH HIM?
THOOM THOOM
NO.
THOOM
INSTEAD, I *TRIBUTE* HIM.
?!
SPECIAL SUMMONS!! D/D/D DESTINY KING ZERO LAPLACE!!!
SHICK
A PARADIGM LURKS IN THE DARKNESS OF TIME!
AND AN INEXORABLE POWER AWAKENS THE DEMON OF CAUSALITY!

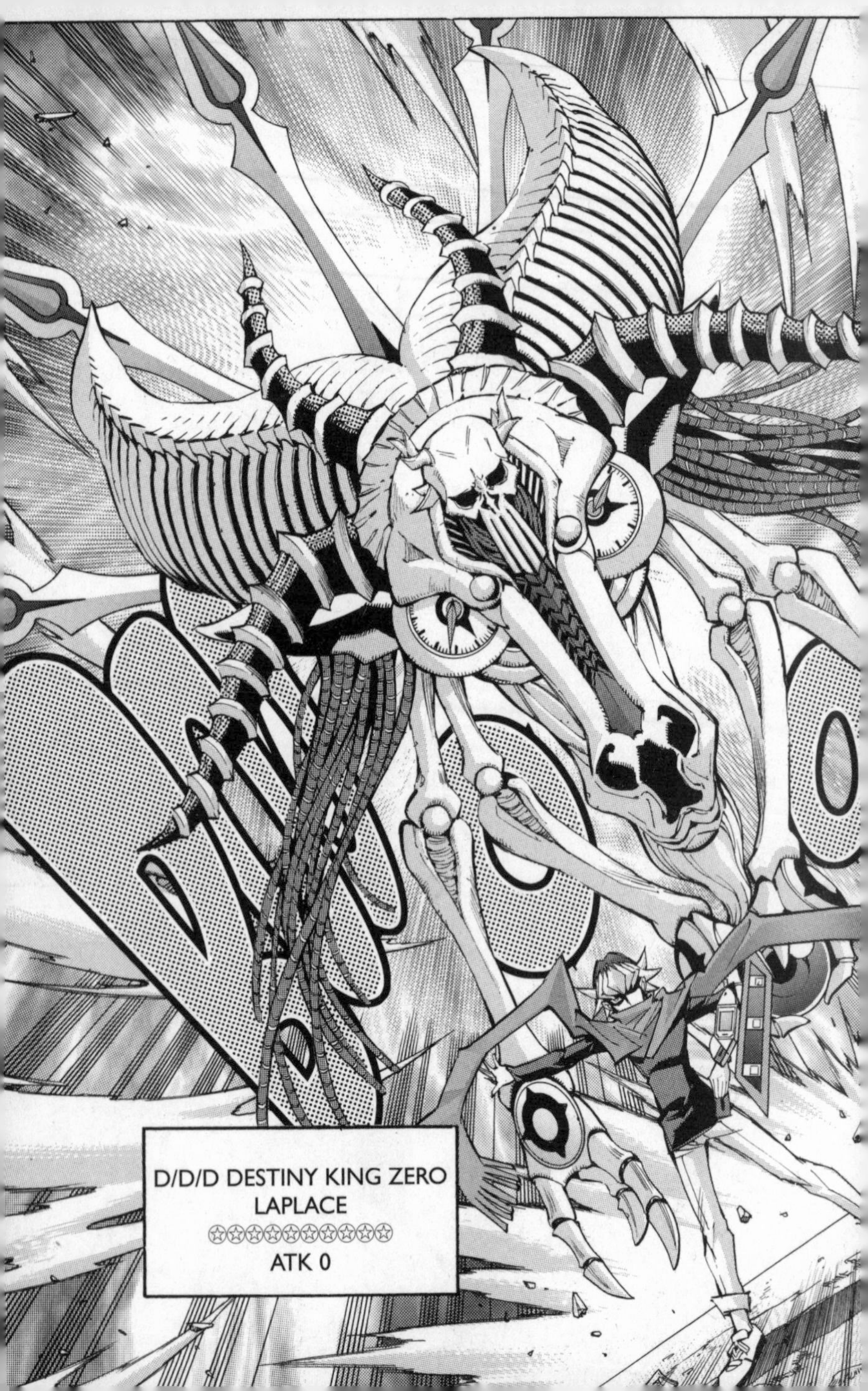
D/D/D DESTINY KING ZERO LAPLACE
☆☆☆☆☆☆☆☆☆☆☆☆
ATK 0

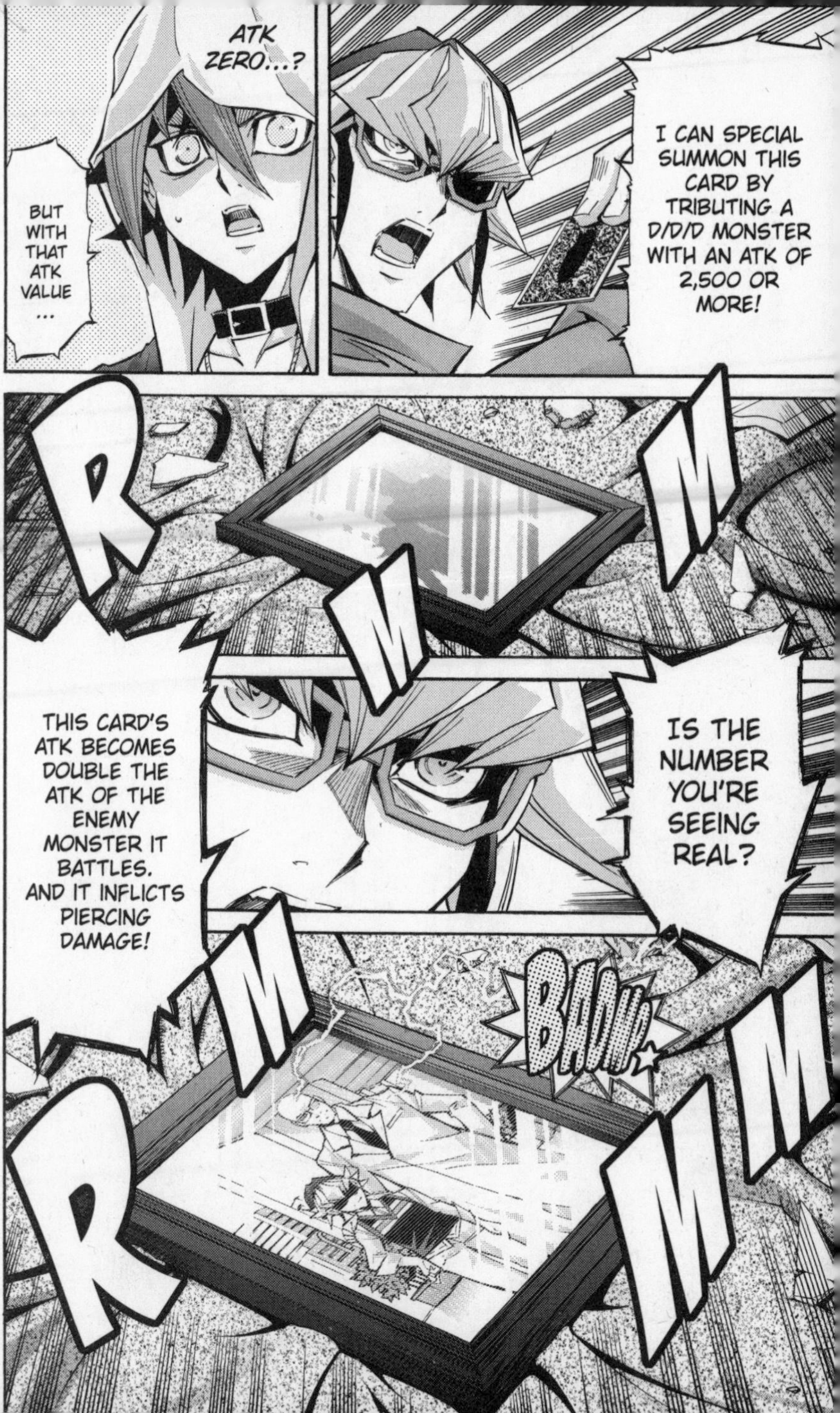
I CAN SPECIAL SUMMON THIS CARD BY TRIBUTING A D/D/D MONSTER WITH AN ATK OF 2,500 OR MORE!
ATK ZERO...?
BUT WITH THAT ATK VALUE ...
RMM
IS THE NUMBER YOU'RE SEEING REAL?
THIS CARD'S ATK BECOMES DOUBLE THE ATK OF THE ENEMY MONSTER IT BATTLES. AND IT INFLICTS PIERCING DAMAGE!
BADUM
RMMMM

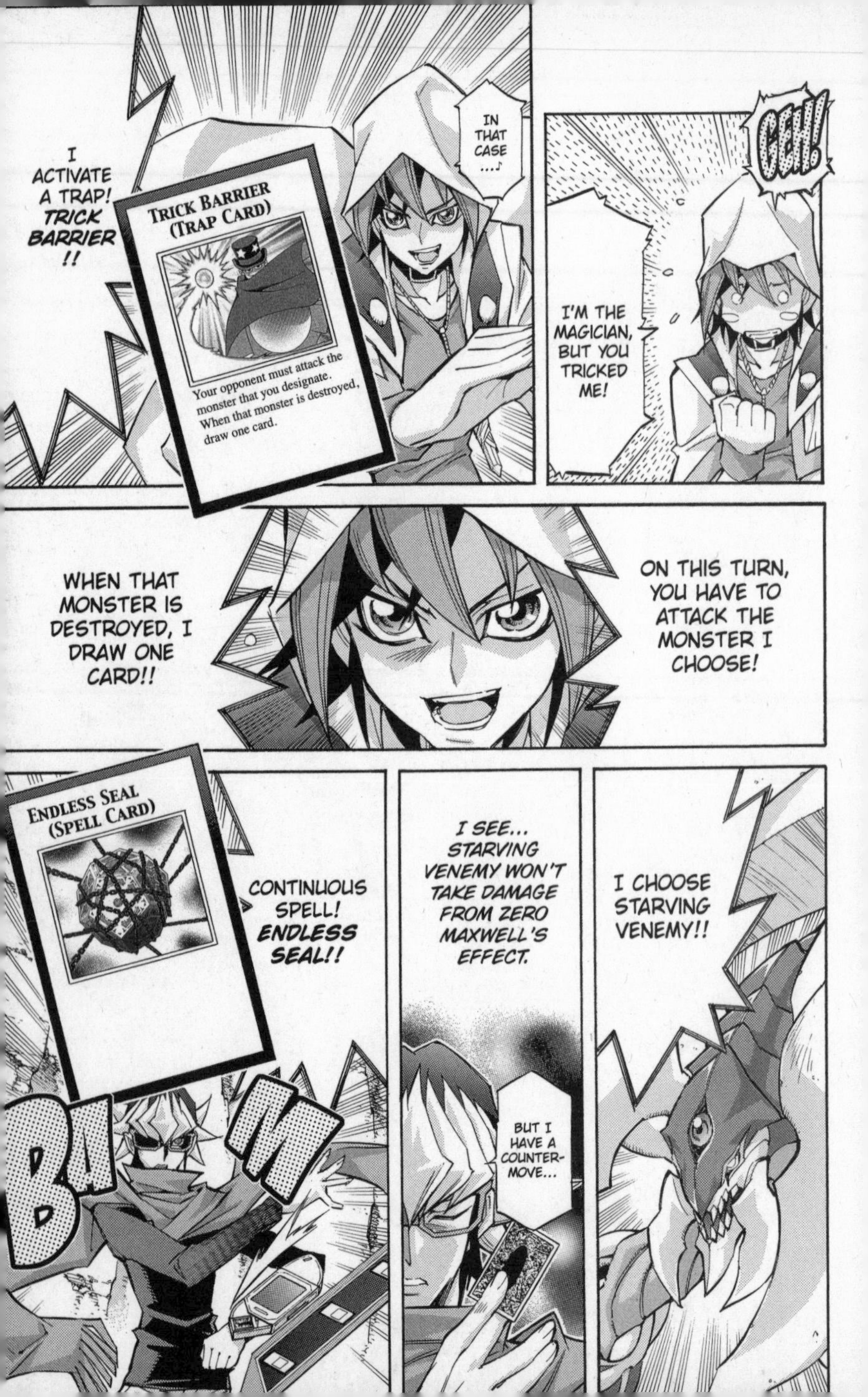
GEH!
I'M THE MAGICIAN, BUT YOU TRICKED ME!
IN THAT CASE ....♪
I ACTIVATE A TRAP! TRICK BARRIER!!
TRICK BARRIER (TRAP CARD)
Your opponent must attack the monster that you designate. When that monster is destroyed, draw one card.
ON THIS TURN, YOU HAVE TO ATTACK THE MONSTER I CHOOSE!
WHEN THAT MONSTER IS DESTROYED, I DRAW ONE CARD!!
I CHOOSE STARVING VENEMY!!
I SEE... STARVING VENEMY WON'T TAKE DAMAGE FROM ZERO MAXWELL'S EFFECT.
BUT I HAVE A COUNTER-MOVE...
CONTINUOUS SPELL! ENDLESS SEAL!!
ENDLESS SEAL (SPELL CARD)
BAM

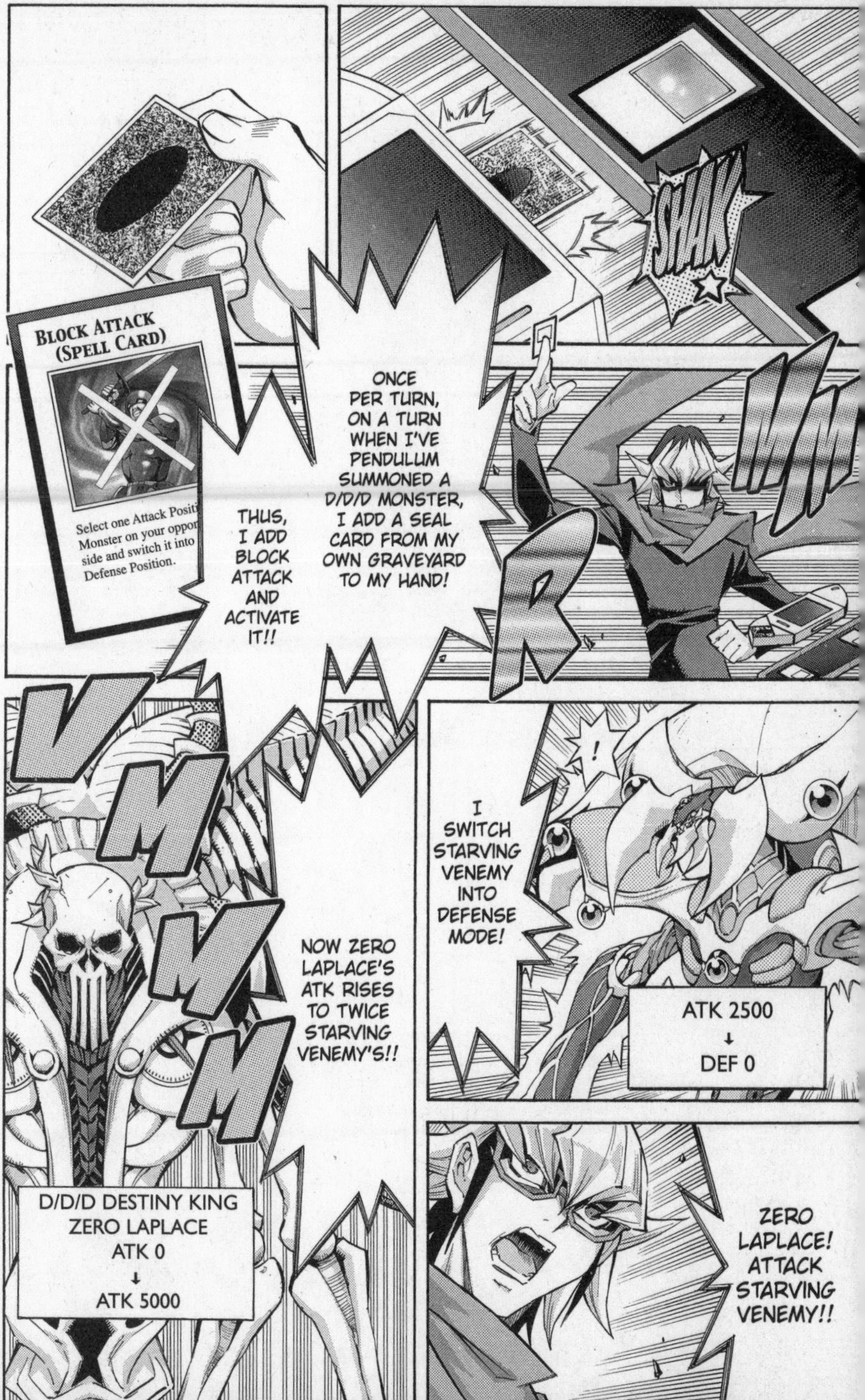
SHAK
MMM
R
ONCE PER TURN, ON A TURN WHEN I'VE PENDULUM SUMMONED A D/D/D MONSTER, I ADD A SEAL CARD FROM MY OWN GRAVEYARD TO MY HAND!
THUS, I ADD BLOCK ATTACK AND ACTIVATE IT!!
BLOCK ATTACK (SPELL CARD)
Select one Attack Positi
Monster on your oppon
side and switch it into
Defense Position.
!
I SWITCH STARVING VENEMY INTO DEFENSE MODE!
ATK 2500 ↓ DEF 0
ZERO LAPLACE! ATTACK STARVING VENEMY!!
VMMM
NOW ZERO LAPLACE'S ATK RISES TO TWICE STARVING VENEMY'S!!
D/D/D DESTINY KING ZERO LAPLACE ATK 0 ↓ ATK 5000

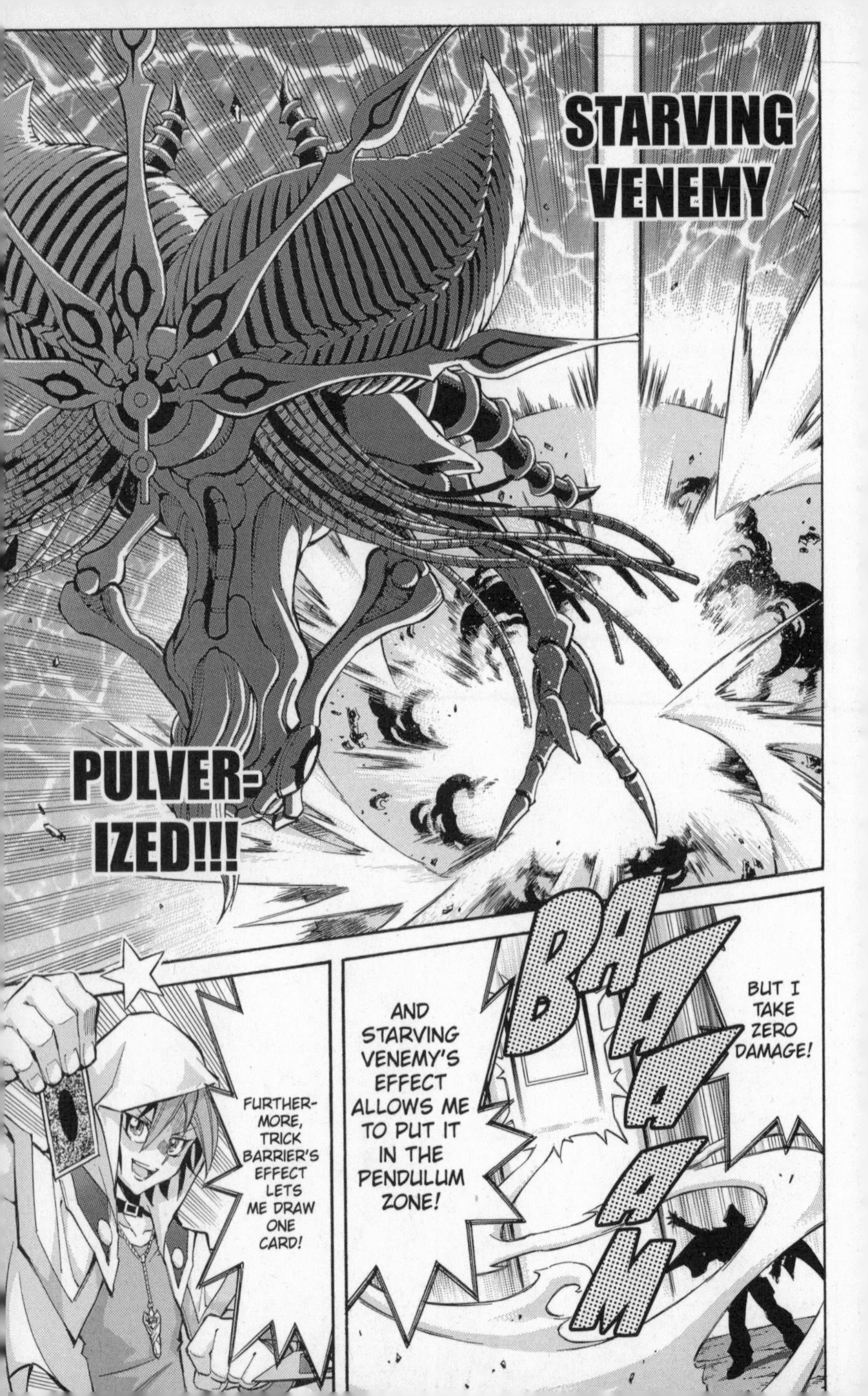
STARVING VENEMY
PULVER-IZED!!!
BUT I TAKE ZERO DAMAGE!
BAAAAM
AND STARVING VENEMY'S EFFECT ALLOWS ME TO PUT IT IN THE PENDULUM ZONE!
FURTHER-MORE, TRICK BARRIER'S EFFECT LETS ME DRAW ONE CARD!

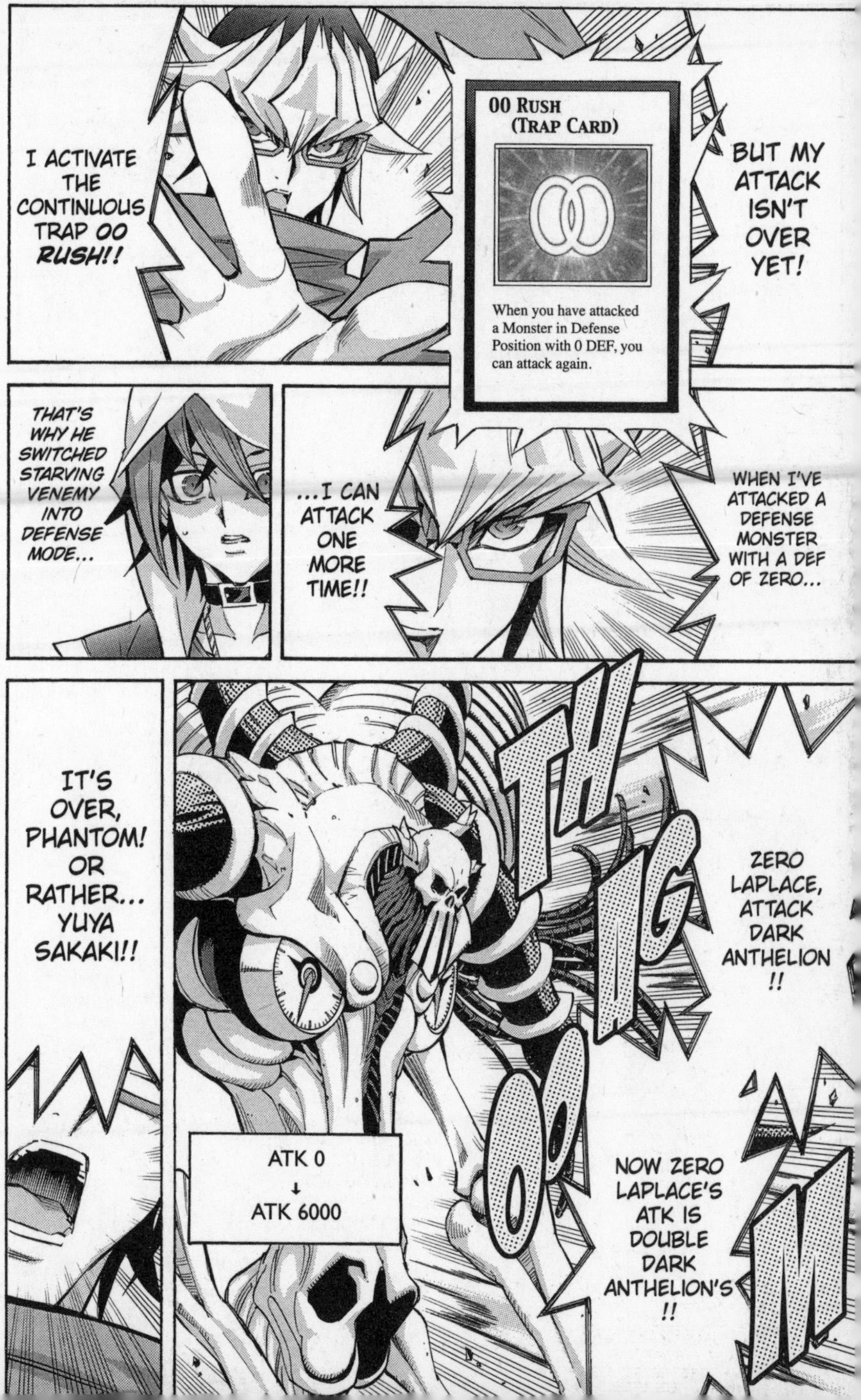
BUT MY ATTACK ISN'T OVER YET!
00 RUSH (TRAP CARD)
When you have attacked a Monster in Defense Position with 0 DEF, you can attack again.
I ACTIVATE THE CONTINUOUS TRAP 00 RUSH!!
WHEN I'VE ATTACKED A DEFENSE MONSTER WITH A DEF OF ZERO...
...I CAN ATTACK ONE MORE TIME!!
THAT'S WHY HE SWITCHED STARVING VENEMY INTO DEFENSE MODE...
ZERO LAPLACE, ATTACK DARK ANTHELION!!
NOW ZERO LAPLACE'S ATK IS DOUBLE DARK ANTHELION'S!!
ATK 0
↓
ATK 6000
IT'S OVER, PHANTOM! OR RATHER... YUYA SAKAKI!!

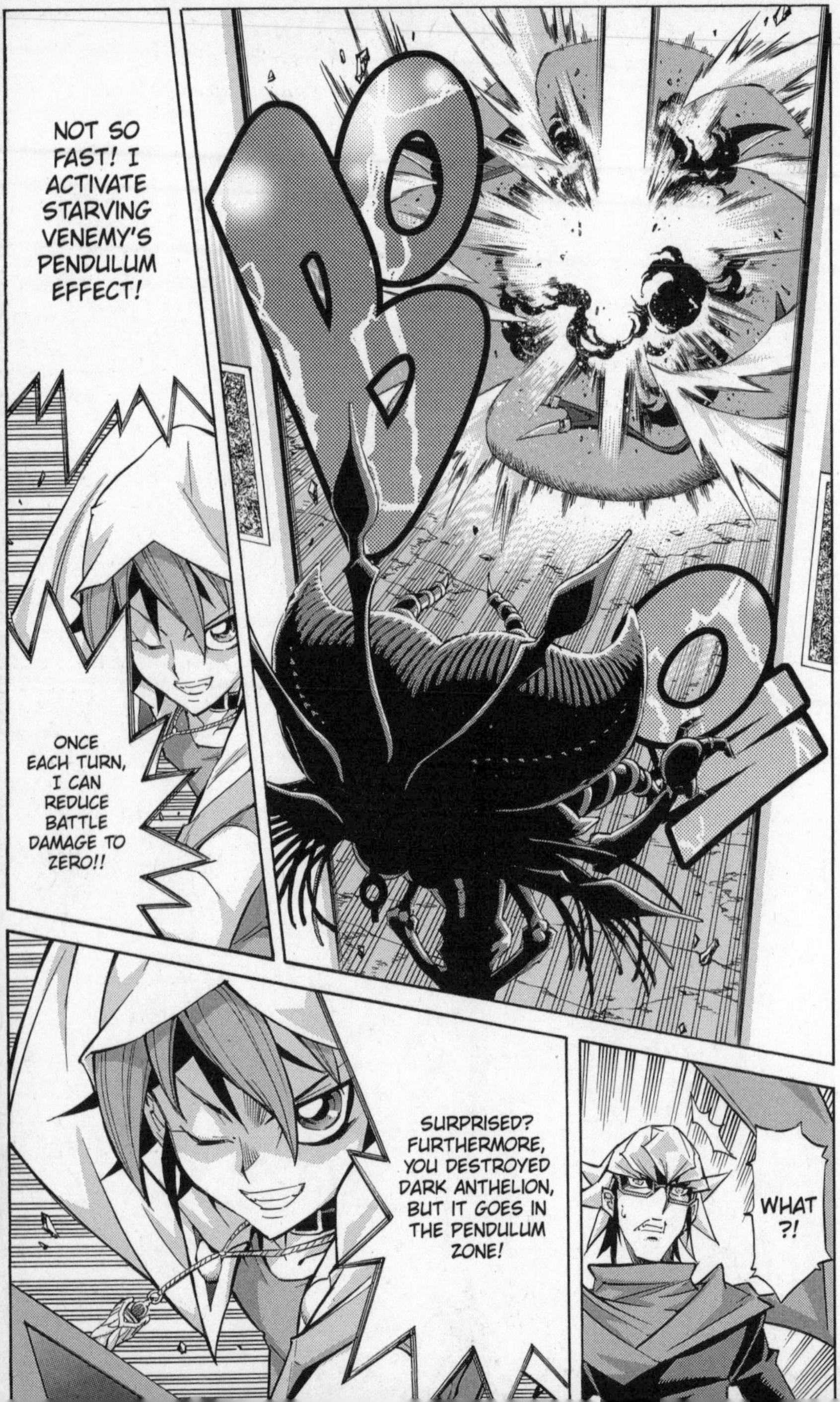
NOT SO FAST! I ACTIVATE STARVING VENEMY'S PENDULUM EFFECT!
ONCE EACH TURN, I CAN REDUCE BATTLE DAMAGE TO ZERO!!
WHAT ?!
SURPRISED? FURTHERMORE, YOU DESTROYED DARK ANTHELION, BUT IT GOES IN THE PENDULUM ZONE!

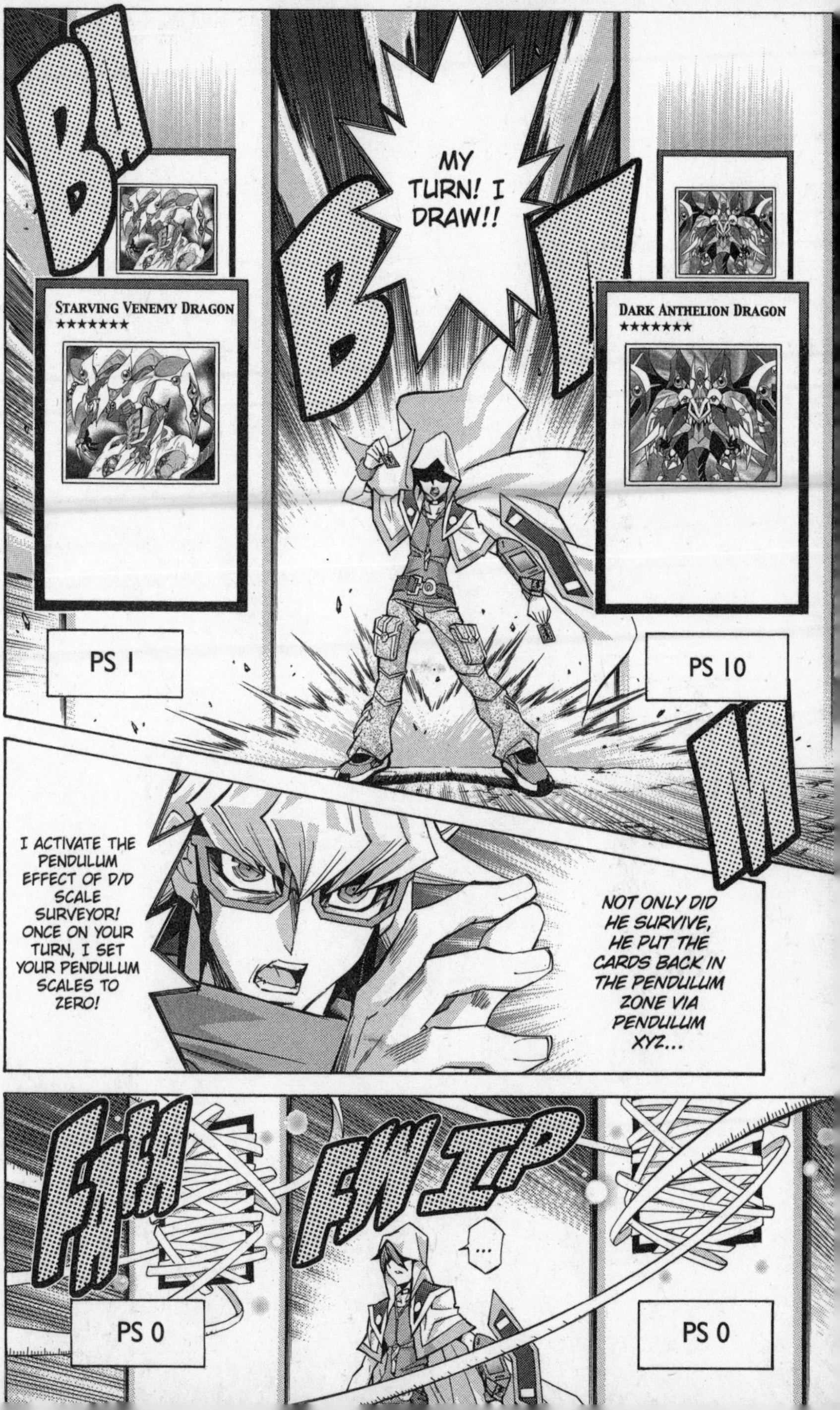
DARK ANTHELION DRAGON
★★★★★★★
PS 10
MY TURN! I DRAW!!
STARVING VENEMY DRAGON
★★★★★★★
PS 1
NOT ONLY DID HE SURVIVE, HE PUT THE CARDS BACK IN THE PENDULUM ZONE VIA PENDULUM XYZ...
I ACTIVATE THE PENDULUM EFFECT OF D/D SCALE SURVEYOR! ONCE ON YOUR TURN, I SET YOUR PENDULUM SCALES TO ZERO!
PS 0
...
PS 0

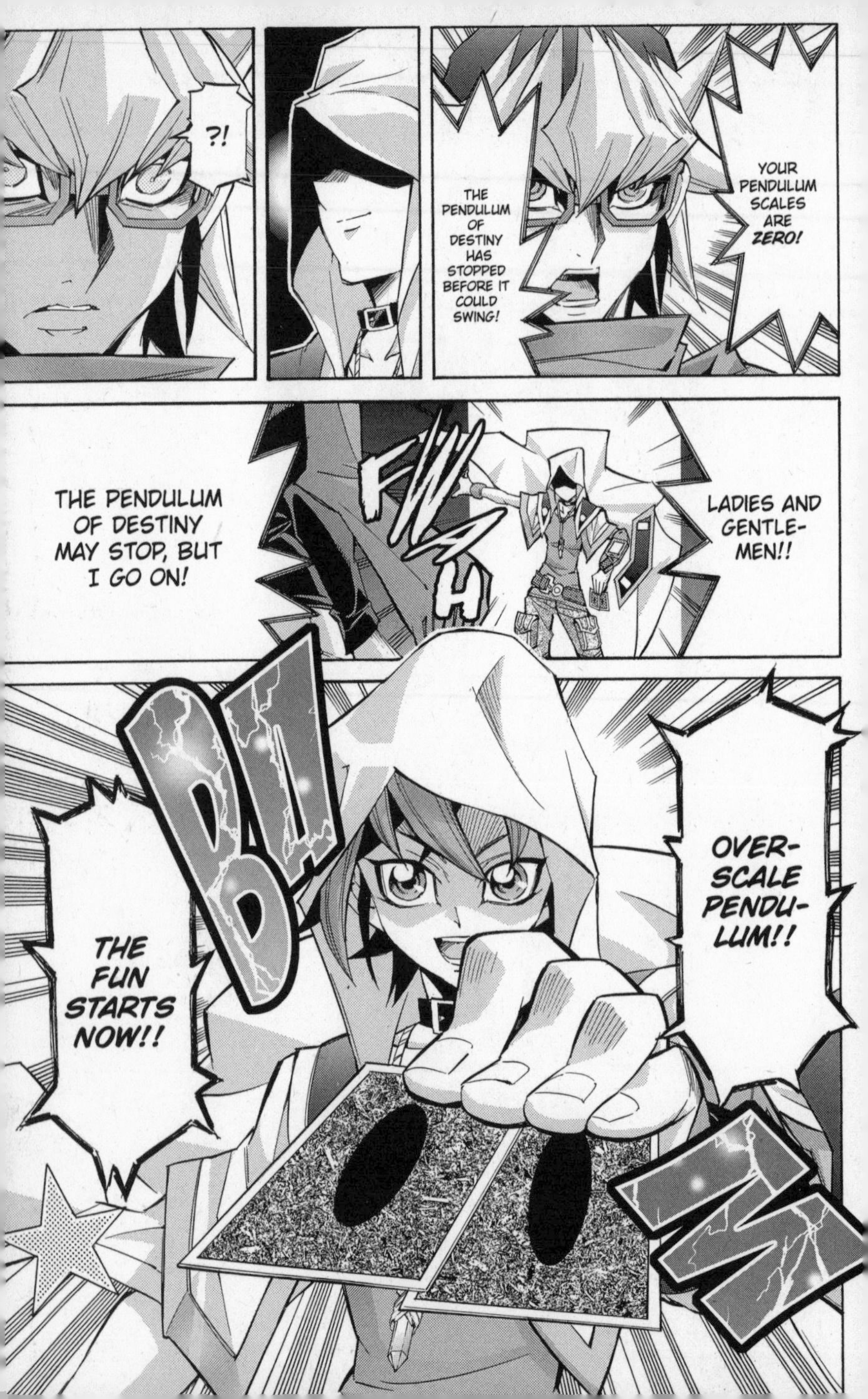
YOUR PENDULUM SCALES ARE ZERO!
THE PENDULUM OF DESTINY HAS STOPPED BEFORE IT COULD SWING!
?!
LADIES AND GENTLE-MEN!!
THE PENDULUM OF DESTINY MAY STOP, BUT I GO ON!
OVER-SCALE PENDU-LUM!!
THE FUN STARTS NOW!!

PRESENTING MIYOSHI SENSEI'S EARLY DESIGNS!

scale 14

ARC-V CHARACTER SKETCHES

EVE

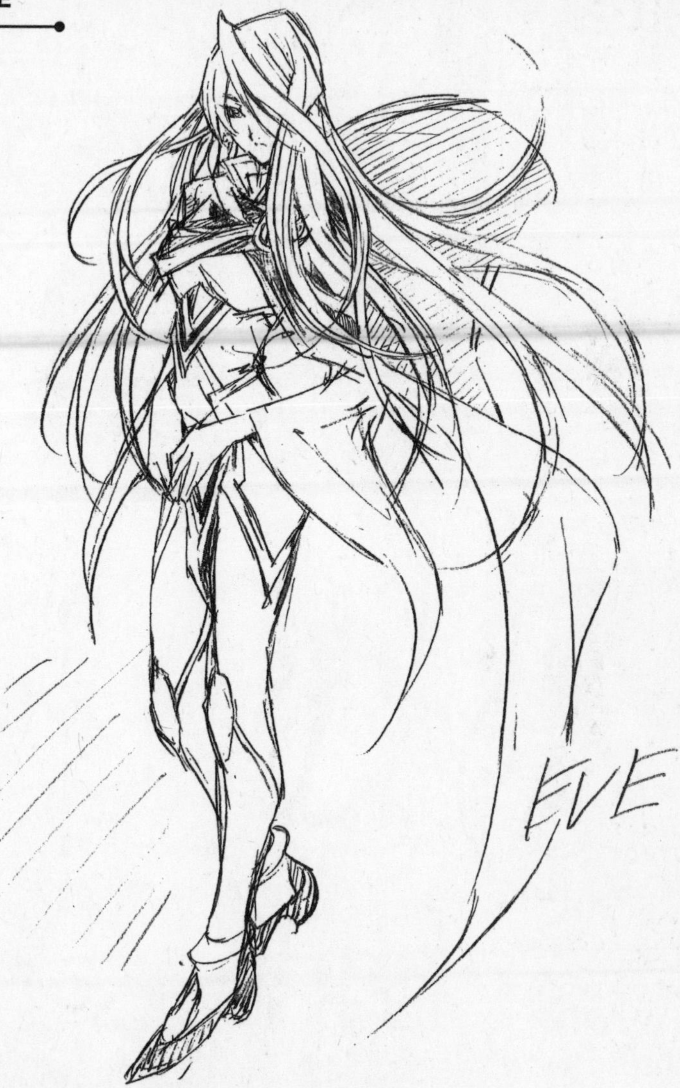
EVE

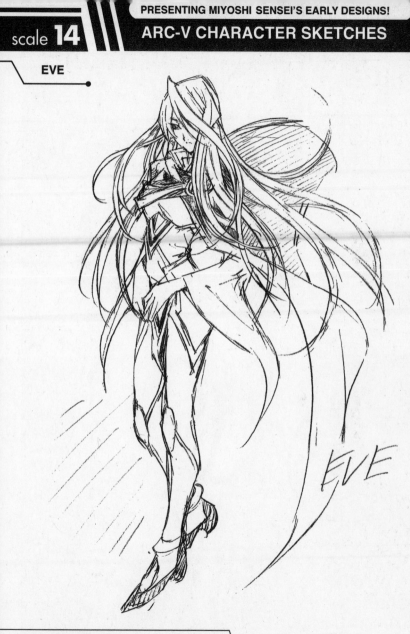

Eve is the central figure of a mysterious organization at the heart of the battle for the Genesis Omega Dragon. Why does she really want Yuya's Adam Factor?

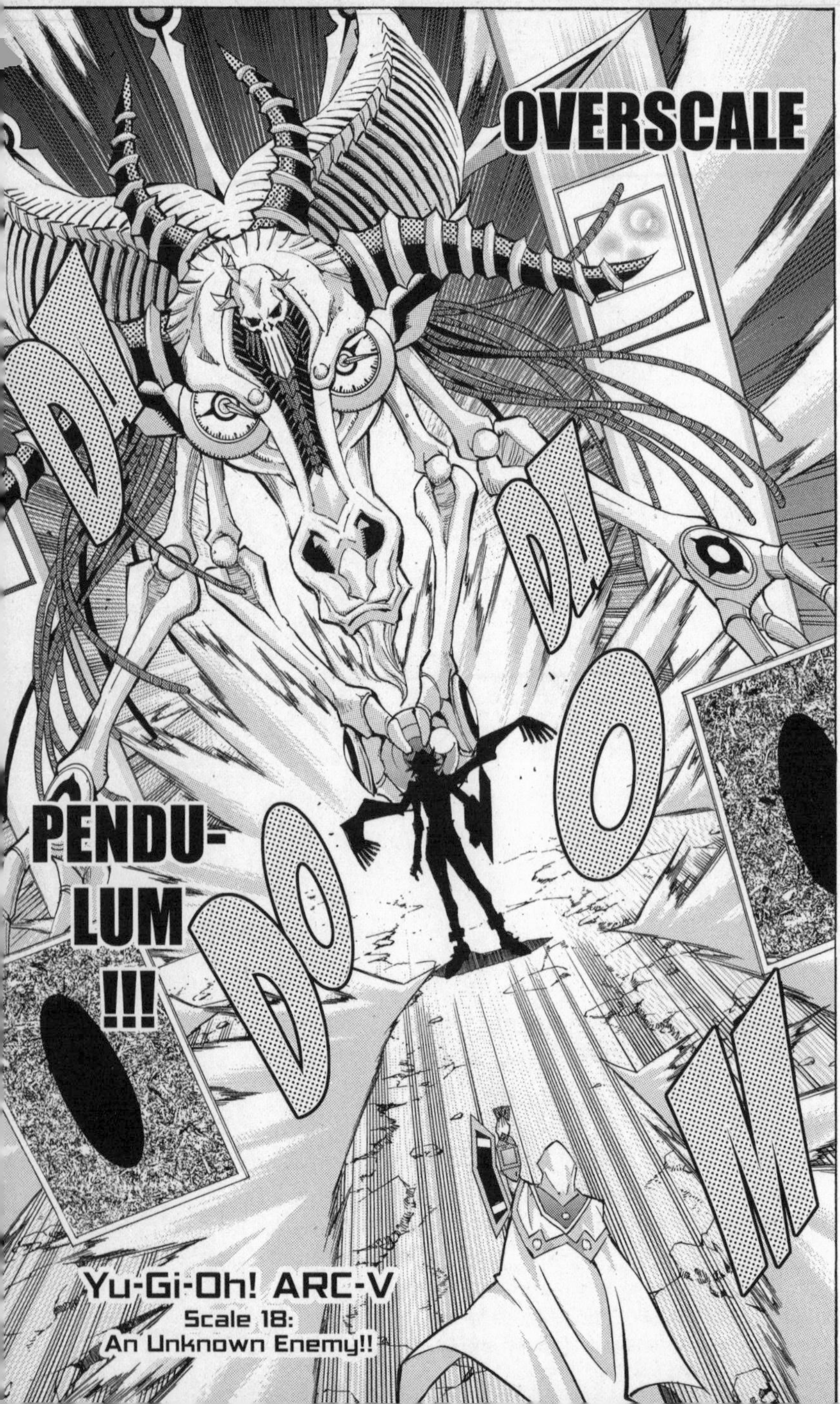
OVERSCALE
PENDU-
LUM
!!!
Yu-Gi-Oh! ARC-V
Scale 18:
An Unknown Enemy!!

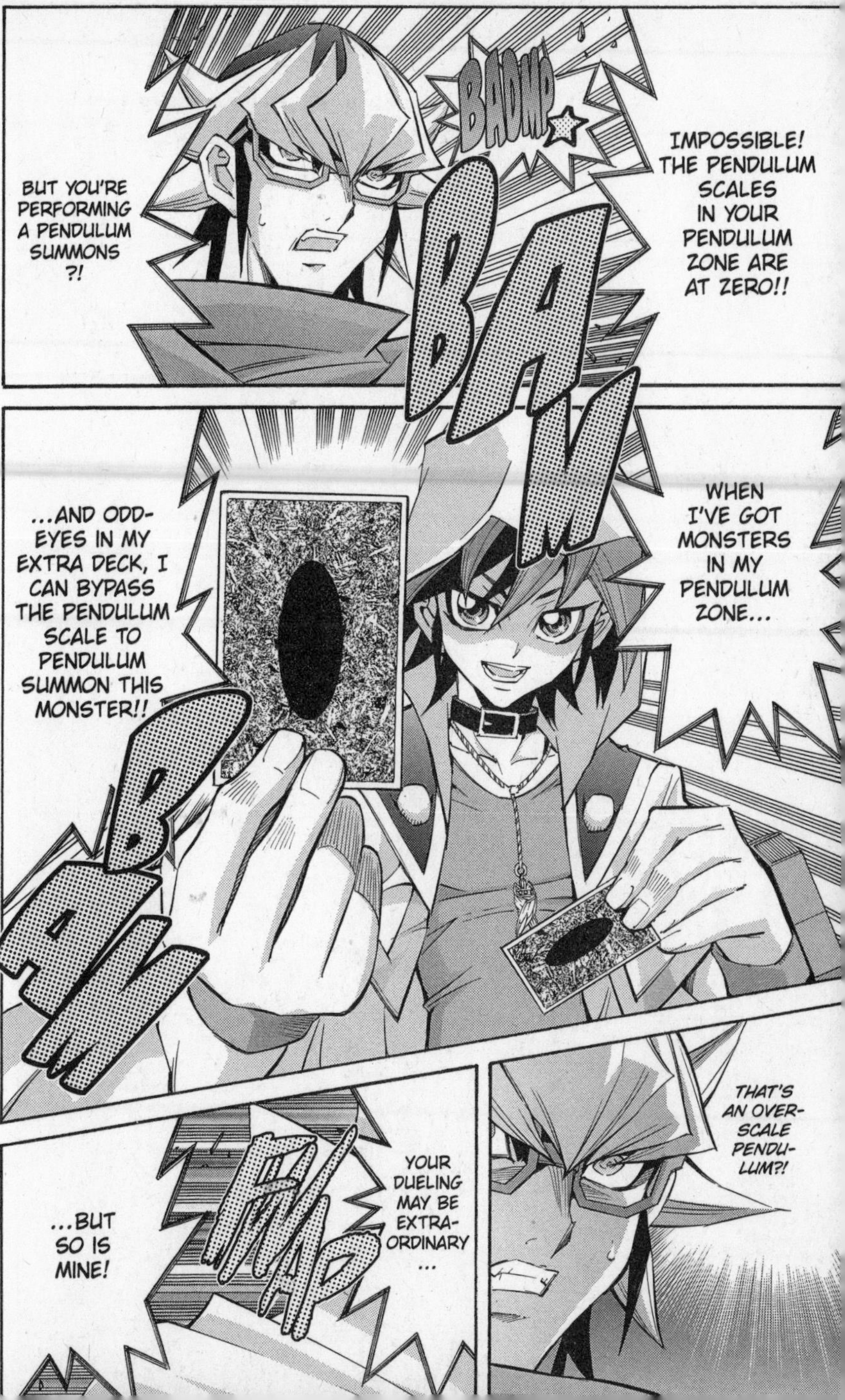
BADOMP
IMPOSSIBLE! THE PENDULUM SCALES IN YOUR PENDULUM ZONE ARE AT ZERO!!
BUT YOU'RE PERFORMING A PENDULUM SUMMONS ?!
BAM
WHEN I'VE GOT MONSTERS IN MY PENDULUM ZONE...
...AND ODD-EYES IN MY EXTRA DECK, I CAN BYPASS THE PENDULUM SCALE TO PENDULUM SUMMON THIS MONSTER!!
BAM
THAT'S AN OVER-SCALE PENDULUM?!
YOUR DUELING MAY BE EXTRA-ORDINARY ...
...BUT SO IS MINE!
FWAP

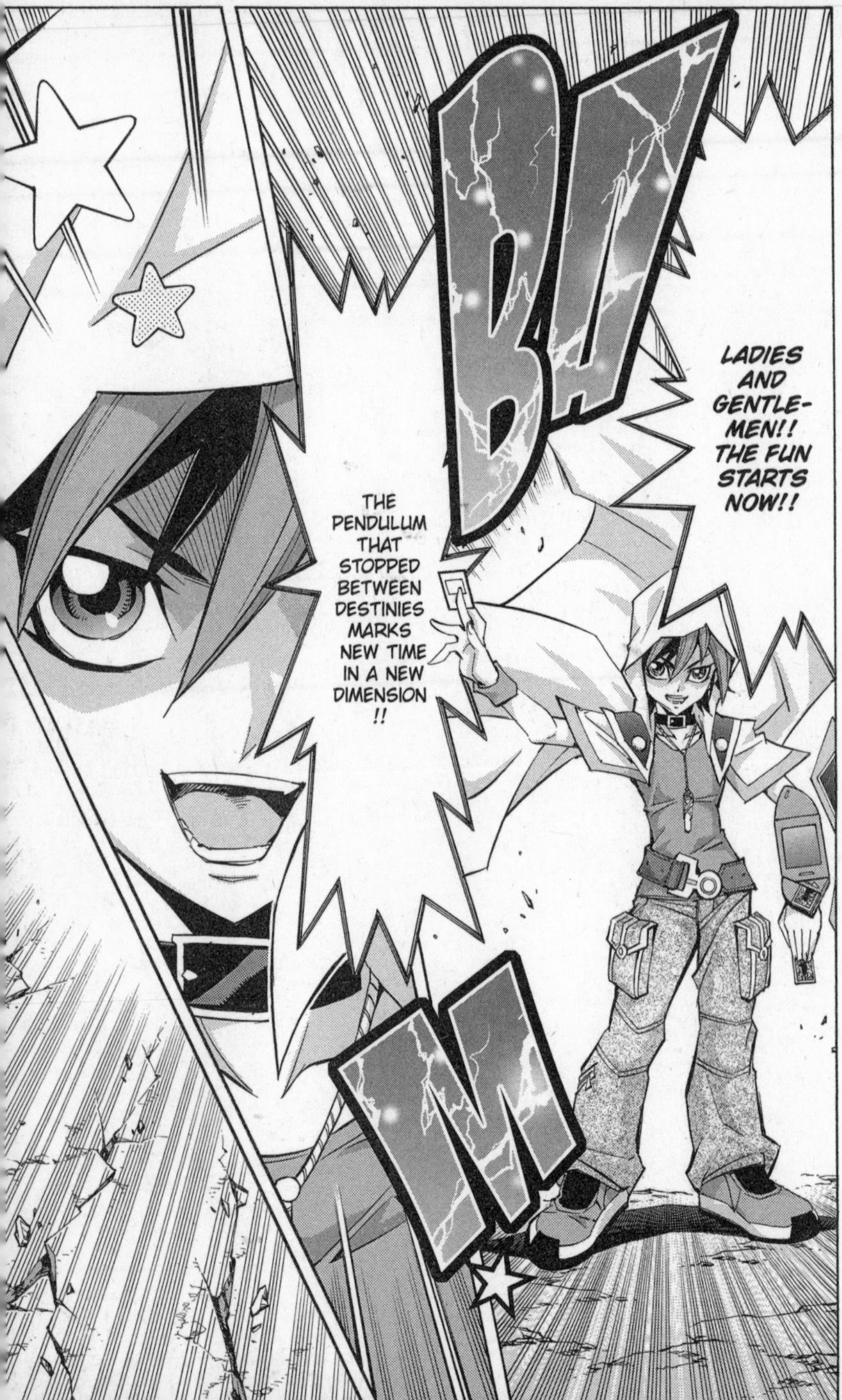

LADIES AND GENTLE-MEN!! THE FUN STARTS NOW!!
BA
M
THE PENDULUM THAT STOPPED BETWEEN DESTINIES MARKS NEW TIME IN A NEW DIMENSION!!

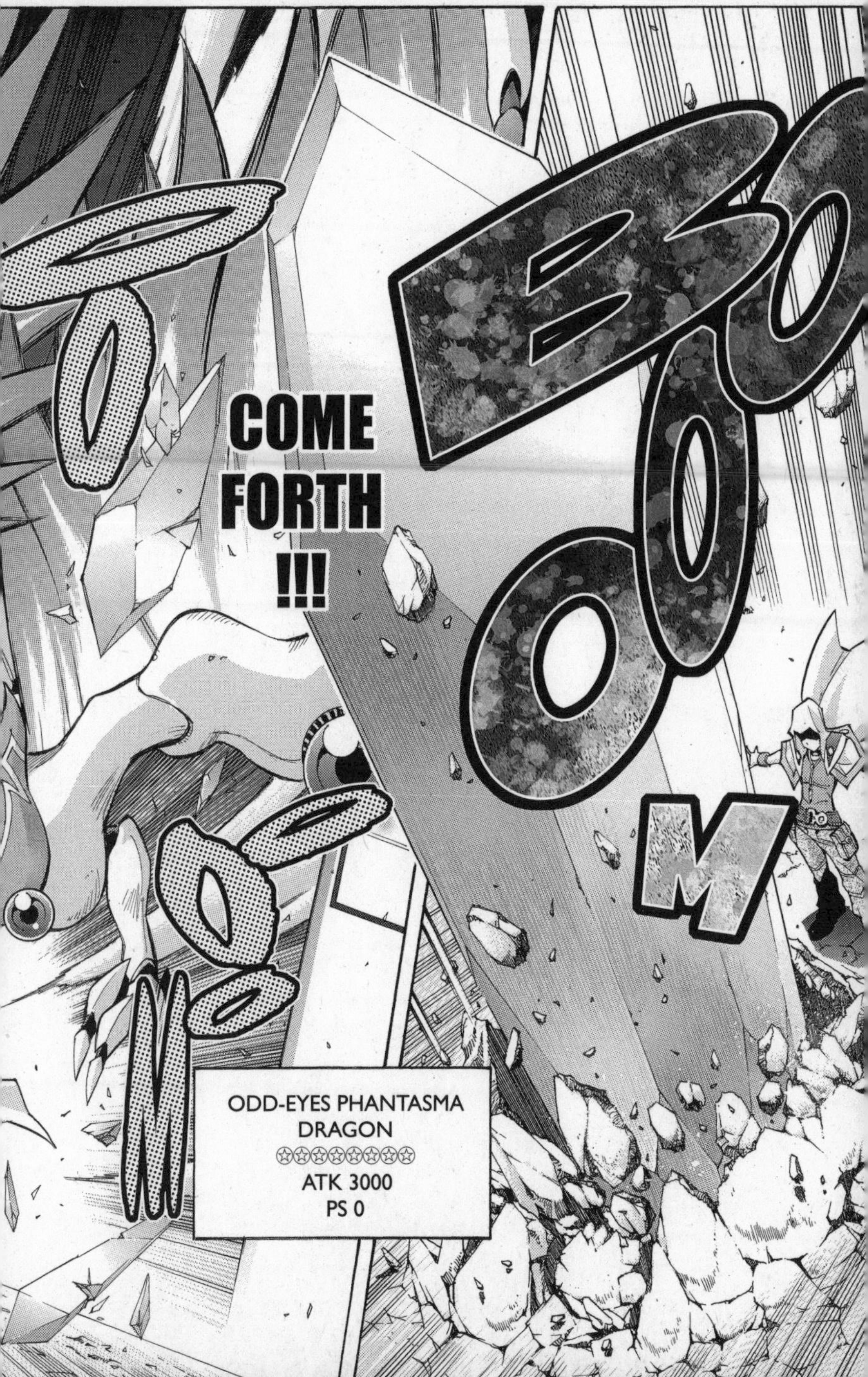
BOOOM
COME FORTH !!!
ODD-EYES PHANTASMA DRAGON
✪✪✪✪✪✪✪✪
ATK 3000
PS 0

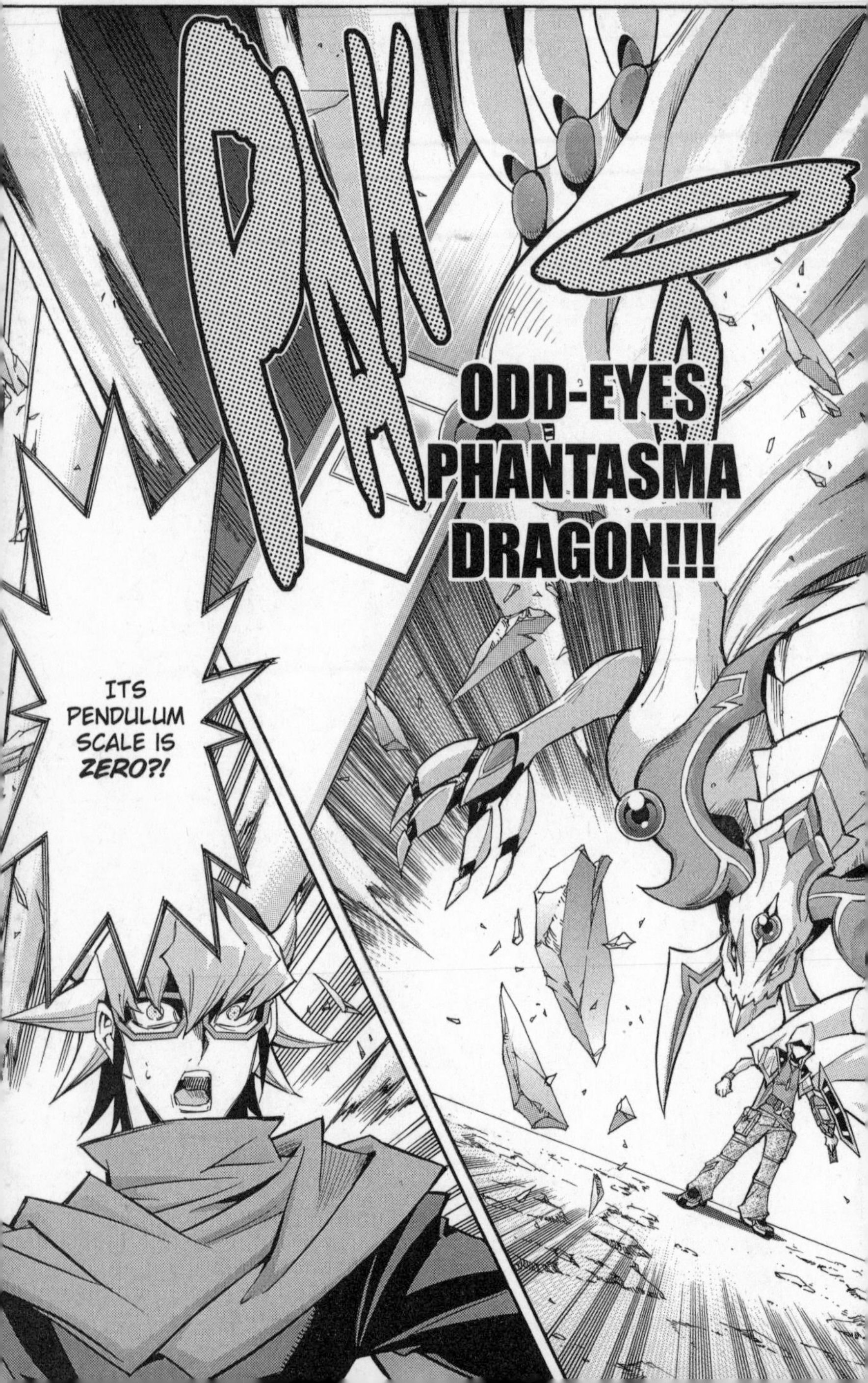
ODD-EYES PHANTASMA DRAGON!!!
ITS PENDULUM SCALE IS ZERO?!

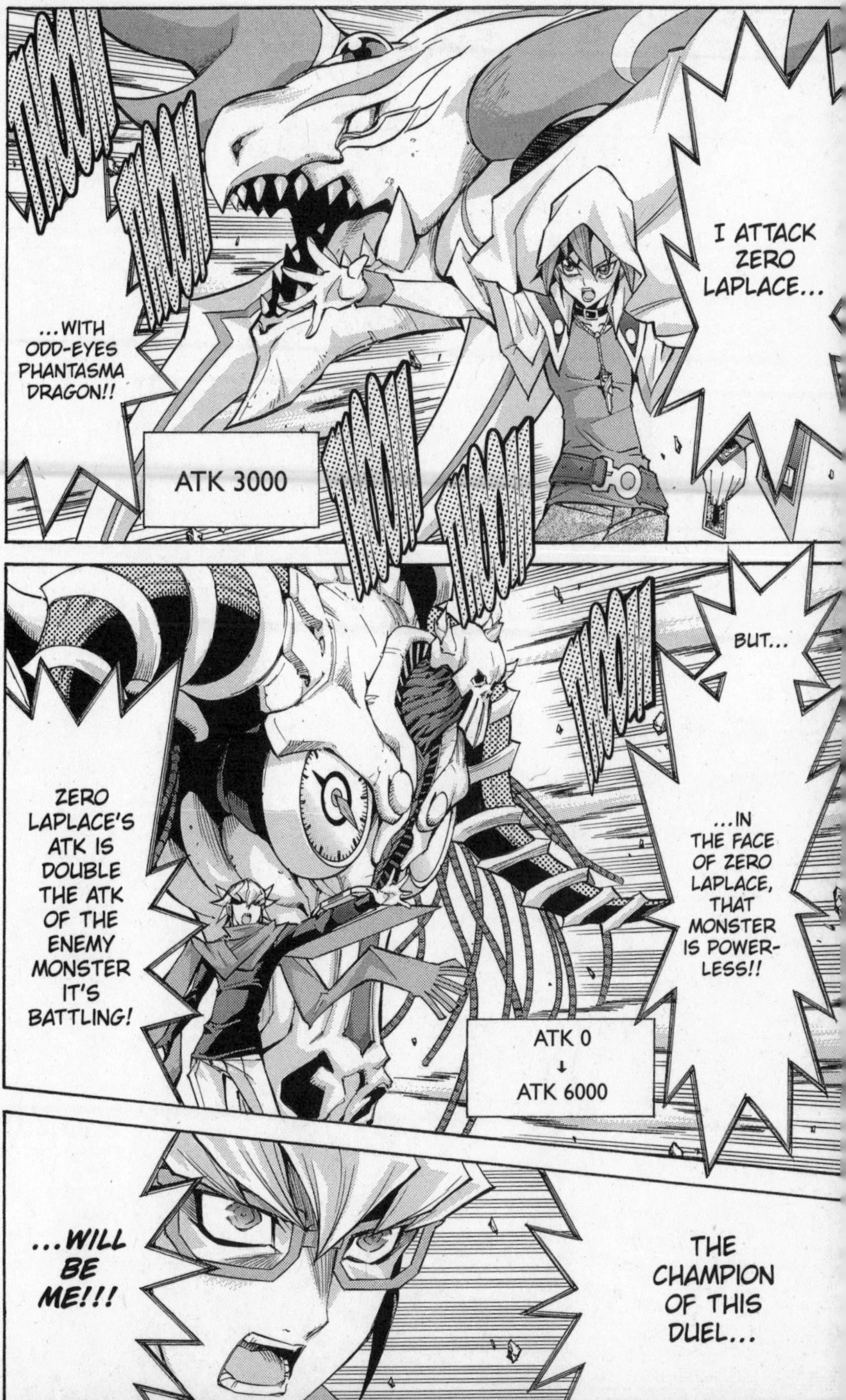
I ATTACK ZERO LAPLACE...
...WITH ODD-EYES PHANTASMA DRAGON!!
ATK 3000
BUT...
...IN THE FACE OF ZERO LAPLACE, THAT MONSTER IS POWERLESS!!
ZERO LAPLACE'S ATK IS DOUBLE THE ATK OF THE ENEMY MONSTER IT'S BATTLING!
ATK 0
↓
ATK 6000
THE CHAMPION OF THIS DUEL...
...WILL BE ME!!!

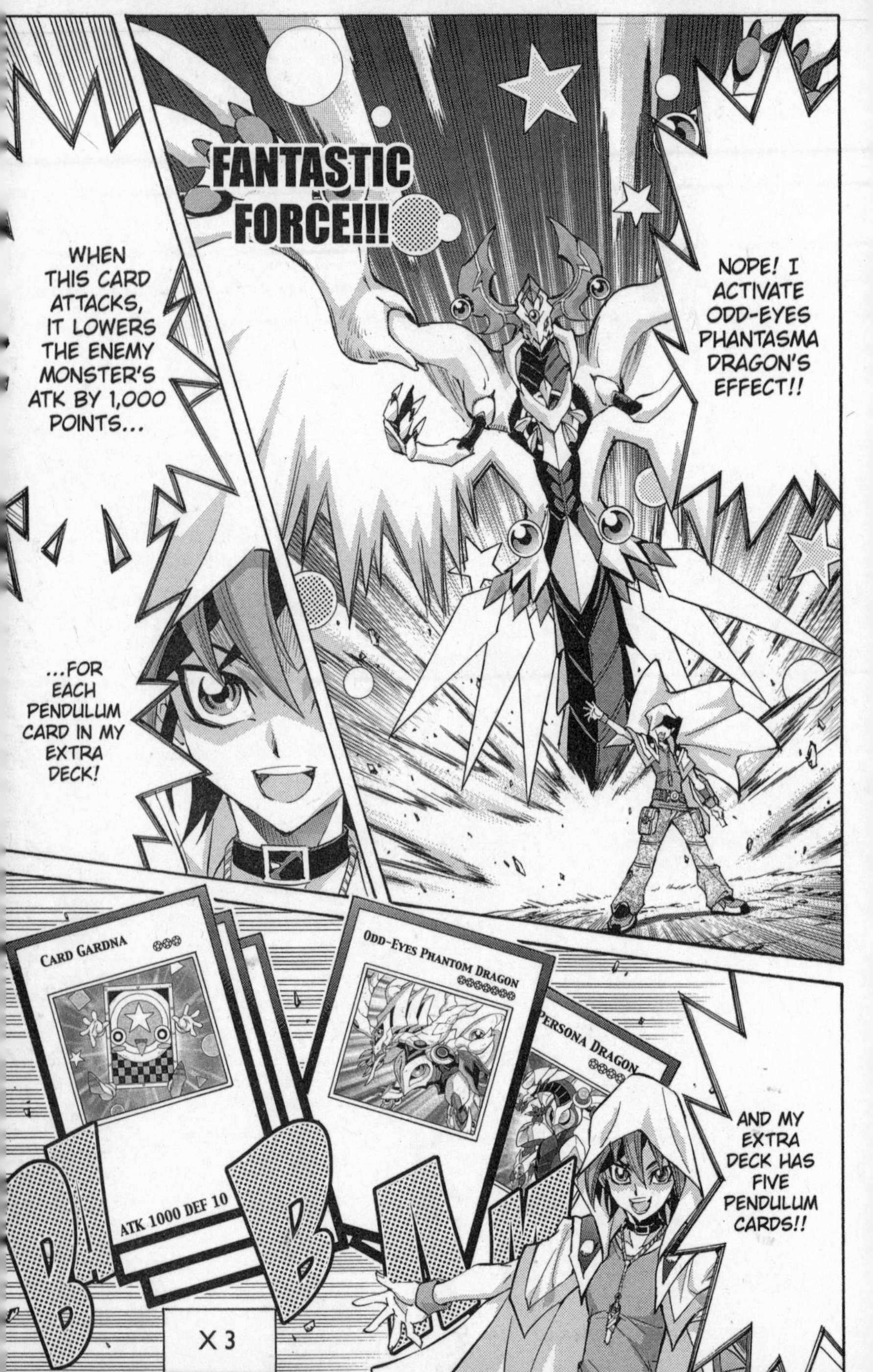
FANTASTIC FORCE!!!
NOPE! I ACTIVATE ODD-EYES PHANTASMA DRAGON'S EFFECT!!
WHEN THIS CARD ATTACKS, IT LOWERS THE ENEMY MONSTER'S ATK BY 1,000 POINTS...
...FOR EACH PENDULUM CARD IN MY EXTRA DECK!
AND MY EXTRA DECK HAS FIVE PENDULUM CARDS!!
PERSONA DRAGON
ODD-EYES PHANTOM DRAGON
CARD GARDNA
ATK 1000 DEF 10
X 3

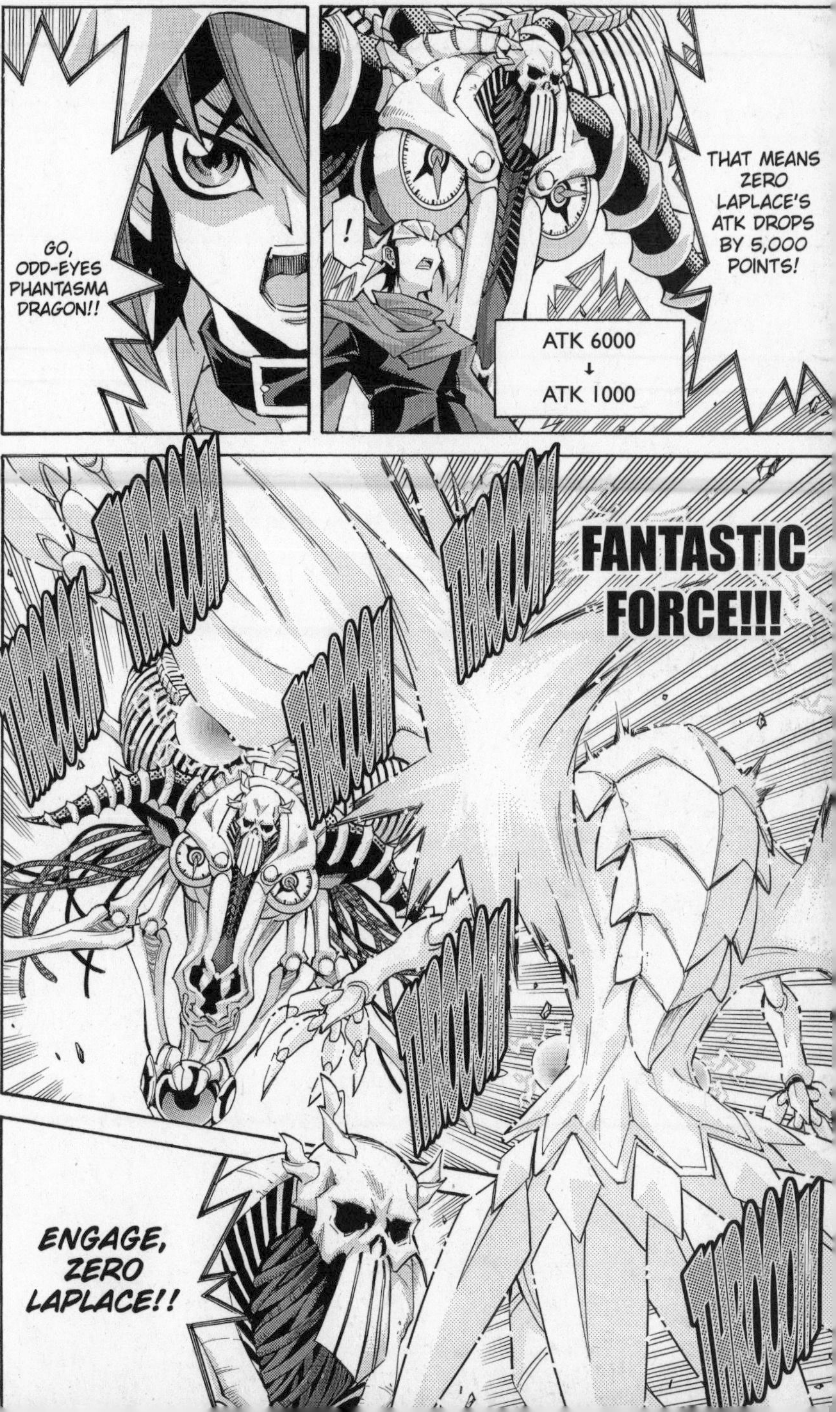
THAT MEANS ZERO LAPLACE'S ATK DROPS BY 5,000 POINTS!
!
ATK 6000 ↓ ATK 1000
GO, ODD-EYES PHANTASMA DRAGON!!
FANTASTIC FORCE!!!
ENGAGE, ZERO LAPLACE!!

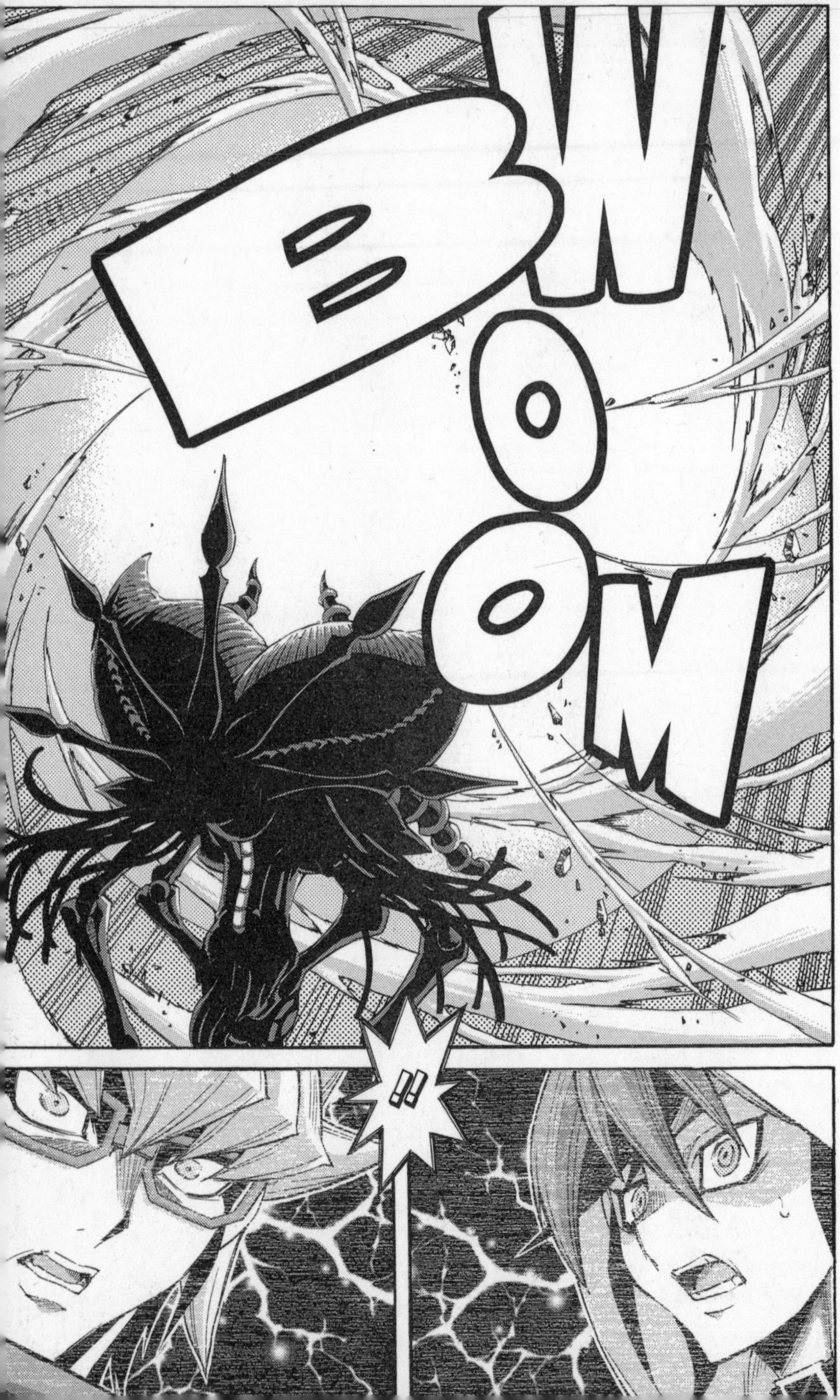
BWOOOM
!!

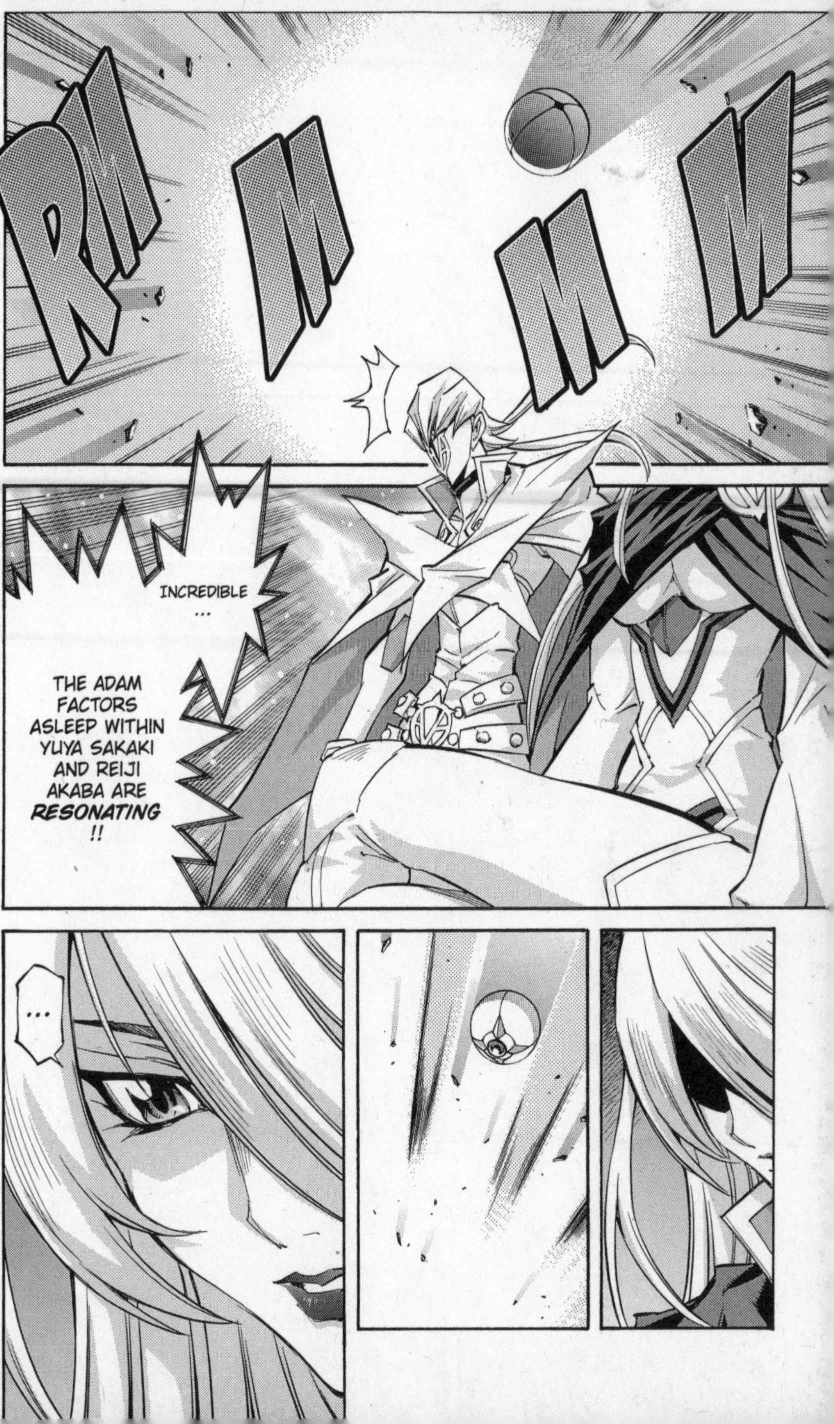
RMMMM
INCREDIBLE ...
THE ADAM FACTORS ASLEEP WITHIN YUYA SAKAKI AND REIJI AKABA ARE ***RESONATING*** !!
...

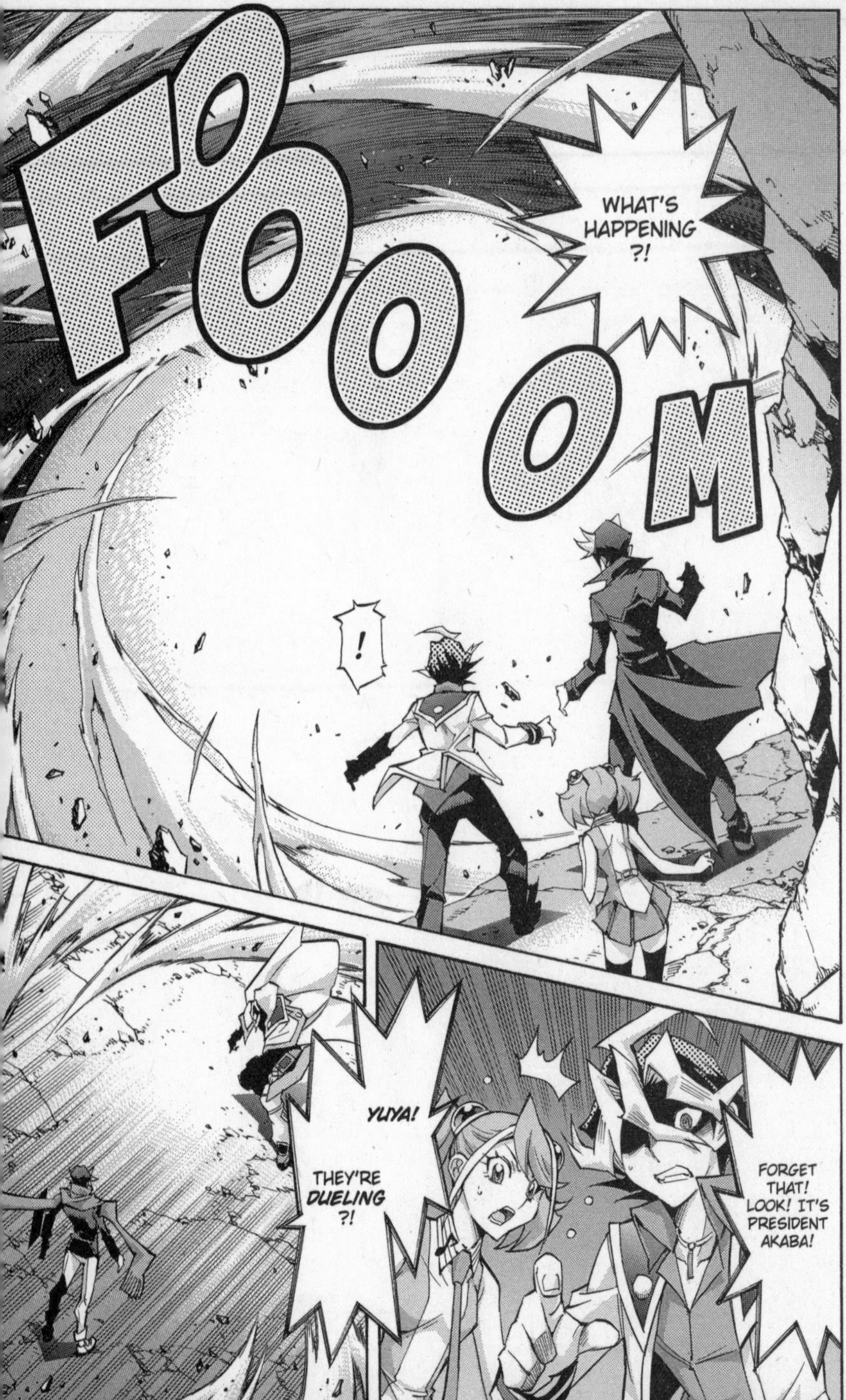
WHAT'S HAPPENING ?!
FOOOOM
!
YUYA!
THEY'RE DUELING ?!
FORGET THAT! LOOK! IT'S PRESIDENT AKABA!

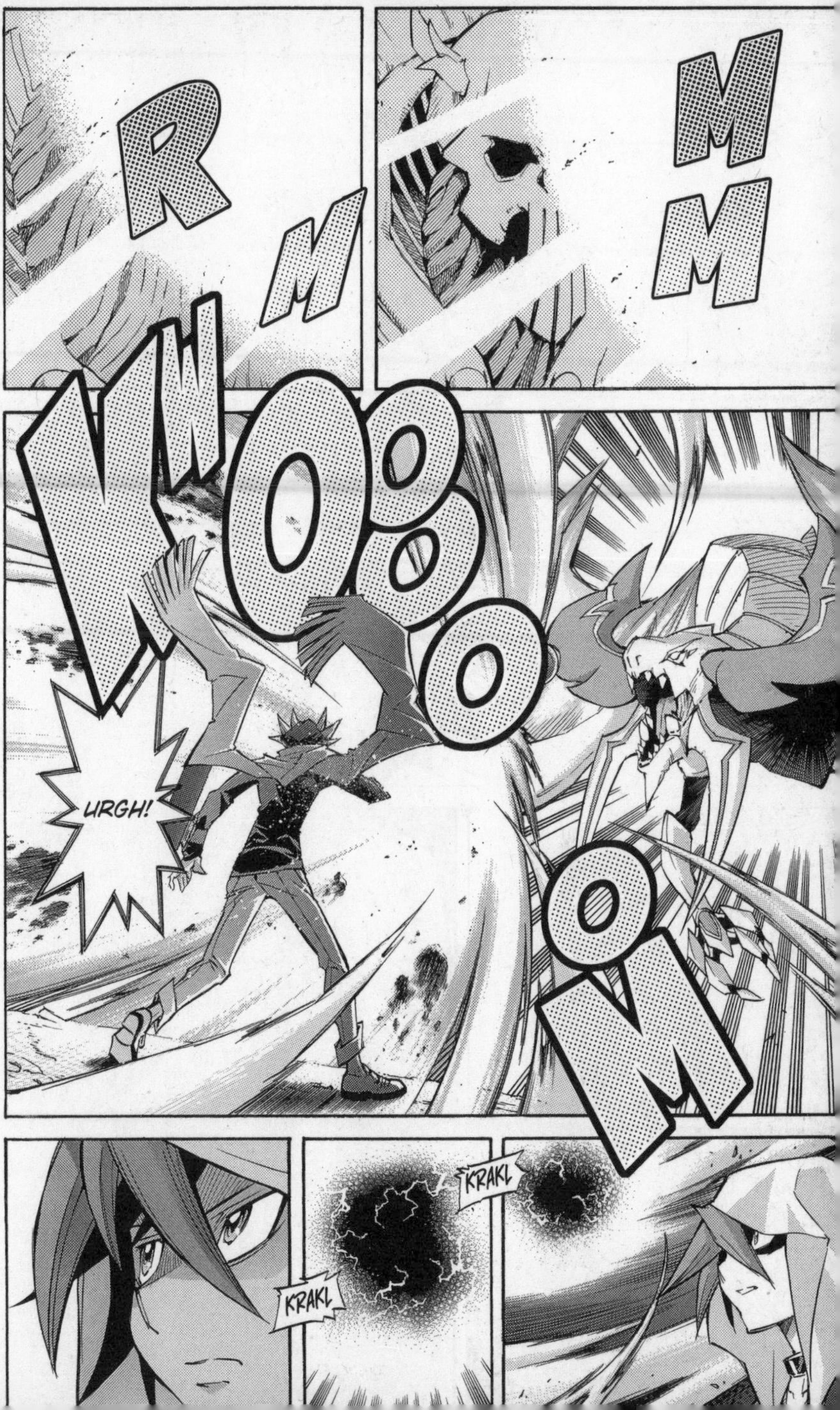
MMM
RM
WHOOOOOOM
URGH!
KRAKL
KRAKL

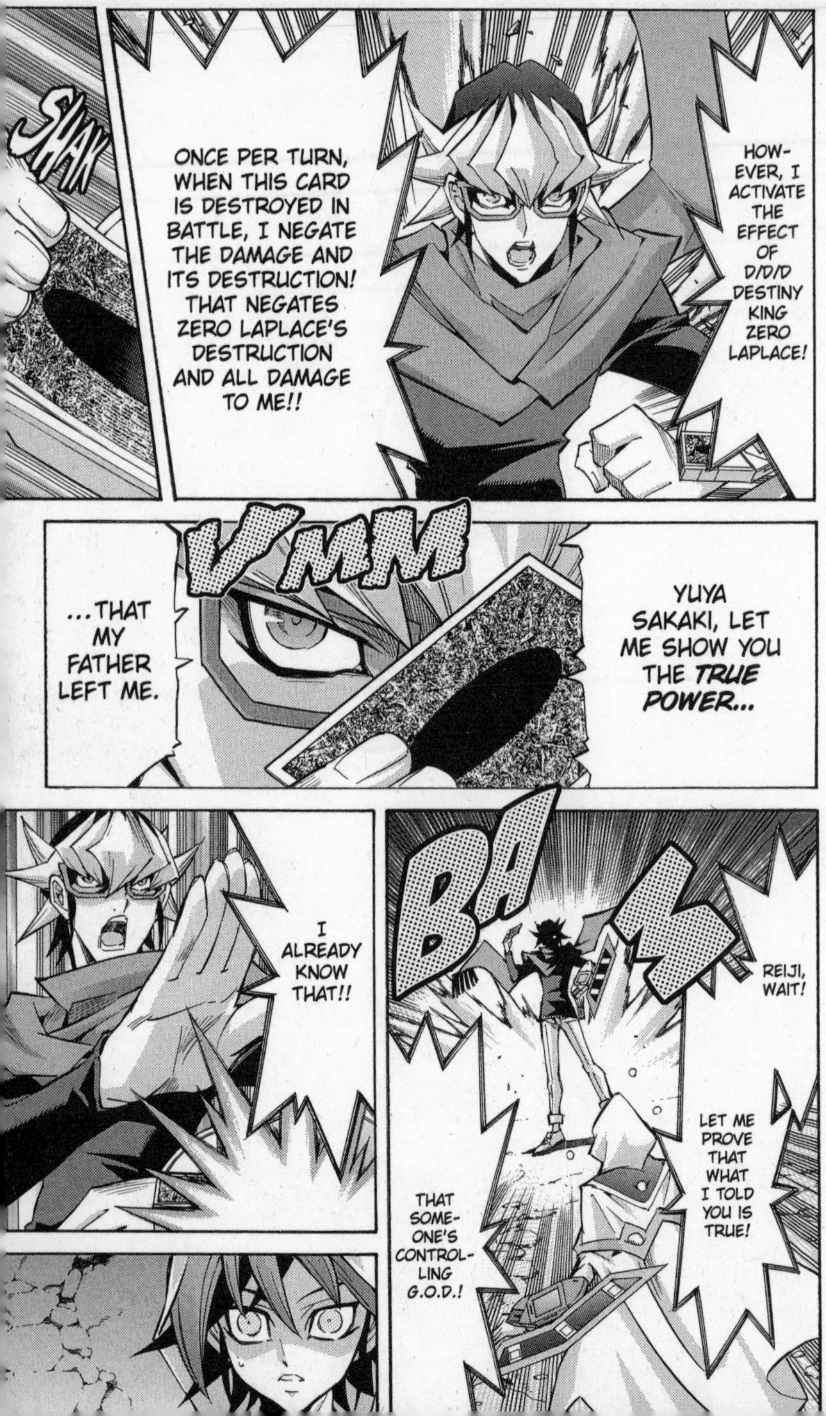
HOW-EVER, I ACTIVATE THE EFFECT OF D/D/D DESTINY KING ZERO LAPLACE!
ONCE PER TURN, WHEN THIS CARD IS DESTROYED IN BATTLE, I NEGATE THE DAMAGE AND ITS DESTRUCTION! THAT NEGATES ZERO LAPLACE'S DESTRUCTION AND ALL DAMAGE TO ME!!
SHAK
VMM
YUYA SAKAKI, LET ME SHOW YOU THE *TRUE POWER*...
...THAT MY FATHER LEFT ME.
BAM
REIJI, WAIT!
LET ME PROVE THAT WHAT I TOLD YOU IS TRUE!
THAT SOME-ONE'S CONTROL-LING G.O.D.!
I ALREADY KNOW THAT!!

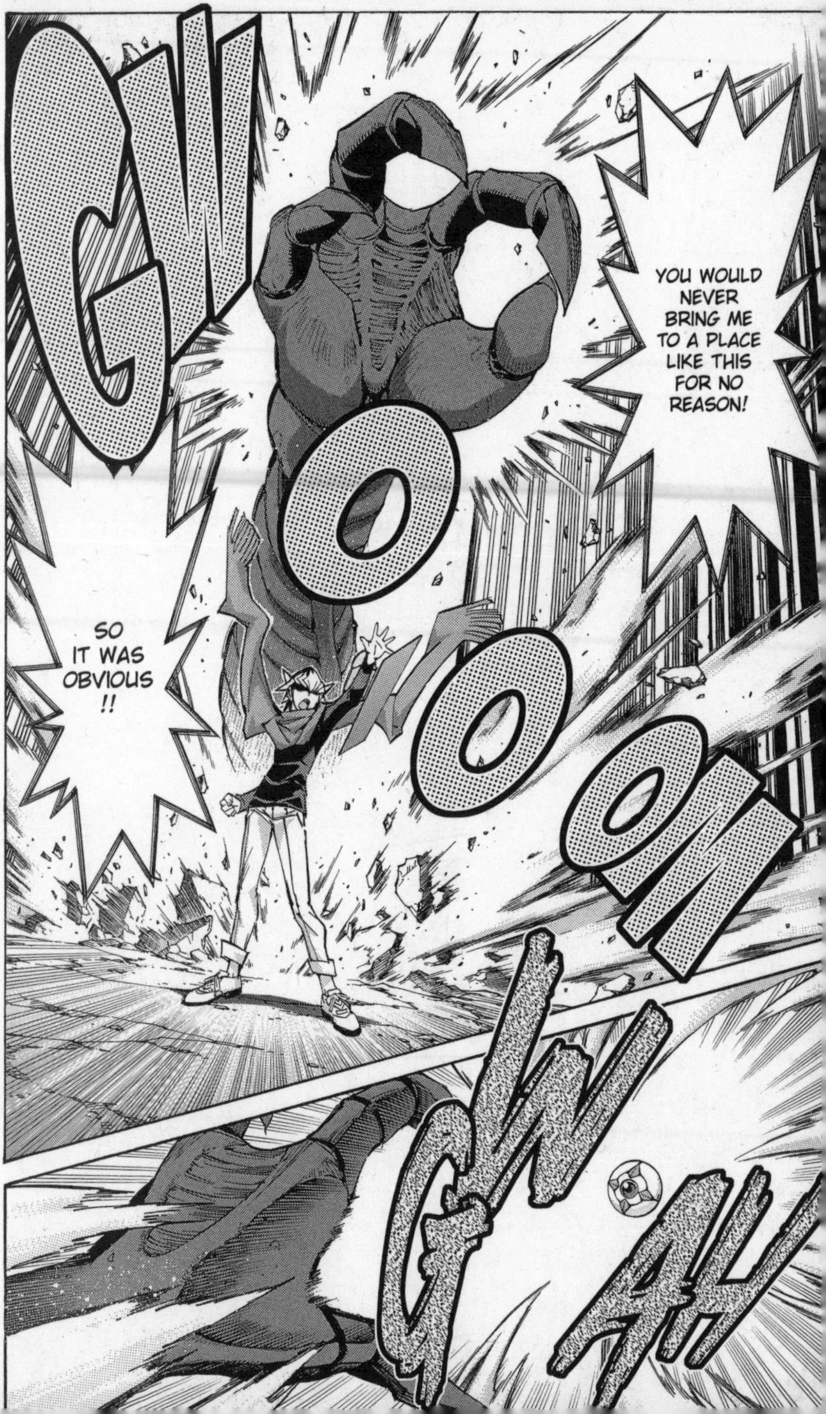
YOU WOULD NEVER BRING ME TO A PLACE LIKE THIS FOR NO REASON!
GWOOOM
SO IT WAS OBVIOUS!!
GWAH

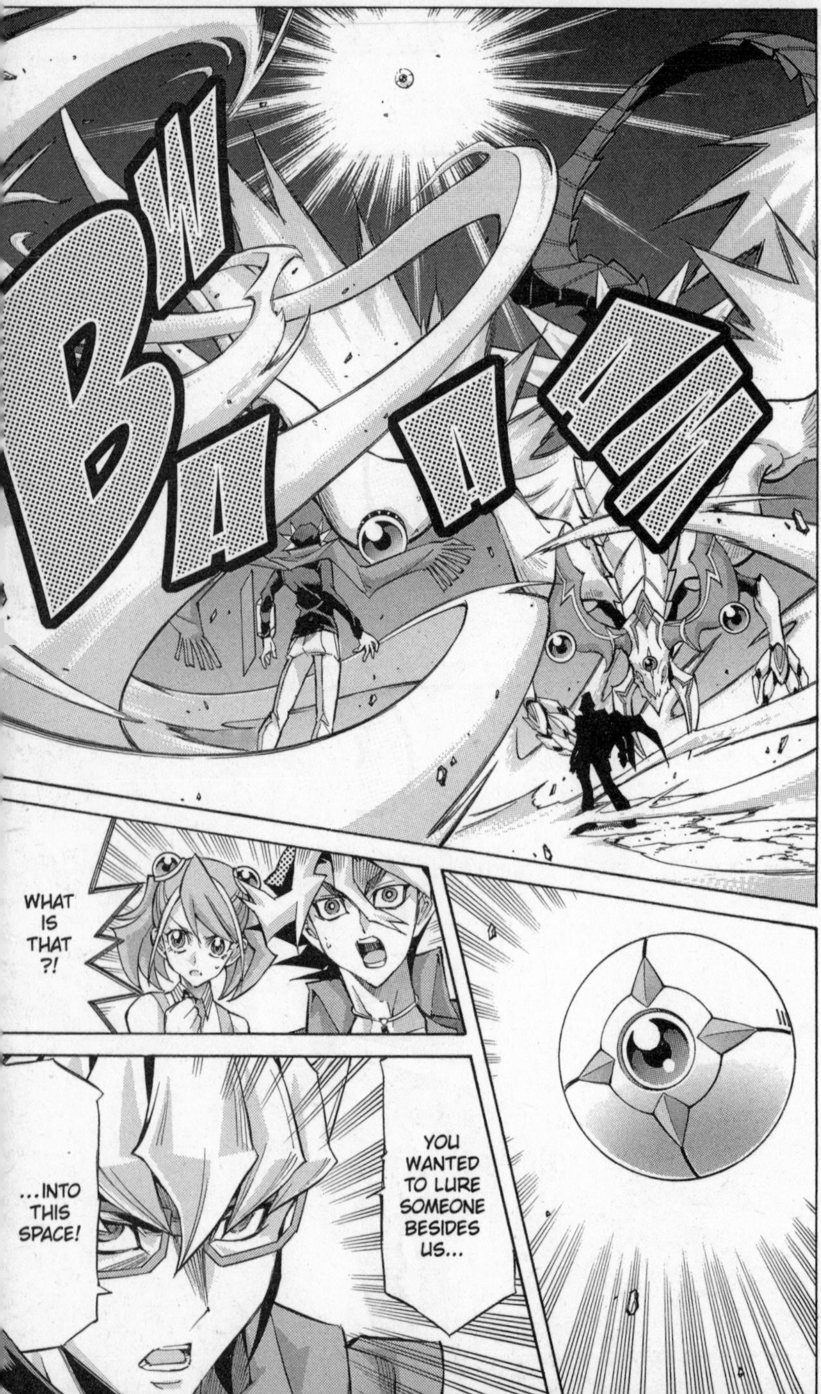
BWAAM!!
WHAT IS THAT?!
YOU WANTED TO LURE SOMEONE BESIDES US...
...INTO THIS SPACE!

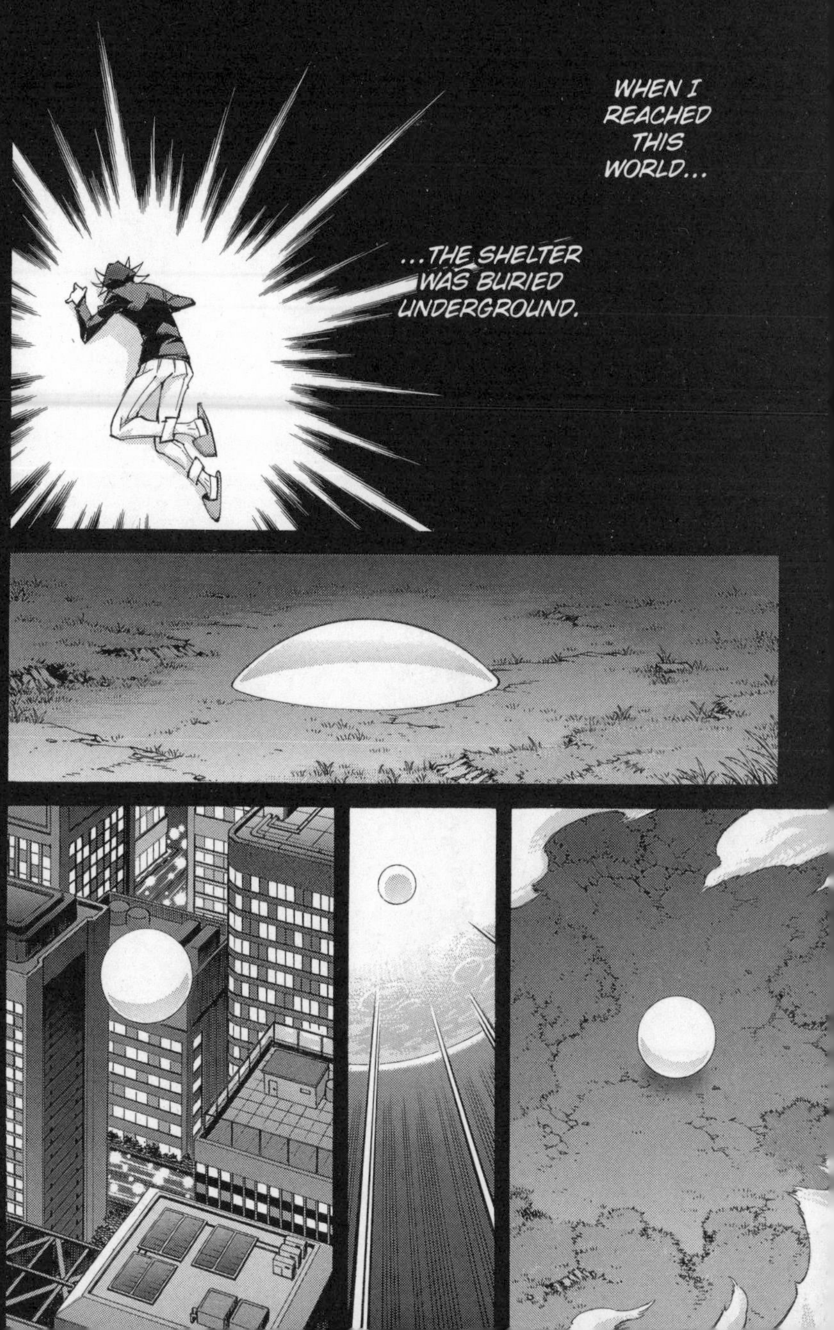
WHEN I REACHED THIS WORLD...
...THE SHELTER WAS BURIED UNDERGROUND.

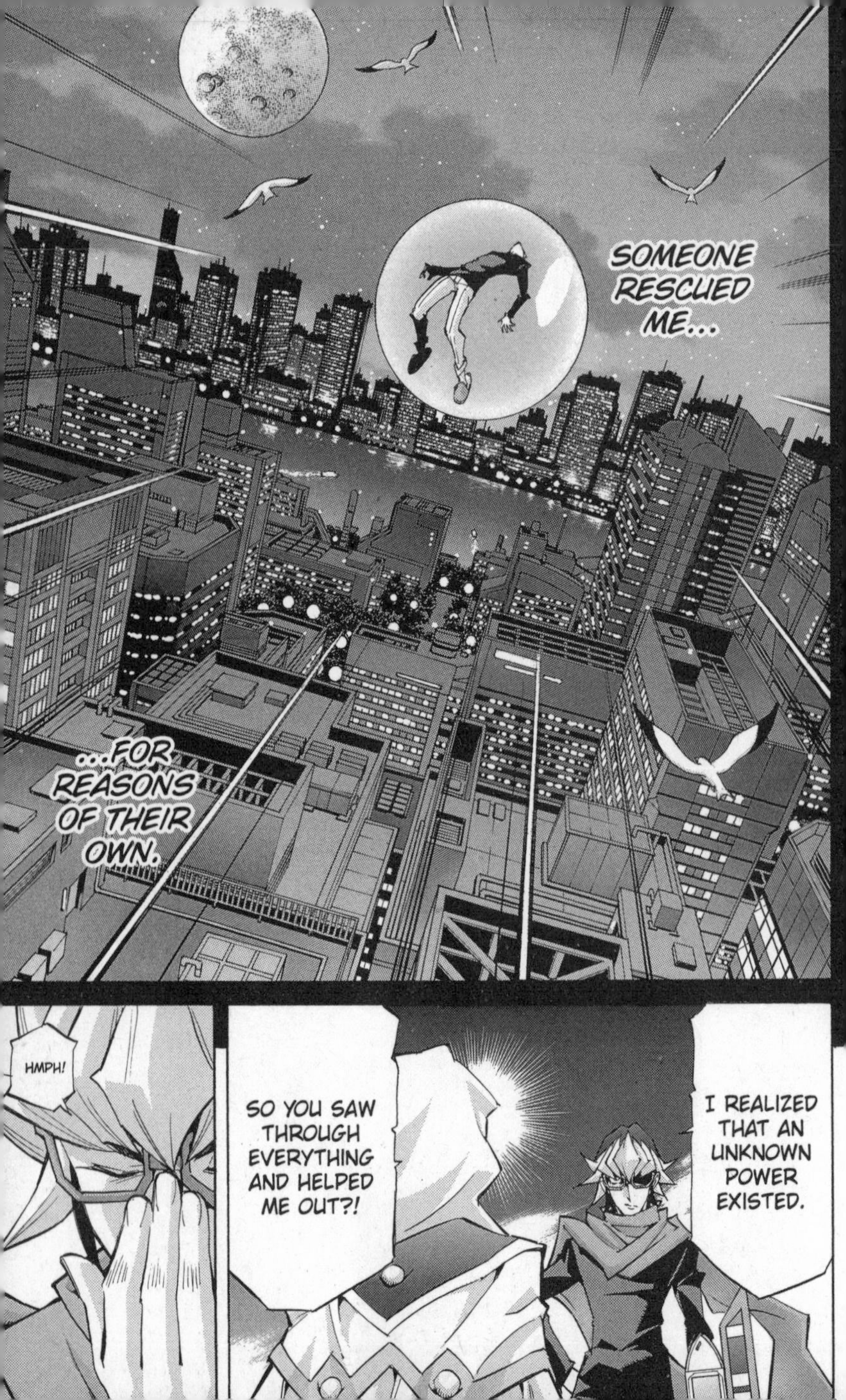
SOMEONE RESCUED ME...
...FOR REASONS OF THEIR OWN.
I REALIZED THAT AN UNKNOWN POWER EXISTED.
SO YOU SAW THROUGH EVERYTHING AND HELPED ME OUT?!
HMPH!

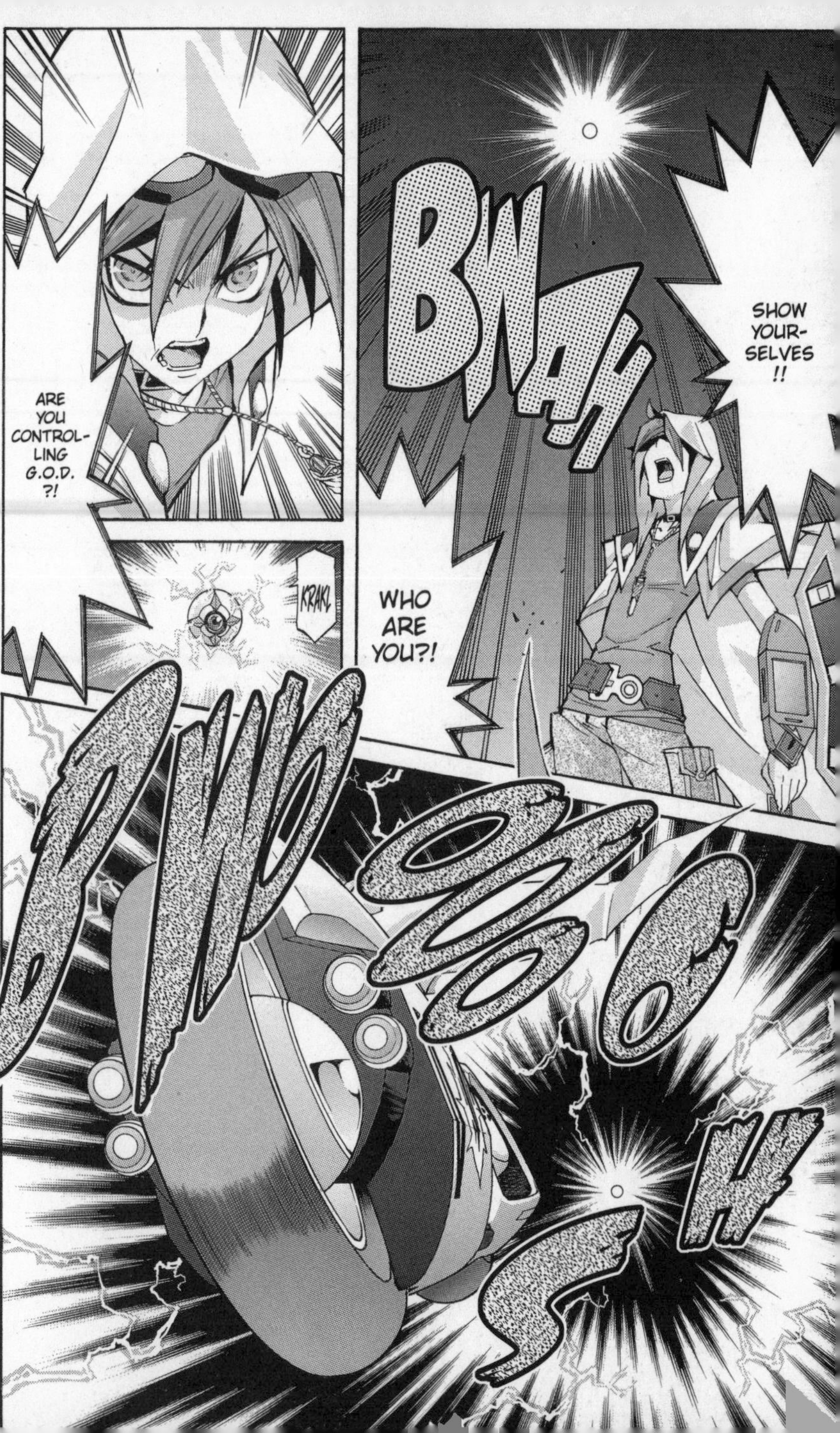
BWAH!!
SHOW YOUR-SELVES!!
WHO ARE YOU?!
ARE YOU CONTROL-LING G.O.D.?!
KRAK!
DWOOOSH

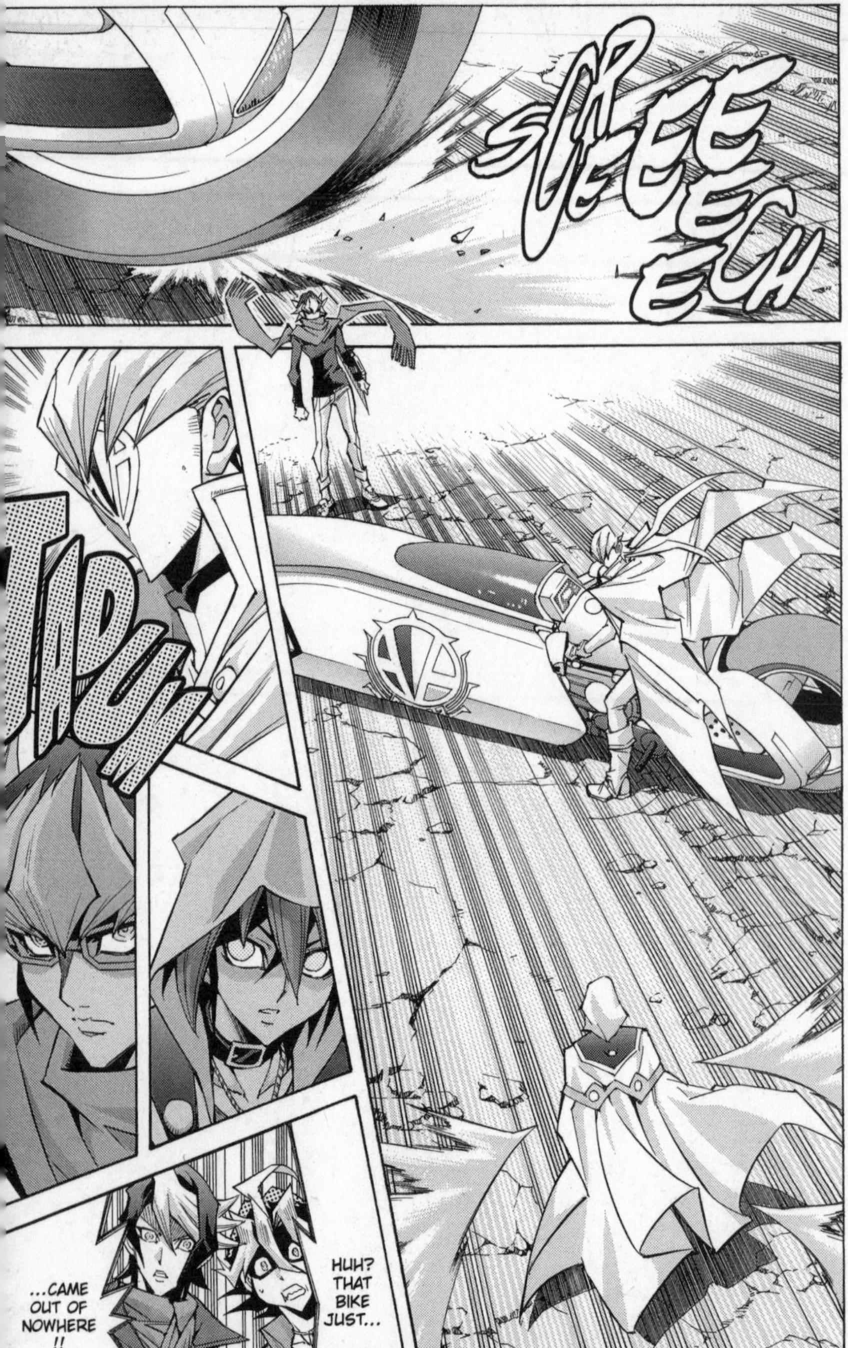
SCREEEEEECH
THDUNK
HUH? THAT BIKE JUST...
...CAME OUT OF NOWHERE!!

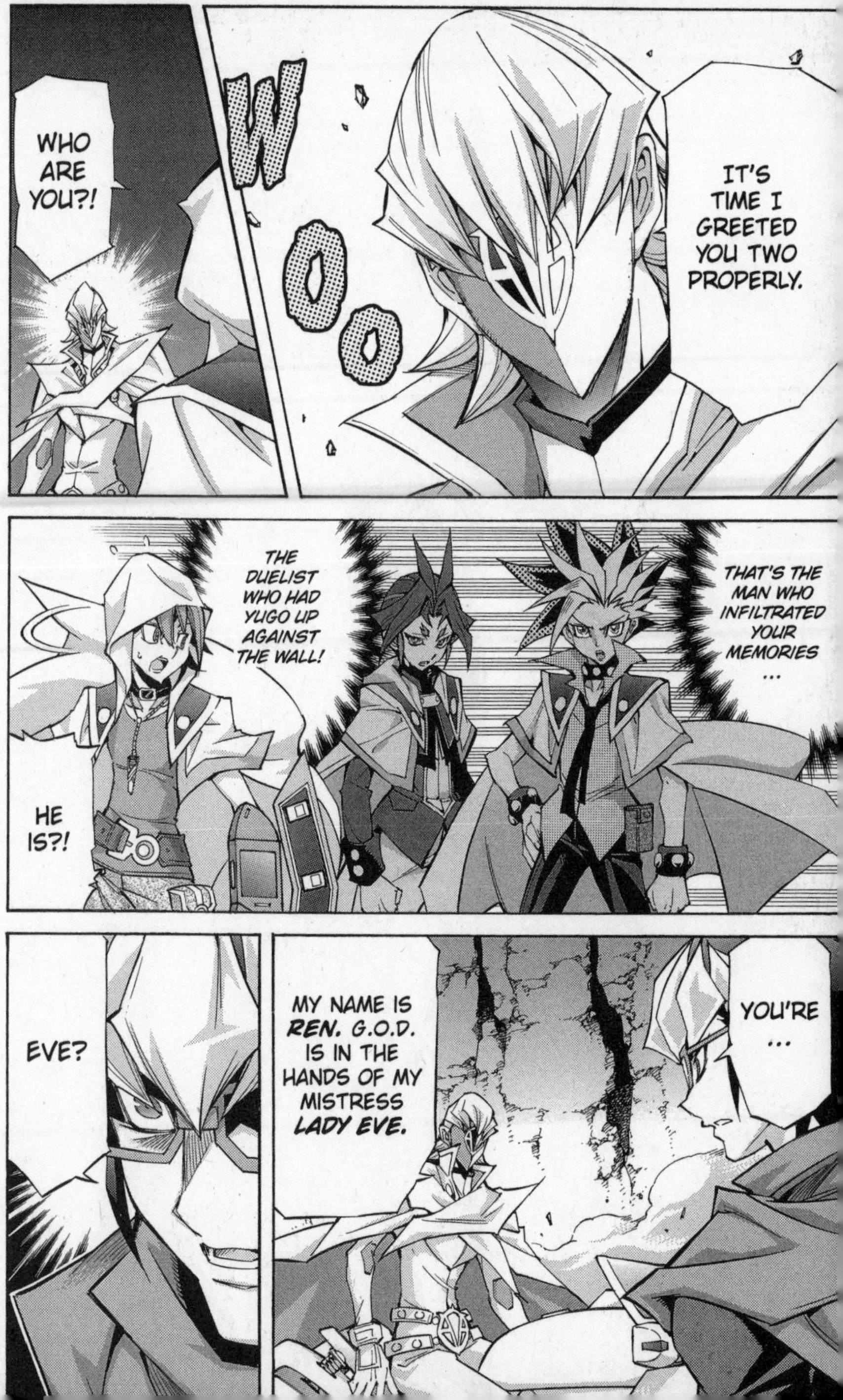
IT'S TIME I GREETED YOU TWO PROPERLY.
WOOO
WHO ARE YOU?!
THAT'S THE MAN WHO INFILTRATED YOUR MEMORIES...
THE DUELIST WHO HAD YUGO UP AGAINST THE WALL!
HE IS?!
YOU'RE...
MY NAME IS REN. G.O.D. IS IN THE HANDS OF MY MISTRESS LADY EVE.
EVE?

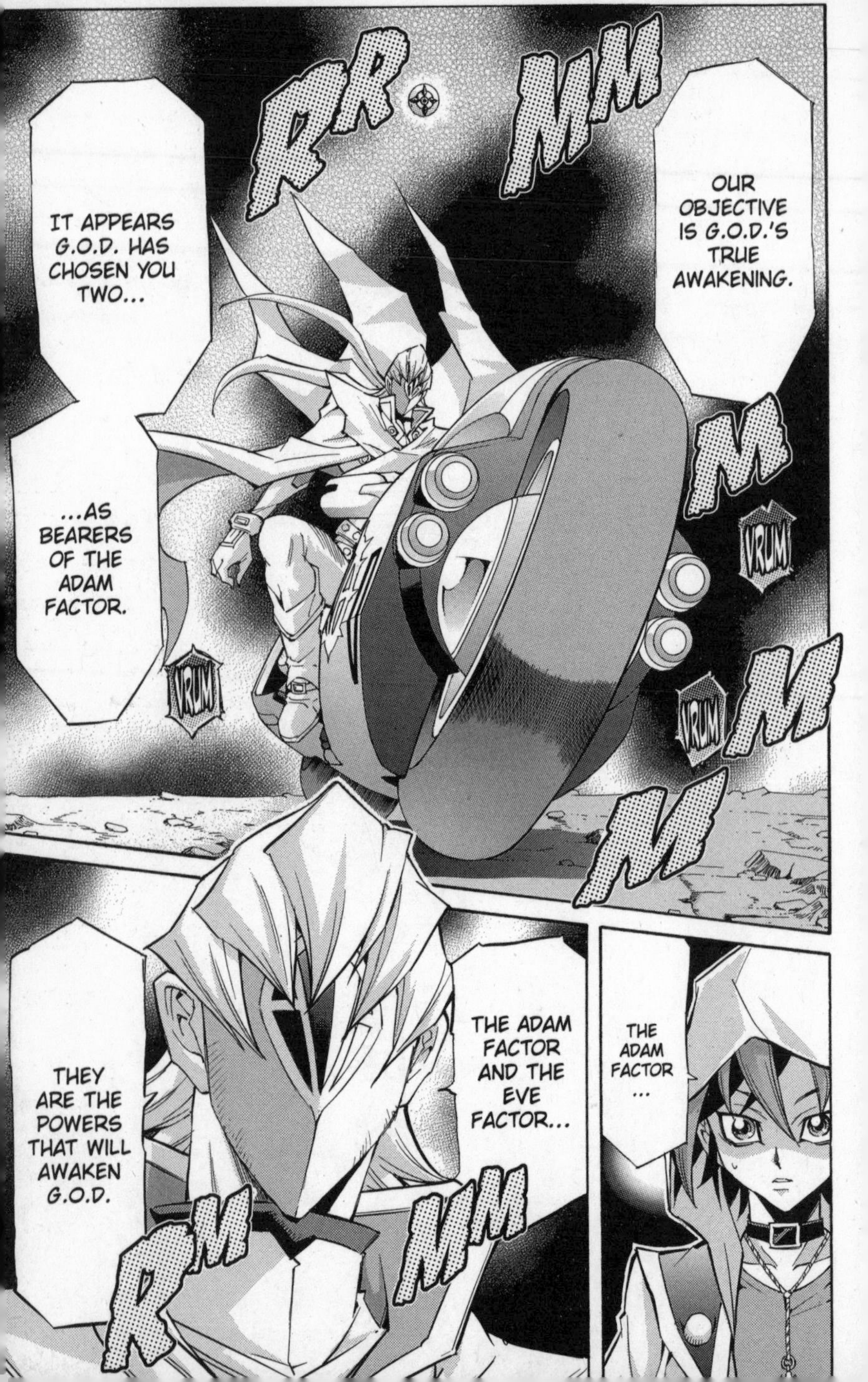
RR MM
OUR OBJECTIVE IS G.O.D.'S TRUE AWAKENING.
IT APPEARS G.O.D. HAS CHOSEN YOU TWO...
...AS BEARERS OF THE ADAM FACTOR.
M
VRUM
VRUM
M M M
VRUM
THE ADAM FACTOR...
THE ADAM FACTOR AND THE EVE FACTOR...
THEY ARE THE POWERS THAT WILL AWAKEN G.O.D.
RMMM

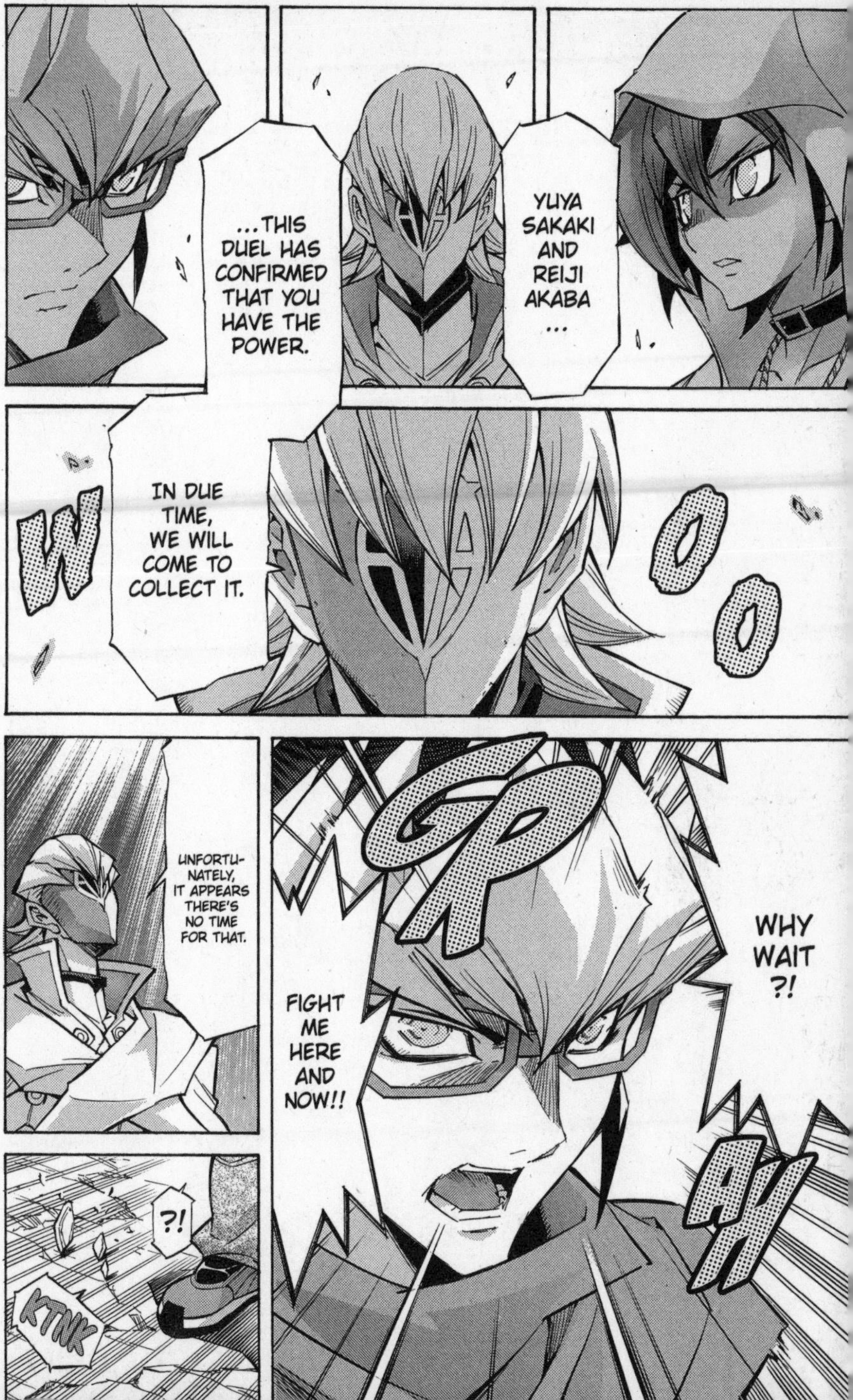

YUYA SAKAKI AND REIJI AKABA...
...THIS DUEL HAS CONFIRMED THAT YOU HAVE THE POWER.
IN DUE TIME, WE WILL COME TO COLLECT IT.
WOO
GR
WHY WAIT?!
FIGHT ME HERE AND NOW!!
AH
UNFORTU-NATELY, IT APPEARS THERE'S NO TIME FOR THAT.
?!
KTNK

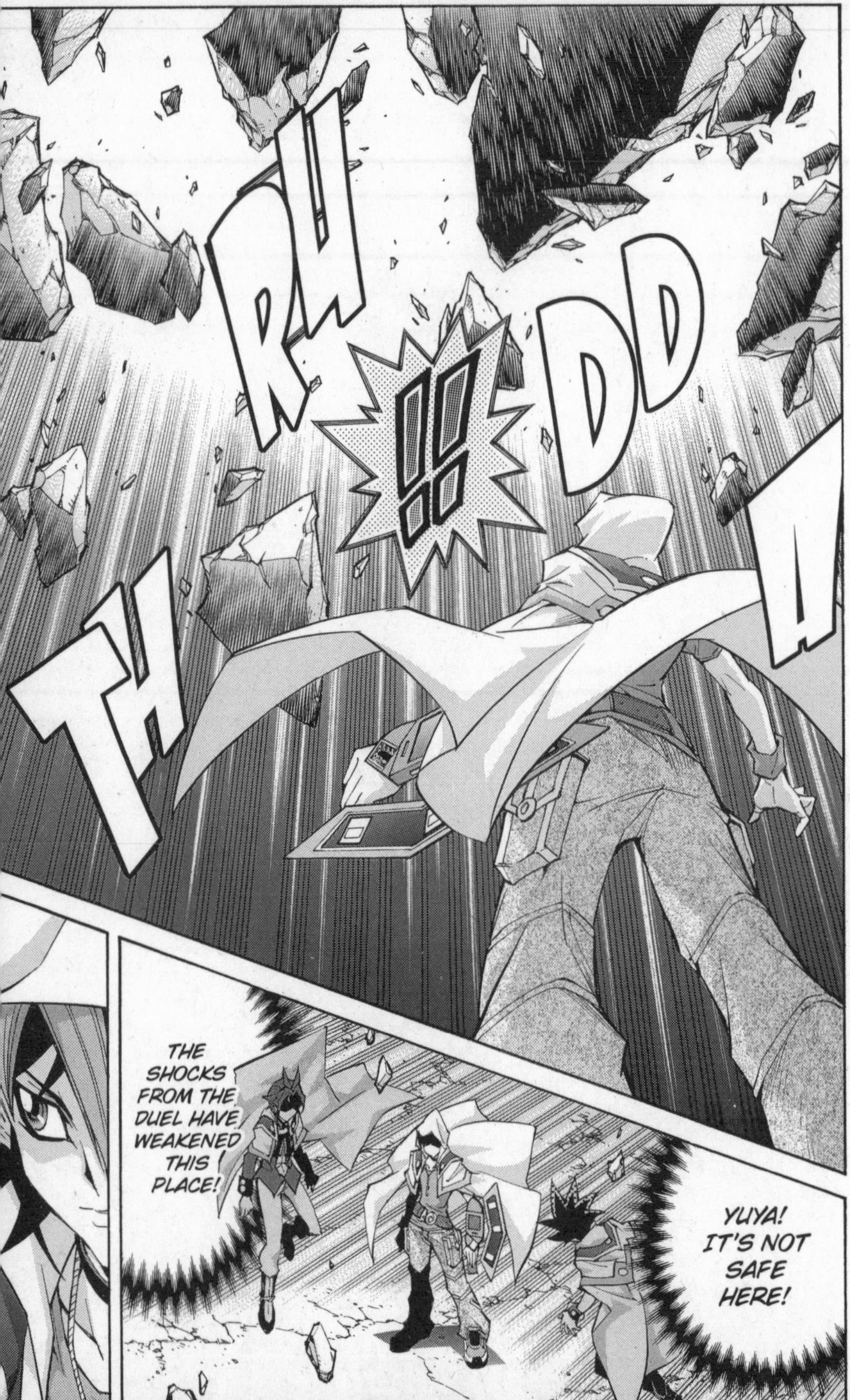
YUYA! IT'S NOT SAFE HERE!
THE SHOCKS FROM THE DUEL HAVE WEAKENED THIS PLACE!

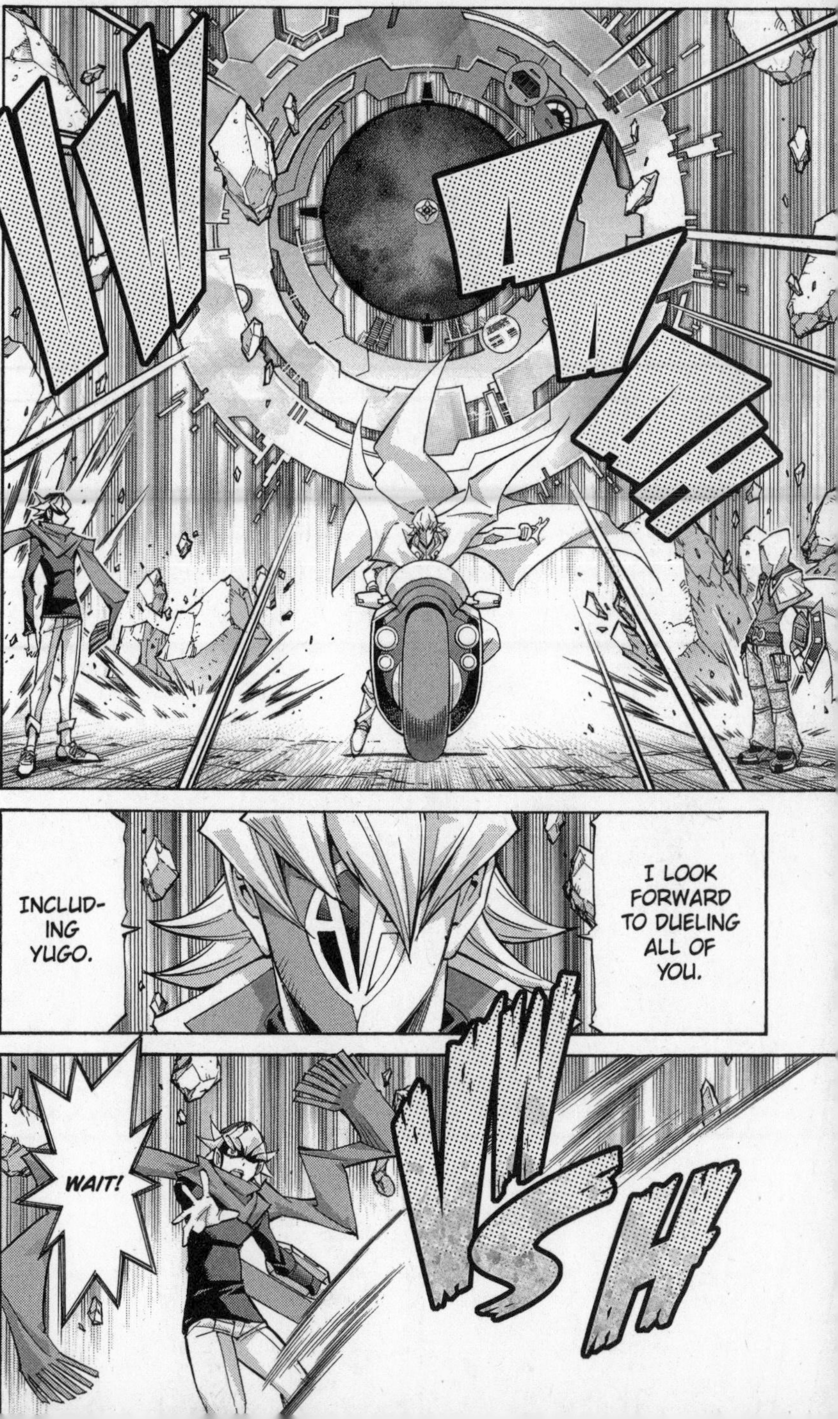
I LOOK FORWARD TO DUELING ALL OF YOU.
INCLUD-ING YUGO.
VWSH
WAIT!

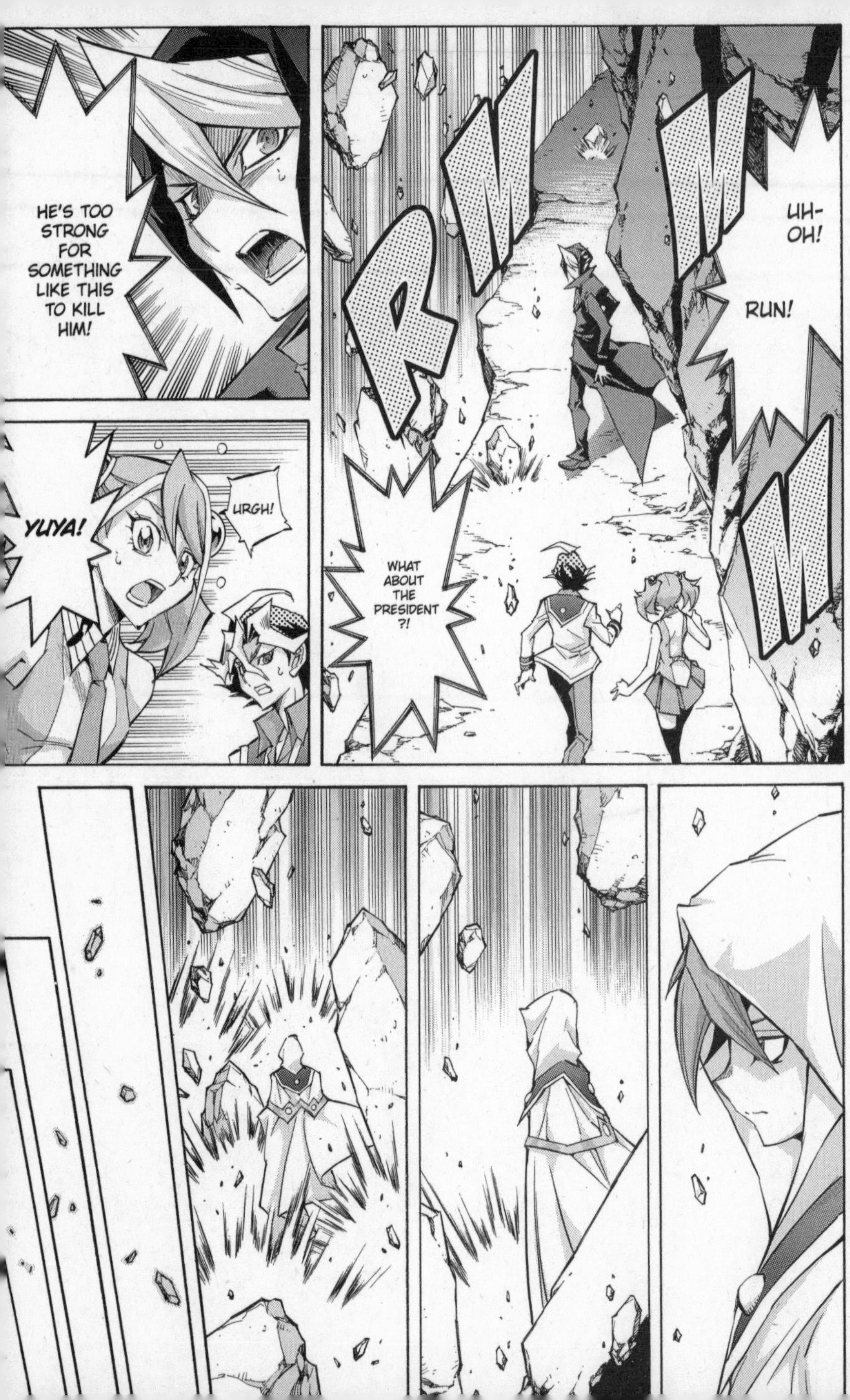
UH-OH!
RUN!
RMMMM
WHAT ABOUT THE PRESIDENT?!
HE'S TOO STRONG FOR SOMETHING LIKE THIS TO KILL HIM!
URGH!
YUYA!

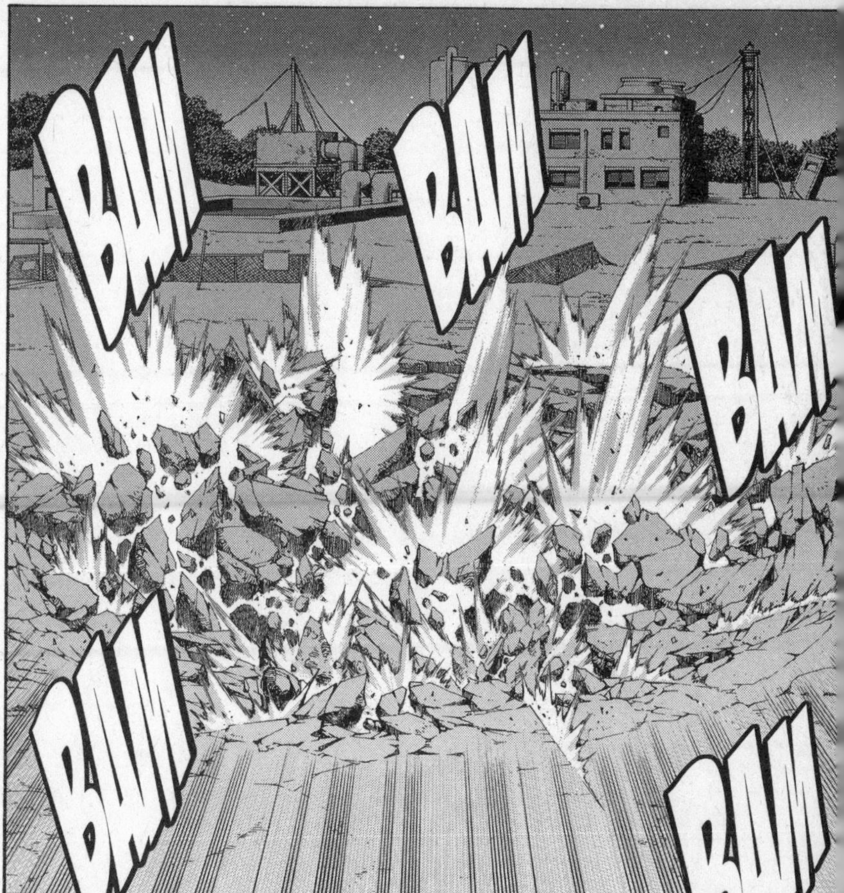
BAM
BAM
BAM
BAM
BAM
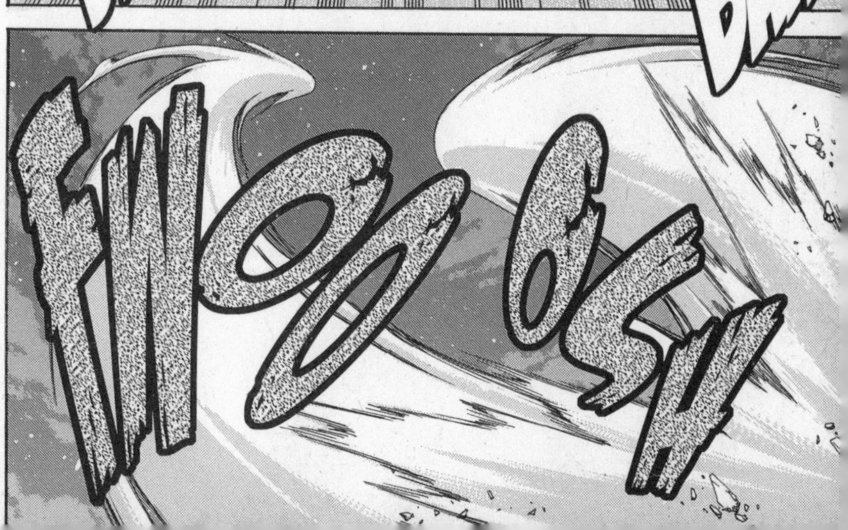
FWOOOSH

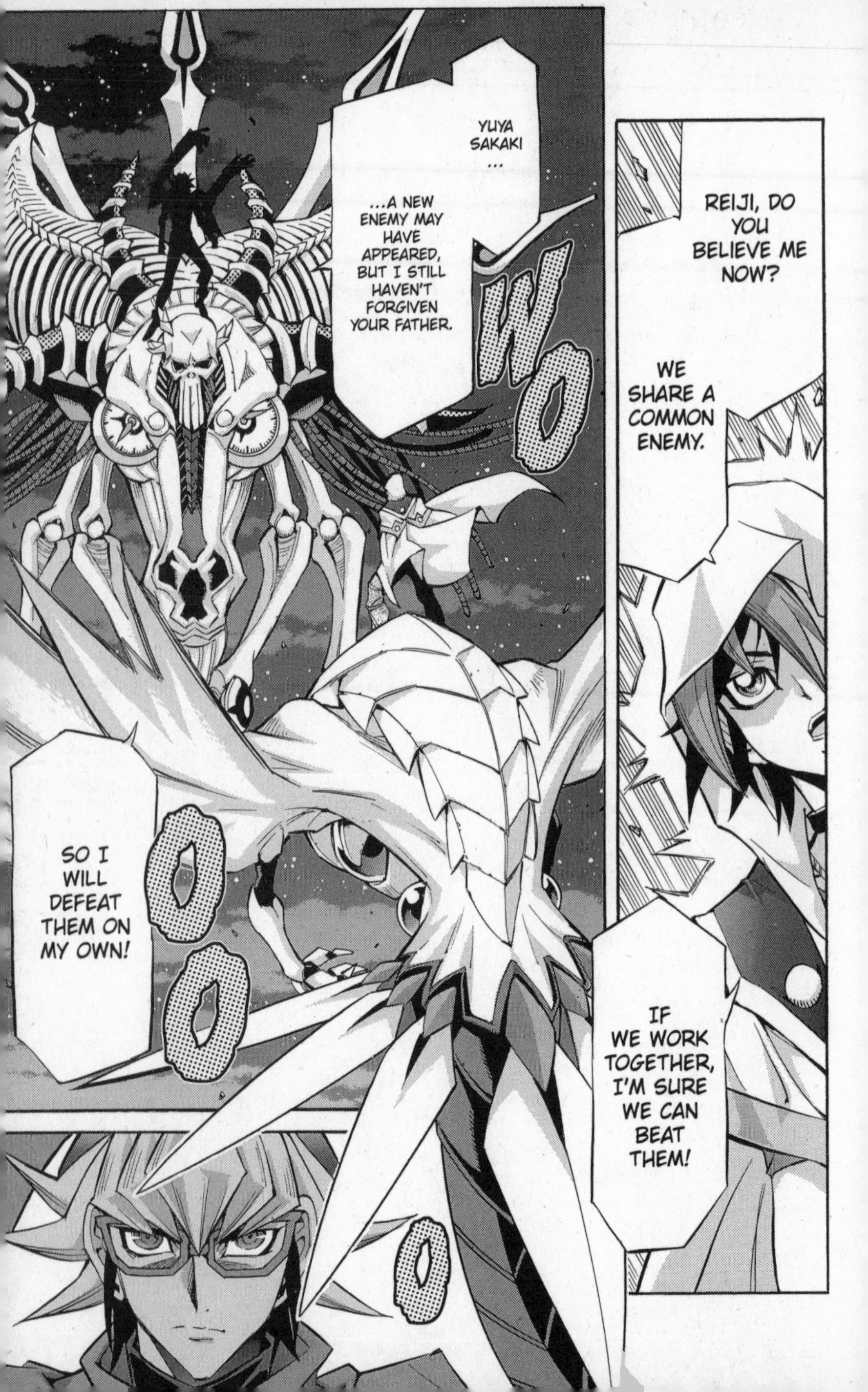
REIJI, DO YOU BELIEVE ME NOW?
WE SHARE A COMMON ENEMY.
IF WE WORK TOGETHER, I'M SURE WE CAN BEAT THEM!
YUYA SAKAKI ...
...A NEW ENEMY MAY HAVE APPEARED, BUT I STILL HAVEN'T FORGIVEN YOUR FATHER.
WOOOO
SO I WILL DEFEAT THEM ON MY OWN!

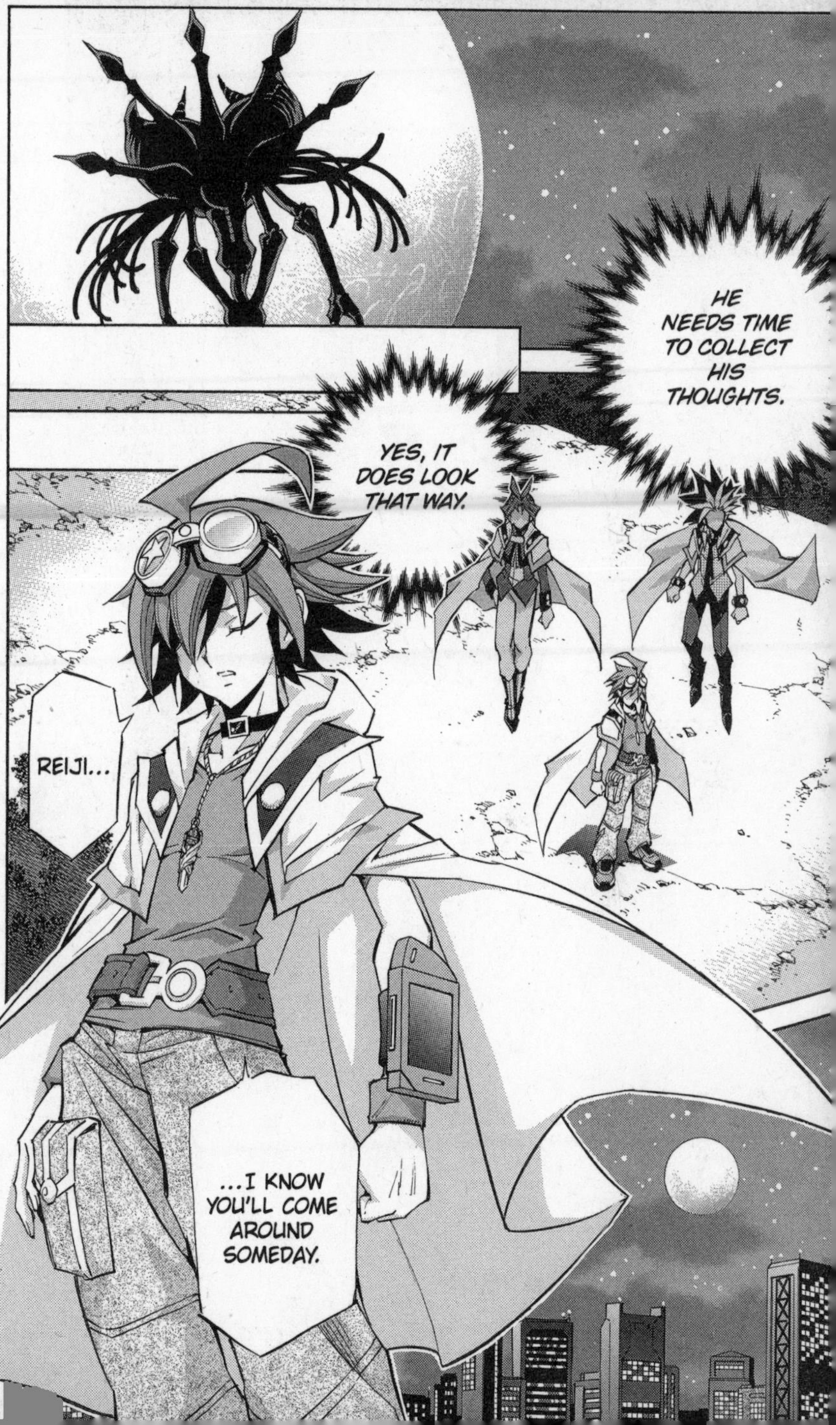
HE NEEDS TIME TO COLLECT HIS THOUGHTS.
YES, IT DOES LOOK THAT WAY.
REIJI...
...I KNOW YOU'LL COME AROUND SOMEDAY.

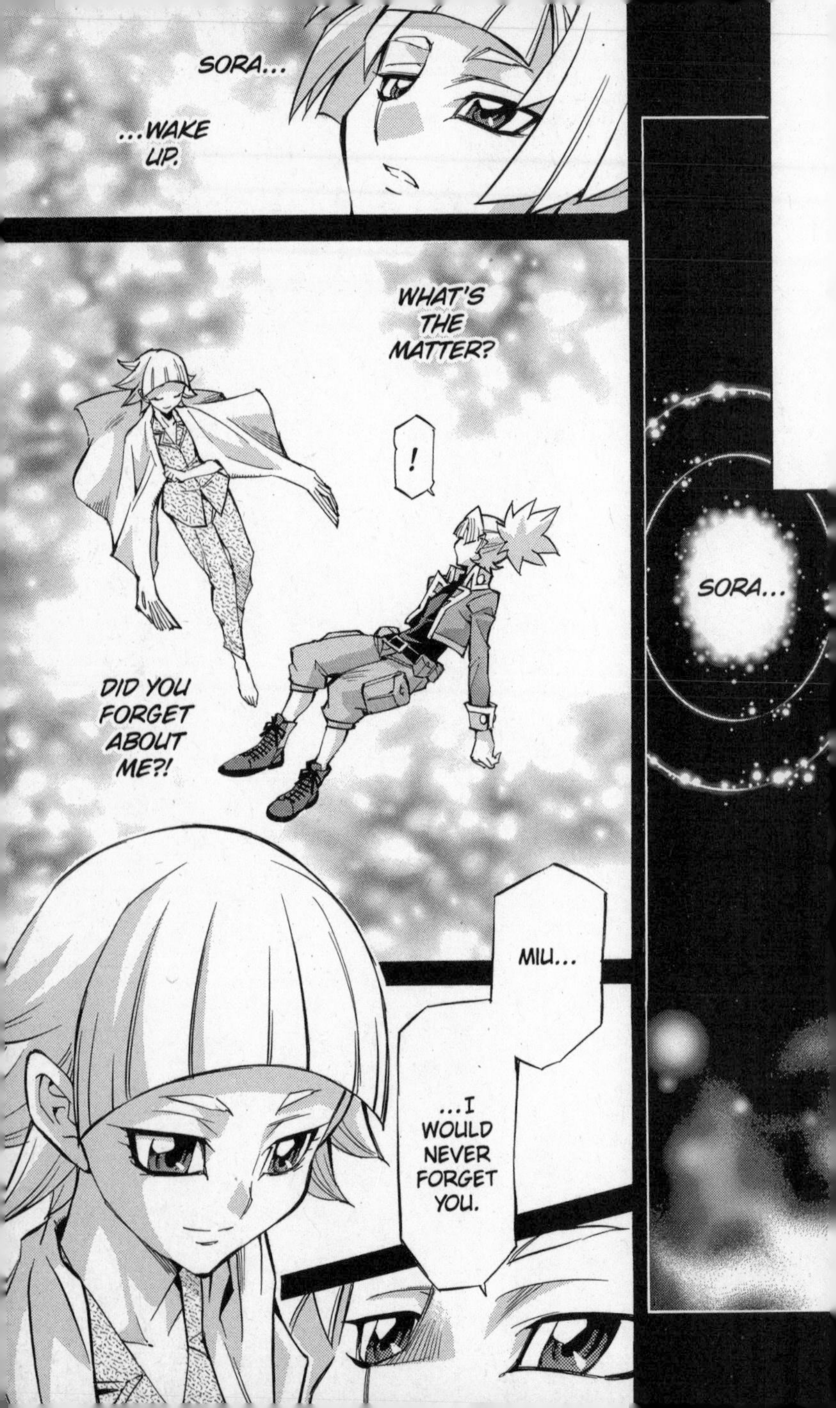
SORA...
SORA...
...WAKE UP.
WHAT'S THE MATTER?
!
DID YOU FORGET ABOUT ME?!
MIU...
...I WOULD NEVER FORGET YOU.

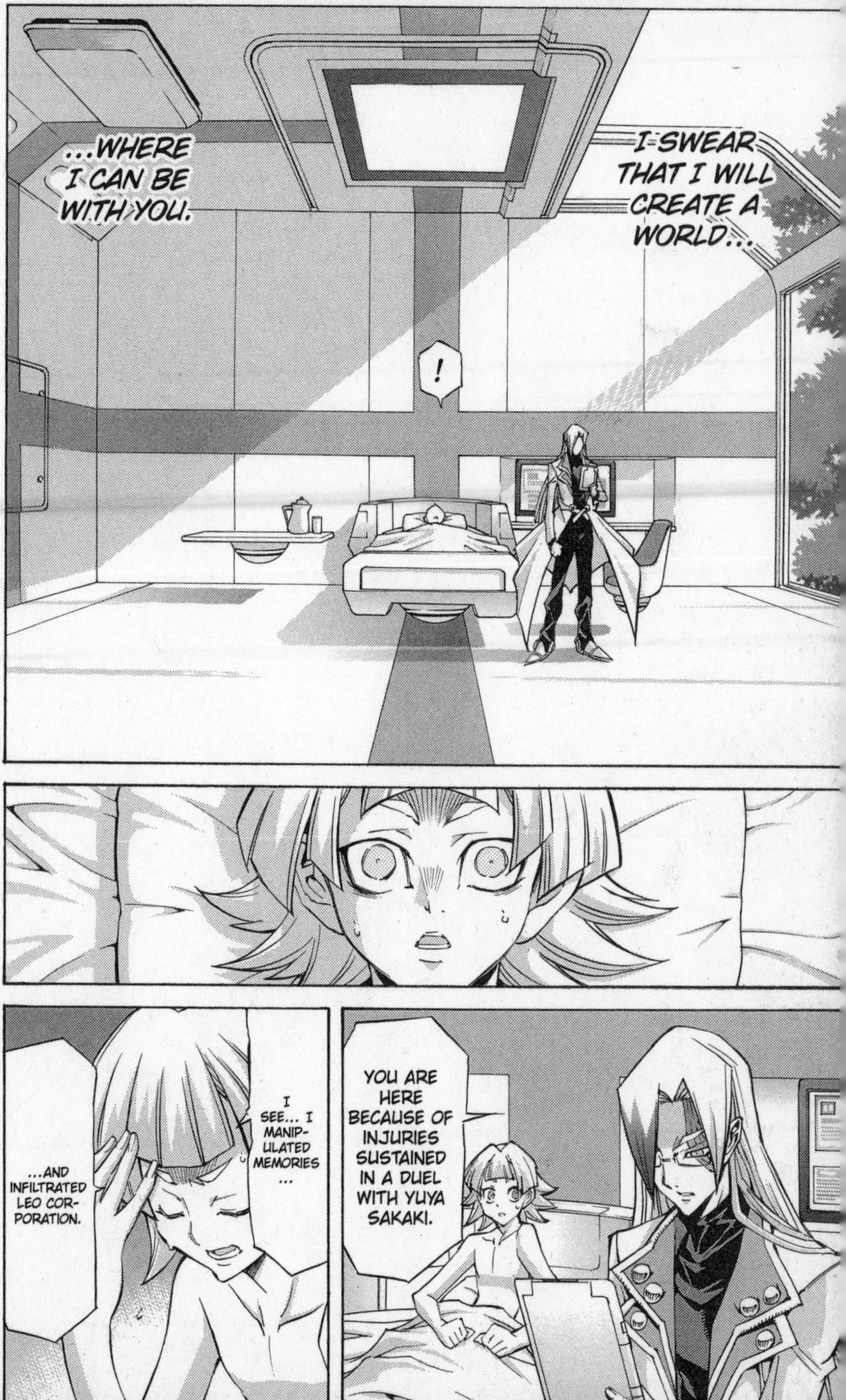
I SWEAR THAT I WILL CREATE A WORLD...
...WHERE I CAN BE WITH YOU.
!
YOU ARE HERE BECAUSE OF INJURIES SUSTAINED IN A DUEL WITH YUYA SAKAKI.
I SEE... I MANIPULATED MEMORIES...
...AND INFILTRATED LEO CORPORATION.

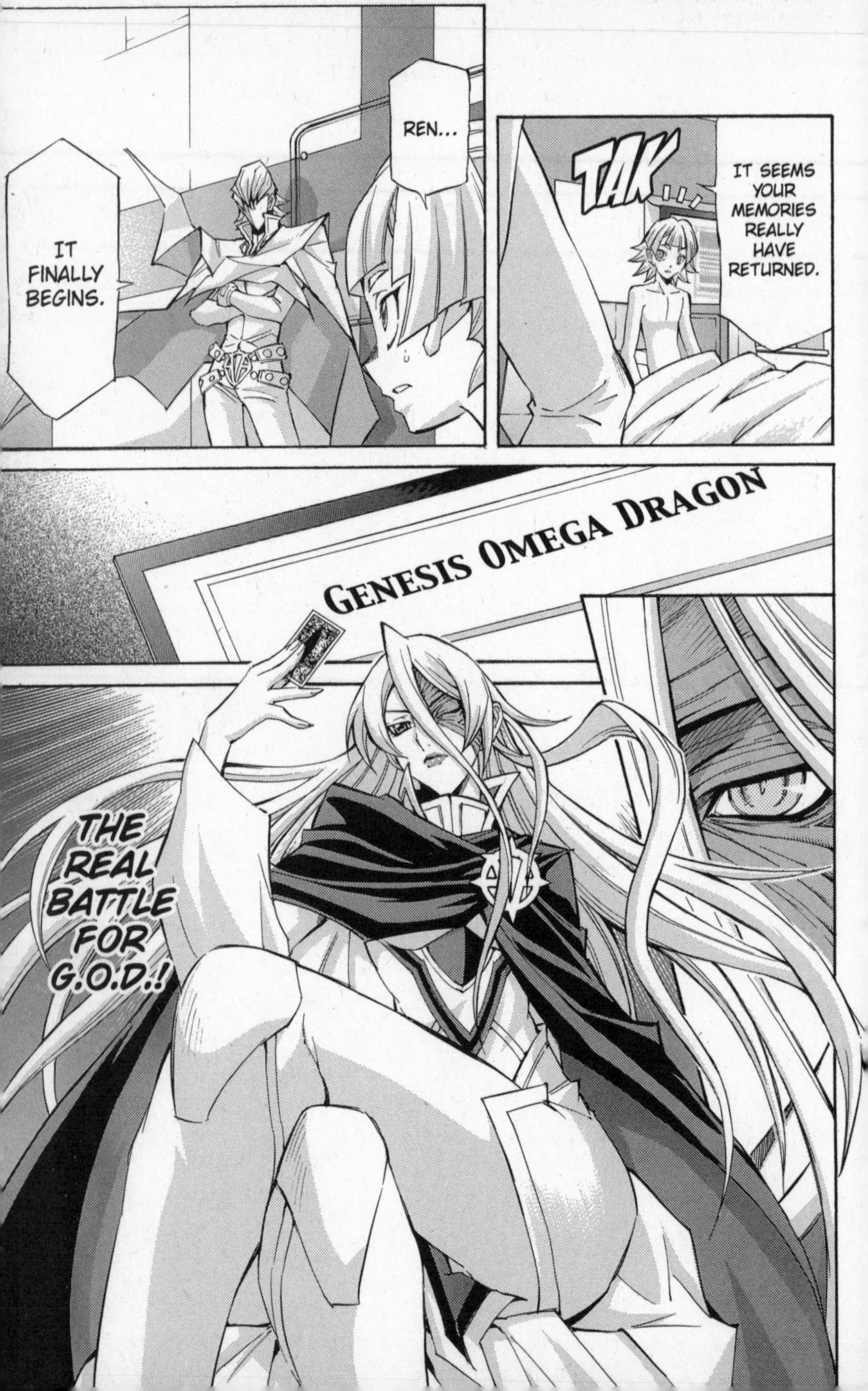
TAK...
IT SEEMS YOUR MEMORIES REALLY HAVE RETURNED.
REN...
IT FINALLY BEGINS.
GENESIS OMEGA DRAGON
THE REAL BATTLE FOR G.O.D.!

Yu-Gi-Oh! ARC-V

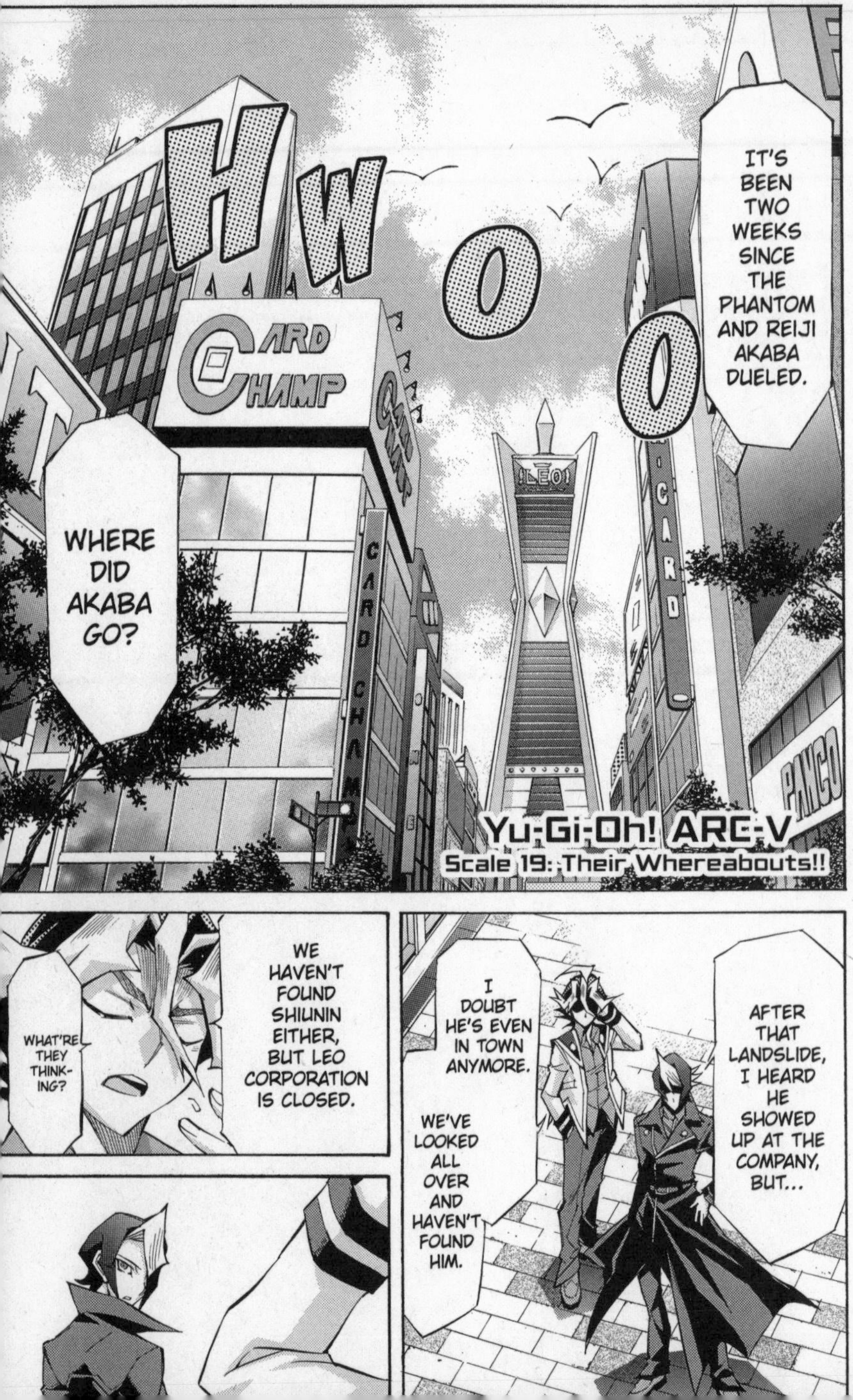
HWOO
IT'S BEEN TWO WEEKS SINCE THE PHANTOM AND REIJI AKABA DUELED.
CARD CHAMP
LEO
CARD
PANGO
WHERE DID AKABA GO?
Yu-Gi-Oh! ARC-V
Scale 19: Their Whereabouts!!
AFTER THAT LANDSLIDE, I HEARD HE SHOWED UP AT THE COMPANY, BUT...
I DOUBT HE'S EVEN IN TOWN ANYMORE.
WE'VE LOOKED ALL OVER AND HAVEN'T FOUND HIM.
WE HAVEN'T FOUND SHIUNIN EITHER, BUT LEO CORPORATION IS CLOSED.
WHAT'RE THEY THINKING?

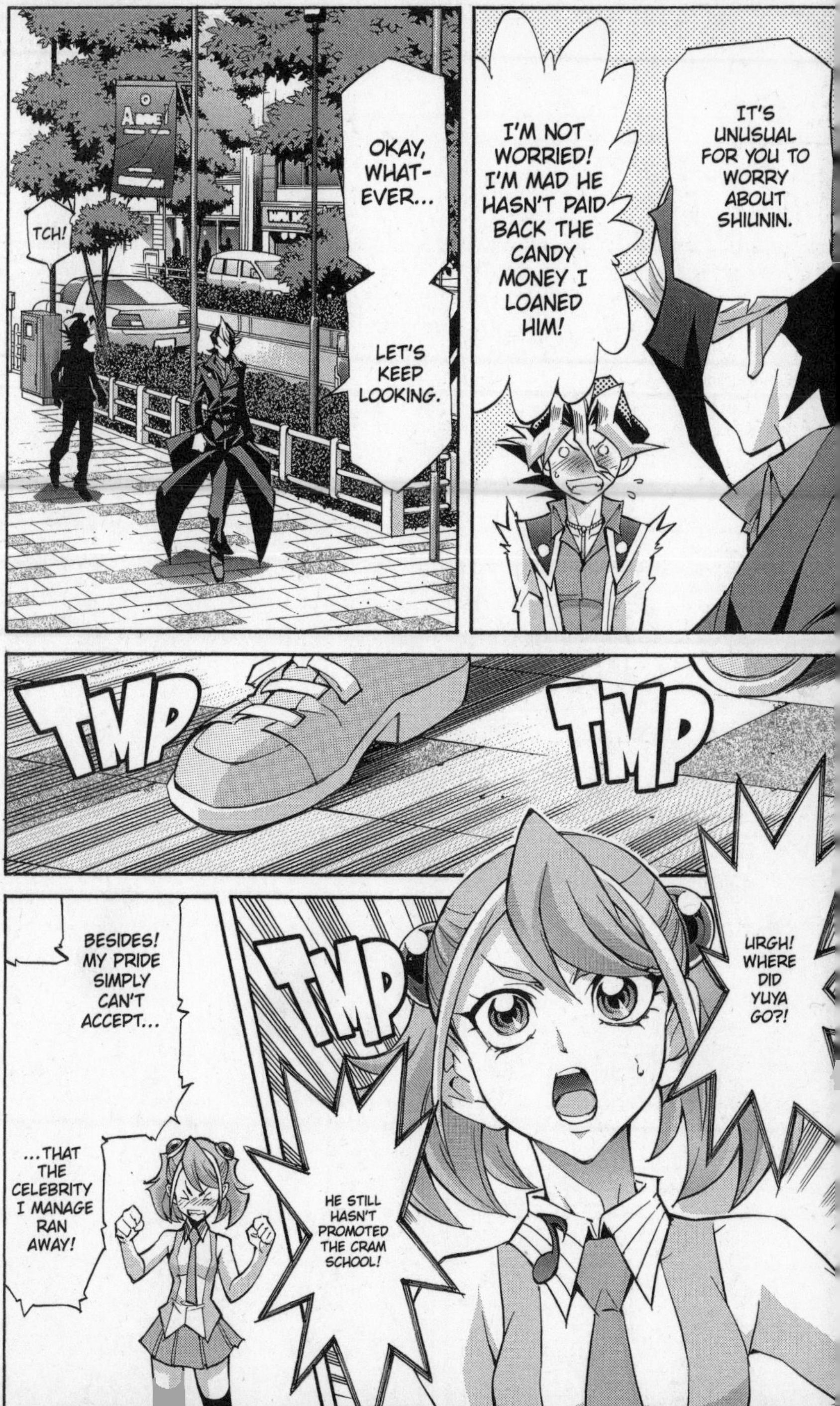
IT'S UNUSUAL FOR YOU TO WORRY ABOUT SHIUNIN.
I'M NOT WORRIED! I'M MAD HE HASN'T PAID BACK THE CANDY MONEY I LOANED HIM!
OKAY, WHAT-EVER...
LET'S KEEP LOOKING.
TCH!
TMP
TMP
URGH! WHERE DID YUYA GO?!
TMP
HE STILL HASN'T PROMOTED THE CRAM SCHOOL!
BESIDES! MY PRIDE SIMPLY CAN'T ACCEPT...
...THAT THE CELEBRITY I MANAGE RAN AWAY!

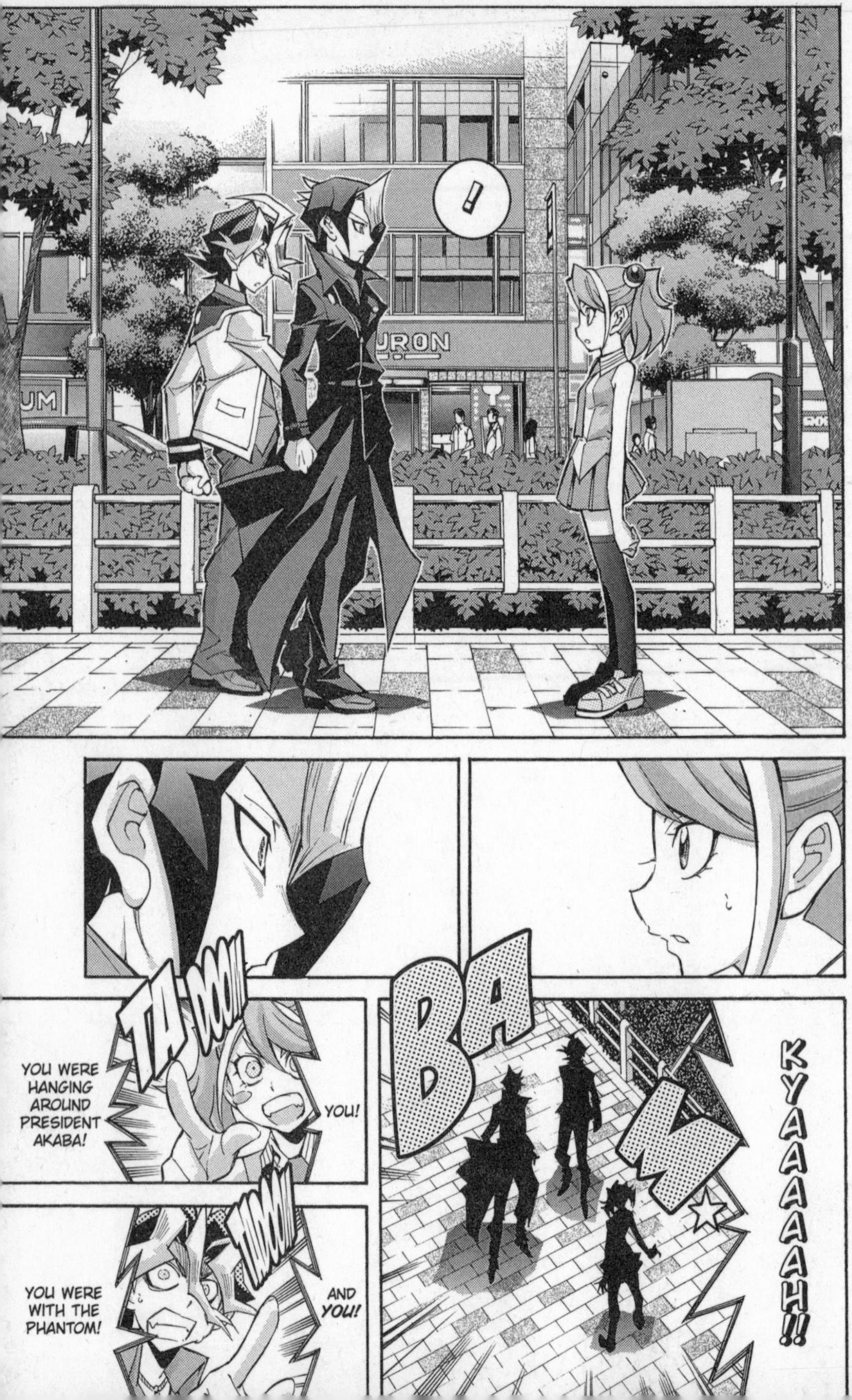
!
KYAAAAAAH!!
BAM
TA-DOOM!
YOU!
YOU WERE HANGING AROUND PRESIDENT AKABA!
AND YOU!
YOU WERE WITH THE PHANTOM!

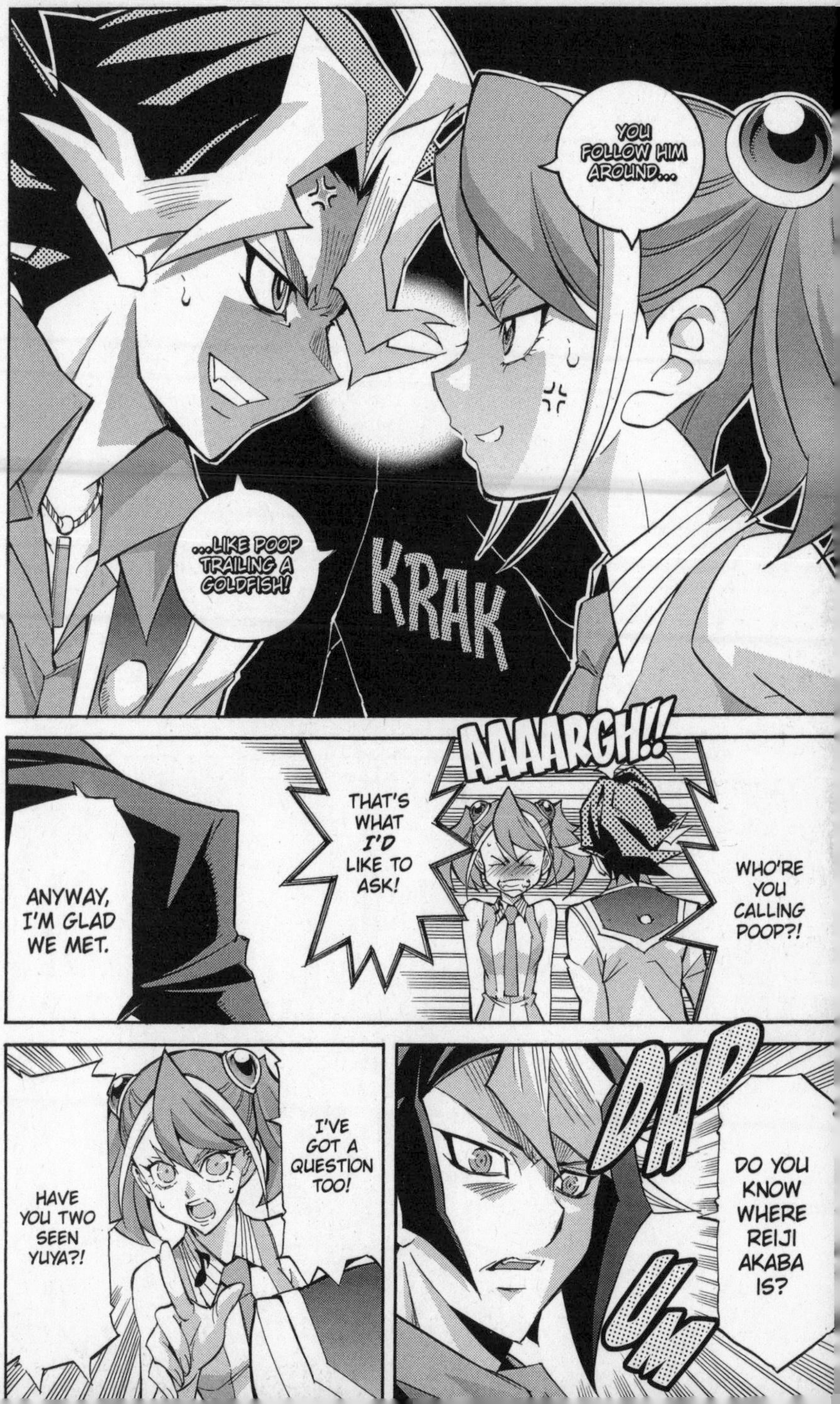
YOU FOLLOW HIM AROUND...
...LIKE POOP TRAILING A GOLDFISH!
KRAK
WHO'RE YOU CALLING POOP?!
AAAARGH!!
THAT'S WHAT *I'D* LIKE TO ASK!
ANYWAY, I'M GLAD WE MET.
DO YOU KNOW WHERE REIJI AKABA IS?
DAP
UM
I'VE GOT A QUESTION TOO!
HAVE YOU TWO SEEN YUYA?!

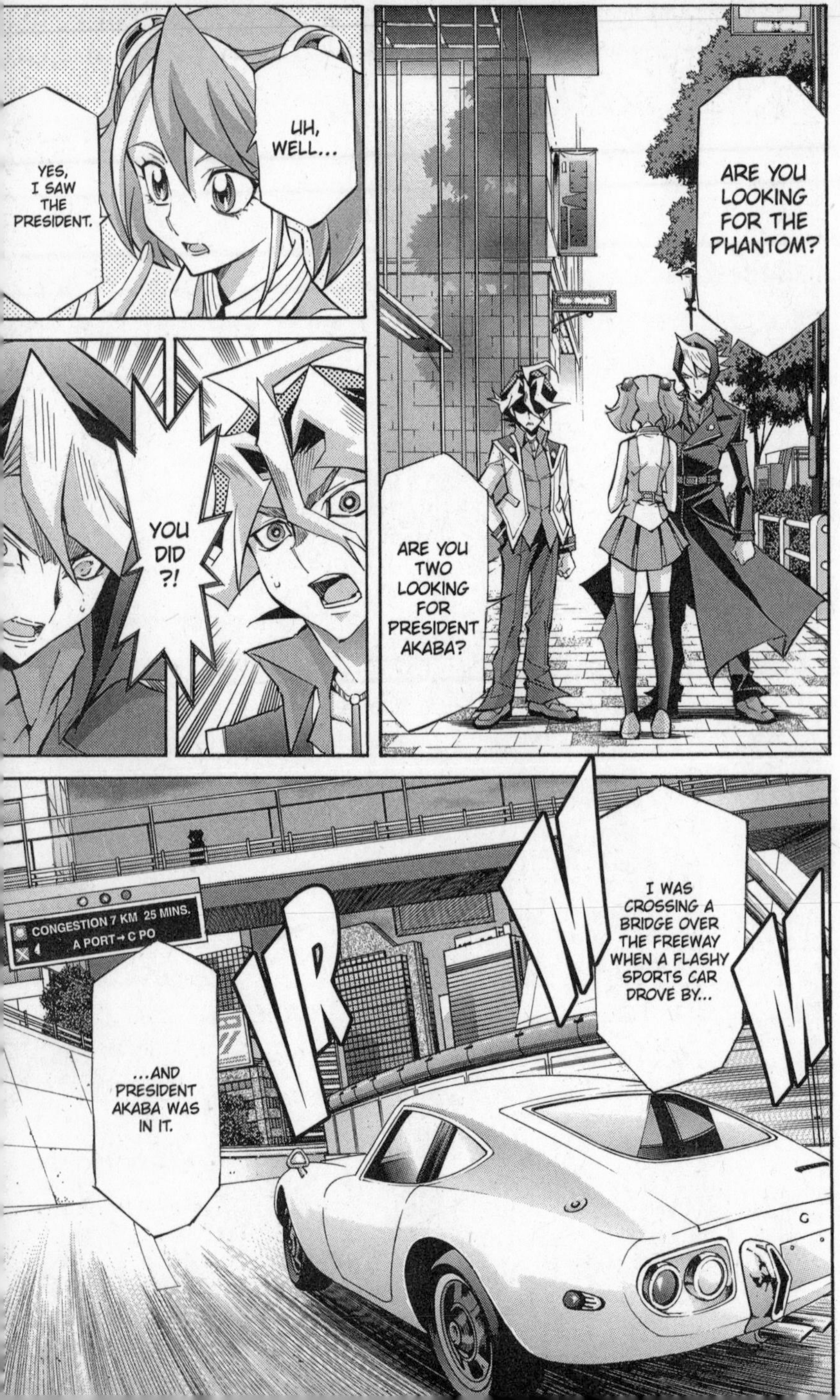
ARE YOU LOOKING FOR THE PHANTOM?
ARE YOU TWO LOOKING FOR PRESIDENT AKABA?
UH, WELL...
YES, I SAW THE PRESIDENT.
YOU DID ?!
I WAS CROSSING A BRIDGE OVER THE FREEWAY WHEN A FLASHY SPORTS CAR DROVE BY...
VRMM
CONGESTION 7 KM 25 MINS.
A PORT → C PO
...AND PRESIDENT AKABA WAS IN IT.

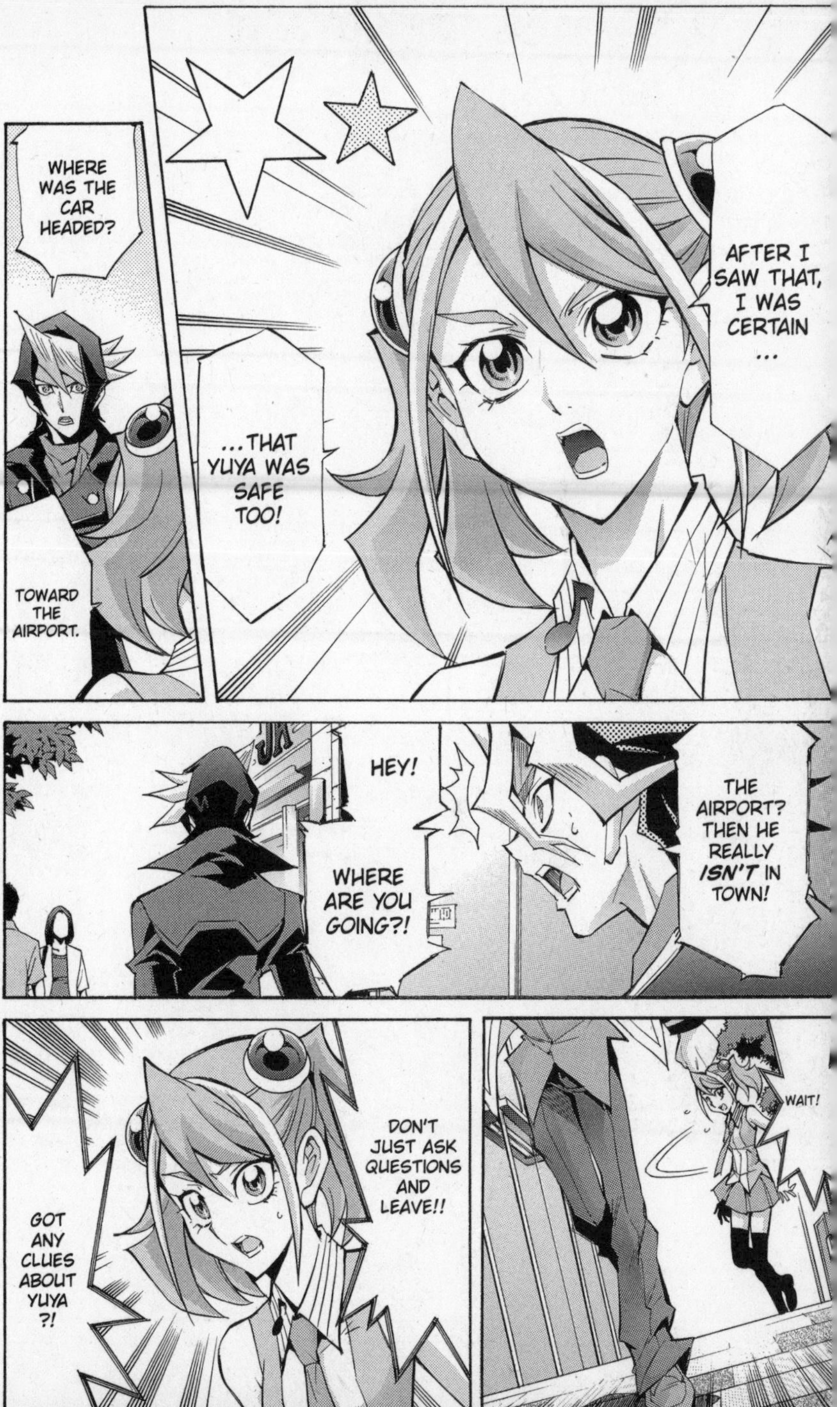
AFTER I SAW THAT, I WAS CERTAIN ...
...THAT YUYA WAS SAFE TOO!
WHERE WAS THE CAR HEADED?
TOWARD THE AIRPORT.
THE AIRPORT? THEN HE REALLY *ISN'T* IN TOWN!
HEY!
WHERE ARE YOU GOING?!
WAIT!
DON'T JUST ASK QUESTIONS AND LEAVE!!
GOT ANY CLUES ABOUT YUYA?!

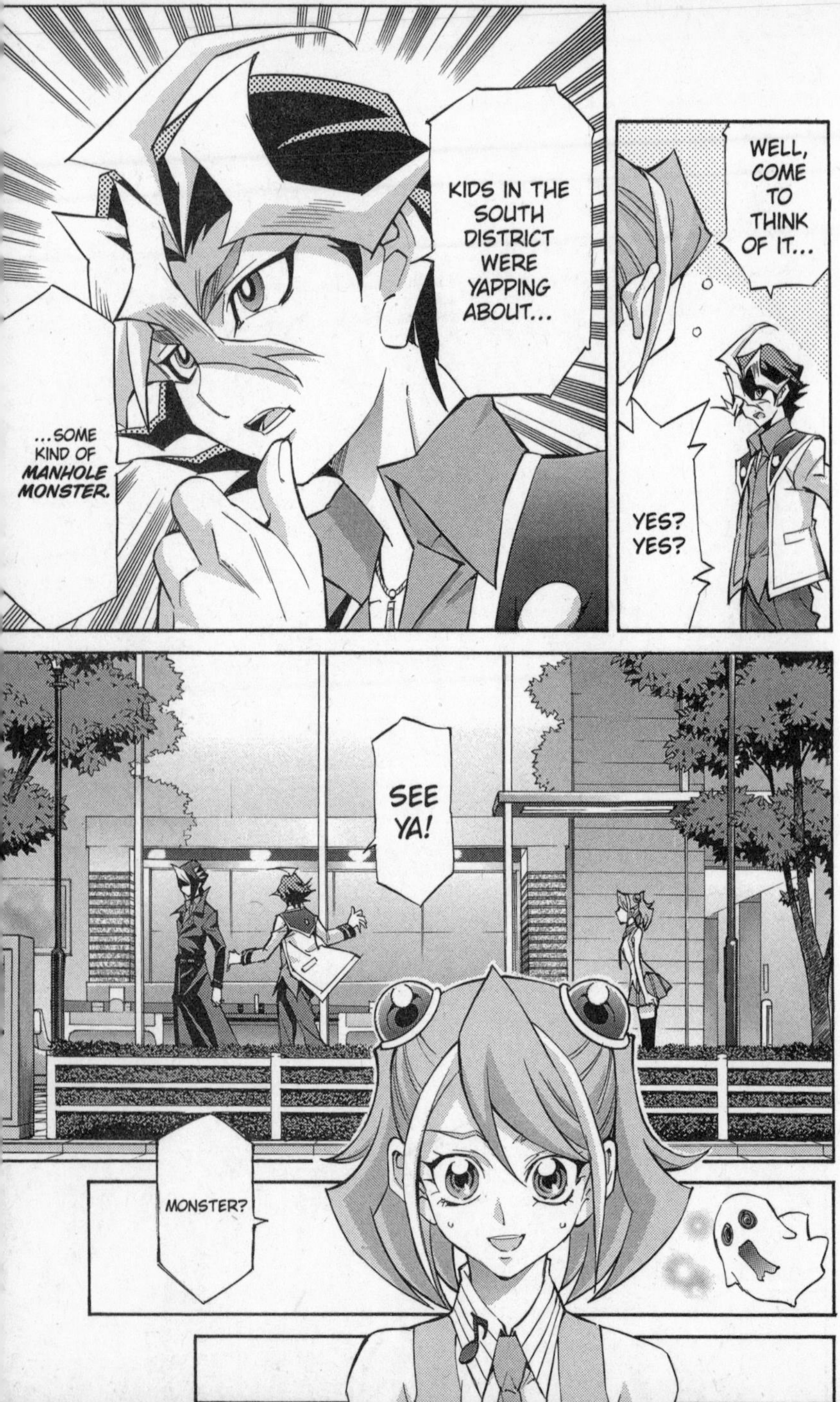
WELL, COME TO THINK OF IT...
YES? YES?
KIDS IN THE SOUTH DISTRICT WERE YAPPING ABOUT...
...SOME KIND OF *MANHOLE MONSTER.*
SEE YA!
MONSTER?

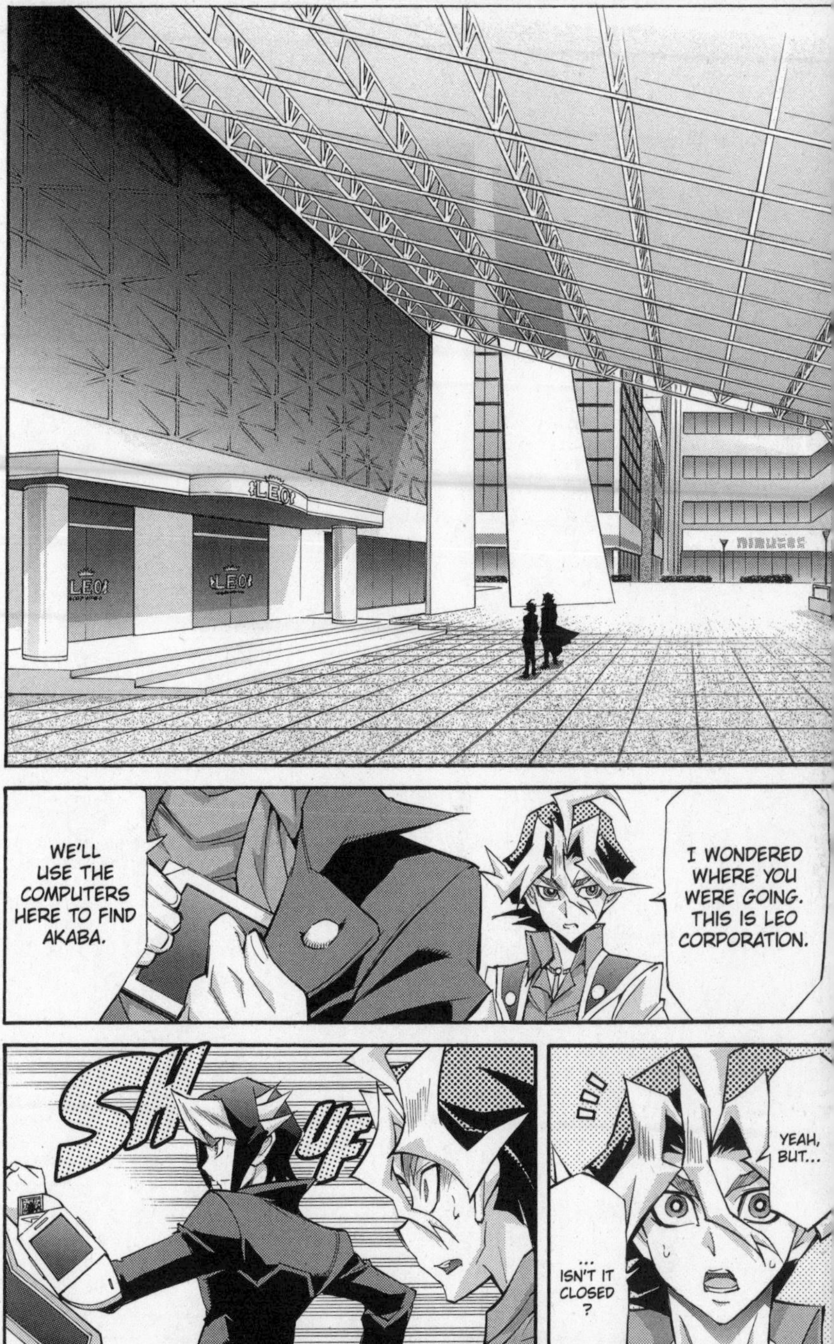
I WONDERED WHERE YOU WERE GOING. THIS IS LEO CORPORATION.
WE'LL USE THE COMPUTERS HERE TO FIND AKABA.
YEAH, BUT...
...ISN'T IT CLOSED?
SHUF

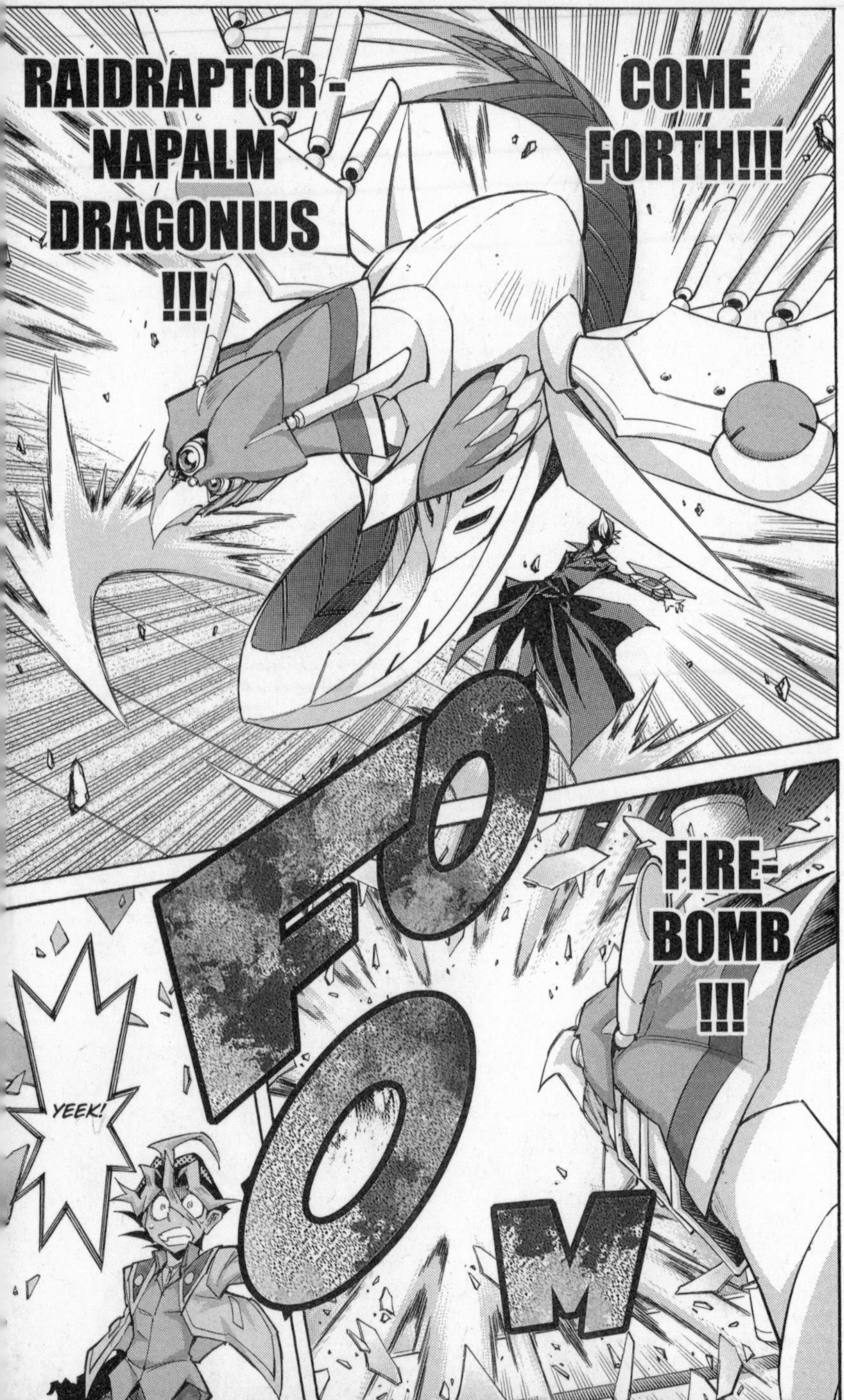
COME FORTH!!!
RAIDRAPTOR - NAPALM DRAGONIUS!!!
FIRE-BOMB!!!
FOOM
YEEK!

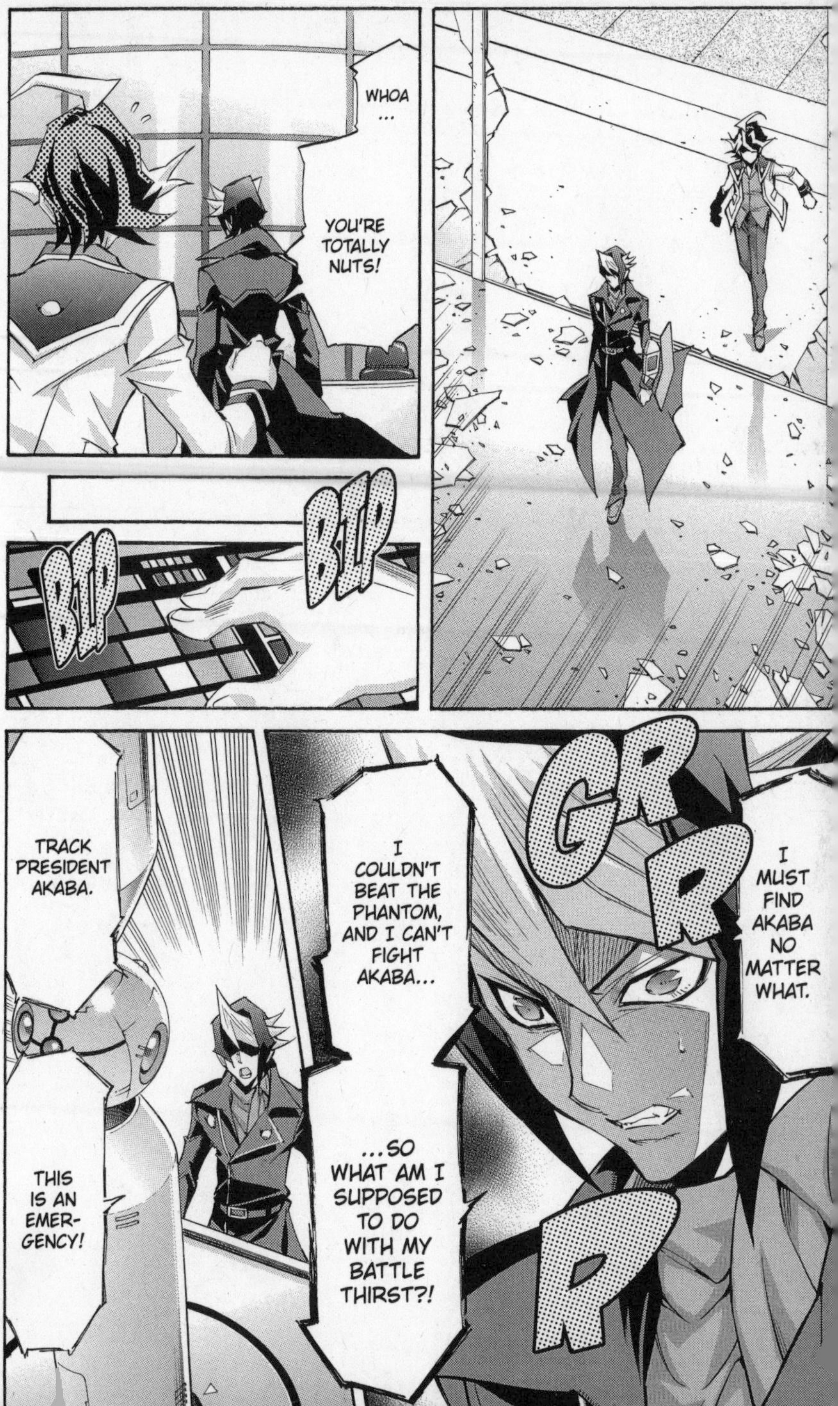
WHOA ...
YOU'RE TOTALLY NUTS!
BIP
BIP
GRR
I MUST FIND AKABA NO MATTER WHAT.
I COULDN'T BEAT THE PHANTOM, AND I CAN'T FIGHT AKABA...
...SO WHAT AM I SUPPOSED TO DO WITH MY BATTLE THIRST?!
R
TRACK PRESIDENT AKABA.
THIS IS AN EMER-GENCY!

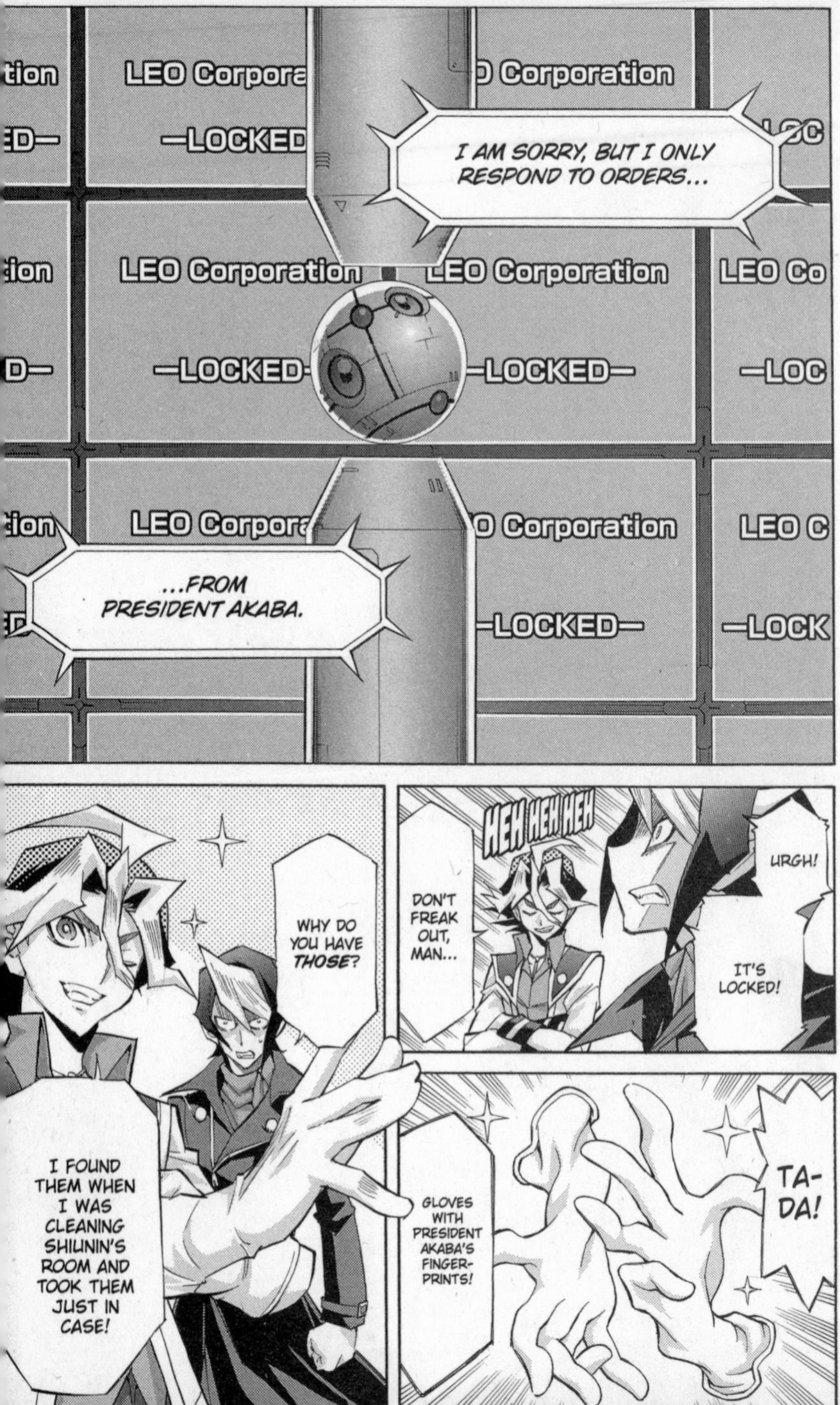
LEO Corporation
—LOCKED—
I AM SORRY, BUT I ONLY RESPOND TO ORDERS...
...FROM PRESIDENT AKABA.
URGH!
IT'S LOCKED!
HEH HEH HEH
DON'T FREAK OUT, MAN...
TA-DA!
GLOVES WITH PRESIDENT AKABA'S FINGER-PRINTS!
WHY DO YOU HAVE *THOSE*?
I FOUND THEM WHEN I WAS CLEANING SHIUNIN'S ROOM AND TOOK THEM JUST IN CASE!

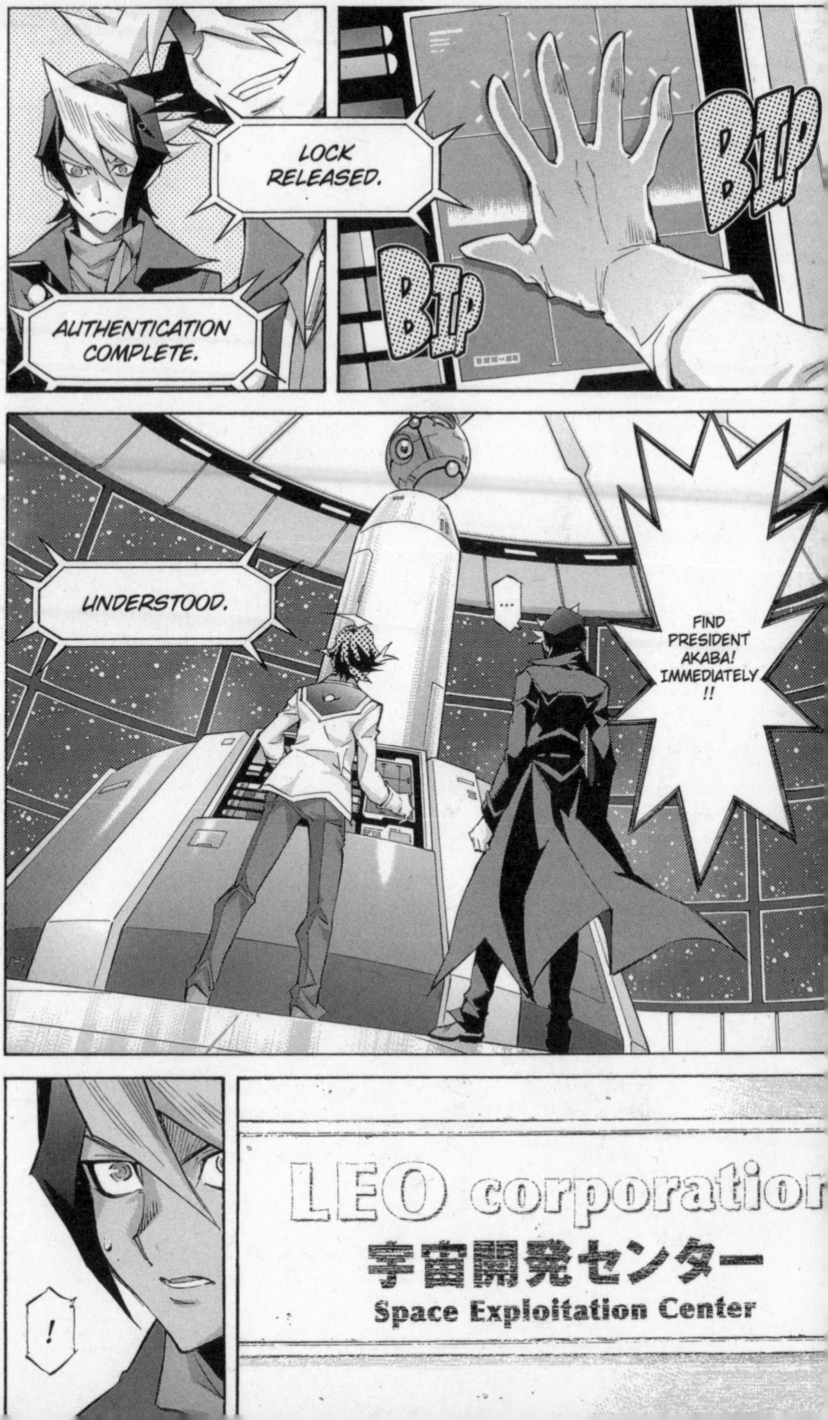
BIP
BIP
LOCK RELEASED.
AUTHENTICATION COMPLETE.
FIND PRESIDENT AKABA! IMMEDIATELY!!
...
UNDERSTOOD.
LEO corporation
宇宙開発センター
Space Exploitation Center
!

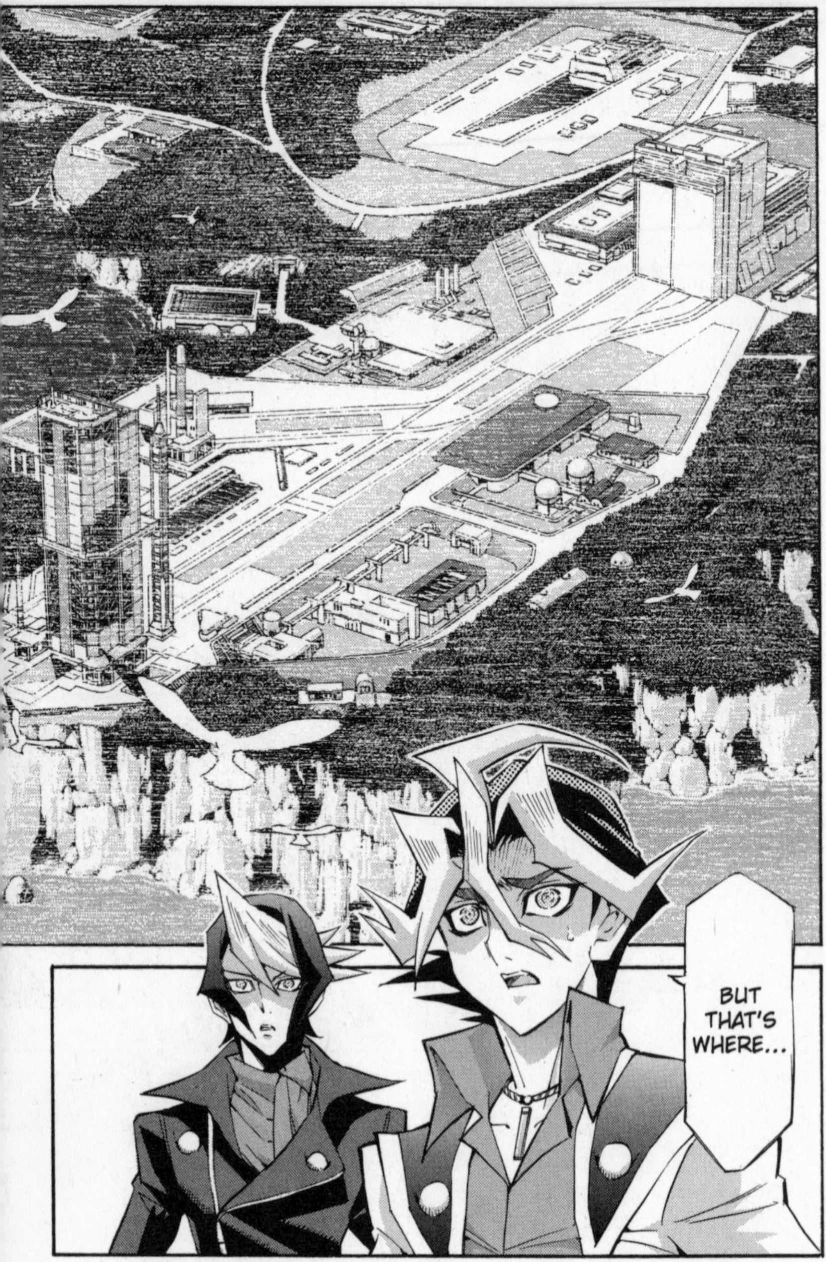
BUT THAT'S WHERE...

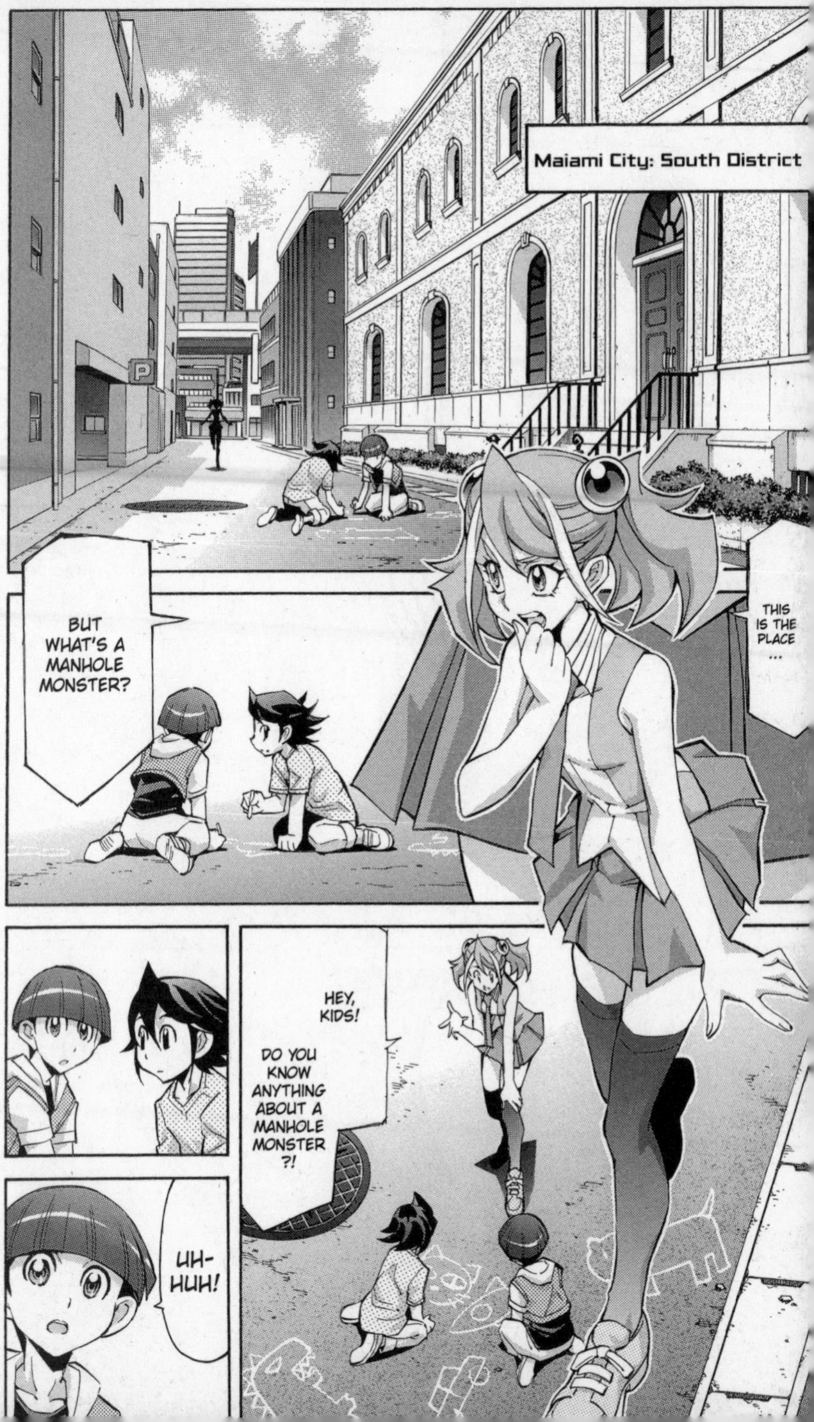
Maiami City: South District
THIS IS THE PLACE...
BUT WHAT'S A MANHOLE MONSTER?
HEY, KIDS!
DO YOU KNOW ANYTHING ABOUT A MANHOLE MONSTER?!
UH-HUH!

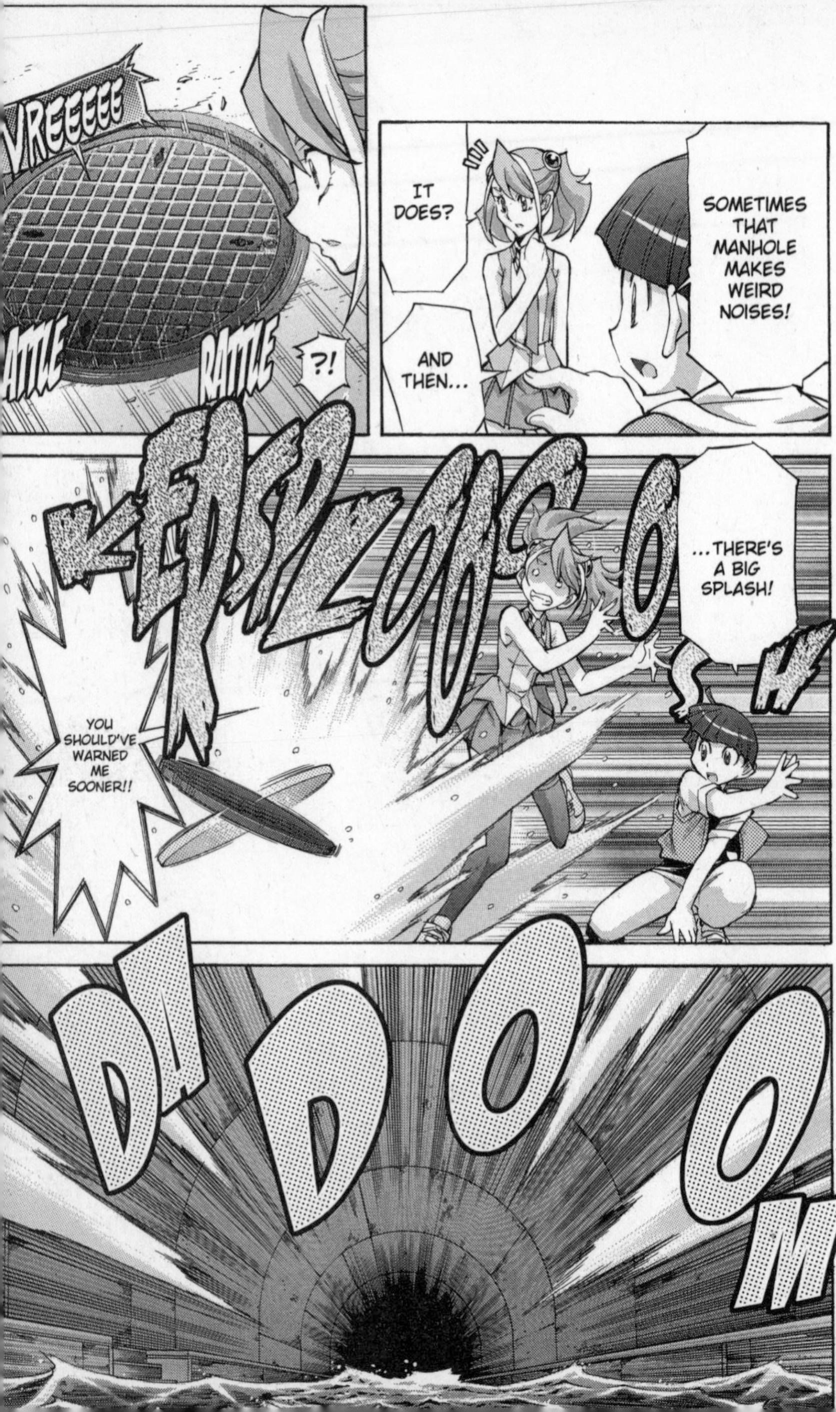
SOMETIMES THAT MANHOLE MAKES WEIRD NOISES!
!!!
IT DOES?
AND THEN...
VREEEEE
RATTLE
RATTLE
?!
...THERE'S A BIG SPLASH!
YOU SHOULD'VE WARNED ME SOONER!!

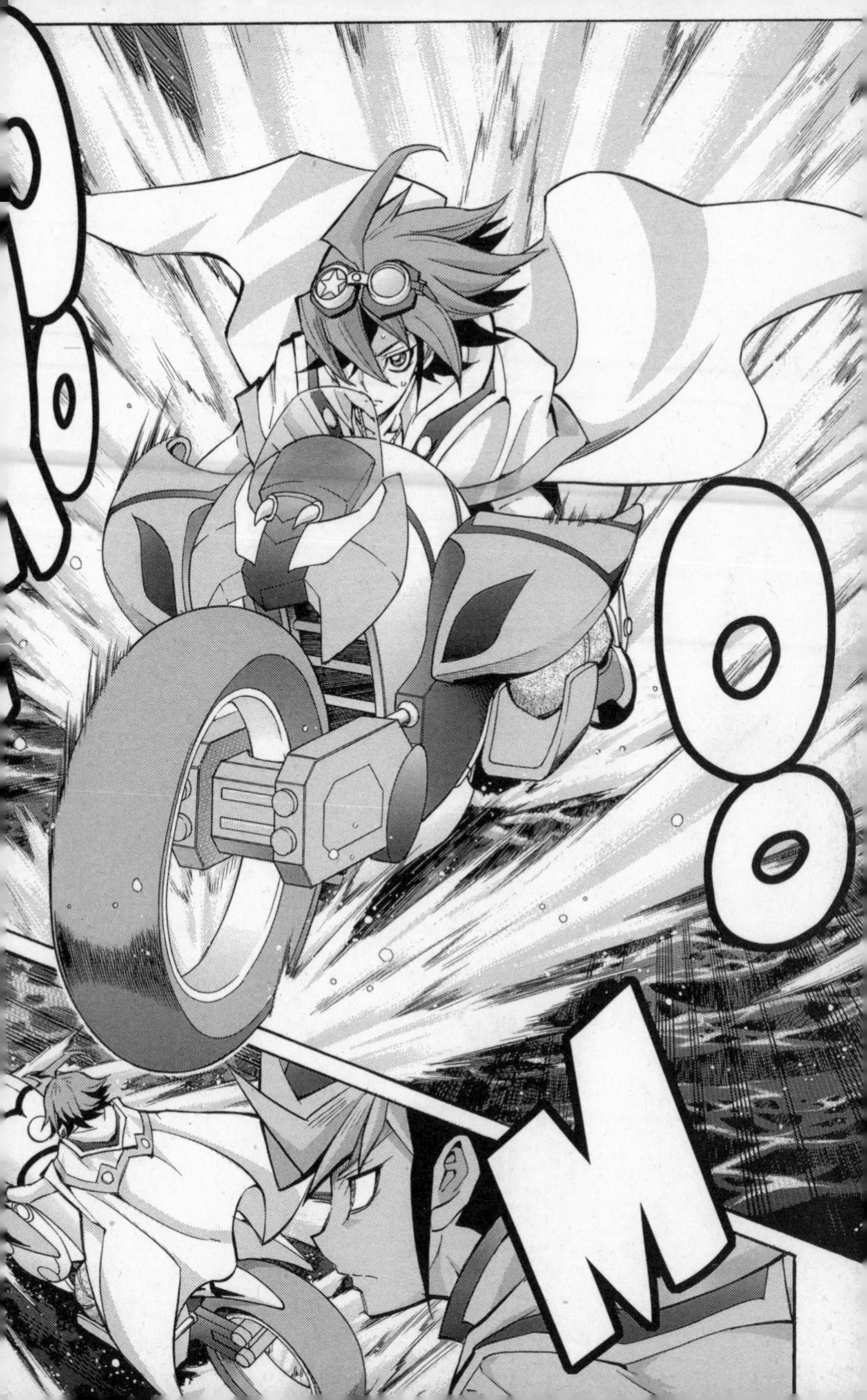
OOOOM

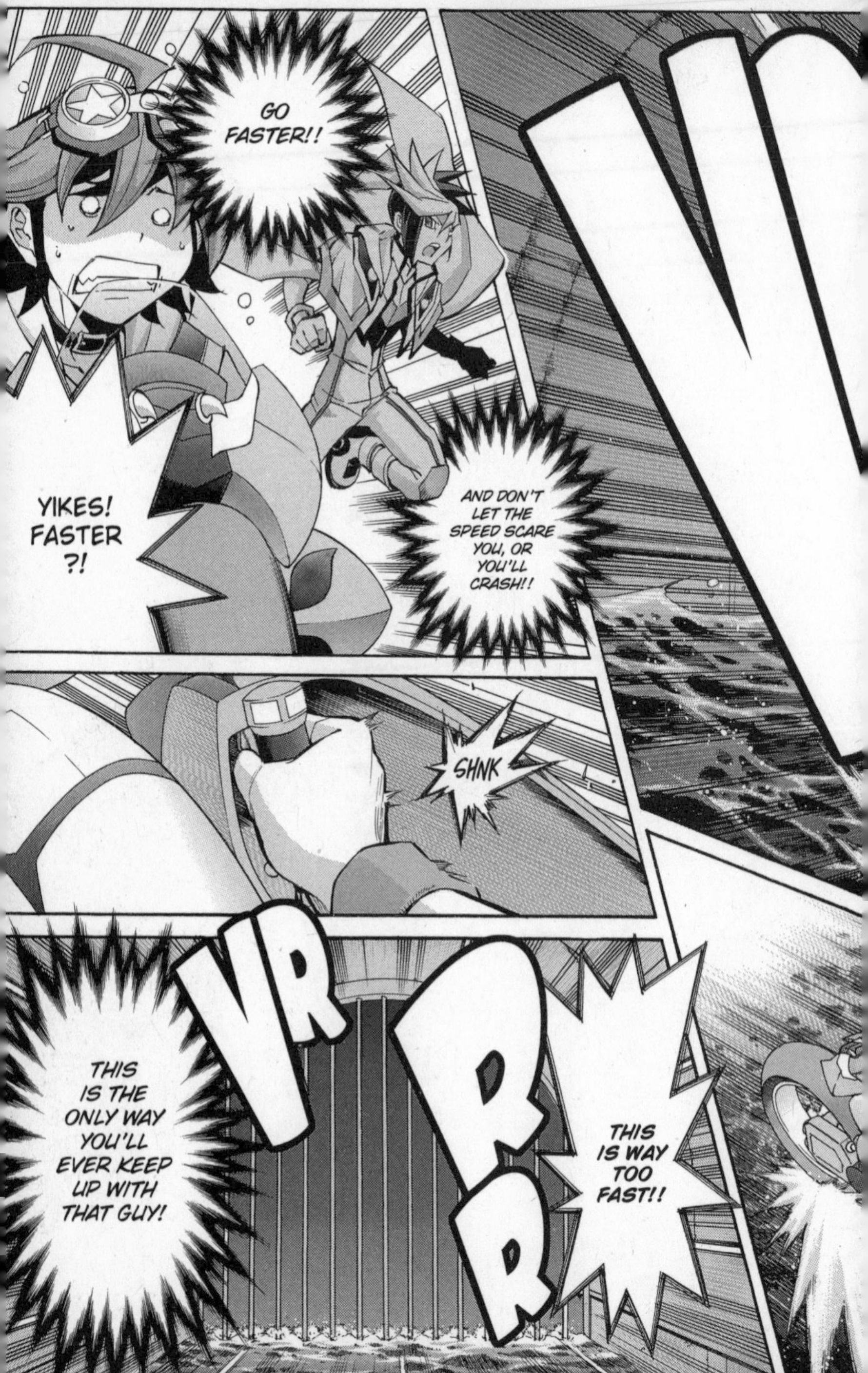
GO FASTER!!
AND DON'T LET THE SPEED SCARE YOU, OR YOU'LL CRASH!!
YIKES! FASTER ?!
SHNK
THIS IS WAY TOO FAST!!
VRRR
THIS IS THE ONLY WAY YOU'LL EVER KEEP UP WITH THAT GUY!

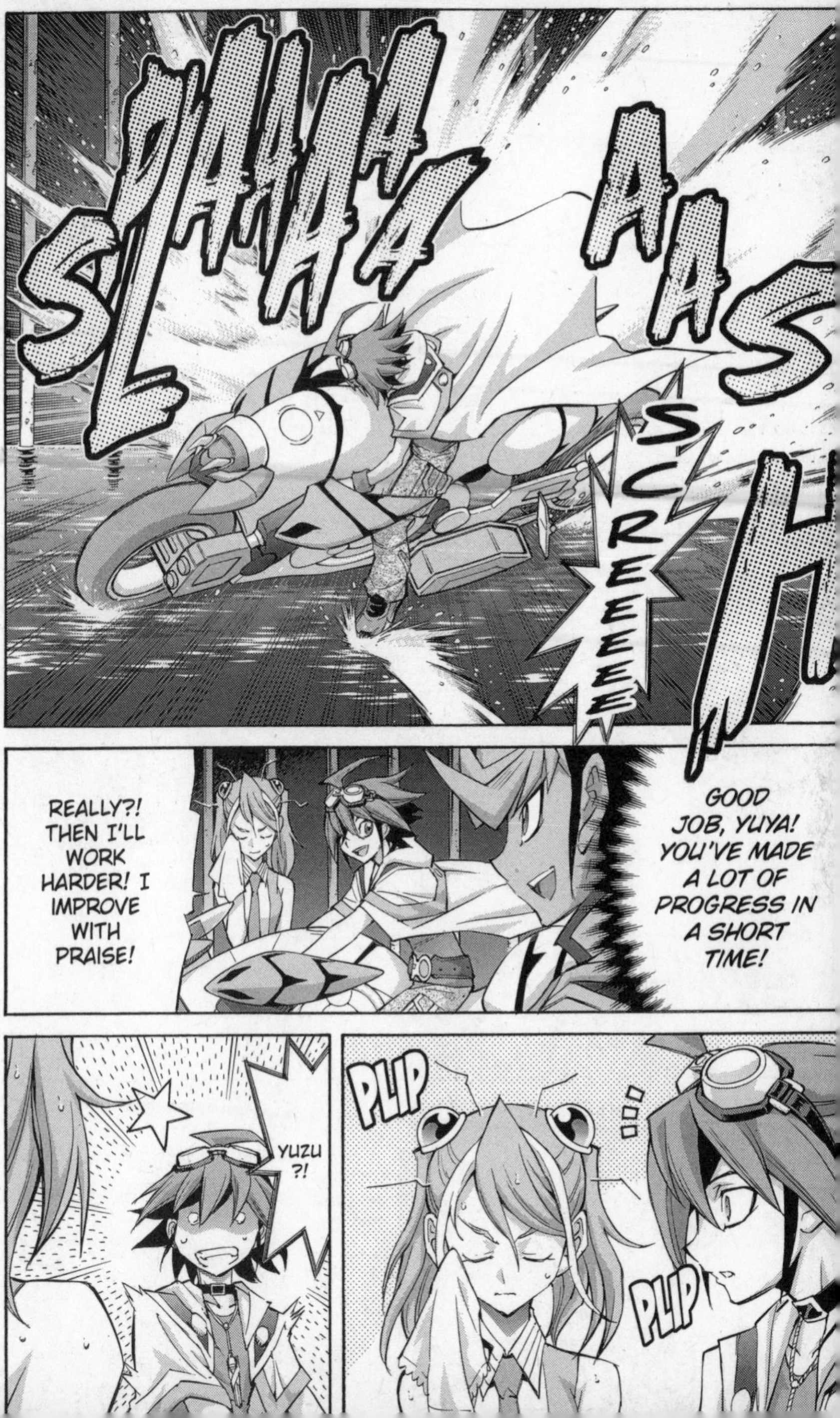
SLAAAAAASH
SCREEEEEE
GOOD JOB, YUYA! YOU'VE MADE A LOT OF PROGRESS IN A SHORT TIME!
REALLY?! THEN I'LL WORK HARDER! I IMPROVE WITH PRAISE!
PLIP
...
PLIP
YUZU ?!

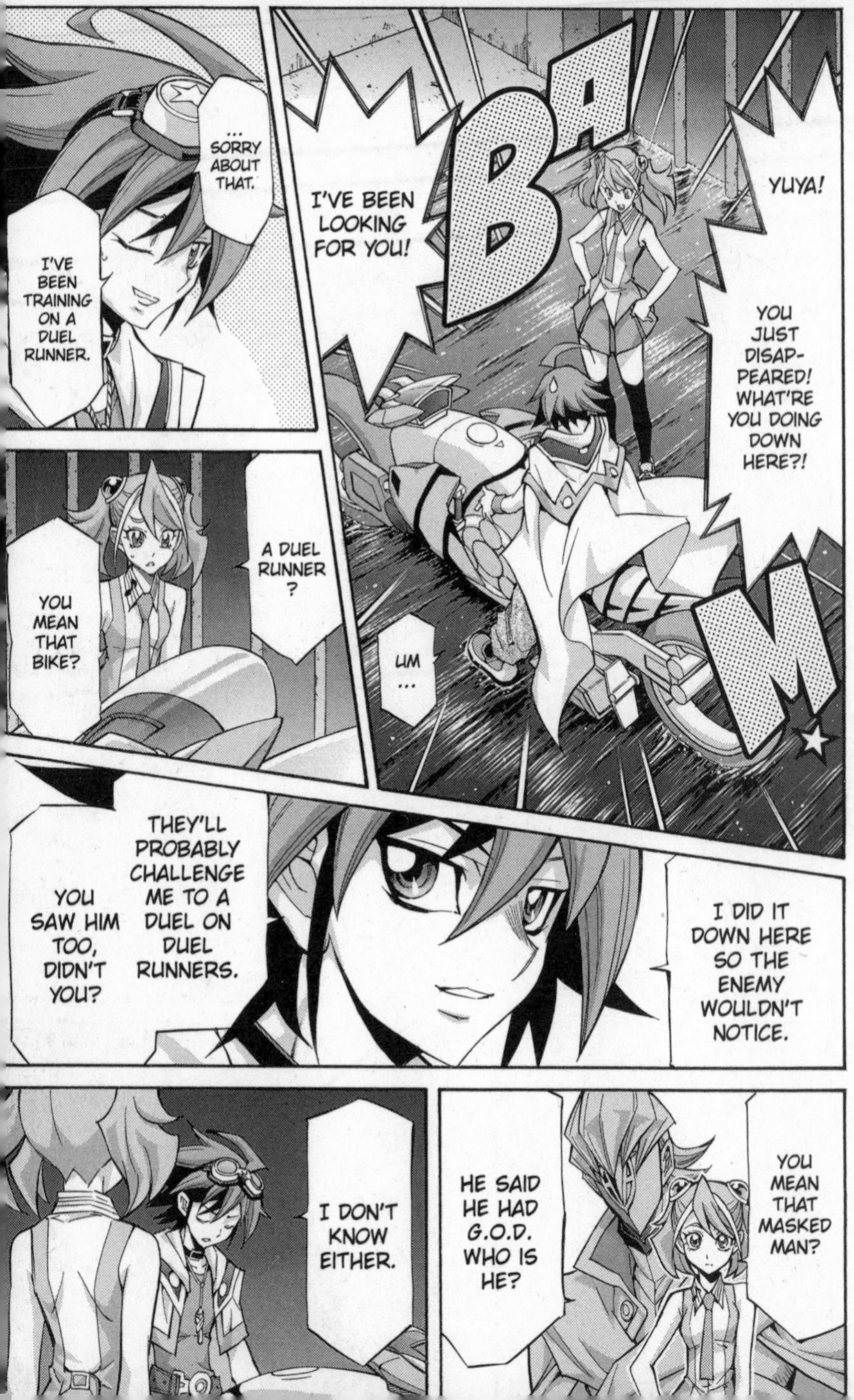
YUYA!
I'VE BEEN LOOKING FOR YOU!
BAM
YOU JUST DISAP-PEARED! WHAT'RE YOU DOING DOWN HERE?!
UM ...
... SORRY ABOUT THAT.
I'VE BEEN TRAINING ON A DUEL RUNNER.
A DUEL RUNNER ?
YOU MEAN THAT BIKE?
I DID IT DOWN HERE SO THE ENEMY WOULDN'T NOTICE.
THEY'LL PROBABLY CHALLENGE ME TO A DUEL ON DUEL RUNNERS.
YOU SAW HIM TOO, DIDN'T YOU?
YOU MEAN THAT MASKED MAN?
HE SAID HE HAD G.O.D. WHO IS HE?
I DON'T KNOW EITHER.

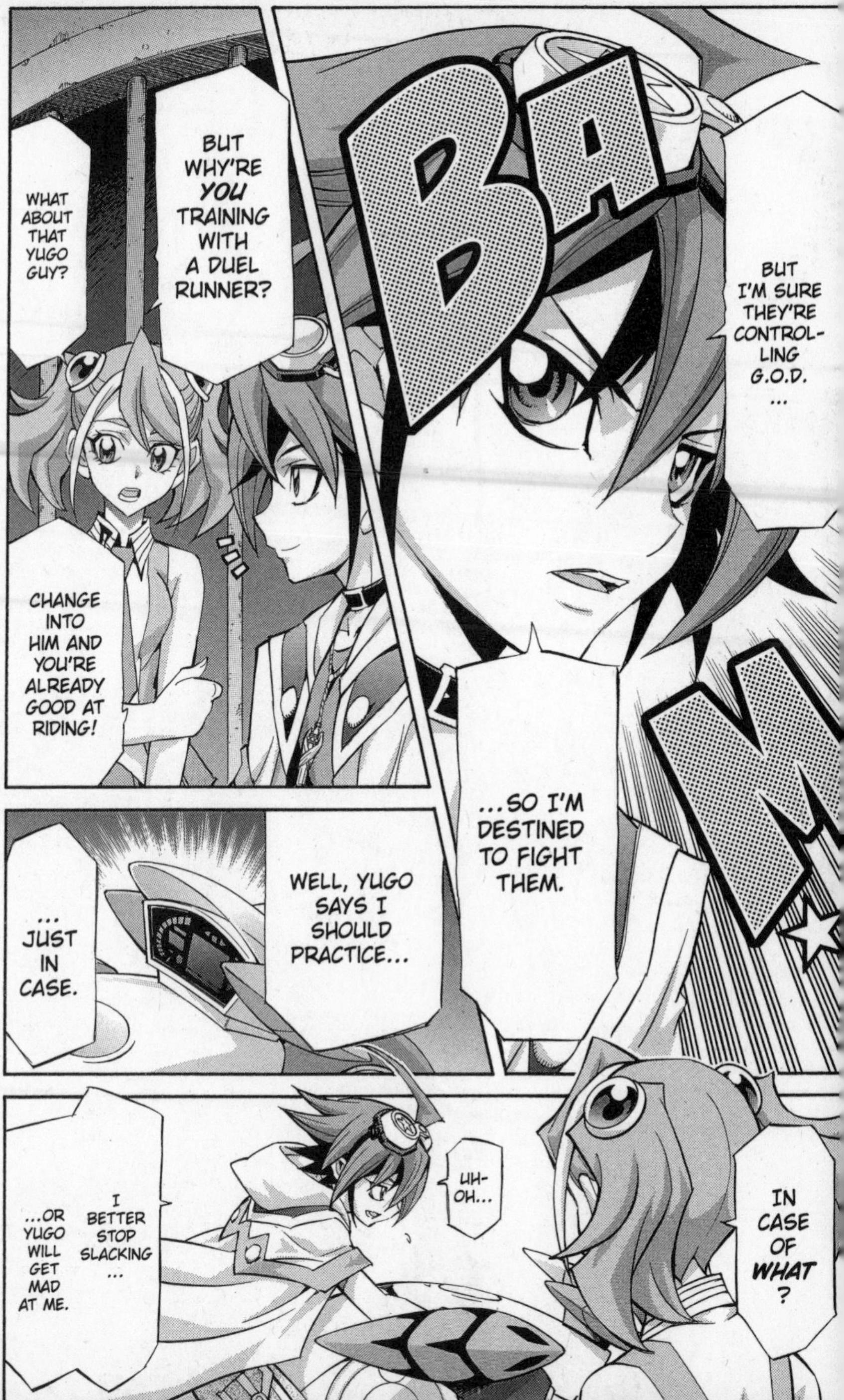
BAM
BUT I'M SURE THEY'RE CONTROLLING G.O.D. ...
...SO I'M DESTINED TO FIGHT THEM.
BUT WHY'RE *YOU* TRAINING WITH A DUEL RUNNER?
WHAT ABOUT THAT YUGO GUY?
CHANGE INTO HIM AND YOU'RE ALREADY GOOD AT RIDING!
WELL, YUGO SAYS I SHOULD PRACTICE...
... JUST IN CASE.
IN CASE OF *WHAT*?
UH-OH...
I BETTER STOP SLACKING ...
...OR YUGO WILL GET MAD AT ME.

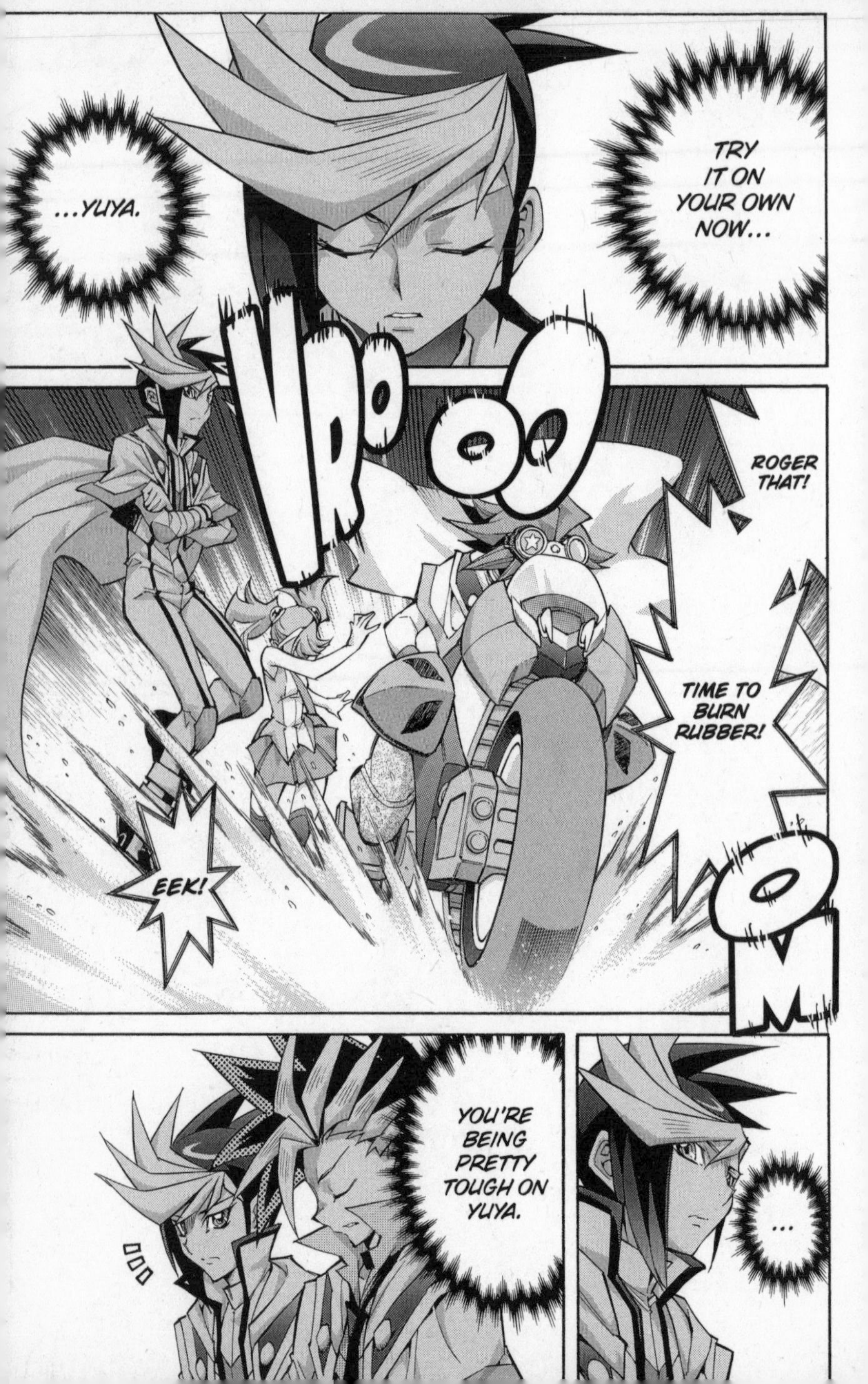
TRY IT ON YOUR OWN NOW...
...YUYA.
ROGER THAT!
TIME TO BURN RUBBER!
VROOOOM
EEK!
...
YOU'RE BEING PRETTY TOUGH ON YUYA.

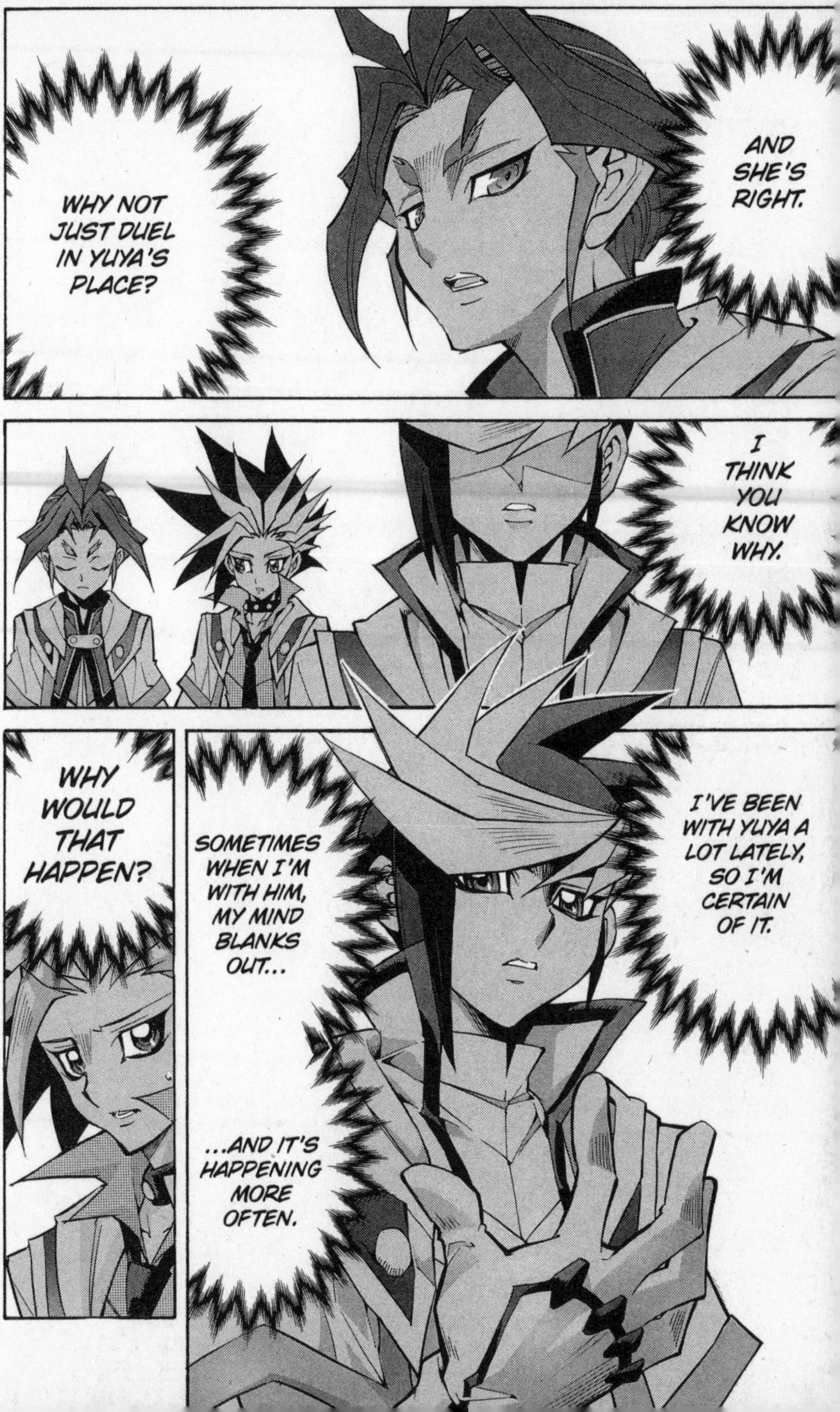
AND SHE'S RIGHT.
WHY NOT JUST DUEL IN YUYA'S PLACE?
I THINK YOU KNOW WHY.
I'VE BEEN WITH YUYA A LOT LATELY, SO I'M CERTAIN OF IT.
SOMETIMES WHEN I'M WITH HIM, MY MIND BLANKS OUT...
...AND IT'S HAPPENING MORE OFTEN.
WHY WOULD THAT HAPPEN?

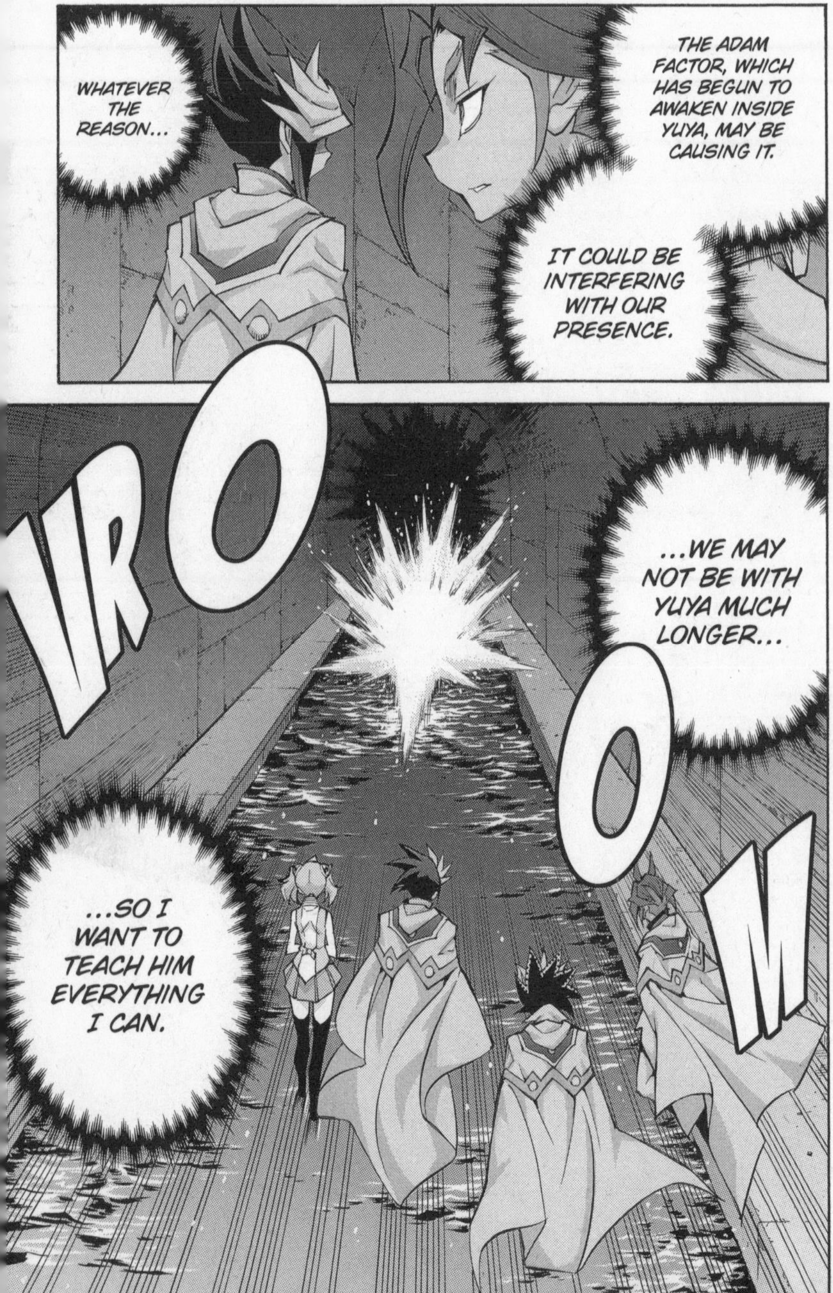
THE ADAM FACTOR, WHICH HAS BEGUN TO AWAKEN INSIDE YUYA, MAY BE CAUSING IT.
IT COULD BE INTERFERING WITH OUR PRESENCE.
WHATEVER THE REASON...
...WE MAY NOT BE WITH YUYA MUCH LONGER...
VROOOM
...SO I WANT TO TEACH HIM EVERYTHING I CAN.

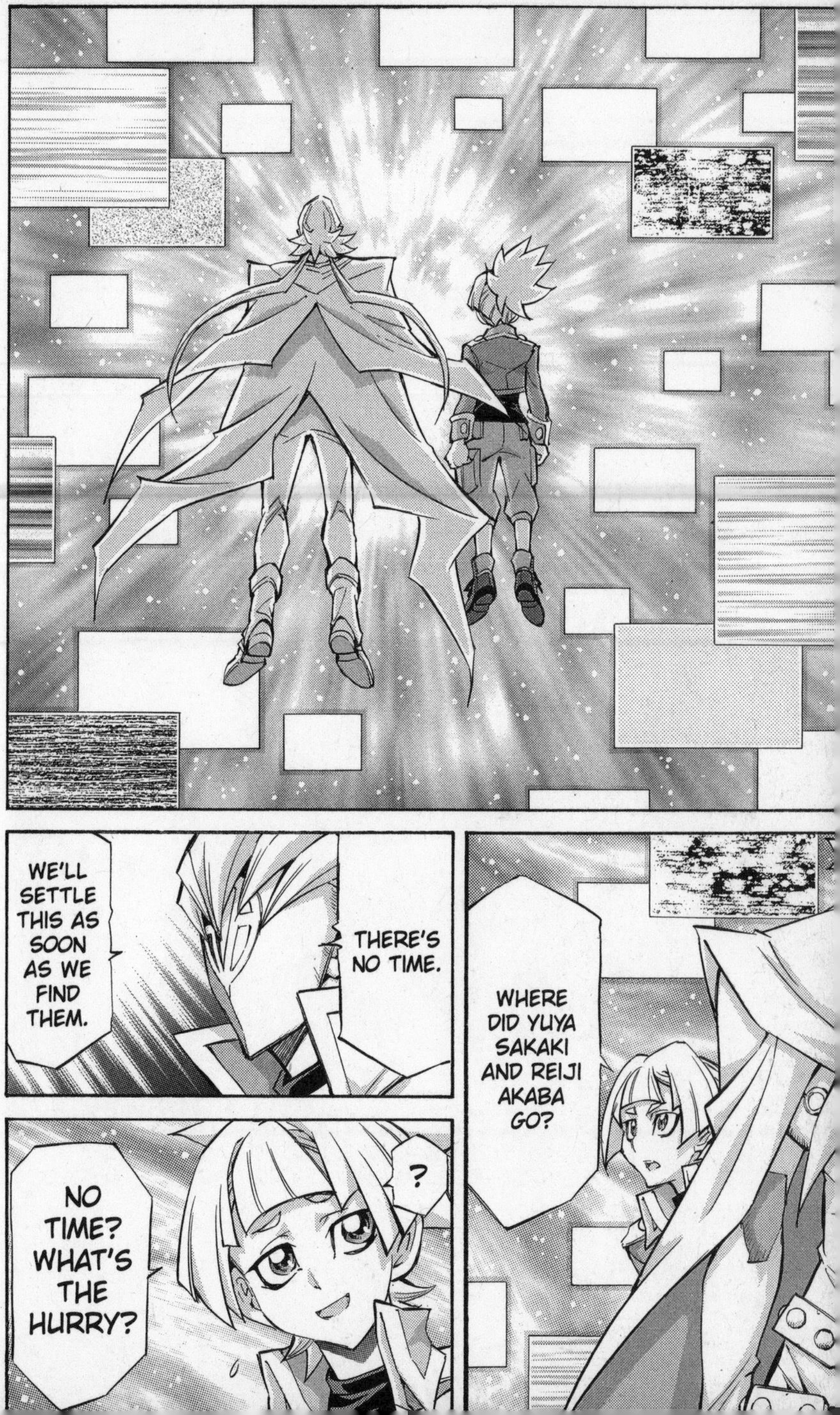
WHERE DID YUYA SAKAKI AND REIJI AKABA GO?
THERE'S NO TIME.
WE'LL SETTLE THIS AS SOON AS WE FIND THEM.
?
NO TIME? WHAT'S THE HURRY?

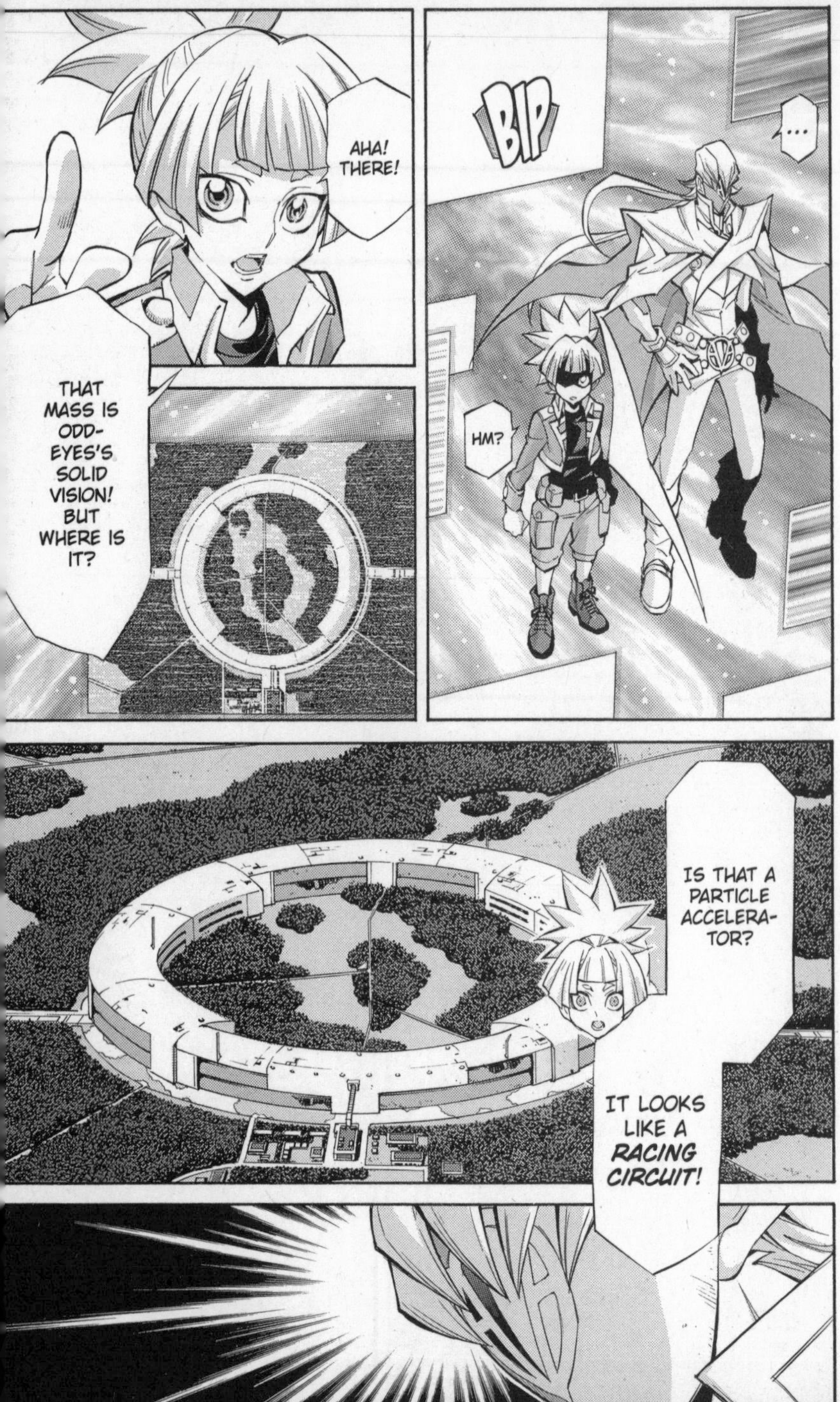
BIP
...
HM?
AHA! THERE!
THAT MASS IS ODD-EYES'S SOLID VISION! BUT WHERE IS IT?
IS THAT A PARTICLE ACCELERATOR?
IT LOOKS LIKE A *RACING CIRCUIT*!

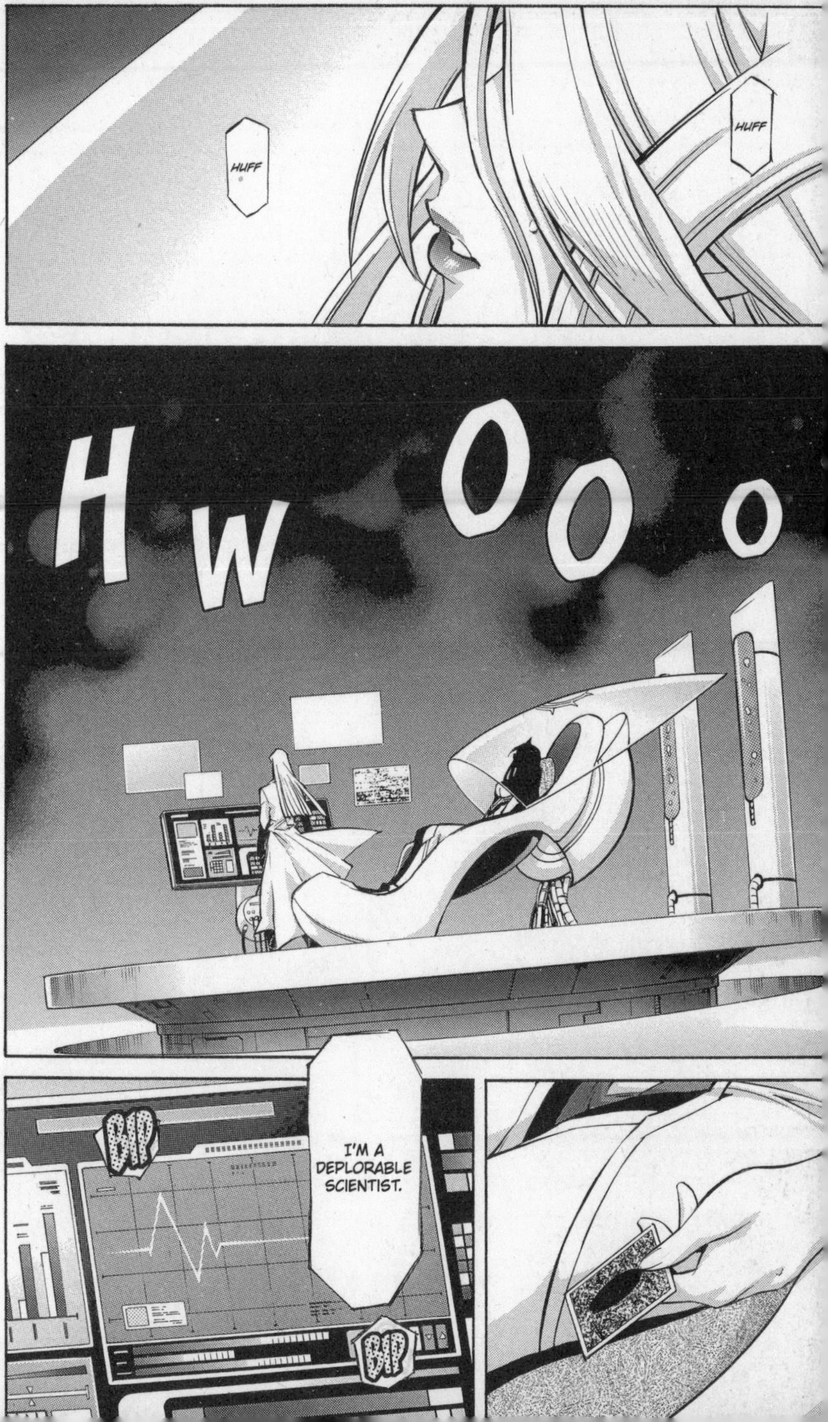
HUFF
HUFF
HWOOO
I'M A DEPLORABLE SCIENTIST.
BIP
BIP

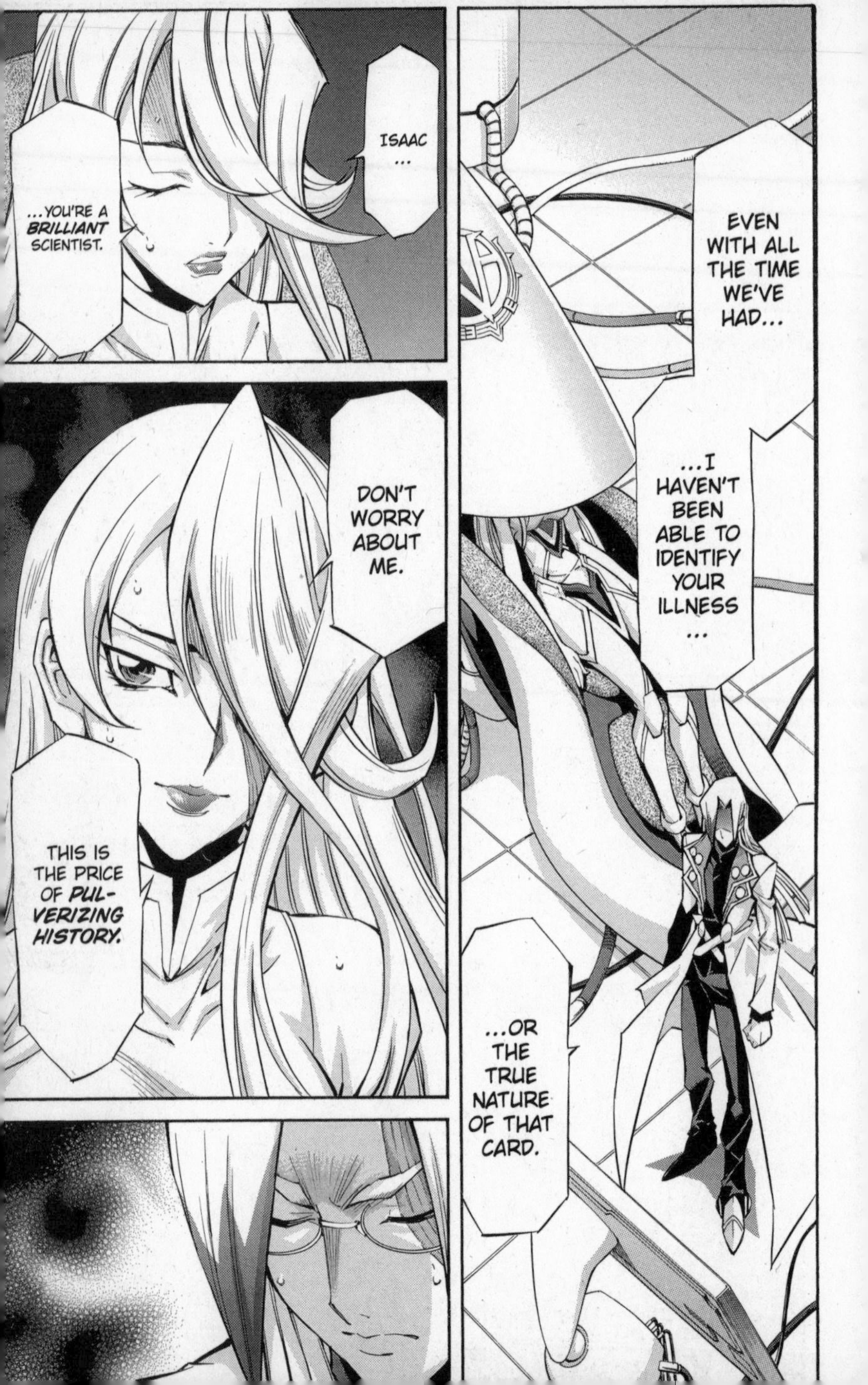
EVEN WITH ALL THE TIME WE'VE HAD...
...I HAVEN'T BEEN ABLE TO IDENTIFY YOUR ILLNESS ...
...OR THE TRUE NATURE OF THAT CARD.
ISAAC ...
...YOU'RE A *BRILLIANT* SCIENTIST.
DON'T WORRY ABOUT ME.
THIS IS THE PRICE OF *PUL-VERIZING HISTORY.*

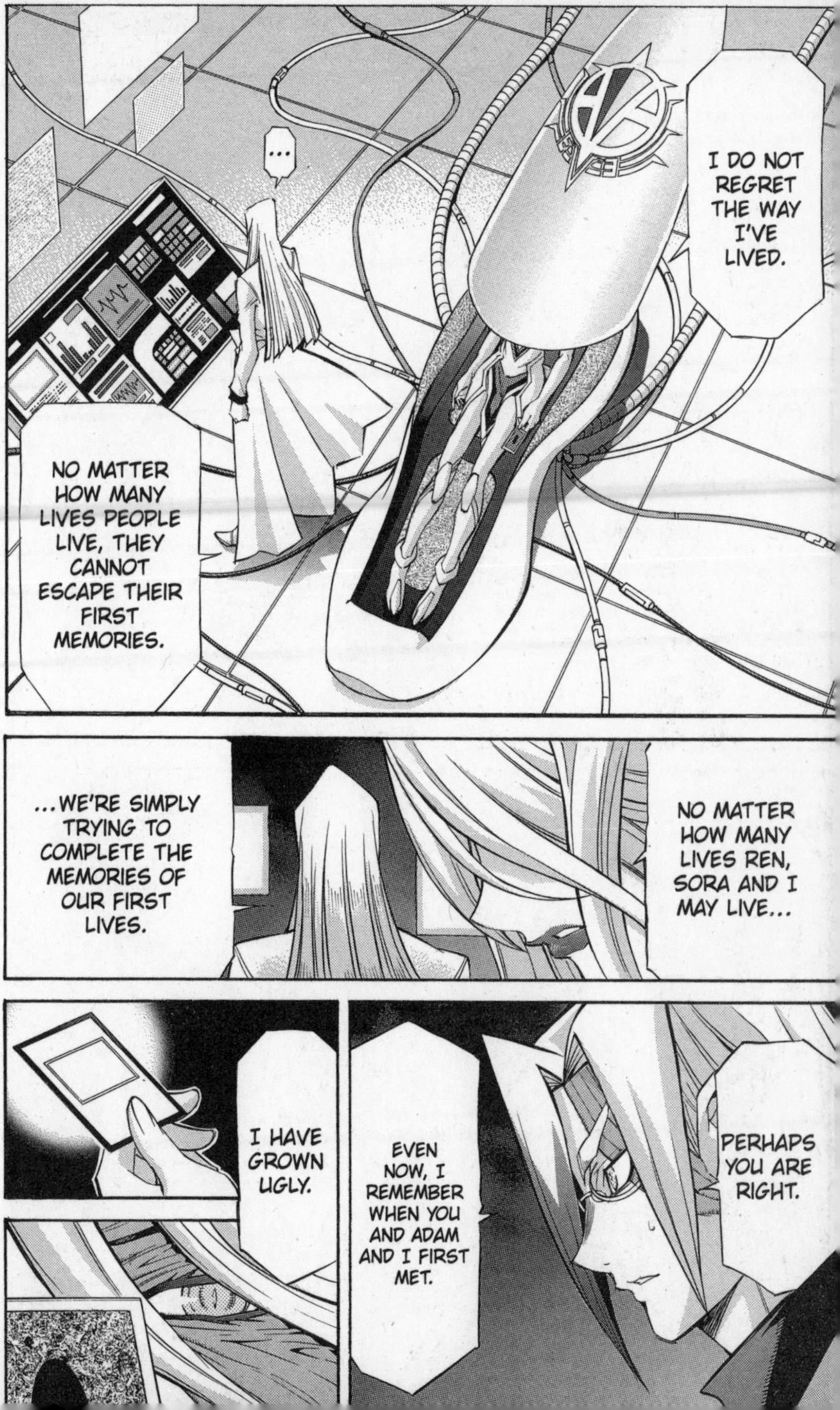
I DO NOT REGRET THE WAY I'VE LIVED.
...
NO MATTER HOW MANY LIVES PEOPLE LIVE, THEY CANNOT ESCAPE THEIR FIRST MEMORIES.
NO MATTER HOW MANY LIVES REN, SORA AND I MAY LIVE...
...WE'RE SIMPLY TRYING TO COMPLETE THE MEMORIES OF OUR FIRST LIVES.
PERHAPS YOU ARE RIGHT.
EVEN NOW, I REMEMBER WHEN YOU AND ADAM AND I FIRST MET.
I HAVE GROWN UGLY.

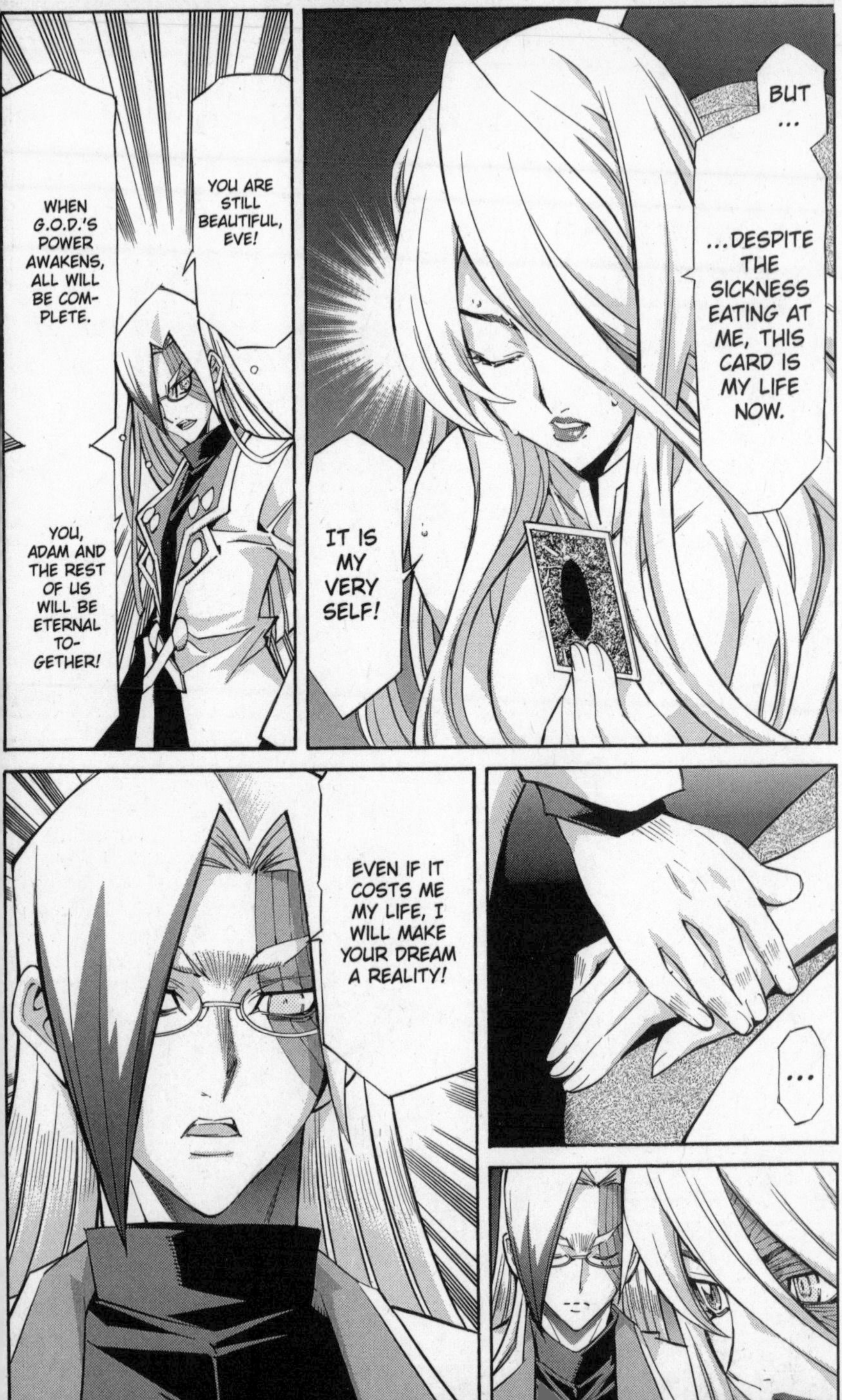
BUT ...
...DESPITE THE SICKNESS EATING AT ME, THIS CARD IS MY LIFE NOW.
IT IS MY VERY SELF!
YOU ARE STILL BEAUTIFUL, EVE!
WHEN G.O.D.'S POWER AWAKENS, ALL WILL BE COM-PLETE.
YOU, ADAM AND THE REST OF US WILL BE ETERNAL TO-GETHER!
...
EVEN IF IT COSTS ME MY LIFE, I WILL MAKE YOUR DREAM A REALITY!

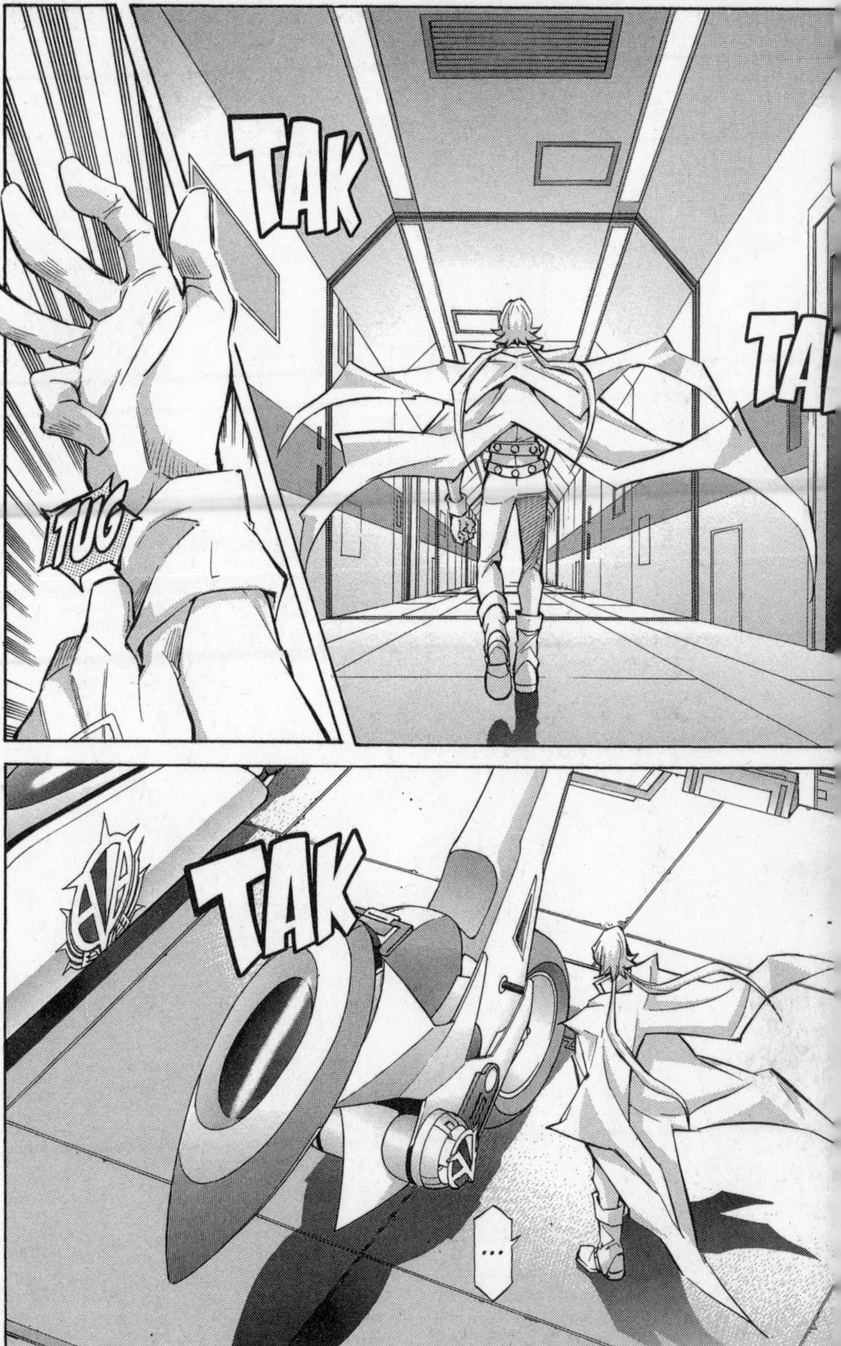
TAK
TA
TUG
TAK
...

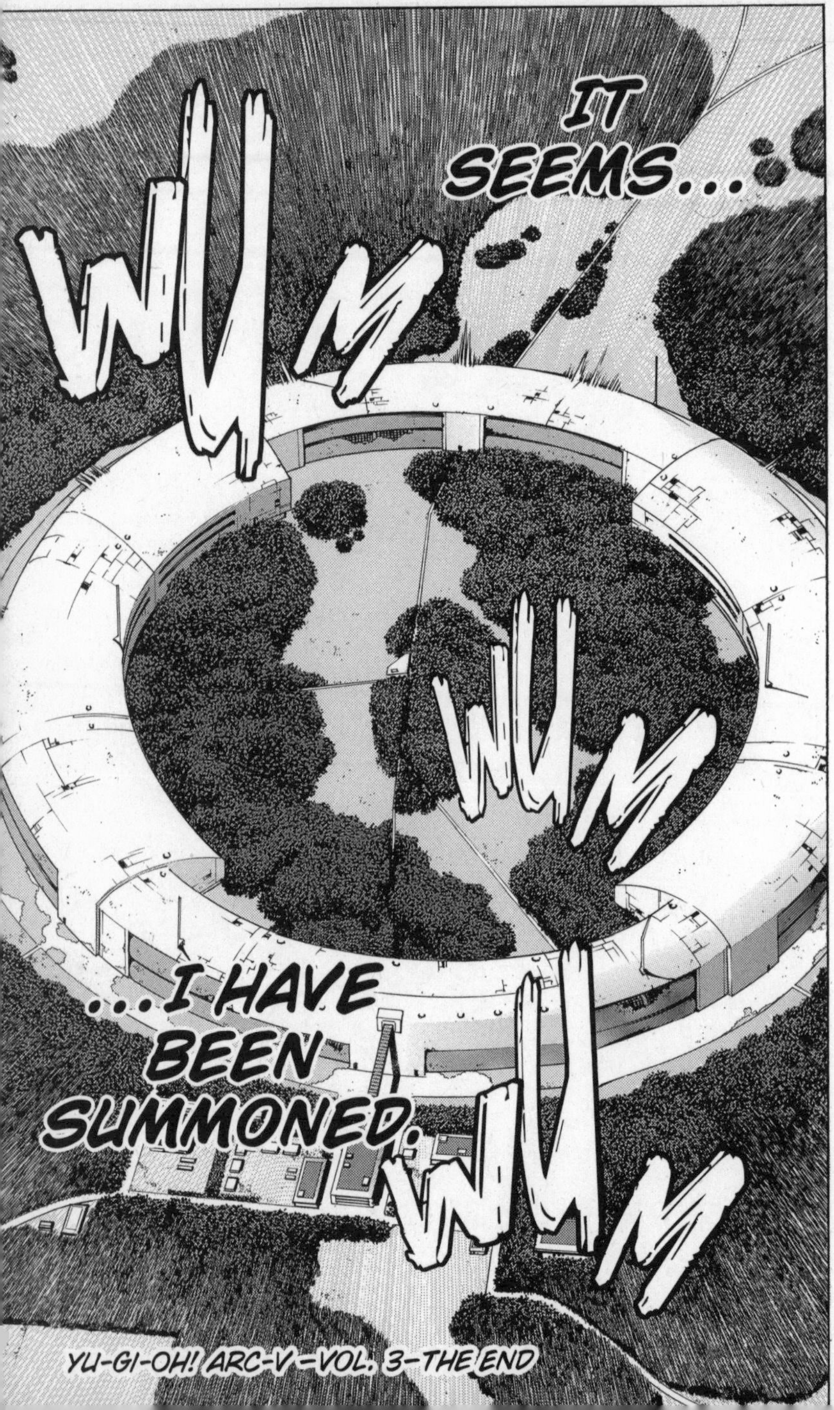
IT SEEMS...
WUM
WUM
...I HAVE BEEN SUMMONED.
WUM
YU-GI-OH! ARC-V -VOL. 3-THE END

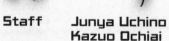

Staff   Junya Uchino
            Kazuo Ochiai

Coloring   Toru Shimizu

Editing   Takahiko Aikawa

Support   Gallop
            Wedge Holdings

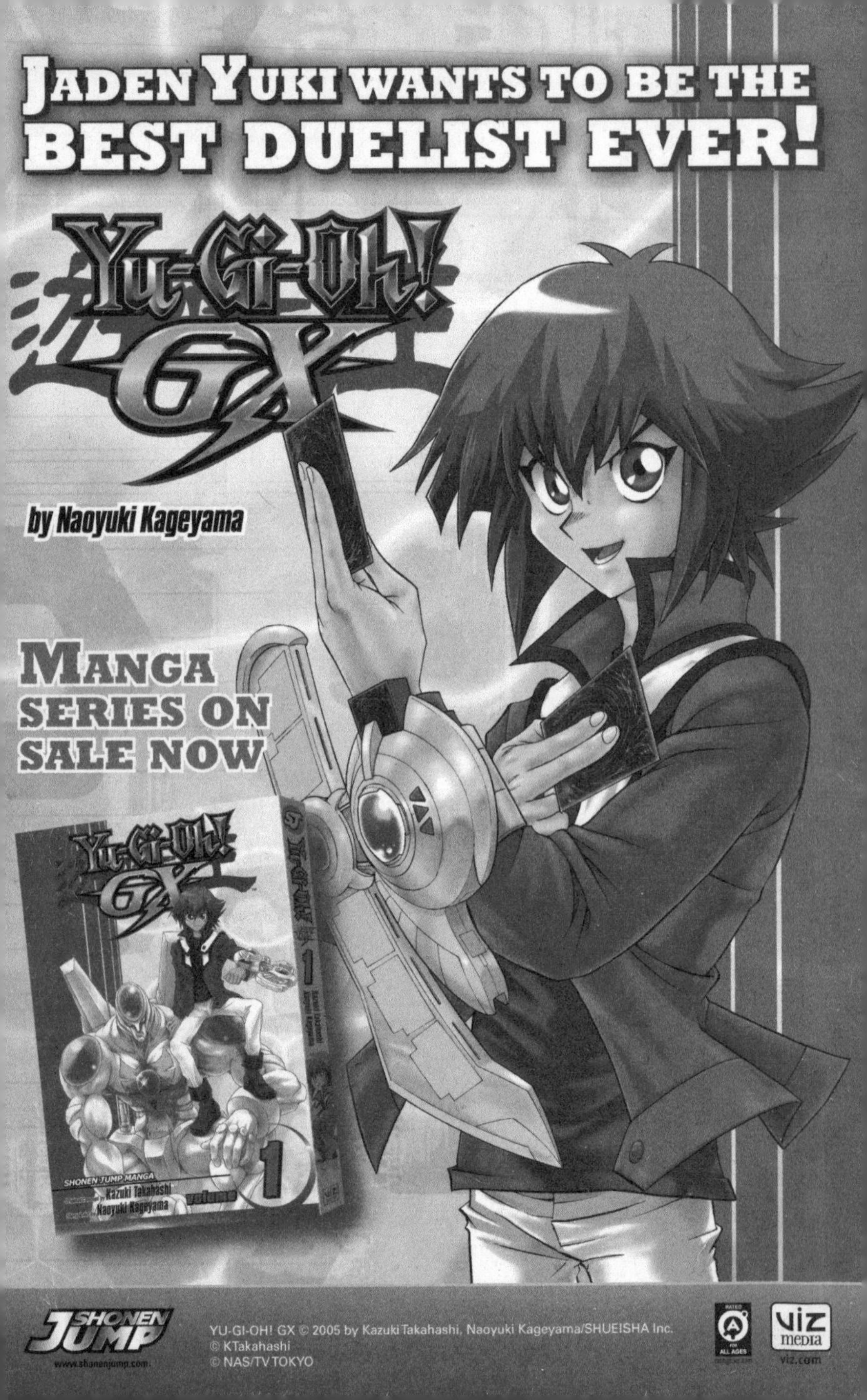

STOP!

YOU'RE READING THE WRONG WAY!

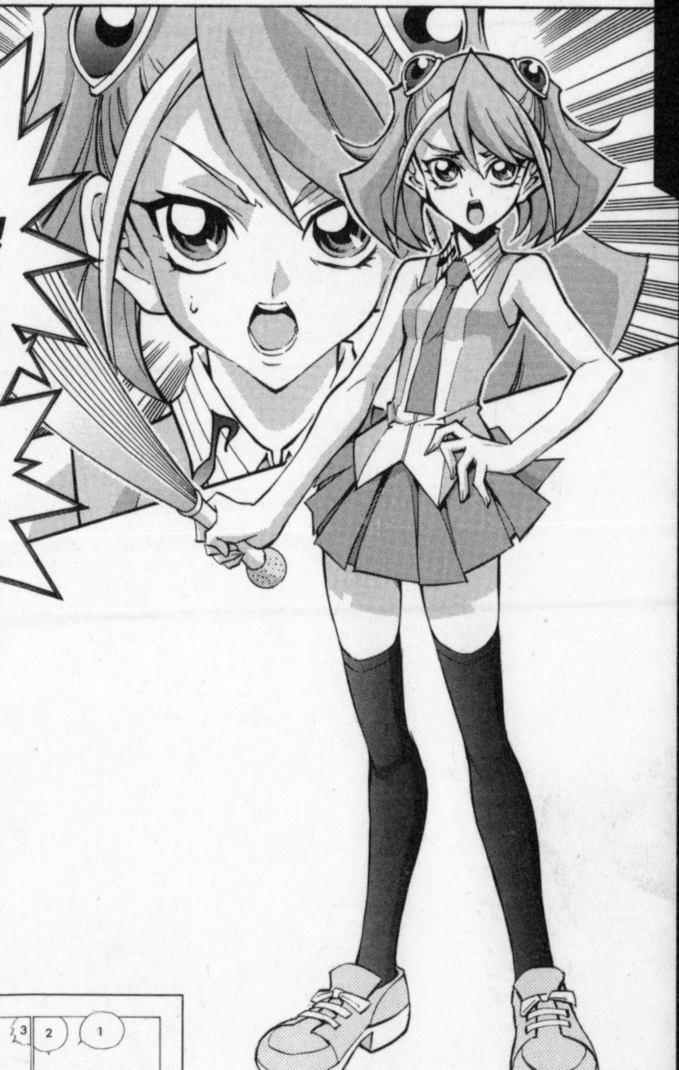

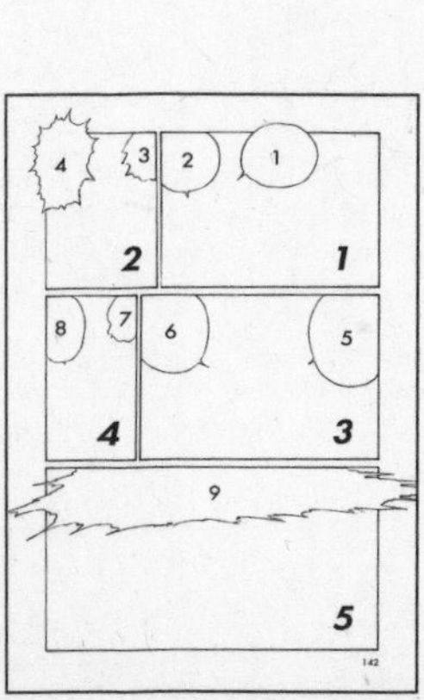

Yu-Gi-Oh! ARC-V

reads from right to left, starting in the upper-right corner. Japanese is read from right to left, meaning that action, sound effects and word-balloon order are completely reversed from English order.

3

SHONEN JUMP MANGA EDITION

ORIGINAL CONCEPT BY
Kazuki Takahashi

PRODUCTION SUPPORT: **STUDIO DICE**

STORY BY
Shin Yoshida

ART BY
Naohito Miyoshi

DUEL COORDINATOR
Masahiro Hikokubo

TRANSLATION + ENGLISH ADAPTATION
Taylor Engel and John Werry, HC Language Solutions, Inc.

TOUCH-UP ART + LETTERING **John Hunt**

DESIGNER **Stacie Yamaki**

EDITOR **Mike Montesa**

YU-GI-OH! ARC-V © 2014 by Kazuki Takahashi, Shin Yoshida, Naohito Miyoshi, Masahiro Hikokubo/SHUEISHA Inc.
Based on Animation TV series YU-GI-OH! ARC-V
© 1996 Kazuki Takahashi
© 2014 NAS • TV TOKYO

Printed in the U.S.A.

Published by VIZ Media, LLC
P.O. Box 77010
San Francisco, CA 94107

10 9 8 7 6 5 4 3 2 1
First printing, March 2018

www.viz.com   www.shonenjump.com

SHIN YOSHIDA

The two giants, Yuya and Reiji, finally clash! And the mystery surrounding them becomes clearer! The fun is just getting started!

NAOHITO MIYOSHI

The *Yu-Gi-Oh! ARC-V* anime is complete! I'm filled with emotion. I'll never forget how I felt when I saw Yuya and the others running around on TV. To everyone on the staff, congrats on a job well done!

MASAHIRO HIKOKUBO

Reiji's D/D/D is an abbreviation for Different Dimension Demon! It doesn't stand for *Duel Daisuki Desu* (I Love Duels) or *Dondon Detekuru Dodekai Monster* (Huge Monsters Show Up One After Another)!